Sport in the Global Society

General Editor: J.A. Mangan

SPORT IN THE GLOBAL SOCIETY

General Editor: J.A. Mangan

The interest in sports studies around the world is growing and will continue to do so. This unique series combines aspects of the expanding study of *sport in the global society*, providing comprehensiveness and comparison under one editorial umbrella. It is particularly timely, with studies in the political, cultural, anthropological, ethnographic, social, economic, geographical and aesthetic elements of sport proliferating in institutions of higher education.

Eric Hobsbawm once called sport one of the most significant practices of the late nineteenth century. Its significance was even more marked in the late twentieth century and will continue to grow in importance into the new millennium as the world develops into a 'global village' sharing the English language, technology and sport.

Other Titles in the Series

THE
COMMERCIALISATION
OF SPORT

Editor

TREVOR SLACK
University of Alberta

Routledge
Taylor & Francis Group

LONDON AND NEW YORK

First published in 2004
by Routledge
2 Park Square, Milton Park, Abingdon, Oxon, OX14 4RN

Simultaneously published in the USA and Canada
by Routledge
270 Madison Ave, New York, NY 10016

Routledge is an imprint of the Taylor & Francis Group

© 2004 Selection and editorial matter: Trevor Slack,
individual chapters: the contributors

Typeset in Times by Taylor & Francis Books Ltd
Printed and bound in Great Britain by Antony Rowe Ltd, Chippenham, Wiltshire

The publisher makes no representation, express or implied, with regard to the accuracy of
the information contained in this book and cannot accept any legal responsibility or
liability for any errors or omissions that may be made.

Every effort has been made to ensure that the advice and information in this book is true
and accurate at the time of going to press. However, neither the publisher nor the authors
can accept any legal responsibility or liability for any errors or omissions that may be
made. In the case of drug administration, any medical procedure or the use of technical
equipment mentioned within this book, you are strongly advised to consult the
manufacturer's guidelines.

British Library Cataloguing in Publication Data
A catalogue record for this book is available from the British Library

Library of Congress Cataloging in Publication Data
A catalog record for this book has been requested

ISBN 0–7146–5021–8 (HB)
ISBN 0–7146–8078–8 (PB)

Dedicated to the memory of my parents

Gladys Slack
26 July 1922 – 24 August 2000

Herbert Slack
29 July 1921 – 26 October 2002

Contents

PART III: THE COMMERCIALISATION OF 'AMATEUR' SPORT

PART IV: TELEVISION AND THE COMMERCIALISATION OF SPORT

PART V: SPORT SPONSORSHIP

Contributors

David L. Andrews is an Associate Professor of Sport and Cultural Studies in the Department of Human Movement Sciences and Education at the University of Maryland, and a visiting research fellow at De Montfort University, in the UK. He is an Associate Editor of the *Journal of Sport and Social Issues*, and has published on a variety of topics related to the critical analysis of sport as an aspect of contemporary commercial culture. He recently edited two anthologies, *Michael Jordan, Inc.: Corporate Sport, Media Culture, and Late Modern America* (SUNY Press, 2001) and (with Steven J. Jackson) *Sport Stars: The Cultural Politics of Sporting Celebrity* (Routledge, 2001).

John Amis is an Associate Professor at the University of Memphis where he holds joint appointments in the Department of Health & Sport Sciences and the Department of Management. He obtained a Ph.D. in sport management from the University of Alberta in 1998. Amis' research interests have predominantly centered on organisational change and the identification, utilisation and management of intangible resources. He has had thirty articles and book chapters published in journals such as *Academy of Management Journal, Journal of Applied Behavioural Science, Journal of Sport Management, European Marketing Journal, European Sport Management Quarterly*, and *Leisure Studies*.

Richard Batty received his Ph.D. from Penn State University. He is an Assistant Professor at the University of California, Sacramento. He teaches courses in sport management, sport organisations and event management. His research interests include volunteers in sports, event management, and sport and social policy.

Wendy Frisby is Associate Professor in the School of Human Kinetics at the University of British Columbia. Her research interests include sport and community development, participatory action research, inter-organisational partnerships, and the application of organisation theory to understanding sport and leisure organisations. She was the Editor of the *Journal of Sport Management* from 2000–2003 and in 2004 she was the recipient of the Earle

F. Zeigler Award from the North American Society for Sport Management. Her research has appeared in *Avante*, *Canadian Journal of Public Health*, *Canadian Women's Studies*, *European Sport Management Quarterly*, *Journal of Park and Recreation Administration*, *Journal of Sport Management*, *Managing Leisure: An International Journal, Society & Leisure*, and the *Journal of Travel Research*.

Bill Gerrard is Professor of Sport Management and Finance at Leeds University Business School. He is a graduate of the University of Aberdeen, Trinity College, Cambridge, and the University of York. His main research interest is in the economics and finance of professional team sports, with a particular emphasis on soccer. His work on sport has appeared in the *Journal of Sport Management*, *European Sport Management Quarterly*, *Journal of Sports Economics*, *Scottish Journal of Political Economy*, the *Journal of Economic Studies*, *New Political Economy*, and the *International Journal of Sport Marketing and Sponsorship*. He has also published a number of economics articles in mainstream economic journals. He has developed a player valuation system and has acted as a consultant to a number of soccer teams. He is a regular media commentator on the business of sport and an expert witness in several sports legal cases. His work has been featured on the BBC's *Money Programme*. He is Associate Editor of *European Sport Management Quarterly,* a member of the editorial boards of *Journal of Sport Management* and *Journal of Sport Economics*, a season ticket holder at Leeds United, retains an allegiance to his first love, Celtic, and a fully fledged member of the Tartan Army. He has been actively involved in fans' groups campaigning against the poor management of Leeds United and trying to rescue the club from the threat of bankruptcy.

Andrew Grainger is a doctoral student in the Department of Kinesiology at the University of Maryland, College Park. He holds a master's degree from the University of Otago, New Zealand, where his thesis focused on globalisation, sports advertising and cultural resistance through advertising standards. His research interests include the globalisation of American popular sporting culture, and the local consumption of global sporting products and practices. He has recently published articles in *Peace Review* and the *International Journal of Sports Marketing and Sponsorship*.

Jean Harvey is a Professor in the School of Human Kinetics at the University of Ottawa. He is also the director of the Research Centre on Sport in Canadian Society. He is the author of *Le corps programmé* (1983) and was the co-editor of *Not Just a Game: Essays in Canadian Sociology of Sport* (1988); he has also been guest editor of several special issues of refereed journals. He has published extensively in journals and books both in English and in French. His research interests now focus on globalisation, sport policy, the sport industry, and sport and social citizenship.

Barrie Houlihan is Professor of Sport Policy in the Institute of Sport and Leisure Policy at Loughborough University in England. His research interests include the domestic and international policy processes for sport. He has a particular interest in sports development, the diplomatic use of sport and drug abuse by athletes. His most recent books include *Sport, Policy and Politics: A Comparative Analysis* (Routledge, 1997); *Dying to Win: The Development of Anti-doping Policy* (Council of Europe Press, second edition, 2002); and *The Politics of Sports Development: Development of Sport or Development through Sport?* (co-authored with Professor Anita White, Routledge, 2002). His recent articles have been published in *Public Administration, Journal of Sport Management* and *Managing Leisure: An International Journal*. In addition to his work as a teacher and researcher, he has undertaken consultancy projects for Sport England, UK Sport and the Department for Education and Skills. He was also chair of the committee that reviewed the joint Sport England/CCPR/NPFA strategy on playing pitches.

Steven J. Jackson is an Associate Professor in the School of Physical Education, University of Otago, New Zealand, where he teaches courses in sport, media and culture, and the sociology of sport. His research interests include sport media, globalisation, and sport and identity politics in sports. He is currently General Secretary for the International Sociology of Sport Association and a member of the editorial board for the *International Review for the Sociology of Sport*. Steve has recently published (with David Andrews) *Sport Stars: The Cultural Politics of Sporting Celebrity* (Routledge) and will soon publish an edited volume titled *Sport, Culture and Advertising* (Routledge).

Lisa M. Kikulis is Associate Professor in the Department of Sport Management at Brock University. Her research interests are in strategic and institutional change of sport and leisure organisations and organisational design, governance, decision-making and government/non-government organisation relations. She has published in the *Journal of Sport Management, Managing Leisure: An International Journal, International Review for the Sociology of Sport, Human Relations*, and the *Journal of Management Studies*.

Lance Kinney received his Ph.D. in mass communication from Florida State University in 1995. He has presented his research at national and international marketing and advertising conferences, including those of the

North American Society for Sport Management, the American Academy of Advertising, the Association for Education in Journalism and Mass Communication, and the American Marketing Association. His work has appeared in the *International Journal of Sports Marketing and Sponsorship*, *Psychology and Marketing*, the *Journal of Promotion Management*, *Street & Smith's Sports Business Journal* and the *Journal of Sport Management*. He is Assistant Professor of Advertising and Public Relations at the University of Alabama, Tuscaloosa.

Marc Lavoie is Professor in the Department of Economics at the University of Ottawa. He has published two books on the economics of ice hockey – *Avantage numérique, l'argent dans la Ligue nationale de hockey* (1997) and *Désavantage numérique, les francophones dans la LNH* (1998) – and two graduate textbooks on post-Keynesian economics, the latest being *Foundations of Post-Keynesian Economic Analysis* (1992). He was also the co-editor of a book on the works of Milton Friedman (1993) and an associate editor of the *Encyclopaedia of Political Economy* (1999). He has published over 100 articles in refereed journals and books, mostly on monetary economics and growth, but also 15 on the economics of sport. He has been a visiting professor at the universities of Bordeaux, Nice, Rennes, Dijon and Grenoble, as well as Curtin University in Perth, Australia.

Tara Magdalinski is a Senior Lecturer in the Faculty of Arts and Social Sciences at the University of the Sunshine Coast. She has published widely in the area of sports studies, focusing most recently on the cultural construction of performance enhancement. In addition, she examines the 'natural' in the bodies and site of the Sydney 2000 Olympics, the cultural reception of Fastskin, and the corporate motives of Olympic education. She is the co-editor of *With God on their Side: Sport in the Service of Religion* (2002).

Daniel S. Mason is an Associate Professor with the Faculty of Physical Education and Recreation at the University of Alberta, where he received his Ph.D in 1999. His research interests focus on the structure, function, and implications of organisations, and their effects on organisational stakeholders and environments. His research currently explores the manner through which cities leverage sporting events and sports franchises as part of their broader development initiatives. He has published his work in *Economic Development Quarterly*, the *Journal of Sport Management*, *Journal of Services Marketing*, *European Journal of Marketing*, *European Sport Management Quarterly*, *Journal of Sport History*, *Urban History Review*, *Sport History Review*, *Sport Management Review*, *Marquette Sports Law Journal*, *Journal of Legal Aspects of Sport*, and *Journal of Sport and Social Issues*.

Michael K. Mauws is an Associate Professor in the Faculty of Physical Education and Recreation at the University of Alberta. His research interests include organisation studies, post-structuralism, moral theory and discourse analysis. The journals in which his writings have been published include the *Journal of Applied Behavioral Science*, the *Journal of Business Venturing*, *Organization Science*, the *Sociology of Sport Journal* and *Quest*.

Stephen R. McDaniel holds a Ph.D. in mass communication from Florida State University (1995). He is an Associate Professor in the Kinesiology Department at the University of Maryland, where he also holds an affiliate appointment with the Department of Communication. His teaching and research are focused on consumer behaviour phenomena in the areas of marketing promotions and media. He has written extensively on the topic of sport sponsorship. He has presented his research to a number of academic groups, including the Association for Consumer Research, the American Marketing Association and the American Academy of Advertising. His research has also appeared in such publications as the *Journal of Promotion Management*, the *Journal of Services Marketing*, the *Journal of Sport Management*, *Psychology & Marketing*, *Social Behavior and Personality*, *Sport Management Review* and *Teaching Business Ethics*.

John Nauright teaches and directs research in the Division of Sport, Health and Leisure at the University of Abertay Dundee, Scotland. He is the author of nine books, including *Making Men: Rugby and Masculine Identity* (1996) and *Making the Rugby World* (1999) (both co-edited with Timothy Chandler); and *Sport, Cultures and Identities in South Africa* (1997) and *The Political Economy of Sport* (2002) (co-edited with Kimberly Schimmel). He edits the journals *Football Studies* and *International Sports Studies*.

Danny O'Brien holds a Ph.D. from De Montfort University, Bedford, England. While undertaking his doctoral studies, Danny won the 1997 North American Society for Sport Management (NASSM) Student Research Paper Competition. His other degree qualifications were earned from California State University, Long Beach; and Australian Catholic University. Currently, Danny lectures in sport organisation and governance, strategic management, and sport event management in Griffith University's Department of Tourism, Leisure, Hotel and Sport Management on the Gold Coast in Queensland, Australia. He has published a number of book chapters, as well as articles in *Journal of Sport Management* and *Sport Management Review*. His research interests have focused primarily on organisational and strategic change in sport organisations, and more recently, on the strategic business leveraging of sport events.

Mark Rosentraub is Professor and Dean at the Maxine Goodman Levin College of Urban Affairs at Cleveland State University. His research interests focus on the effects of professional sports teams and the facilities they use on urban areas; the financing, organisation and delivery of urban services; and economic development issues. His work has included studies of urban change and growth, public-private partnerships, economic development strategies, and the relationship between sport, economic development and the public sector. His *Major League Losers: The Real Costs of Sports and Who's Paying For It* was published in 1997 and 1999. His research has also appeared in *Public Administration Review, American Review of Public Administration, Economic Development Quarterly,* the *Journal of Sport and Social Issues,* the *Journal of Urban Affairs, Urban Affairs Review,* the *Journal of the American Planning Association, Public Finance Review* and *State and Local Government Review,* as well as several other journals and numerous collections.

George H. Sage is Professor Emeritus at the University of Northern Colorado. He has published several books, including *Sociology of American Sport* (with Stan Eitzen), *Sport and American Society* and, most recently, the second edition of *Power and Ideology in American Sport: A Critical Perspective.* He has also written numerous articles, which have appeared in such journals as the *Sociology of Sport Journal,* the *Journal of Sport and Social Issues, Research Quarterly for Exercise and Sport, Arena Review, Quest* and the *Sociology of Work and Occupations Journal.* He has been president of the North American Society for the Sociology of Sport, is a Fellow of the American Academy of Kinesiology and Physical Education and in 1985–86 was selected as Alliance Scholar for the American Alliance for Health, Physical Education, Recreation, and Dance. His most recent work has been on aspects of the sporting goods industry.

Michael Silk is an Assistant Professor in the Department of Kinesiology at the University of Maryland. He obtained his Ph.D. in 1999 from the University of Otago in New Zealand and his master's from the University of Alberta in 1996. His research and teaching focuses on sporting practices, products, events, celebrities and spectacles within (late) global capitalism, with a particular emphasis on the restructuring of spaces, places and identities, new communications technologies, and the work of cultural intermediaries. He has contributed a number of book chapters to edited collections and has recently published in *Media, Culture & Society,* the *Sociology of Sport Journal,* the *Journal of Sport and Social Issues, International Review for the Sociology of Sport, Culture, Sport & Society* and the *Journal of Sport Management.* He has also published in, and co-edited (with David L. Andrews), a recent special edition of the *International Journal of Sport Marketing and Sponsorship* that focused on 'transnational marketing'.

Trevor Slack is Professor and Canada Research Chair in Sport Management at the University of Alberta. He has previously held positions as Head of the School of Physical Education, Sport and Leisure at De Montfort University in England, and as Visiting Fellow in the Centre for Corporate Strategy and Change at Warwick Business School. His research interests are primarily in the areas of organisational strategy and change. He is currently engaged in work on changes in sporting organisations in emerging economies. He was previously the Editor of the *European Sport Management Quarterly* and the *Journal of Sport Management*. His work has appeared in such journals as *Organization Studies*, *International Review for the Sociology of Sport*, the *Journal of Sport Management*, the *Journal of Management Studies*, *Human Relations*, the *European Journal of Marketing*, *Leisure Studies* and the *Journal of Leisure Research*.

Ellen J. Staurowsky is a Professor of Sport Sociology and Chair of the Department of Sport Management and Media at Ithaca College, New York. A former college athlete, coach and athletic director, she has been actively involved in the research of social justice issues in sport for almost 20 years. Her major areas of scholarly interest include the implications of racialized 'American Indian' imagery in sport, gender equity in intercollegiate athletics, economics and intercollegiate athletics, and sport and violence. She has published over 30 articles, and made 60 presentations at international, national and regional conferences. In 1998 she co-authored, with Allen L. Sack of the University of New Haven, the book *College Athletes for Hire: The Evolution and Legacy of the NCAA Amateur Myth*. Among the honours she has received, she was named a fellow in the AAHPERD Research Consortium in 1999, awarded the Young Alumni Achievement Award by Temple University in 1998 and selected as the 1996 Margaret Paulding Lecturer.

Lucie Thibault is Associate Professor in the Department of Sport Management at Brock University. Her research interests include sport policy, the Canadian sport system, strategy in non-profit sport organisations, and inter-organisational linkages in leisure and sport. Her work has been published in the *Journal of Sport Management*, *Journal of Sport and Social Issues*, *Loisir et Société*, the *International Review for the Sociology of Sport*, *Human Relations*, and *Leisure Studies*.

David Whitson is a Professor in the Department of Political Science at the University of Alberta. He is co-author of *The Game Planners: Transforming Canada's Sport System* (McGill-Queen's, 1990) and *Hockey Night in Canada: Sport, Identities, and Cultural Politics* (Garamond, 1993). He has also published numerous scholarly articles on the sociology and politics of sport. His research interests now focus on the effects of globalisation on Canadian cities and regions, and he has just published an anthology (with Roger Epp) entitled *Writing Off the Rural West: Globalization, Governments, and the Transformation of Rural Communities* (University of Alberta Press, 2001).

Series Editor's Foreword

Serena Williams smiles dazzlingly at her audience with a toothpaste from a world-famous multi-national in one hand and a tennis racket clutched to her bosom in the other – commercialism above the belt![1] Simultaneously, Tom Bower reveals that in professional football there could be more dummies sold off the field than on it, 'Where quiet, connivance, bland denials and the pocketing of millions [in the form of bungs] are the rule'[2] – commercialism below the belt!

In their different ways both Williams and Bower point up a widespread reality in modern sport; commercialism – fair and foul.

Of course, this reality is complex. By the mid-1980s this was shrewdly appreciated by commentators on sport. One wrote sensibly, 'It is important … to distinguish the *different* (emphasis added) ways sport can be related to capital', and specified them:[3] some sports are essentially profit-maximising business enterprises; some sports are commercialised but essentially to cover costs in order to survive; some sports assist capital accumulation both indirectly and directly by offering opportunities to enterprises to provide essentials (equipment) and accessories (clothing and the like); some sports enter closely into partnership with commerce and the media through retailing, sponsorship and advertising – and increasingly 'product' sales; finally, some sports may attempt some, if not all, of these things simultaneously.[4] It is necessary also to appreciate that money is not invariably the exclusive motive for commercial involvement in sport; there is reflected glory to be achieved, social approval to be gained, personal or corporate enthusiasm to be indulged.

In short, the relationship between sport and commerce is complicated. In a very different context many centuries ago, Horace came close to a succinct summary of the seductive nature of modern sport for the entrepreneur: 'He has gained every point who has mixed profit with pleasure',[5] while André Gide went even deeper to the heart of the matter: ' "M" est d'avis … que le profit n'est pas toujours ce qui mène l'homme; qu'il y a des actions desintéressées.'[6] The recent widespread praise heaped on the late Paul Getty II makes this point perfectly.

Nevertheless, what is clear, increasingly, from a rather messy mélange of situations that comprise the contemporary 'liaison' between sport and commerce, is that many modern sports in their new commercial existence, like the famous creation of Harriet Beecher Stowe '… never had no father and mother, nor nothing' but were 'raised by a speculator, with lots of others'.[7]

As Trevor Slack, in the opening sentence of the Prologue of his globally ground-breaking book, declares, 'one of the most visible aspects of modern sport is its strong links to commercial enterprises',[8] while he adds cautiously but confidently that, although the several attempts to estimate the value of commercial interest in sport are highly subjective, what can be deduced from them 'is that there is a large commercial involvement in sport and the level of involvement is growing'.[9] Only too true.

Finally, an attractive feature of *The Commercialisation of Sport* which gels smoothly with the approach of the Sport in the Global Society series, is the varied academic backgrounds of the contributors, which allow a fascinating diversity of perspectives. As a result, *The Commercialisation of Sport* has an appealing eclecticism – usefully informative, healthily critical, and in totality, wholly original.

Professor J. A. Mangan

IRCSSS,

De Montfort University (Bedford)

NOTES

1. See 'Business', 20 April 2003, p.1.
2. See the review by Russell Davies, 'Pay up, pay up, and pay the game' in 'Review', 23 February 2003, p.13.
3. John Hargreaves, *Sport, Power and Culture* (Cambridge: Polity Press, 1987), p.114. His analysis has been slightly adapted to take account of more recent developments.
4. Ibid., pp.14–15.
5. Angela Partington (ed.), *The Oxford Dictionary of Quotations* (Oxford: OUP, revised fourth edition, 1996), p. 347.
6. 'I believe … that profit is not always what motivates man; there are disinterested actions.' See Partington (1996), p. 303.
7. An appropriate adaptation of the plaintive statement by Topsy in Harriet Beecher Stowe's *Uncle Tom's Cabin*, many editions.
8. Trevor Slack, *The Commercialisation of Sport* (London: Frank Cass, 2004), Prologue, p.xiii.
9. Ibid., p.xiv.

Foreword

It is a difficult job to write a foreword to a book – there are no established formats and no guidelines to follow. Using one's close friend and a member of one's family to assist me in the writing of this foreword may be seen as self-serving or tantamount to nepotism; however, such a charge would deny my daughter Chelsea's status as a student of cultural studies at Nottingham Trent University. Chelsea has shared her insights below:

> I feel a great honour by being asked to write part of the foreword and contribute to my Dad's book. Not only because I am able to do this for my Dad, but also because the book itself represents a collection of great authors working together. I am familiar with most of them through various conferences, visits to our house, and other events that have taken place over the years. I know that my Dad has great respect for each of them and is thoroughly impressed with the work they have contributed. I am hoping that my contribution to the book through this foreword will be a reflection of how hard my Dad works, not only in an academic sense, but also most importantly to him, as a family member.

> Another thing my Dad mentioned when I asked him about this foreword was to talk about the people who made contributions. Yet after looking at the contents and the significant amount of people that have been involved in the creation of this book, it would be a very lengthy task. As I mentioned previously, it just goes to show the hard work and commitment so many people have put in, and also the vast array of areas that are being explored and researched within the field of sport management. I know my Dad values the contributions of the authors very much, and without them this book would not have been published. For those of you reading this who have contributed to this book, on behalf of myself and my family I thank you for the hard work, effort and patience you have exhibited in order to make this book a success.

I would now like to share with you my good friend Bill Gerrard's insights into the book. Bill is well trained in both the theoretical and practical aspects of economics. His theoretical training was gained at Trinity College, Cambridge University, probably England's finest seat of learning. His practical experience was gained at the less celebrated but equally relevant terraces of Leeds United Football Club. As Bill explains:

This book has had a long genesis in part due to Trevor's ill health. The contributors are all leading researchers in the field of sport management. Some are Trevor's students and research collaborators. Some are colleagues, past and present. Many are good friends. All share Trevor's vision of sport management as a field drawing on leading-edge developments in the parent business disciplines. Trevor thanks them for providing such an interesting set of perspectives on the commercialisation of sport and he also appreciates their understanding and co-operation during the editorial process.

In sum, this book is divided into five parts. Each deals with an aspect of the sport industry which has been subject to increased links to the commercial sector. The chapters are not intended to provide definitive summaries of their respective areas of the sport industry, but merely serve as examples of the types of work that can be done on the commercialisation of sport.

Acknowledgements

I would like to thank Tony Mangan and the support of a former doctoral student of mine (now a colleague at the University of Alberta), Dan Mason, who has been a tower of strength during my illness. I would also like to thank a close friend, Dr. Bill Gerrard, who has supported my recovery, my academic work and my family during this difficult period. Without the help of these individuals this book would not have been completed.

My wife, Janet, 'Shorty', must be recognised for her tireless advocacy and help with the book, along with my two daughters, Chelsea and Meghan who have shown their love and understanding while their Dad has been ill.

Finally, I would like to thank my rehab team, Dr. Henriette Groeneveld, Dr. Tammy Hopper, Mr. Stuart Cleary and Miss Debbie Steadward, who have kept me going.

Series Editor's Note

Prior to the publication of *The Commercialisation of Sport*, Trevor Slack became seriously ill. All who worked with him at Frank Cass, especially J. A. Mangan and Jon Manley, who worked most closely with him, wish him the speediest of recoveries.

Prologue

One of the most visible aspects of modern sport is its strong links to commercial enterprise. Stadiums and arenas bear the names of businesses that pay to buy the naming rights to these venues. Commercial sponsors' logos appear on athletes' clothing and equipment, on the facilities in which they play, and in the titles of the events in which they compete. Media companies spend vast sums of money on rights to broadcast sporting events, and advertisers pay to promote their products and services in the commercial breaks during the screening of these events. Cities invest large sums of money, often at the expense of other more important social projects, to stage major sporting events or to attract professional teams to their area. Star athletes are transferred for millions of dollars or pounds and professional sport franchises are sold for sums that are higher than the Gross Domestic Products (GDPs) of some countries. Even recreational athletes are subject to a constant barrage of pressures to improve their game by purchasing the latest high-tech sports equipment, and very few children's sport teams and events operate without an omnipresent sponsor. There are few businesses today that do not have, or have not had, some link to sport and there are even fewer sport leagues, teams, events or organisations that do not have some commercial aspect to their operation.

While sport has always had links to business, the number, frequency and intensity of the links between the two have increased considerably over the past 25 to 30 years. Estimating the size of the commercial interest in sport is an inexact science. There is no Standard Industrial Classification (SIC) code for sport and business, while related activities that would be commonly recognised as being part of the sport industry are recorded under a variety of SIC codes. Disney, for example, which has part of its operations in sport, is listed under 'recreational activities'. Nike is listed in the 'footwear' SIC, Spalding under 'recreational products', Churchill Downs under 'casinos and gaming', and Russell under 'apparel'.[1]

Despite the difficulties in clearly demarcating what constitutes the sport industry, there have been several attempts to estimate the value of commercial interest in sport. In 1986 a study by the now defunct publication *Sports Inc.* estimated that what it termed 'the US Gross Domestic Sport Product (USGDSP)' was worth US$47 billion[2]. In 1990 an article in *The Sporting News* described sport as a $63.1 billion industry.[3] A 1995 article by

Meek in *Sport Marketing Quarterly* estimated the USGDSP at $152 billion, indicating a growth rate of 8.8 per cent per annum since 1986,[4] and a figure that was significantly higher than the overall growth in GDP. Most recently, a 1999 *Sport Business Journal* article estimated the US sports industry as having a value of $213 billion, with a real per-capita growth rate of 7.8 per cent.[5] The size of the sport industry in other countries is not as well-researched as in the US, but those data that do exist show a similar picture. Gratton suggests that consumer spending on sport in the UK reached a record £15.2 billion in 2000. The comparative figure for 1990 was £8.9 billion, giving an overall market increase over the ten years of 70 per cent. The commercial sport sector was described as accounting for 1.8 per cent of GDP and employing 450,000 people or 1.6 per cent of the UK's total employment.[6] A 1997 Australian study found that that country's sport and recreation sector involved 11,000 businesses, produced goods and services valued at around $12 billion, and contributed 1.2 per cent to GDP.[7]

Despite the fact that the studies cited above are highly subjective, what can be deduced from them, with reasonable confidence, is, first of all, that there is a large commercial involvement in sport and, second, that the level of involvement is growing. In many of the world's economies sport makes a significant contribution to GDP. However, despite the increasing commercialisation of sport, the topic has been subjected to little academic analysis. There are numerous trade journals devoted to aspects of the industry and every day newspapers are replete with details of the commercial activity that has come to characterise sport, but few of these contain any type of scholarly critique. There are also books about the management of sport,[8] the economics of sport[9] and the marketing of sport,[10] as well as books that contain chapters on commercial aspects of sport.[11] There are also books that focus on the development of sport leagues and teams,[12] and books that look at the staging of events such as the Olympic Games[13] or the relationship between television and sport.[14] However, to date the only volume that focuses solely on the commercialisation of sport and provides some level of scholarly analysis is Lawrence and Rowe's 1986 book *Power Play*, which restricts its focus to Australia.[15]

The intent of this current work is, then, to fill a gap in the literature and provide a scholarly critique of some of the current commercial practices influencing sport. It does this by providing a series of essays on five different aspects of the commercialisation of sport: the sports industry; the public sector and the commercialisation of sport; the commercialisation of 'amateur' sport; television and the commercialisation of sport; and sport sponsorship. The authors contributing to this volume come from a variety of academic backgrounds, which include cultural studies, sociology, political science, economics, sport studies, organisation theory, and policy studies. Thus they bring a number of different perspectives to this important area.

In the first chapter of the opening part of the book, David Andrews directs attention to what he sees as 'the most culturally significant sector of the sport industry', the commercial mass media. He argues that, under 'late capitalism', cultural manufacturing, as opposed to the traditional manufacturing process, has become a principal means of capital accumulation. The cultural significance of sport is used by those within the media and communications industries to enhance the profit statements of their companies. Andrews uses two case studies to illustrate this point. First he focuses on the most powerful player in the world of media, Rupert Murdoch's News Corporation. He shows how Murdoch employed the cultural significance of sport to build his media empire. Andrews then turns his attention to the Olympic Games to demonstrate the way in which the power elite of the media world appropriated sport and designed it, promoted it and delivered it in order to maximise levels of capital accumulation.

In the second chapter George Sage looks at the growth of the sporting goods industry, which, as he puts it, has developed from struggling entrepreneurs to national businesses to transnational corporations. Sage describes the social and historical conditions that influenced the growth of the industry. He shows how many sporting goods companies are now integrated into the global economy. Focusing on Nike and Rawlings as examples, Sage describes how within this new economy sporting goods companies such as these have moved the production side of their operations 'off shore', usually to developing countries using female, low-cost, non-unionised labour. He discusses the implications of these moves for the workers in these developing nations, the social movements set up to counter worker exploitation, and the successes that these movements have had. Sage, like Andrews, demonstrates how, in the pursuit of capital, much of the sports industry is based on the appropriation of sport and the exploitation of those who work within the industry.

In the final chapter in the first part of the book, Barrie Houlihan takes a different approach from the first two authors, suggesting that much work on globalisation has tended to marginalise the role of the state. He argues that, with reference to sport, commercial media companies are seen as the primary vehicle of globalisation and international sport organisations are seen as playing an important secondary role. Such views tend to ignore, or, at best, pay little attention to, the significance of the state in the process of globalisation. In contrast, Houlihan argues that the state and international governmental organisations play key roles in the globalisation of sport. He then examines two recent incidents – player transfers and broadcasting rights in soccer, and then Olympic reform – to demonstrate the capacity of states to shape global sport. In the first instance Houlihan focuses on the Bosman case and the broadcasting of listed sports events. He shows how sport organisations have to operate within a framework of national and, in the European Union (EU), supranational regulation, and how this has slowed the pace of integration of commercial media organisations and sport clubs, and also played a role in reversing some of the changes that came about as a result of the Bosman case. In relation to Olympic reform, Houlihan focuses on the role of the European Union and the US government, which set up an investigation into the corruption scandals that rocked the International Olympic Committee (IOC) in the late 1990s. He shows how pressures from the US and the EU helped to shape the way in which global sport could develop under the IOC, and this, he suggests, is more a characteristic of internationalised sport than global sport.

The second part of the book focuses on the involvement of the public sector in the commercialisation of sport. In the first chapter in this part David Whitson, Jean Harvey and Marc Lavoie examine the question of government subsidisation of professional sport teams. Many such teams in Canadian cities do not have fan bases comparable to those of their US counterparts, nor do they enjoy similar levels of public subsidy. This, as the authors point out, has resulted in the departure of several Canadian teams to locations in the US. (Indeed, since this chapter was written the teams identified have been joined by the NBA's Vancouver Grizzlies, who have moved to Memphis.) The authors analyse the establishment and findings of the Mills Committee, which recommended tax measures that would provide financial support to Canadian professional sport; the rejection of these recommendations by the Canadian government; the subsequent Manley proposals; and the public outcry that resulted from these. Whitson and his colleagues go on to show how studies commissioned by industry supporters and civic boosters interested in securing or retaining professional sport franchises for their cities often distort the economic benefits of franchises to local communities.

In the second chapter on the role of the public sector, Mark Rosentraub continues the theme of public subsidies to professional sport teams. He first explores the evolution of the 'American system' for professional sports and the status of the four main leagues (the NHL, the NFL, the NBA and the MLB) as cartels. He then argues that the cartel structure of professional sport has meant that the leagues, owners and players have enjoyed economic success. In contrast, host communities have suffered financially. Through their ability to control the numbers of teams, leagues have been able to extract significant subsidies from the communities that host franchises. In addition, Rosentraub suggests that, with the cartel structure of professional sport, fans are being short-changed, because ticket prices have risen and the competitiveness of the leagues is being undermined. He suggests that the current system is not immutable and he offers two scenarios that he feels would help to reduce the requirement for public subsidies of sport teams and make teams more competitive, without making a major impact on either the property rights of owners or the players' wage structures.

Continuing the theme of public sector involvement in the commercialisation of sport, Lucie Thibault, Lisa Kikulis and Wendy Frisby examine the partnerships that have been created between public sector organisations involved in the delivery of sport and those in the commercial sector. Such partnerships require managerial orientations and practices that are significantly different from those traditionally found in the public sector. Thibault and her colleagues explore the economic, social and political factors that have led to partnerships with commercial operators becoming accepted as mechanisms for the delivery of sport, the complexities of these partnerships and the consequences for key stakeholders. They suggest that, unless they are carefully managed, partnerships between public and commercial providers of sport may result in the traditional social mission of the public sector being overtaken by the economic motives of commercial providers. As more and more public sector agencies engage in partnerships with commercial agencies and use market mechanisms in their service provision, the questions that these authors raise about the advantages and disadvantages of such interorganisational relationships are becoming increasingly important.

In addition to the increasingly commercial orientation of public sector organisations involved in sport, we have also seen the 'amateur' side of sport become more and more subject to commercial forces. The three chapters in the third part of this book explore this issue. In the first chapter Ellen Staurowsky examines intercollegiate athletics in the US, where athletes who are ostensibly 'amateurs' raise large sums of money and generate considerable prestige for the colleges and universities they attend. Staurowsky shows how the ideals of amateurism, education and not-for-profit status around which college sport is based have been replaced (if they ever existed) by professionalism, entertainment and profit motives. She suggests that a corporate veil based on the ideology of amateurism helps the NCAA to position itself as an amateur/educational sport governing body, rather than an athletic corporation/cartel. With the increasing pressures of commercialisation, such a masquerade is resulting in the economic interests of college sport undermining the ideals of education on which such activities are allegedly based.

In Chapter 8 Danny O'Brien and Trevor Slack discuss a sport that was once described as the last bastion of amateurism: rugby union. They provide a case study that looks at how, following the 1995 'Paris Declaration', one first-division English club responded to the pressures to adopt a more professional and commercialised form of operation. Their work shows the dynamics of the change process and, specifically, how powerful actors with commercial interests were able to take over the club. It also illustrates the sources of resistance to change and the variety of strategic responses employed by those who were opposed to the change. In doing so it brings a 'fine-grained' understanding to the commercialisation process in what was traditionally a non-commercially oriented sport.

In the last chapter of this part, Tara Magdalinski and John Nauright focus on the Olympic Games, the sporting spectacle that, from its relatively humble and amateur-oriented beginnings, has turned into what they describe as 'the largest corporatised multi-sport event' in the world. They show that, while the Olympics have always depended on local economic and political elites for their success, the more recent Games have been heavily financed by corporate sponsors and commercial partners. The Games are described as being commercially saturated to the point where educational programmes for children and Olympic mascots (which are primarily directed at children) are used as tools of the sponsorship program.

In the opening chapter of this book David Andrews describes the media as 'the most culturally significant sector of the sport industry'. Certainly, there are strong media links to many of the processes of commercialisation that have taken place within sport. The most significant branch of the media in this regard is television: consequently, the focus in the fourth part of this book is on television and the commercialisation of sport. In the opening chapter of this part (Chapter 10), Steven Jackson, Andrew Grainger and Richard Batty focus first on rugby union. They outline the transformation of what is described as New Zealand's national game and the commercial forces that helped to bring about this transformation. Their paper shows how, as part of the transformation process, the primary sponsor of the All Blacks used images of the Maori Haka and *moko* (facial tattoos) in its advertising campaigns, which led to a legal challenge by members of a Maori tribe. Jackson and his co-authors go on to show that such incidents are not isolated. They describe a Nike commercial that was removed from New Zealand television for being too violent and a Reebok commercial featuring the basketball star Shawn Kemp that never made it on to the country's television screens for the same reason. These incidents suggest that, while the commercial forces of television advertising are strong, there is resistance to this advertising, and that there are lines that must not be crossed as companies seek to market sport and sport products to consumers.

In the following chapter Michael Silk continues the focus on television. Silk sets out to rethink the relationship between cultures and economies. Focusing specifically on the practices of Television New Zealand (TVNZ) at the 1998 Kuala Lumpur Commonwealth Games, he shows how the production of cultural forms affects cultural identities. The paper demonstrates how TVNZ attempted to produce a 'preferred' sense of national identity, yet at the same time had to be sensitive to the requirements of its main sponsor, Air New Zealand, which was trying to promote positive images of Malaysia. This resulted in TVNZs broadcasts containing 'preferred' interpretations of Malaysia over 'local' New Zealand performances.

In the final chapter in this part of the book Bill Gerrard explains what he sees as the three stages of the commodification of team sports. He argues that television has played a major role in changing the commercial structure of professional sport, to such an extent that the competitive and financial viability of some leagues has been threatened by the disparities between teams, as well as by conflicts between players and owners. The latest trend in the commodification of professional sport has, Gerrard suggests, been the total or partial acquisition of teams by media groups. Media companies are vertically integrating sport teams into their operations, following a trend that goes somewhat against current business practices. Gerrard suggests that media companies' need for access to sport broadcasting rights and the ability to limit uncertainty in the professional sport industry are the two main reasons why such counter-intuitive trends are occurring in professional sport. He concludes that media ownership of sport teams is not likely to diminish in the near future.

The final part of this book deals with another of the main drivers of the commercialisation of sport: sponsorship. In the opening chapter, Trevor Slack and John Amis bring a critical perspective to the practice of sponsorship. They argue that most scholars who have studied the sponsorship activities of companies have not looked critically at the rationale for this involvement or the consequences of such involvement. Challenging the traditional notion of sponsorship as an exchange relationship, Slack and Amis demonstrate the unequal nature of the exchange. They show how sponsorship enhances the capital accumulation of sponsoring companies, changes the way sport is experienced and practised, and can serve to disadvantage fans. In pointing out these concerns Slack and Amis provide one of the first substantial critiques of a practice that has become inextricably linked to sport. Given the increased amount of money that is being spent on sponsorship,[16] such a critique serves to question the 'common sense' rationales that have frequently been presented for sport sponsorship.

In Chapter 14 Stephen McDaniel, Daniel Mason and Lance Kinney examine the sponsorship of sport by companies involved in producing 'sin products' – that is, tobacco, alcohol and gambling. There has been considerable discussion at the political level[17] and within the academic literature[18] about this issue. As McDaniel and his colleagues point out, with the hyper-commercialisation of sport and with sport organisations, both state-supported and professional, seeking increasing finances to maintain their levels of operation, the debate over companies involved in alcohol, tobacco or gambling sponsoring sport has received increased attention.

However, as is explained in this chapter, this relationship is not new, and the acceptability of such financial support varies by both product and by the type of sport being sponsored.

In the final chapter Michael Mauws offers a further critique of sponsorship practices. He uses a post-structuralist perspective to examine the ethical implications that arise from the sponsorship of athletes. Sponsorship, Mauws argues, acts as a form of disciplinary practice that serves to affect the behaviours of athletes. As Mauws correctly argues, interpretations of these effects will be influenced by the ethical perspectives adopted. Mauws favours post-structuralism of a type that he sees as best expressed in the work of Bauman. From this perspective athletes engage in sponsorship for purely economic reasons, to the detriment of the essence of the game and their sporting experience.

What can be found in the pages that follow is, then, a somewhat eclectic collection of essays written by scholars from a variety of academic backgrounds. What the chapters have in common is that they all raise critical questions about the commercialisation of sport. Given the rapid pace at which commercial practices have pervaded sport and the widespread nature of these practices, it is important that we do not unquestioningly accept the changes that are being wrought upon us. Raising issues about commercialisation can only help to make sport better. If this book helps to stimulate discussion about such issues then it has met the aims that were set for it.

NOTES

1. D. Rascher, 'What is the Size of the Sports Industry?', online at www.sportseconomics.com/newsletter/nl_display.php?TheNLName=Current; extracted on 23 April 2002.
2. Rascher, 'What is the Size of the Sports Industry?'.
3. E. Comte and C. Stogel, 'Sports: A \$63.1 Billion Industry', *The Sporting News* (Jan. 1990), 60–1.
4. A. Meeks, 'An Estimate of the Size and Supported Economic Activity of the Sports Industry in the United States', *Sport Marketing Quarterly*, 6, 4 (1997), 15–21.
5. D. Broughton, J. Lee and R. Nethery, 'The Answer: \$213 Billion', *Sport Business Journal*, 23, 26 (20 Dec. 1999).
6. C. Gratton, 'Sport and Economic Regeneration', online at www. britishcouncil.org/ work/sport/ed.htm; extracted 24 April 2002.
7. Australian Bureau of Statistics, 'Twelve Billion Dollars from Sport and Recreation', online at www.abs.gov.au/ausstats/abs@.nsf/5fle01afb32859f9ca25697500217f48/f876el; extracted 24 April 2002.
8. See, for instance, C. Gilson, M. Pratt, K. Roberts and E. Weymes, *Peak Performance* (London: HarperCollins Business, 2000); T. Slack, *Understanding Sport Organizations* (Champaign, IL: Human Kinetics, 1996); S. Szymanski and T. Kuypers, *Winners and Losers* (London: Penguin, 2000).
9. See, for instance, J. Fizel, E. Gustafson and L. Hadley, *Sport Economics: Current Research* (Westport, CT: Praeger, 1999); H. Preuss, *Economics of the Olympic Games* (Sydney: Wala Walla Press, 2000); J. Quirk and R. Fort, *Hard Ball* (Princeton, NJ: Princeton University Press, 1999).
10. See, for instance, G. Milne and M. McDonald *Sport Marketing* (Sudbury, MA: Jones and Bartlett Publishers, 1999); B. Mullin, S. Hardy and W. Sutton, *Sport Marketing* (2nd edition, Champaign, IL: Human Kinetics, 2000).
11. See, for instance, M.. Polley, *Moving the Goalposts* (London: Routledge, 1998); J. Coakley, *Sport in Society* (Columbus, OH: McGraw-Hill, 2001).

12. See J. Morgan, *Glory for Sale* (Baltimore, MD: Bancroft Books, 1997) for an analysis of the NFL; D. Wyatt, *Rugby Disunion* (London: Victor Gollancz, 1995) for the changes that occurred in rugby union before the Paris Declaration; and J. Sugden and A. Tomlinson, *FIFA and the Contest for World Football* (Cambridge: Polity Press, 1998) for details of the governing body of football (soccer).

13. See, for instance, K. Reich, *Making It Happen* (Santa Barbara, CA: CAPRA Press, 1986); F.W. King, *It's How You Play the Game* (Calgary: Script: the writers' group inc., 1991).

14. See, for instance, L. Wenner, *Media Sport* (London: Routledge, 1998); G. Whannel, *Fields in Vision: Television Sport and Cultural Transformation* (London: Routledge, 1992); J.F. Larson and Heung-Soo Park, *Global Television and the Politics of the Seoul Olympics* (Boulder, CO: Westview Press,1993).

15. G. Lawrence and D. Rowe, *Power Play* (Sydney: Hale & Iremonger, 1986).

16. T. Meenaghan and P. O'Sullivan, 'Playpower – Sports Meets Marketing', *European Journal of Marketing*, 33 (1999), 241–9.

17. 'Germany Backs Tobacco Lobby', *The Guardian* (6 Dec. 1997), p.5; 'Sport Left in Lurch by Tobacco Ban', *The Guardian* (28 Feb. 1999), p. 4.

18. J. Hoek, P. Gendall and M. Stockdale, 'Some Effects of Tobacco Sponsorship Advertisements on Young Males', *International Journal of Advertising*, 12 (1993), 25–35; R. Sparks, 'Youth Awareness of Tobacco Sponsorship as a Dimension of Brand Equity', *International Journal of Sport Marketing and Sponsorship*, 1 (1999), 236–60.

PART I:
THE SPORTS INDUSTRY

Sport in the Late Capitalist Moment

DAVID L. ANDREWS

Ignoring MediaSport today would be like ignoring the role of the church in the Middle Ages or ignoring the role of art in the Renaissance; large parts of society are immersed in media sports today and virtually no aspect of life is untouched by it.[1]

Any journalist making such trite observations as 'it's no longer "only a game"', 'it's all about the money these days' or, heaven forbid, the interminable 'sport has become big business' should have his or her salary docked and press pass revoked for stating the mind-numbingly obvious. During earlier phases in the evolution of the capitalist system, sport may have possessed a degree of autonomy from profit-driven rhythms and regimes. If misty-eyed nostalgia exaggerates the extent of this long lost independence, then the sports industry's gross annual revenues of some $324 billion worldwide – nearly half of which is generated in the United States alone[2] – make it inconceivable to think of sport as anything but an important arm of the global capitalist order. Yet the very term sport industry is misleading. The production and consumption of sport-related goods and services spans any number of industrial sectors, including (but not restricted to) manufactured products and apparel, travel, biomedicine, building construction and education. Yet it is the pervasive presence and influence of the commercial mass media that direct us to the most culturally significant sector of the sport industry. For, as Rowe notes, 'sport and the sports media, as cultural goods par excellence, are clearly a central element in a larger process (or set of processes) that is reshaping society and culture'.[3]

Within the context of the contemporary US political economy, the explosion of sporting content on network and cable television, radio, in newspapers, magazines and on the Internet has transformed sport into an intrusive and influential cultural practice; one that profoundly contributes to the shaping of everyday understandings, identities and experiences, as it swells the coffers of the wider economy. Propelled by media machinations, sport has risen to replace work, religion and community as the cultural 'glue of collective consciousness in latter twentieth century America', while simultaneously becoming the 'most potent of global "idioms"'.[4]

Hence this chapter focuses on the popular cultural phenomenon variously described as 'mediasport', the 'sports/media complex', the 'sport-business-TV nexus', 'sportainment' or 'the high-flying entertainment-media-sports industry'.[5]

Far from providing a comprehensive overview of the subject,[6] this chapter analyses the relationship between contemporary sport culture and the media industry. Despite the growing awareness of what one writer calls the 'institutional alignment of sports and media in the context of late capitalism',[7] sport continues to be fetishised by large sections of the general populace as a cultural form somehow removed from the invasive influences of late capitalism. Even the most critical of cultural commentators can slip into a whimsical romanticism whenever sport is mentioned, thereby totally ignoring its broader social and economic derivations or ramifications. Countering such naivety, and invoking Marshall McLuhan's dictum 'fish don't know water till beached',[8] this discussion encourages readers to think outside common-sense, uncritical and myopic understandings of sport by highlighting two exemplars of this most evocative of late capitalist synergies (that between sport and the commercial media), namely News Corporation and the Olympic Games. For the minimum requirement for becoming a productive contributor within the sport industry, an accomplished sport studies scholar and – perhaps most importantly – an informed sport consumer, is the ability to discern and dissect the political-economic nexus of sport-media-commerce.

Contextualising Contemporary Sport

If cultural fields are 'always constituted with and constitutive of a larger context of relationships',[9] then sport cultures are unavoidably – indeed dialectically – linked to contemporaneous economic, political, social and technological arrangements. Sports that prevailed in both pre-industrial and industrial eras were, in a cultural Marxist sense, a 'product of historical conditions ... and are fully applicable only to and under those conditions'.[10] For instance, the maturation of nation-state-based capitalism in Western Europe and North America during the second half of the nineteenth century, was accompanied by the emergence of institutionalised sport as – at least partially – an agent of social control for the urban industrial masses. By codifying sporting practice (regulated participation) and sanctioning cathartic release (mass spectatorship), the patrician-industrialist power bloc ensured that sport helped constrain working bodies to the demands and discipline of the industrial workplace, while simultaneously contributing to the commercialisation of urban leisure culture.[11] As labour historian Harry Braverman puts it:

the filling of the time away from the job also becomes dependent upon the market, which develops to an enormous degree those passive amusements, entertainments, and spectacles that suit the restricted circumstances of the city and are offered as substitutes for life itself. Since they become the means of filling all the hours of 'free' time, they flow profusely from corporate institutions which have transformed every means of entertainment and 'sport' into a production process for the enlargement of capital.[12]

Thus within the modern industrial era, institutionalised sport became an emergent site of 'surveillance, spectacle, and profit'[13] in a newly defined realm of 'free' time.

Despite a few examples of sport's commercialisation in the United States before the industrial era (for example in the promotional activities of colonial taverns[14]), many sport organisations and institutions continued outwardly to resist the lure of capitalist economic forces well into the twentieth century (some undoubtedly conditioned by residues of de Coubertin-esque idealism). Sport in this sense remained a 'semiautonomous sphere of culture',[15] that is, only *somewhat* removed from the practices and pressures of the marketplace. After the Second World War, however, the intensification of corporate-based consumer capitalism accelerated the 'infiltration'[16] of market forces into almost every facet of human existence, including sport. Corporate capitalism's inexorable appropriation of sport culture replaced the amateur(ish) volunteerism of official 'Old Boy' sporting values with the scientific business principles and rationalities espoused by 'men and women of the Corporation'.[17] These new values infiltrated sport via 'modern forms of domination, such as "business administration", and techniques of manipulation, such as market research and advertising'.[18] Sport was thereafter effectively and efficiently reorganised in accordance with corporate values and a logic of profit maximisation. Initially in the post-war United States, and subsequently in the corporatising economies of Western Europe, Japan and Australasia, this imperious corporate model transformed sport into *big* business, undermining once and for all any claim that sport enjoyed a semiautonomous relation to the political economy.

Once conclusively appropriated by corporate capitalism, the very constitution and delivery of sport culture became dialectically implicated in subsequent changes in the economic order. Today's media-driven sport culture can only be understood in relation to what Jameson famously described as the cultural logics of late capitalism that have crystallised in the final decades of the twentieth century.[19] Before this phase of late capitalism, the political economy had been dominated by mass *material* manufacturing carried out by large-scale manual workforces, in traditional factory settings, using heavy industrial machinery. During the 1970s declining industrial productivity rates, and the inflationary effects of global oil crises, incited the gradual unravelling of industrial capitalism after almost a century of relatively stable growth. Within this climate of economic stringency, the desire for reduced labour costs, and the lure of streamlined high-tech communication industries (both sources of increased profits), prompted the large-scale relocation of the labour-intensive material manufacturing sector to the industrialising peripheries of the global economy. In contrast, within core economies, in addition to a flourishing and multifaceted service sector, a manufacturing void was filled by a novel order centred on culture industries (advertising, marketing and the commercial media), whose emphasis on a mode of information[20] facilitated an economic transition from the material to the cultural, mirrored in the shift from production to consumption as the primary activity within the contemporary economy.

To a certain extent, then, mass *cultural* manufacturing (realised through the utilisation of sophisticated communications technology by a highly educated and well compensated technical elite) acts as a principal *mechanism* and *source* of capital accumulation within the late capitalist condition. As S. Connor has noted, the contemporary economy revolves around the 'production, exchange, marketing and consumption of cultural forms – considered in their widest sense and therefore including advertising, TV and the mass media generally – as a central focus and expression of economic activity'.[21] Since overseas labour reduced manufacturing costs to absolute minima, there has been a reconfiguring of the commodity value chain;[22] specifically, promotional (marketing, advertising and the commercial media) links have been mobilised as the primary means of creating the inflated surplus values required for economic profitability. Hence, the monetary value of late capitalist commodities is largely shaped within the cultural (or symbolic) realm of the 'Consciousness Industries',[23] as opposed to traditional industries' adding of value through the mass manufacturing of raw materials into finished products. With reference to a noted sport example, the exorbitant price of a pair of Nike Air Jordan shoes is practically unrelated to the relatively minuscule cost of manufacturing them in overseas industrialising economies. In marketing parlance, the competitive advantage held by Air Jordan's over rival sport footwear products (almost all of which are made in similar socio-economic locations, frequently in the same factories) is added (or manufactured) during the product's promotional phases in the United States, often involving the use of sporting celebrities. Through innovative advertising campaigns that both capitalised on, and indeed accentuated, basketball star Michael Jordan's cultural prominence, Air Jordan shoes were furnished with a symbolic value that effectively transformed a gaudy concoction of leather, nylon, and rubber into a prized cultural commodity; a commodity whose media-nurtured desirability was the key determinant in establishing an inflated economic value within today's informational-symbolic order.[24]

The Sport-Media Complex

Without question this discussion of the political economy of sport could focus exclusively on Nike. Nike is, after all, the brand that has most effectively blurred the boundaries between sport, the economy and contemporary media culture. Goldman and Papson have even suggested that we live in a 'Nike culture'.[25] Nevertheless, and with a nod to Nike, we must take a broader view of contemporary sport culture, and turn instead to the merger of media and sport which has fostered a process that Rowe calls the 'culturalization of economics'.[26] In an era in which *Business Week* could remark that 'entertainment has replaced the defense and auto industries as the driving force of the US economy',[27] the media-sport entertainment complex can be shown to stand out as a key *source* of wealth creation.

The recent reinvention of Westinghouse provides a graphic example of how the US political economy has been transformed by cultural industrial logics and shows sport's role in this process. At one time an industrial giant with thriving interests in the consumer-durable, commercial engineering, defence and nuclear industries, Westinghouse had amassed $15 billion in debt by 1993, because it had failed to respond expediently to the macroeconomic changes that signalled the demise of the traditional manufacturing sector. The threat of financial collapse was resolved by hiring (the other) Michael Jordan from PepsiCo in 1993 to direct the corporation's transformation. Jordan initiated a five-year plan that, while including more than 20,000 job losses, saved Westinghouse for its shareholders. His solution: make it a media corporation. This was achieved by selling off traditional businesses in order to fund the purchase of the CBS media group for $5.4 billion in 1995 and the Infinity Broadcasting radio group in 1996. As if finally to signal the death knell of its industrial capitalist past, and indeed its rebirth as a major force in the media sector, Westinghouse officially changed its name to CBS Corporation in 1998. This was followed by the $34.5 billion purchase by Viacom (owners of Paramount Pictures, MTV, VH1, Nickelodeon and Simon & Schuster publishers) of the CBS Corporation in 1999, which effectively created a diversified media entertainment giant to compete with Time Warner, Disney and News Corporation.

Sport played a central role in this industrial restructuring process. CBS had reached its nadir after losing television broadcast rights for National

Football Conference (NFC) games to the maverick Fox network, which made an unprecedented $1.58 billion bid in December 1993, ending CBS's 38-year relationship with professional football.[28] Few were surprised in 1998 when the newly reorganised and competitive CBS regained an NFL foothold with its $4 billion purchase of rights for American Football Conference games for the period 1998–2005. Leslie Moonves, then president of CBS television, said the deal put CBS 'back in the game'. In the words of Don Hewitt, executive producer of *60 Minutes*, 'I think it's like restoring a piece of the CBS logo' (*60 Minutes* ratings suffered more than others from the loss of NFL coverage, which aired before it on Sunday evenings).[29] As if to further consolidate the network's standing, in late 1999 CBS signed an unprecedented $6.2 billion contract for world-wide multi-platform (television, radio, Internet, licensing, sponsorship and publishing) rights to the NCAA men's basketball tournament for the 11-year period from 2003 to 2013, thus consolidating a 'relationship' that dated back to 1981.[30]

Although increasingly challenged by new cable, satellite, digital and Internet-based media – as well as the resurgent movie sector – commercial network television was still the entertainment industry's central force at the end of the 1990s. Networks had become subsidiaries of large media or industrial conglomerates, including ABC (Disney), CBS (Viacom), Fox (News Corporation) and NBC (General Electric). Since revenue from the sale of advertising space represents network television's principal revenue stream (augmented by sponsorship income and syndication fees), the size and composition of programme audiences assumes critical importance; audiences effectively become commodities sold by media outlets to advertisers.[31] Under this economic system, the boundaries between advertiser and programmer interests have been virtually erased. With scant regard for television's educative and informative potential, commercial television networks routinely originate repetitious and bland menus of entertainment-oriented programming (game shows, situation comedies, docudramas and infotainment), designed solely to secure mass audiences. Sport is on the menu too, offering a number of unique qualities: It is relatively inexpensive and easy to produce (certainly compared with equivalent programming lasting upwards of two hours); it is practically the only live television genre involving uncertain outcomes; it has a historically and culturally entrenched popular appeal; and, perhaps most significantly, it can boast the rare ability to attract high concentrations of the 18–34 year-old male consumers prized by corporate advertisers.[32] So, in purely pecuniary terms (and that is primarily what they are motivated by) live sport coverage is an attractive proposition for the major networks. As G. Sage neatly summarised: 'The media have no inherent interest in sport. It is merely a means for profit making. ... For TV and radio, sport gets consumers in front of their sets to hear and see commercials; in effect, TV and radio rent their viewers' and listeners' attention.'[33]

The clamour for audience ratings has led to network television moguls' perpetual engagement in a circus of spiralling bidding wars for the exclusive rights to these high-profile events. For example, in order to maintain its position as the 'Olympic network', NBC invested $3.55 billion for television rights to the three summer and two winter Olympiads between 2000 and 2008.[34] Broadcast rights for the Super Bowl also represent a significant part of the shared $17.6 billion eight-year contract signed by the NFL and ABC/ESPN, CBS and Fox in 1998. Having effectively purchased the US population's sporting attention, it is subsequently leased for exorbitant sums to corporate advertisers. Jon Mandel of Grey Advertising noted: 'When you think that virtually half the country's watching the Super Bowl ... this makes a hell of a statement.'[35] Mandel was referring to Super Bowl XXII in 1997 which tied for the third most-watched television show in US history. Hence in 1999 the popular appeal of the Super Bowl spectacle enabled Fox to charge $1.6 million for each of the 30-second advertisement spots (of which there were 58 in total), a figure which was expected to rise to $1.9 million per spot for 2000.[36] Similarly, NBC charges elevated advertising rates for its near three weeks of prime-time Olympic coverage, making its television rights a highly profitable investment (see later discussion of the Olympic Games).

While high-profile sport mega-events draw huge audiences from a broad spectrum of the population, regular major-league sport programming – often with seemingly modest television audiences in terms of volume – routinely attracts high concentrations in the more narrow male demographic category prized by corporate advertisers. This explains the significant sums networks payfor the television rights to the USA's professional sporting big four: $17.6 billion (ABC/ESPN, CBS and Fox) for NFL rights from 1998 to 2005; $2.4 billion (NBC and Turner) for NBA rights from 1998–9 to 2001–2; $1.7 billion (NBC, Fox and ESPN) for MLB rights from 1996 to 2000; and $600 million (ABC/ESPN/ ESPN2) for NHL rights from 1999–2000 to 2003–4. Although losing portions of its core male viewership to the media culture phenomenon that is TNT's *WCW Monday Nitro* and USA Network's *WWF Raw* (World Wrestling Federation),[37] ABC's *Monday Night Football* continues to preoccupy the North American male adult gaze to such a degree that it receives a staggering $380,000 for every 30-second advertising spot.[38] Lower down the television sport food chain, despite being expected to garner modest viewing figures, the very fact that approximately 40 per cent of the audience for its telecasts is drawn from the cherished 18–34 year old male demographic means ABC's NHL television coverage commands between $30,000 and $35,000 per 30-second spot.[39]

As well as regular network coverage catering to televised sport's traditional adult male constituency, sport programming targeted at specific market niches has recently come to the fore. Whereas *Monday Night Football*'s adult male demographic was once the almost exclusive quarry of sport programmers, now late capitalism's broadening exploitative reach has brought female, youth, ethnic and grey markets into the televised sport universe, as evidenced by the presence of the Women's National Basketball Association (WNBA) on NBC and Lifetime; the X Games on ABC/ESPN, ESPN2; Major League Soccer (MLS) on ABC/ESPN/ ESPN2; and numerous Senior PGA events on various channels. This trend is vividly exemplified by NBC's creation and coverage of the Gravity Games; a response to the network losing the rights to broadcast AFC football to CBS in 1999.

As the sports audiences created by television continue to diversify in terms of *size* (sporting mega-events) and *specificity* (regular and niche sport programming), the media-sport complex strengthens its strategic hold on the structure and logic of commercial television, proving to be an almost unassailable means of attracting advertiser dollars. For this reason, and as Jary has lamented, there exists an 'increasing tendency for sport organisations in particular to become indirectly controlled or monopolised by media organisations and/or major advertisers'.[40] In the light of this trend, the remainder of this discussion focuses on two case studies, News Corporation and the Olympic Games, which in different ways are both heavily implicated in late capitalism's 'seductively consumerist union of commerce, sport and television'.[41]

News Corporation

> There is no one in the media world who has a greater commitment to the commercial exploitation of sport than Murdoch.[42]

Rather than Michael Eisner (Disney's Chairman and CEO), Charles Dolan (Cablevision's Chairman) or John Malone (TCI's Chairman and CEO), it is Rupert Murdoch (News Corporation's long-time Chairman and CEO) who is perched atop the global sport-media complex. This is no mean feat for someone with a professed lack of interest in sport per se. Yet it is wholly indicative of a masterly entrepreneur who recognises the importance of sport's cultural significance for the process of capital accumulation within the media and communications industries. For, in Murdoch's terms, throughout the 1990s News Corporation used sport as a primary '"battering ram" for entry into new markets' throughout the world.[43] As Peter Chernin, News Corporation's President and Chief Operating Officer, outlined: 'This company is so defined by sports right now because what we have found in building our worldwide TV ventures – which are essentially pay-TV – is that the two things that drive them are movies and sports. And sports is the more important.'[44] In this manner, Murdoch used sport's popular appeal, and the economic benefits derived from it, as a means of elevating News Corporation to the level of Disney, Time Warner, Viacom et al. within the global media oligopoly.[45]

Sport was certainly not a primary focus of Murdoch's initial forays in the media business. Beginning in Australia, then moving into New Zealand, the United Kingdom and the United States, News Corporation acquired a vast stable of newspapers that presently numbers 132 separate properties,[46] magazines (e.g. *TV Guide*, the *Weekly Standard* and the *Times Literary Supplement*) and publishing houses (HarperCollins, Regan Books, Zondervan). While this array of print holdings helped establish Murdoch's media empire, News Corporation's elevation to the status of a 'main player in the global media system'[47] was realised through key movie and television industry acquisitions made during the 1980s. In 1985, Murdoch purchased a 50 per cent stake in the struggling Twentieth Century Fox film and television studio for $325 million.[48] This transaction provided News Corporation with a familiar brand identity, film and television production facilities, and a library of over 2,000 films. All three factors proved instrumental in Murdoch's subsequent creation of a fourth national television network to challenge ABC, CBS and NBC. In May 1985, News Corporation purchased seven television stations from Metromedia for $2 billion,[49] instantaneously providing the newly founded Fox Television Incorporated with a presence in the United States' major television markets (New York, Los Angeles, Chicago, Washington, Houston and Dallas).[50] Twentieth Century Fox's production facilities also proved an important resource for originating network programming, as did access to its vast film library. Murdoch subsequently brought his populist (some may argue consciously lowbrow) production values – honed in the highly competitive newspaper business – to network audiences, as *In Living Color*, *The Simpsons*, *Beverly Hills 90210* and tabloidic telejournalism signalled the arrival of Fox Television.[51] News Corporation became increasingly television-oriented, as evidenced by the fact that TV presently generates more than one-third (35 per cent in 1998) of the company's earnings.[52]

Having secured a foothold in the all-important US television market, Murdoch's ambitions expanded to colonising the new media platforms that emerged in the 1980s from the worldwide spread of communications deregulation and privatisation policies. So News Corporation embarked on a globally-oriented satellite television expansion that included Foxtel (Australia), JSkyB (Japan), Zee TV (India), Sky (New Zealand), Vox (Germany) and Star TV (Asia). However, perhaps of most note was the launch of British Sky Broadcasting (BSkyB) in the United Kingdom which foretold important elements of News Corporation's future involvement in sport. Following a short yet acrimonious and financially draining struggle between Murdoch's Sky Television and British Satellite Broadcasting, these rival fledgling satellite providers eventually merged in 1990 to form BSkyB. Because it was a subscriber service, BSkyB's profitability – indeed its and News Corporation's very existence following the massive losses incurred before the merger – depended on the ability to attract *paying* customers; something abhorrent to many media consumers in the United Kingdom. Murdoch's saviour was none other than the much-maligned English soccer fan. One would be hard pressed to find another cultural product with anything like the same popular appeal of English soccer. The entrenched popularity of soccer meant that it was 'the only sport that was clearly capable of attracting significant numbers of new customers to satellite TV'.[53] Consequently, in 1992, Sky Sport (BSkyB's sport channel) paid £304 million (an increase of some 600 per cent over the previous contract) for an exclusive five-year deal with the newly formed English Premier League to televise live games.[54] Without question English Premier League soccer became the 'jewel in the crown'[55] in BSkyB's consciously populist diet of trite situation comedies, sensationalist news coverage and blockbuster movies. Yet Murdoch also recognised the potential of other sporting contests. BSkyB subsequently embarked on a seemingly relentless, and usually successful, pursuit of Britain's most coveted sporting events which saw it acquire most of the English national soccer team's games, England's cricket test matches played abroad, many major rugby union games, rugby league in its entirety and the Ryder Cup.[56] This sports-oriented strategy certainly proved effective, as satellite dishes began adorning the outside of Britain's houses and flats in sizeable numbers, signifying a rapid rise in BSkyB subscribers that guaranteed the network's existence (and provoking Prince Charles, with his less than populist sensibilities, to describe them as 'architectural acne'). When Sky Sport's initial contract with the Premier League ended in 1997, not surprisingly Murdoch moved quickly to quash any competitors by agreeing to pay £670 million for a four-year deal.

Murdoch's experiences in the United Kingdom alerted him to the importance of sport in the process of shaping News Corporation into a truly global media power. As Murdoch himself outlined in 1996, News Corporation 'will be investing and acquiring long-term rights and becoming part of the sports establishment. … Football, of all sports, is number one.'[57] This philosophy underpinned Fox Television's wrestling of television broadcasting rights to NFC games away from CBS in December 1993. Fox paid the National Football League a staggering $1.58 billion for the four-year contract, a vastly inflated price designed to deter the more established, and perhaps more conservative, networks. Justifying Fox's huge outlay, Murdoch brazenly admitted: 'We put that $380 million a year on the table to help build Fox. We didn't do it so some quarterback can make another half million a year. ... That's just a by-product. What we did, we did selfishly, to build the network. It was a selfish business decision.'[58] And build the network it did. The acquisition of NFC football proved so successful in establishing and defining Fox's network status that it plainly solidified a necessary relationship between network television and the NFL as a whole, prompting one unnamed network executive to later rue: 'I just don't think you can be a network anymore without NFL football.'[59] This sentiment was ably reflected in the frenzied negotiation that led to the signing in early 1998 of an eight-year contract for NFL television rights, for a combined $17.6 billion (or $2.2 billion annually), divided between ABC/ESPN ($9.2 billion), Fox ($4.4 billion) and CBS ($4.0 billion). Fox Television was not only playing with the 'big boys', it had helped establish the criteria for membership to this exclusive sport-media order.

Having hugely benefited as a network from its NFL coverage, Fox Television then turned to Major League Baseball (MLB) and the National Hockey League (NHL) with similar expectations. Largely due to the lure of World Series coverage (even if shared with NBC), Fox's joint involvement with NBC and ESPN in a $1.7 billion five-year contract (1996–2000) for MLB coverage has proved moderately successful. Conversely, despite numerous innovations designed to popularise televised coverage of the game (including the infamous glowing puck), Fox's involvement with the NHL proved less than satisfactory in terms of national viewing figures, leading to ABC/ESPN's uncontested $600 million bid for a five-year television contract beginning in the 1999–2000 season. Of course by this time News Corporation had developed a significant sporting presence within the US cable television market through its setting up of the Fox Sports channel in 1993. Nine regional cable sports networks were subsequently purchased in 1996, providing the groundwork for the innovative Fox Sports Net, a network of 22 regionally-based cable sports channels linked by the national nightly highlight show *Fox Sports News* and other nationally aired programming, but also incorporating a large proportion of regionally focused sports coverage. Fox Sports Net presently control the local cable television rights to 71 of the 76 US-based MLB, NBA and NHL teams, placing it in a significantly stronger position than ABC's more established, but less regionally flexible, ESPN and ESPN2 cable sports channels. Indeed, such is its vigorous good health that one commentator recently referred to the '8,000-pound gorilla that Fox Sports Net has become'.[60]

Television coverage rights and networks are but two aspects of Murdoch's broader vision of creating a vertically integrated and globally encompassing sport-media delivery system. Countering the broader trend towards corporate outsourcing and institutional disaggregation, News Corporation has sought to secure central ownership and control over the various revenue-generating nodes of the sport entertainment industry.[61] For this reason, the late 1990s saw News Corporation engage in a global quest focused on the acquisition of entire sport leagues, individual teams and even stadia.

Murdoch's most comprehensive sporting coup was his purchase of British Rugby League for £87 million in 1995. With the purpose of securing inexpensive programming for its Sky Sport cable network, News Corporation effectively bought a 100-year-old sporting culture ingrained in the working class and history of northern England. Rugby League was thus transformed from a financially troubled and poorly administered sport, into a single 'corporate entity' owned and controlled by BSkyB, which implemented divisional restructuring, new pseudo-American team names (such as the Bradford Bulls, Wigan Warriors and Halifax Blue Sox) and merchandising initiatives.[62] The takeover also saw a century of Rugby League tradition conveniently erased when the game was switched from a winter to a summer playing season. Whether beneficial or not in the long run for spectators and players alike, this profound alteration in the game's very complexion was solely motivated by corporate exigencies. Specifically, the shift ensured that coverage of the Sky Sport's newly formed 'Super League' would not clash with English Premier League soccer, Murdoch's prize possession within a British broadcasting rights context. To a lesser extent, he also wanted to avoid scheduling and player conflicts with the rival rugby union code in which he had a considerable investment.

At the same time, News Corporation was fighting a more contested takeover battle within the Australian sport market. Murdoch had long coveted Kerry Packer's domination of cricket and Australian Rugby League (ARL), both of which figured prominently on Packer's Nine Network (Packer was Murdoch's arch media rival within the Australasian context). Sensing an opportunity to loosen Packer's grip on rugby league in early 1995, and desperate for popular programming to provide impetus for his new Foxtel cable TV network, Murdoch announced plans to establish a rival 'Super League' in 1996 made up of elite players and six entire teams prised away from the ARL. After much legal wrangling, the competing leagues went into direct competition. Both fared poorly in terms of game attendance and television viewership due to the perceived fractured and diluted nature of either product. In late 1997, the inevitable ensued with the merger of the ARL with the Super League to form the National Rugby League, jointly owned between the two camps.[63] The merger meant the closure of a number of teams and the eventual merger of others. As a result

Murdoch was castigated for precipitating the ruin of a national institution and a community resource. Not that he would have been perturbed by such criticism as ultimately he realised his goal of gaining (at least joint) control of Australia's premier rugby code. The ARL-Super League scenario merely underscored Murdoch's conscienceless modus operandi; the ruthless 'determination to secure whatever corporate advantage he can, regardless of the cultural or commercial obstacles'.[64]

Not all sports leagues are as vulnerable to News Corporation's advances, forcing Murdoch to turn his avaricious gaze to professional teams as a means of expanding his sporting media network. In Miller's terms:

> 'software' is what media empires call the teams they own. Fans may see the Los Angeles Dodgers or the New York Knicks as home teams with illustrious histories, but the new breed of owners – Rupert Murdoch's News Corp., Time Warner, Disney, Cablevision, Comcast – view them as content, programming fodder for the insatiable beast called television.[65]

Doubtless initially coveting a large television market-based NFL franchise, within the US context Murdoch's football aspirations were stifled by the NFL's prohibition on corporate ownership of league franchises. According to NFL Commissioner Paul Tagliabue, a media corporation's involvement in the league 'would present a conflict of interest in competitive situations' over rights fees negotiations. 'We always want our interests to have but one interest. That might be compromised.'[66] With such restrictions in place, Murdoch turned to the USA's other major professional sports.[67] Most notably in March 1998, and after protracted negotiations with MLB, Fox purchased the entire Los Angeles Dodgers organisation for $311 million, thus commandeering 'one of the great brand names in America in a world where brand names are increasingly important'.[68] Through this investment in the Los Angeles Dodgers, Fox Entertainment effectively purchased a permanent and high-profile presence in one of the US's largest television markets, by being able to offer a marquee programming attraction to the local viewing audience.[69]

Although successful in acquiring the Dodgers, Murdoch's even more audacious £623 million bid for Manchester United was ultimately blocked by the British government's Mergers and Monopolies Commission (MMC) in April 1999.[70] The rationale for this denial centred on the deleterious effects on competition in the broadcast sport industry arising from the competitive advantage BSkyB would command – as owners of the arguably most popular and watched English Premier League club – when negotiating for the league's television rights. In the words of the MMC:

The adverse effects of the merger, in particular the reduction of competition for Premier League rights and the consequential reduction of competition in the sports premium channel market and the wider pay TV market, appear to us to be very serious. As it is our view that no undertakings would remove these adverse effects, we conclude that prohibiting the merger is both an appropriate and a proportionate remedy, and we recommend accordingly.[71]

Murdoch consequently changed tack and has, through stealth as opposed to brute force, sought to garner influence over the future destination of English Premier League television rights. To this end, BSkyB embarked on a 'buying spree' of up to 9.9 per cent (the maximum percentage allowed for ownership in multiple clubs) of shares in individual clubs. With Manchester United, Manchester City and Leeds United already in his portfolio, Murdoch turned his attention to, among other clubs, Aston Villa, Chelsea, Tottenham, Newcastle and Sunderland as targets for future investment.[72]

Sport league and team ownership provides guaranteed popular television content on a truly worldwide scale, and has thus been a crucial element in establishing News Corporation as the 'first vertically integrated entertainment-and-communications company of truly global reach'.[73] The control afforded by ownership also provides networks with the ability to generate significant revenue from the 'migration' of game coverage to lucrative pay-per-view television platforms.[74]

With a multi-channel global television footprint such as that possessed by News Corporation, the cross-fertilisation of sport programming has become yet another lucrative option: BSkyB feeds of English Premier League soccer represent a staple part of Fox Sports World's offerings in the US, with live games on Saturday and Sunday mornings also available to pay-per-view satellite systems. Given the multiple opportunities for revenue generation afforded by News Corporation's local, national and global reach, it's no wonder that Murdoch makes high-priced bids for sporting properties and thereby 'inflates cost and undercuts competitive balance'. Put another way, News Corporation approaches sport (leagues, teams and stadia) not as profit centres but as 'cog[s] in the machine' of global media capitalism for which it is willing to pay substantial amounts.[75]

As NBC Sports chairman Dick Ebersol commented in response to Murdoch's repeat ranking at the top of *The Sporting News Power 100*, the annual list of the top 100 most powerful people in sports, 'It isn't even remotely a race. You could make him Nos. 1 through 5.'[76]

Olympic Games

> Whenever we switched on the tube, we saw what Ebersol wanted us
> to see, when he wanted us to see it. … Whether we like it, we watched.
> But we weren't watching the Olympics; we were watching Ebersol's
> vision of the Olympics.[77]

The previous case study focused primarily on an illustration of the
structure underlying the political economy of contemporary sport media
culture. The discussion now turns to the Olympic Games, a true sporting
'mega-event'[78] that grabs the attention of the global populace and reveals
how the media leviathans of late capitalism creatively appropriate sport
content as a means of furthering their rapacious agendas. Politics,
corruption and commercialism have been an ever-present aspect of the
modern Olympic movement since its inception with the Athens games of
1896.[79] Nevertheless, even in the hypercommercial world of late
twentieth-century sport, the Olympic Games somehow managed to
maintain an aura – however spurious and symbolic – of sporting purity
and unity seemingly unsullied by the world around it.[80] Williams would
perhaps argue that the Olympics' wholesome appeal is derived from 'the
joys of performance and the excitement of unpredictable drama [that] still
have the ability to transcend the commodification of sport'.[81] Within the
television universe, however, such an assertion could not be further from
the truth.

The drama of the Olympic Games as broadcast to millions of Americans
by NBC has been neither unpredictable nor is it divorced from the pervasive
commodification of sport.[82] Instead, NBC's televisual Olympics are a
'media event'[83] consciously designed, promoted and delivered to serve the
network's profit-driven purposes. Focusing on NBC's coverage of the 1996
summer Olympic Games in Atlanta,[84] this discussion unearths the motives,
manifestations and consequences of the network's reviewing, massaging
and repackaging of Olympic reality.[85]

In 1995, NBC signed two contracts with the International Olympic
Committee (IOC), amounting to $3.55 billion, which secured the
broadcasting rights to the summer Olympic Games in 2000, 2004 and 2008,
and to the winter Olympic Games in 2002 and 2006.[86] For the foreseeable
future, NBC effectively bought the rights to becoming the USA's Olympic
channel. In doing so, Dick Ebersol, President of NBC Sport (and executive
producer of NBC's coverage of the Atlanta Games) had purchased the right
to creatively suture the network's trademark peacock logo to the
accumulated and emotive symbolism of the Olympic rings. As Richard
Pound, the principal marketer of the Olympic Games brazenly admitted, 'If
you owe them [the bank] $10,000, you're a customer. If you owe them

$10,000 billion you're a partner.'[87] With the 'thoroughly modern marriage'[88] forged between NBC and the IOC, in a US context the Olympic Games are as much, if not more, about the advancement of NBC stock than about covering the event itself. This was particularly true since NBC had *guaranteed* its corporate advertisers a 17 Nielsen rating (equating to roughly 16.3 million TV households). Should Olympic broadcasts fall below that mark, the network would provide advertisers with free air time; an unwelcome eventuality that would eat into the anticipated return on the $465 million investment paid for the rights to televise the Atlanta Games.[89] Clearly, NBC was substantially more than a channel of transmission for the Olympic event, and the Atlanta Games were destined to become an NBC-directed, prefabricated Olympic spectacle: a 'highly artificial construct, designed for maximum sentiment and ratings'.[90]

In the lead-up to the Atlanta Games, Ebersol predicted people will get the 'results from CNN or the Internet ... but they'll get the stories from NBC'.[91] This Olympic production strategy was certainly nothing new; it merely represented the latest, and perhaps most sophisticated, attempt to transform televised sport in such a way that it could better compete with other forms of mass entertainment.[92] Ebersol even acknowledged his role and influence at the helm of NBC's Olympic fiction factory: 'I get to arrange how all these things are perceived in the world.'[93]

Driven by the economics of the marketplace, Ebersol freely admitted that 'ratings are the yardstick by which it [NBC] will judge its Olympic Games coverage'.[94] As a result he had to 'keep in mind appealing to the widest audience'.[95] For Ebersol, ensuring a *wide* audience meant capturing and sustaining the interest of women viewers.[96] Women were of particular interest to network executives because, through its ongoing research into the Olympic television audience, NBC had deduced that 'men will watch the games no matter what'.[97] This research also identified that, unlike other sporting events, women are drawn to the spectacle of the Olympics in roughly equal numbers to men. Consequently, the size of NBC's female viewership would determine the difference between commercial success and failure: between reaping the financial benefits of charging up to $700,000 per 30 seconds of advertising and being forced to offer free advertising space as a way of alleviating corporate customer dissatisfaction with poor ratings. Hence NBC's brief involved packaging the Olympics in such a way 'that women will stay glued'.[98] This fact predetermined that, despite the merit or otherwise of the forthcoming exploits of female Olympians, the Atlanta Games would be a celebration of Olympic womanhood. Within its battery of promotions which prepared the American audience for the upcoming spectacle, NBC openly declared that its focus would be on women's sports.[99] Before the ceremonial flame had been lit, and despite the fact that male athletes continued to profoundly outnumber female athletes 6,582 (63.53 per cent) to 3,779 (36.47 per cent),[100] a complex illusion of Olympic gender equality and emancipation was already artificially piloting NBC's mediation of the Atlanta Games.

NBC's strategy for the actual coverage of the Atlanta Games involved manufacturing a stereotypically 'feminine' Olympic spectacle. In creating this prime-time 'Oprah Olympics',[101] NBC manufactured its own Olympic reality centred around events deemed appropriate to female viewers, and infused with sentiment designed to resonate with the female psyche. According to production executives, NBC's conscious manipulation of the content and structure of Olympic reality 'was based on a scientific campaign to shape their broadcasts to a feminine sensibility'.[102] NBC's crude interpretation of its Olympic audience research findings reduced the complexities of consumer motivations and predispositions to a binary and essentialist model of gender norms and differences. In accordance with this reductionist model, certain sports are viewed as being popular among women simply because they incorporate and celebrate traditionally feminine traits such as bodily beauty, grace and expression. Conversely, male sports are deemed to be unpopular among women because their embodied masculine characteristics are viewed as an anathema to feminine sensibilities. In an Olympic context, this point was succinctly – if crudely – expressed by Ebersol: 'If you put boxing in the middle of the greatest family entertainment in all of sports, you're going to drive people away. …Women and children won't stand for it.'[103]

NBC's Atlanta Olympic coverage highlighted events that represented women in ways that the network deemed would be gender-appropriate for a *mainstream* US audience. Predictably, NBC's prime-time coverage focused on a surplus of meanings associated with the presumed hyperfemininity of certain events.[104] This perspective foregrounded gymnasts such as Shannon Miller, Dominique Dawes, Dominique Moceanu and Kerri Strug; swimmers such as Janet Evans, Amanda Beard and Amy Van Dyken; and, divers such as Mary Ellen Clark and Becky Ruehl. Of course there is nothing inherently feminine about these sporting activities, or any other activity for that matter. However, all of them have long been culturally coded as signifying the type of vulnerable, aesthetic and heterosexualised embodied femininity, around which NBC chose to centre its Olympic reality.[105]

Feminising the content of the prime-time Olympic schedule was aided by the economic leverage held by NBC over the IOC: a clear example of 'the television tail wagging the sports dog'.[106] As John Krimsky, US Olympic Committee deputy secretary-general and managing director for business affairs, admitted, the Olympic Games are essentially a 'made-for-TV event … and there are a number of things we can do to enhance that.

That's our job, to enhance the brand.'[107] Hence, among other measures, the IOC sanctioned the expansion of the gymnastics competition from seven to nine nights of prime-time coverage, the inclusion of a made-for-TV champions gala as an audience grabbing finale to the gymnastics competition, the enlargement of the swimming programme from six to seven days and the promotion of the diving programme within the Olympic schedule. Presumably because they were deemed not to have exuded the appropriate feminine aura, the highly successful US women's basketball, soccer and softball teams received nothing like the same prime-time coverage. Meanwhile, even less telegenic 'boxers, wrestlers and weightlifters – hairy, sweaty undesirables' were left to compete in the 'daytime ratings wars': 'The structure of NBC Olympic production was similarly framed by an essentialist understanding of gender as a binary category, within which the rational sports loving male was positioned against the emotionally driven sentiment loving female.' [108]

The goal of fashioning the Atlanta Games into a feminine product designed to bring 'a tear to the eye and bullion to the coffers'[109] necessitated NBC manipulating the structure of Olympic reality into a 'highly elastic style narrative' that artificially dramatised the event through the pre-programmed, and frequently delayed, manipulation and amplification of Olympic televisual discourse.[110] It has been noted that sport's unique quality over other forms of televised popular entertainment is the immediacy and uncertainty of sporting spectacles.[111] Recognising, yet subverting, the primacy of the live sporting event, NBC's Olympic televisual spectacle was consciously fashioned into a timeless and unreal space that, to the casual observer, appeared as if it were live (even though up to 40 per cent of it was not).[112] According to Dick Ebersol, 'In our minds, we'll be live at all times',[113] and certainly the network's announcers expressed nothing that indicated to the contrary. In actuality, NBC's nightly broadcasts were considerably more complex:

> Within NBC's broadcast of the Games, there are three types of production. The first is purely live, when something is shown in real time. ... The second is called live-on-tape ... What viewers see is called live by the announcers but is shown several minutes or several hours later. ... The third is taped coverage, which is usually easy to distinguish because there are breaks in continuity.[114]

The motive behind the intermingling of purely live, live-on-tape and taped coverage under NBC's deceptive rubric of being 'plausibly live' was plain. 'Its job was to build interest and drama in the unfolding panorama of the Olympic Games.'[115] The adoption of multiple programming formats allowed NBC's Olympic production team to artificially heighten and intensify the dramatic content of its broadcasts, giving them a degree of creative flexibility that simply does not exist in 'purely live' production. The network utilised 'plausibly live' programming to mould seamless and engaging narratives that were invariably built to a suspenseful climax, but whose relation to unfolding real-time events was largely irrelevant. NBC simply chose to blur 'reality in the name of a good story',[116] the network's logic being that if you 'tell them stories ... they will watch'.[117]

The most conspicuous example of NBC's 'plausibly live' strategy centred on the delaying, rearranging and massaging of Kerri Strug's final vault in the women's gymnastics team competition. The 'historic' vault actually took place in the late afternoon, but it was not shown on NBC until approaching midnight Eastern time. Seizing upon the emotive narrative offered up by the exploits of the injured Strug, NBC's prime-time programming served as a vehicle for gradually intensifying the drama surrounding this admittedly heroic, triumphant, yet ultimately irrelevant vault (the US had already won the gold medal prior to the vault). The result was NBC's 'highest, most emotional, most poignant moment', which garnered a phenomenal 27.2 Nielsen rating.[118] Despite the notoriety of this particular event, the repackaging of Strug's vault was indicative of NBC's production strategy throughout the Games: 'To NBC, the Olympics are episodes or segments in a prime-time show. It is all about stories, tales to be told, athletes to admire. Results are incidental. The events need not be presented on television in the linear fashion in which they unfold in real life.'[119] As well as creating a 'zone of fictional time',[120] an equally significant, and related, element of NBC's narrativizing of the Olympic schedule involved the strategic insertion of taped personal profiles as a means of creating emotive attachments between the television audience and particular athletes, and thereby events.[121]

The influential Roone Arledge developed 'Up Close and Personal' profiling for ABC's ground-breaking coverage of the 1972 Munich Olympics.[122] For the Atlanta Games, Ebersol enthusiastically appropriated this technique, and commissioned 135 two- to three-minute emotion-laced segments featuring various athletes, personalities, countries and events drawn from the televisual vaults of Olympic history past, present *and* future. These syrupy examples of 'formulaic hagiography' focused on a broad array of athletes, from predictable features on high-profile USA hopefuls such as Michael Johnson and Janet Evans, to stories on foreign notables such as the Belarusian gymnast Vitali Scherbo, the British triple-jumper Jonathan Edwards and the Canadian rower Silken Laumann.[123] These humanising segments personalised 'the competitors with feature stories that emphasise[d] family tragedies, childhood physical ailments and heartbreaking disappointments'.[124] By narrating contests through the stories of particular individuals, NBC framed the coverage of events in order to influence the way they were consumed. These 'motivational infomercials' acted as affective anchors by orchestrating viewers' emotional investment in the simulated narrative evolving before their eyes.[125]

In sum, the real-time Olympics became completely lost in the midst of the multiple temporal zones engaged during the carefully scripted production of these 'soap opera games'.[126] NBC's fabrication of highly emotive narratives framed the Olympics into a '17-day marathon *Melrose Place*'[127] for women who, according to the network, are 'addicted to melodrama'. NBC's conscious decision to fashion the Games into a distinctly feminine televisual spectacle was certainly a ratings and financial success. This gendered Olympic strategy was seemingly vindicated by an average 21.6 Nielsen rating (equating to roughly 20.7 million TV households), an impressive 41 per cent share of the television audience, which equated to a weighty 25 per cent increase over the viewing figures for the Barcelona Games.[128] In the crucial 18-to-34 female demographic segment, NBC's ratings had improved 16 per cent from the Barcelona figures, and a staggering 69 per cent from Seoul.[129] NBC's ratings far surpassed the guaranteed mark set for securing full payments for advertising air time. As a consequence, and even after sharing 10 per cent of its profits with the IOC, NBC made a $70 million profit on its initial $465 million Olympic investment.[130]

Yet these figures fail to express how the typically diverse and unpredictable viewing patterns were rendered irrelevant by NBC's media machine, which directly – and uncritically – attributed the reasons for higher Olympic viewing figures to its 'innovative' production strategies. No other explanation was even plausible. As a result, the widespread scepticism and resistance to the NBC Olympics expressed by many consumers was neutered, and became wholly submerged, under the symbolic weight of the network's increasingly reified, strategically concretised and evidently satisfied imaginary female consumer.[131] Fabricated 'with Mrs Six-pack and the kids in mind', NBC's clean, face-lifted and engineered emotional spectacle was modelled on stereotypical and demeaning models of women as both hyperfeminine objects of production and hypersensitive subjects of consumption.[132]

The progressive political potential of an increased female presence in the Olympic spectacle thus was neutralised by the demeaning way in which NBC chose to represent and engage women. Yet, given the economics of the television industry, Ebersol has already announced that money talks in regard to the network's Olympic production strategies; thus his antiquated gendered world is set for a reprise. 'Get used to it,' as one commentator put it. 'The ratings were so high that NBC will take the same tack into Sydney and beyond.'[133]

Coda

> In corporate/Americanized sport, the game has become somewhat less important than its capacity to be a vehicle presenting particular messages to a particular select and often massive audience.[134]

This discussion may have unearthed some disheartening revelations pertaining to the political economy of contemporary sport culture. Elsewhere I have argued that sport has, in Fukuyama's terms, reached the end of history precipitated by the 'total exhaustion of viable systematic alternatives'[135] to the sport-media-entertainment complex discussed here.[136] On reflection this sentiment intimates a resigned bitterness which adds little to the critical analysis of contemporary sport. Without question the global sport economy is dominated by brazenly commercial enterprises that make no pretence as to the cardinal importance of delivering entertaining products designed to maximise profit margins. As such it becomes increasingly important to engage in rigorous and thoughtful critiques of the hypercommercial sporting cultures that transfix many of our lives. In other words, while as enthusiastic sport consumers we may be temporarily intoxicated by the intensity of a Dodgers rally in the bottom of the ninth, or a heroic feat by an American Olympian, we should not overlook the economic, technological and political forces that come together to structure our experiences of contemporary sport culture. As the novelist E.M. Forster commanded, 'Only connect! ... Live in fragments no longer.'[137] For only then is it possible to 'give a better understanding of where "we" are so that "we" can get somewhere better':[138] perhaps a place where the *sporting medium* is no longer inextricably tied to a *commercial message*.

NOTES

This chapter is a slightly revised version of D.L. Andrews, 'Sport', in R. Maxwell (ed.), *Culture Works: The Political Economy of Culture* (Minneapolis, MN and London: University of Minnesota Press, 2001), pp.131–62.

1. M.R. Real, 'MediaSport: Technology and the Commodification of Postmodern Sport', in L.A. Wenner (ed.), *Mediasport* (London: Routledge, 1998), p.15.
2. A. Meeks, 'An Estimate of the Size and Supported Economic Activity of the Sports Industry in the United States', *Sport Marketing Quarterly*, 6, 4 (1997), pp.15–21.
3. D. Rowe, *Sport, Culture and the Media*: The Unruly Trinity (Buckingham: Open University Press, 1999), p.67.
4. R. Goldman and S. Papson, *Nike Culture* (London: Sage, 1998), p.66; D. Jary, 'The McDonaldization of Sport and Leisure', in B. Smart (ed.), *Resisting McDonaldization* (London: Sage, 1999), p.124.
5. Wenner, *Mediasport*; S. Jhally, 'Cultural Studies and the Sports/Media Complex', in L.A. Wenner (ed.), *Media, Sports, and Society* (Newbury Park, CA: Sage, 1989), pp.70–93; D Rowe, 'The Global Love-Match: Sport and Television', *Media, Culture & Society*, 18, 4 (1996), p.565; R. Lipsyte, 'Little Girls in a Staged Spectacle for Big Bucks? That's Sportainment!', New York

Times, 4 August 1996, p.14; S. Marantz, 'The Power of Air', *The Sporting News*, 24 December 1997, p.1.

6. See S. Barnett, *Games and Sets: The Changing Face of Sport on Television* (London: British Film Institute, 1990); R.V. Bellamy, 'Professional Sport Organizations: Media Strategies', in Wenner, *Media, Sports, and Society*, pp.120–33; R.V. Bellamy, 'The Evolving Television Sports Marketplace', in Wenner, *Mediasport*, pp.73–87; J. Chandler, *Television and National Sport: The United States and Britain* (Urbana, IL: University of Illinois Press, 1988); S.T. Eastman and T.P. Meyer, 'Sports Programming: Scheduling, Costs, and Competition', in Wenner, *Media, Sports, and Society*, pp.97–119; R.W. McChesney, 'Media Made Sport: A History of Sports Coverage in the United States', in Wenner, Media, Sports, and Society, pp.49–69; Jhally, 'Cultural Studies and the Sports/Media Complex'; B.G. Rader, *American Sports: From the age of Folk Games to the Age of Spectators* (Englewood Cliffs, NJ: Prentice-Hall, 1983); Real, 'MediaSport', pp.14–26; R.E. Rinehart, *Players All: Performances in Contemporary Sport* (Bloomington, IN: Indiana University Press, 1998); Rowe, 'The Global Love-Match', pp.565–82; Rowe, *Sport, Culture and the Media*; L.A. Wenner, 'Media, Sports, and Society: The Research Agenda', in Wenner, *Media, Sports, and Society*, pp.13–48; L.A. Wenner, 'Playing the Mediasport Game', in Wenner, *Mediasport*, pp.3–13; G. Whannel, *Fields in Vision: Television Sport and Cultural Transformation* (London: Routledge, 1992); D. Whitson, 'Circuits of Promotion: Media, Marketing and the Globalization of Sport', in Wenner, *Mediasport*, pp.57–72.

7. Real, *MediaSport*, p.15.

8. E. McLuhan and F. Zingrone (eds), Essential McLuhan (New York: Basic Books, 1995).

9. L. Grossberg, *Bringing it All Back Home: Essays on Cultural Studies* (Durham, NC: Duke University Press, 1997).

10. D. McLellan, *Karl Marx: Selected Writings* (Oxford: Oxford University Press, 1977).

11. R. Butsch (ed.), *For Fun and Profit: The Transformation of Leisure into Consumption* (Philadelphia, PA: Temple University Press, 1990).

12. H. Braverman, *Labor and Monopoly Capital: The Degradation of Work in the Twentieth Century*, 25th ed. (NewYork: Monthly Review Press, 1998), p.279.

13. T. Miller and A. McHoul, *Popular Culture and Everyday Life* (London: Sage, 1998), p.61.

14. S. Hardy, 'Where Did You Go, Jackie Robinson? Or the End of History and the Age of Sport Infrastructure', *Sporting Traditions: Journal of the Australian Society for Sports History*, 16, 1(1999), p.85–100.

15. F. Jameson, *Postmodernism, or the Cultural Logic of Late Capitalism* (Durham, NC: Duke University Press, 1991), p.48.

16. This apt metaphor is borrowed from J. Habermas, 'Conservatism and Capitalist Crisis', *New Left Review* , 115 (1979), pp.73–84.

17. J. McKay and T. Miller, 'From Old Boys to Men and Women of the Corporation: The Americanization and Commodification of Australian Sport', *Sociology of Sport Journal*, 8, 1 (1991), p.86.

18. P. Bourdieu, *Acts of Resistance: Against the Tyranny of the Market* (New York: The New Press, 1998), p.35.

19. Jameson, *Postmodernism*.

20. M. Poster, *The Mode of Information: Poststructuralism and Social Context* (Chicago, IL: University of Chicago Press, 1990).

21. S. Connor, *Postmodernist Culture: An Introduction to Theories of the Contemporary* (Oxford: Basil Blackwell, 1989), p.46.

22. G. Gereffi and M. Korzeniewicz (eds), *Commodity Chains and Global Capitalism* (Westport, CT, Greenwood Pres and London, 1994).

23. Jameson, *Postmodernism*, p.68.

24. M. Castells, *The Rise of the Network Society* (Oxford: Blackwell Publishers, 1996).

25. For a broad-ranging semiotically informed analysis of Nike's cultural significance, see Goldman and Papson, *Nike culture*. For insightful discussions of other aspects of the Nike phenomenon refer to: J. Ballinger, 'Nike in Indonesia', *Dissent* , 45, 4 (1998), pp.18–21; L.B.A. Brewer, 'There is No Finish Line: Telling the Nike Story with Signs, Video, and Doorknobs', *Identity*, (May/June 1995), pp.44–9; C.L. Cole and A.S. Hribar, 'Celebrity Feminism: *Nike Style* – Post-Fordism, Transcendence, and Consumer Power', *Sociology of Sport Journal*, 12, 4 (1995), pp.347–69; M. DeMartini, 'The Great God Nike: Good or Evil?', *Sporting Goods Dealer*, March 1997, pp.34–9; N.K. Denzin, 'Dennis Hopper, McDonald's and Nike', in B. Smart (ed.), *Resisting McDonaldization*, (London: Sage, 1999); M.T. Donaghu and R. Barff, 'Nike Just Did

It: International Subcontracting and Flexibility in Athletic Footwear Production', *Journal of The Regional Studies Association*, 24, 6 (1990), pp.537–51; N. Ind, 'Nike: Communicating a Corporate Culture', in *Great Advertising Campaigns: Goals and Accomplishments* (Lincolnwood, IL: NTC Business Books, 1993), pp.171–86; D. Katz, *Just Do It: The Nike Spirit in the Corporate World* (New York: Random House, 1994); M. Korzeniewicz, 'Commodity Chains and Marketing Strategies: Nike and the Global Athletic Footwear Industry', in Gereffi and Korzeniewicz, *Commodity Chains and Global Capitalism*, pp.247–65; M.R. Lafrance, 'If You Let Me P.L.A.Y.: Nike's Intersections of Postfeminism and Hyperconsumption', in G. Rail and J. Harvey (ed.), *Sport and Postmodern Times: Culture, Gender, Sexuality, the Body and Sport* (Albany, NY: SUNY Press, 1998); J. McKay, 'Just Do It: Corporate Slogans and the Political Economy of "Enlightened Racism"', *Discourse: Studies in the Cultural Politics of Education*, 16, 2 (1995), pp.191–201; G.H. Sage, 'Justice Do It! The Nike Transnational Advocacy Network: Organization, Collective Actions, and Outcomes', *Sociology of Sport Journal*, 16, 3 (1999), pp.206–35; J.B. Strasser and L. Becklund, *Swoosh: The Unauthorized Story of Nike and the Men Who Played There* (New York: Harcourt Brace Jovanovich, 1991); T. Vanderbilt, *The Sneaker Book: Anatomy of an Industry and an Icon* (New York: The New Press, 1998); and G.E. Willigan, 'High Performance Marketing: An Interview with Nike's Phil Knight', *Harvard Business Review*, (July/August 1992), pp.91–101.

26. Rowe, Sport, *Culture and the Media*, p.70.
27. Anon, 'Editorial: The Expanding Entertainment Universe', *Business Week*, 14 August 1995, p.114.
28. The National Football League is divided into two conferences, the National Football Conference (NFC) and the American Football Conference (AFC), each made up of 16 teams.
29. B. Carter, 'Football Deal Emphasizes NFL's Pre-eminence as Program Supplier', *New York Times*, 14 January 1998.
30. M. Hiestand, 'CBS Locks in College Hoops for $545m', *USA Today*, 19 November 1999, p.1C.
31. L. Grossberg, E. Wartella and D.C. Whitney, *MediaMaking: Mass Media in a Popular Culture* (Thousand Oaks, CA: Sage, 1998).
32. E. Herman and R.W. McChesney, *The Global Media: The New Missionaries of Corporate Capitalism* (London: Cassell, 1997), pp.140–5, 153–4.
33. G.H. Sage, *Power and Ideology in American Sport: A Critical Perspective* (Champaign, IL: Human Kinetics, 1990), p.123.
34. Real, 'MediaSport', pp.14–26.
35. Quoted in Martzke, 'Super Drama', p.1C.
36. See G. Farrell, 'Advertising's Super Day Ruled by the Dot', *USA Today*, 7 September 1999, p.1B; R. Rosenwein, 'The Anatomy of a Super Bowl Ad: 30 Seconds in the End Zone', *Brill's Content*, February 1999, pp.72–7; S. Elliott, 'Despite Millions of Viewers, the Superbowl is not Quite So for Madison Avenue', *New York Times*, 1 February 2002, p.2c.
37. See C. Hess, 'Wake Up, Business: Values Are Shifting', *USA Today*, 7 September 1999, p.17A.
38. See J. Mandese, 'Prime-Time Pricing Woes', *Advertising Age*, 20 September 1999, pp.1, 12, 16.
39. For example, the Fox network averaged a minuscule 1.4 household television rating for its regular-season coverage during the 1998–99 season. See L. Brockinton, 'Networks Begin First Season of Deal', *Street & Smith's Sports Business Journal*, 4–10 October 1999, p.29.
40. Jary, 'McDonaldization', p.120.
41. D Rowe, 'The Global Love-Match', p.566.
42. D. Rowe and J. McKay, 'Field of Soaps: Rupert v. Kerry as Masculine Melodrama', in R. Martin and T. Miller (eds), *SportCult* (Minneapolis, MN: University of Minnesota Press, 1999), p.191.
43. Quoted in R. Snoddy, 'Alliances for a Digital Future', *Financial Times*, 11 December 1996, p.1.
44. Quoted in C. Bruck, 'The Big Hitter', *The New Yorker*, 8 December 1997, p.82.
45. Fronting the new informational economy is a species of economically and culturally imposing global media corporations such as Time Warner, Disney, Viacom, Sony, Seagram, Bertelsmann, Granada and indeed News Corporation. These purveyors of variously formatted mass-mediated cultural products represent the dynamic force in the late capitalist economy, occupying much the same role as mass-manufacturing titans such as Ford, General Motors, General Electric, Dupont and Westinghouse Electric did in the industrial economy. See E. Herman and R.W. McChesney, 'Dominant Firms in the Global Media Market: News Corporation', in Herman and McChesney, *The Global Media*, pp.70–77, for a detailed explication of these 'new missionaries of corporate capitalism'.
46. News Corporation's newspaper acquisitions have included: the Perth Sunday Times in 1956; the

Sydney Mirror and *Sunday Mirror* in 1960; the *Australian* and Wellington *Dominion* in 1964; the London *Sun* and *News of the World* in 1969; the San Antonio *Express, News*, and *Sunday Express* and *News* in 1973; the New York *Post* in 1976; the London *Times* and *Sunday Times* in 1981; the *Boston Herald* in 1982; and the *Chicago-Sun Times* in 1984.

47. Herman and McChesney, *The Global Media*.
48. W. Shawcross, *Murdoch: The Making of a Media Empire* (New York: Touchstone Books, 1997).
49. Under a previous agreement, one of the seven stations, WCVB Boston, was immediately sold to the Hearst Corporation.
50. In 1985, compelled by Federal regulations that forbade an individual owning a newspaper and a television station in the same city, Murdoch was forced to sell the *New York Post*. The rule against foreign ownership of broadcasting licences also forced him to change his citizenship from Australian to American. Fox Television's subsequent purchases brought US television station holdings to 22 – the largest in the nation and a clear indication of Fox's emergence as a truly national network.
51. In November 1998 News Corporation set up a subsidiary company, Fox Entertainment Group Inc. This company comprised US-based assets in the filmed entertainment, television programming and distribution and sports team sectors.
52. In descending order the rest of News Corporation's earnings are derived from: newspapers (25 per cent); magazines and inserts (22 per cent); filmed entertainment (15 per cent); books (2 per cent); and other (1 per cent). See Chief Executive Officer's Review, News Corporation 1998 Annual Report: http://www. newscorp.com/report98/cer.html.
53. J. Williams, 'The Local and the Global in English Soccer and the Rise of Satellite Television', *Sociology of Sport Journal*, 11, 4 (1994), p.387.
54. Ibid, p.387.
55. J. Arundel and M. Roche, 'Media Sport and Local Identity: British Rugby League and Sky TV', in M. Roche (ed.), *Sport, Popular Culture and Identity* (Aachen: Meyer & Meyer Verlag, 1998), p.73.
56. Murdoch's successful procurement of the broadcast rights to many of the key events within Britain's sporting calendar has caused widespread consternation among the viewing public, due to the financial restrictions it places on citizen's access to core aspects of their national culture. This has led to government legislation that attempts to protect eight events deemed of national importance (FIFA. World Cup, the Olympic Games, Wimbledon, the English and Scottish FA Cup Finals, the Epsom Derby, the Aintree Grand National and home test matches for the England cricket team) for 'free to view TV' services (Arundel and Roche, 'Media Sport and Local Identity').
57. Quoted in Shawcross, *Murdoch*, p.406.
58. Quoted in Pierce, Master of the Universe, p.182.
59. Quoted in Carter, 'Football Deal'.
60. J. Rofe, 'The 800-Pound Gorilla Keeps Growing: Fox Discovers That Buying Sports Properties is Cheaper Than Renting – And It Heads Off the Competition', *Street & Smith's Sports Business Journal*, 23–29 August 1999, p.24.
61. For a discussion of the differences between horizontal and vertical integration, see Castells, *The Rise of the Network Society*.
62. Arundel and Roche, 'Media Sport and Local Identity'.
63. For extended discussions of the ARL-Super League conflict see D. Rowe, 'Rugby League in Australia: The Super League Saga', *Journal of Sport and Social Issues*, 21, 2 (1997), pp.221–6; Rowe and McKay, 'Field of Soaps'.
64. M.A. Hiltzik, 'Playing by his Own Rules', *Los Angeles Times*, 25 August 1997.
65. S. Miller, 'Taking Sports to the Next Level: Start with Teams, Add Arenas, Media and You've Got a Sports Empire', *Street & Smith's Sports Business Journal*, 23–29 August 1999, p.23.
66. Quoted in T. Heath and P. Farhi, 'Murdoch Adds Dodgers to Media Empire', *Washington Post*, 20 March 1998, p.A1.
67. As part of Fox Entertainment's purchasing of a 40 per cent share in Rainbow Media Holdings (a Cablevision subsidiary) in 1998, Murdoch gained a 40 per cent interest in both the New York Knicks and the New York Rangers.
68. Peter Chernin, News Corporation's president, quoted in Heath and Farhi, 'Murdoch Adds Dodgers'.
69. Fox's position in the Los Angeles market is destined to be strengthened by Murdoch's stated desire to exercise his option to purchase 40 per cent of the Los Angeles Kings and ten per cent of the Los Angeles Lakers; both clauses associated with his 40 per cent investment in the team's new

arena, the Staples Center in April 1998. Moreover, as well as the Staples Center, and as part of his sport franchise dealings, Murdoch acquired Dodger Stadium and a significant interest in Madison Square Gardens (40 per cent ownership), thus adding control of sport stadia and venues to his vertically integrated sports media delivery system. See Rofe, 'The 800-Pound Gorilla'.

70. See A. Walsh and A. Brown, *Not for Sale! Manchester United, Murdoch and the Defeat of BSkyB* (Edinburgh: Mainstream, 1999).
71. Quoted in T. Freeman, 'The Big Match', *The Student Law Centre* (BPP Law School, London) (1999): http://www.studentlaw.com/match.htm.
72. J. Cassy and J. Finch, 'BSkyB Linked to New Premiership Buying Spree', *The Guardian*, 11 August 1999.
73. Shawcross, *Murdoch*, p.399.
74. See Bruck, 'The Big Hitter'.
75. Miller, 'Taking Sports to the Next Level', p.32.
76. M. Knisley, 'All Rupert, All the Time', *The Sporting News*, 14 December 1998, p.16.
77. M. Knisley, 'Rock Solid', *The Sporting News*, 30 December 1996, p.S5.
78. M. Roche, 'Mega-Events and Micro-Modernization'; *British Journal of Sociology*, 43, 4 (1992) pp.563–600; M.Roche, 'Mega-Events and Urban Policy'.*Annals of Tourism Research*, 21, 1 (1994), pp.1–19; M. Roche *Mega-Events and Modernity: Olympics, Expos and the Growth of Global Culture* (London: Routledge, 2000)
79. See A. Tomlinson and G. Whannel (eds), *Five Ring Circus: Money, Power and Politics at the Olympic Games* (London: Pluto Press, 1984).
80. See R. VanWynsberghe and I. Ritchie, '(Ir)Relevant Ring: The Symbolic Consumption of the Olympic Logo in Postmodern Media Culture', in G. Rail (ed.), *Sport and Postmodern Times* (New York: State University of New York Press, 1998), pp.367–84.
81. Williams, 'The Local and the Global', p.394.
82. This discussion is a significantly abbreviated version of D.L. Andrews, 'Feminizing Olympic Reality: Preliminary Dispatches from Baudrillard's Atlanta', *International Review for the Sociology of Sport*, 33, 1 (1998), pp.5–18.
83. D. Dayan and E. Katz, *Media Events: The Live Broadcasting of History* (Cambridge, MA: Harvard University Press, 1992).
84. NBC broadcast 79 hours of prime-time Olympic coverage, 171.5 hours in total.
85. S. Zipay, 'Atlanta Olympics – Media – Absurdity Dominates Coverage', Newsday, 30 July 1996, p.A60.
86. Real, 'MediaSport'.
87. R. Thurow, 'Lord of the Rings', *Wall Street Journal*, 19 July 1996, p.14.
88. Knisley, 'Rock Solid'.
89. P. Farhi, 'For NBC, Olympics are the Golden Days: Network Sets Records for Viewership and Profitability at Games', Washington Post, 3 August 1996, p.F1.
90. D. Remnick, 'Inside-Out: The NBC Strategy that Made the Games a Hit', *The New Yorker*, 5 August 1996, p.27.
91. J. Impoco, 'Live from Atlanta: NBC Goes for Women Viewers and Platinum Ratings', US News & *World Report*, 15 July 1996, p.36.
92. See Barnett, *Games and Sets*; A. Blake, *Body Language: The Meaning of Modern Sport* (London: Lawrence & Wishart, 1996); Rader, *In its Own Image: How Television has Transformed Sports*; (New York: The Free press, 1984) Whannel, *Fields in Vision*.
93. Quoted in J. Goodbody, 'NBC Sets an Olympic Broadcast Record', *The Times*, 7 August 1996, p.21.
94. Quoted in Anon, 'NBC's Time Warp", *New York Times*, 2 August 1996, p.A26.
95. Quoted in R. Sandomir, 'NBC's Money Shots Prove It: They Love a Parade', *New York Times*, 19 July 1996, p.14B.
96. Zipay, 'Atlanta Olympics'.
97. M. Gunther, 'Get Ready for the Oprah Olympics', *Fortune*, 22 July 1996, p.43.
98. Ibid.
99. J. Schulian, 'Protecting the Investment: NBC's Opening-Night Coverage was as Commercial as the Games Themselves', *Sports Illustrated*, 29 July 1996, p.112.
100. D. Becker, 'More Women Athletes Head for Atlanta', USA Today, 18 January 1996, p.12C.
101. Gunther, 'Oprah Olympics', p.42.
102. Remnick, 'Inside-Out', p.26.
103. Quoted in Gunther, 'Oprah Olympics', p.43.

104. A.M. Feder, '"A Radiant Smile from the Lovely Lady": Overdetermined Femininity on "Ladies" Figure Skating', in C. Baughman (ed.), *Women on Ice: Feminist Essays on the Tonya Harding/Nancy Kerrigan Spectacle* (New York: Routledge, 1995), pp.22–46.
105. M.C. Duncan, 'Sports Photographs and Sexual Difference: Images of Women and Men in the 1984 and 1988 Olympic Games', *Sociology of Sport Journal*, 7, 1 (1990) pp.22–43; J. Ryan, *Little Girls in Pretty Boxes: The Making and Breaking of Elite Gymnasts and Figure Skaters* (New York: Warner Books, 1995); D. Whitson, 'The Embodiment of Gender: Discipline, Domination, and Empowerment', in S. Birrell and C.L. Cole (eds), *Women, Sport, and Culture* (Champaign, IL: Human Kinetics, 1994), pp.353–71.
106. D Rowe, 'The Global Love-Match', p.573.
107. R. Hoffer, 'Putting the Gold on Hold', *Sports Illustrated*, 2 March 1998, p.28.
108. Schulian, 'Protecting the Investment', p.117.
109. Ibid, p.26.
110. Ibid, p.26.
111. Anon, 'Sport and Television: Swifter, Higher, Stronger, Dearer', *The Economist*, 20 July 1996, p.17.
112. B. Hruska, 'What NBC Has Planned: High Tech and High Drama', *TV Guide*, 20 July 1996, pp.8–10.
113. Sandomir, 'NBC's Money Shots'.
114. R. Sandomir, 'Olympics Moments, but Hours Later on TV', *New York Times*, 25 July 1996, p.A1.
115. R. Crain, 'NBC's Sappy Profiles Aid Marketers', *Advertising Age*, 12 August 1996, p.15.
116. Anon, 'NBC's Time Warp'.
117. Impoco, 'Live from Atlanta', p.36.
118. Sandomir, 'Olympic Moments'.
119. Ibid.
120. Anon, 'NBC's Time Warp'.
121. G. Levin, 'Peacock Prancing Proudly at Return on Olympics', *Variety*, 29 July 1996, p.21.
122. See S. Rushin, 'Chapter One: The Titan of Television', *Sports Illustrated*, 16 August 1994, p.35.
123. M. Carlson, 'The Soap Opera Games: Determined to Make Every Event a Tearjerker, NBC Overplays the Personal Stories', Time, 5 August 1996, p.48.
124. Anon, 'NBC's Time Warp'.
125. Carlson, 'The Soap Opera Games'.
126. Ibid.
127. Sandomir, 'NBC's Money Shots'.
128. L. Shapiro, 'In Rating the TV Coverage, It's a Thin Line Between Love and Hate', *Washington Post*, 6 August 1996, p.E6.
129. Levin, 'Peacock Prancing'.
130. P. Farhi, 'For NBC, Olympics are the Golden Days: Network Sets Records for Viewership and Profitability at Games', Washington Post, 3 August 1996, p.F1; G. Levin, 'Peacock Web Basks in Olympian Glory', *Variety*, 5–11 August 1996, p.25.
131. C. Lury and A. Warde, 'Investments in the Imaginary Consumer: Conjectures Regarding Power, Knowledge and Advertising', in M. Nava et al. (eds), *Buy This Book: Studies in Advertising and Consumption* (London and New York: Routledge, 1997), pp.87–102.
132. Gunther, 'Oprah Olympics', p.42.
133. M. Knisley, 'Rock Solid', p.S6.
134. P. Donnelly, 'The Local and the Global: Globalization in the Sociology of Sport', *Journal of Sport and Social Issues*, 20, 3 (1996), p.246.
135. F. Fukuyama, 'The End of History?', *The National Interest*, 16 (1989), p.3.
136. D.L. Andrews, 'Dead and Alive?: Sport History in the Late Capitalist Moment', *Sporting Traditions: Journal of the Australian Society for Sports History*, 16, 1 (1999), pp.73–85.
137. E.M. Forster, *Howards End* (New York: Vintage Books, 1961 [1910]).
138. L. Grossberg, *We Gotta Get Out of This Place: Popular Conservatism and Postmodern Culture* (London: Routledge, 1992), p.21.

2

The Sporting Goods Industry: From Struggling Entrepreneurs to National Businesses to Transnational Corporations

GEORGE H. SAGE

An important component of the increasing commercialisation of sport has been the growth of the sporting goods industry. The Sporting Goods Manufacturers Association (SGMA) in the United States defines this industry as 'a composition of manufacturers of athletic footwear, sports apparel and sporting goods equipment, as well as manufacturers of accessory items to the sports and recreation market'.[1] More specifically, sporting goods are the uniforms, footwear, balls, bats, gloves, protective equipment and so forth that are necessary for playing sport. They constitute a US$170 billion global industry. In the US alone, sporting goods sales, in 2002, at wholesale prices totalled $47.7 billion.[2] Thus the manufacturing of sporting goods is a key component in the commercialised sport industry, and it is the primary focus of this chapter.

Sporting goods and equipment are not, of course, gifts of nature; they are made by people working in manufacturing plants throughout the world. Understanding the manufacture of contemporary sporting goods requires historically situating this segment of the sport industry within the rise of factory manufacturing, the evolution of commercial sport forms, the growth of the sporting goods industry and the recent trend towards a global economy. These are the foundations on which the contemporary sporting goods manufacturing industry rests.

The Industrial Revolution and the Rise of Factory Manufacturing

The system of sporting goods production has evolved over the past 200 years. Today sporting goods are produced in large mechanised factories that employ hundreds, even thousands, of workers. These conditions represent the latest stage in the development of industrial manufacturing. During the seventeenth and eighteenth centuries the vast bulk of all goods were produced in or near people's homes. The industrial process was primarily carried out by means of hand labour and simple tools, and the home and the workplace were often indistinguishable. However, in Britain in the latter part of the eighteenth century a series of inventions mechanised manufacturing and, along with other technological innovations and economic changes, launched what became known as the Industrial Revolution.[3]

Technological innovations and capitalist industrial development spread from Britain to Europe and America, and a factory system of manufacturing evolved wherever industrialisation took place. By the 1830s dozens of early industrialists in the New England states had moved decisively towards factory manufacturing. During the first half of the nineteenth century the most common forms of business organisation in the industrialising countries were partnerships, owned by two or more individuals, and proprietorships, in which a single person owned the entire business. However, as the factory system took root the corporation began to emerge as the pre-eminent institutional form of private enterprise, and it became the dominant form of business organisation in the latter nineteenth century. Owners of the early factories quickly established a pattern of hiring workers as cheaply as possible. They often employed women and children, who could be hired for lower wages than men. These low-paid manufacturing employees worked for as long as 16 hours a day, and many were subjected to various pressures, even physical punishment, in an effort to make them speed up production. Thus the early years of factory manufacturing were characterised by appalling conditions for large numbers of workers.[4]

During the latter four decades of the nineteenth century British, American and European manufacturers in several industries began to build the prominent feature of the modern factory system: mass production of standardised goods. Corporations, with their limited liability and enormous financial power, developed mass-production methods and mass sales. They were also able to drive out small businesses and acquire control over the production and pricing of goods and services in a number of industries. By the 1890s corporations produced nearly three quarters of the total value of manufactured products in the United States.[5]

The tendency towards profit maximisation among manufacturers in the industrialising countries during the latter nineteenth century led to massive exploitation of workers through low wages and a long work-week. Working conditions were often dreadful and dangerous. Labour organisations were formed to force owners to correct some of the worst abuses. Workers agitated for and obtained the right to organise, and they established labour unions. The unions, after considerable struggle and frequent setbacks, won important concessions, including the right to organise workers in factories and to represent them in negotiations.[6]

Although the patterns of industrial expansion varied among the Western industrialising nations, and each experienced the inevitable business cycles, industrial growth continued unabated. However, after the Second World War, most manufacturing enterprises in Britain and Western European countries were devastated. The USA had been spared the ravages of the war and became the leading producer of manufactured goods. During the 1950s manufacturing again began to play a dominating role in the economic expansion of Western countries. The number of manufacturing workers continued to increase in industrialised countries throughout the 1960s and 1970s, as did the value added to their economies by manufacture. However, by the mid-1970s, many manufacturers in the industrialised countries began an accelerated pattern of foreign direct investment in developing countries. Relocation of manufacturing plants to offshore sites increasingly led to factory closings, with accompanying loss of jobs and even economic devastation in some regions. These practices by transnational corporations led to what is now called a global economy.[7]

Before discussing the ascendancy of the global economy, and its relevance to sporting goods manufacture, it is necessary to review the rise of modern sport, the growth and development of the sporting goods industry and how they were intertwined with the Industrial Revolution and the evolution of manufacturing.

The Growth of Commercial Sport Forms

Modern commercial sport forms have, over the past two centuries, evolved hand in hand with the growth of modern industrial society. While this is not the place to provide a detailed chronology of the rise of commercial sport, an overview of its evolution is important for understanding the linkages between this social practice and the manufacture of sporting goods.[8]

Although it may be hard to imagine today, there was little of what could be called organised participant or spectator sport prior to the mid-nineteenth century. Pre-modern societies did have various types of informal play, games and competitive rites which operated on a local basis, but there was no formally organised commercial sport industry. Such an industry requires technologies that support rapid transportation, communication and mass production. It also requires an infrastructure of large numbers of people living in close proximity – an urban population – with substantial amounts of discretionary time and money. These conditions did not exist until the later nineteenth century.[9] An orchestration of expanding industrialisation and urbanisation, enhanced by the revolutionary transformations in communication and transportation and other technological advances, provided the framework for the rise of commercial sport. In Britain, the lure of commercialisation gradually undermined amateurism in a number of sports. By the mid-1880s professional soccer had been accepted, and while the battle to preserve amateurism was fought more fiercely in rugby union, by the end of the nineteenth century a group of players had broken ranks to form the professional game of rugby league. W. Vamplew has argued that 'commercialised spectator sport for the mass market became one of the economic success stories of late Victorian England'. He claims that 'by 1910 there were over 200 first-class professional cricketers plus several hundred county ground staff and league professionals; some 400 jockeys and … in soccer there were 6,800 registered professionals … earning money from playing sport'.[10]

The increasingly commercialised sport industry became divided into three segments: a performance segment, where sporting performance was offered to consumers as a participation or spectator product; a promotion segment, where marketing tools were used to promote the sport product, and a production segment, where products needed or desired for the production of, or to influence the quality of sporting performance, were manufactured. These developments, during the last half of the nineteenth century, set the stage for the remarkable growth in mass popular sport and professional sport which followed during the twentieth century.[11]

During the first half of the 1900s organised sport grew and prospered, becoming a massive commodified industry. Sport became one of the most engrossing of all social interests. The sporting spirit became a prominent part of the social life of large numbers of people. Growing urban areas, better transportation facilities, a growing affluent class, a higher standard of living and more discretionary funds for purchasing sporting equipment fostered sport and facilitated the formation of numerous leagues and teams. Commercialised sport penetrated many levels of the business world: fashion, mass media, transportation, communication, advertising and a variety of marginal enterprises all profited.

In the past 30 years two of the more recent trends in commercial sport have been the colossal expansion of professional spectator sports and the increased active participation by the general public in sport. Professional sports are operated as corporate entities that function very similarly to corporations of any other kind, albeit with certain tax and monopolistic advantages. The professional team sport industry has been one of the most successful growth industries in recent decades. The number of teams in all professional leagues has grown at an unbelievable rate, more than doubling their numbers in the past three decades. At the same time, the number of sports in which there are now professional leagues and tours has expanded rapidly.

The second trend – increased participation in sport by the general public – is a product of increased leisure, mass transportation and communication, as well as increased personal income. The construction of facilities and the manufacture of equipment inexpensive enough for the large mass of working-class people have had an important impact on participant sports. Moreover, a concerned awareness of the increasingly sedentary lifestyle of people in all socio-economic strata, and of the rise in diseases related to this lifestyle, has stimulated mass participation in sport and exercise.

These two trends have had a major impact on the sporting goods industry. Professional athletes as well as the average sport participant require appropriate apparel, footwear and equipment. As professional sports and general public participation has expanded, the demand for sporting goods and equipment has been incredible; thus sporting goods has been a major growth industry during the past 30 years.

The Growth of the Sporting Goods Manufacturing Industry

As the commercial sport industry grew and modern sport forms developed, participants began using special apparel This was for comfort, for safety, to efficiently perform the required tasks for each sport and to distinguish members of different teams. To meet these needs a sporting goods industry took root in parallel with the rise of commercial sport and the growth of mass-produced manufacturing in other industries. Indeed, mass produced manufactured goods and corporate organisation developed in sport just as they did in other industries.

Sporting goods production and distribution were rudimentary and poorly organised until the last three decades of the nineteenth century. Athletes and sportsmen either fashioned their own uniforms and equipment or used equipment and apparel supplied by home-crafting, merchant importers or local artisans who produced sporting goods as a sideline.[12] However, conditions changed rapidly after the 1870s as new economic, social and cultural conditions created a market for standardised manufactured sporting goods and equipment. Increased participation in sports, professionalisation of sports, technological innovations making large-scale manufacturing feasible and a growing urban class of spectators for sporting events combined to form the foundation for a sporting goods industry. Entrepreneurs saw the potential for profits in supplying and fuelling the demand for sporting goods and equipment.

Although the popularity of sport and outdoor recreation was still in the early stages of development in the late nineteenth century, their growing acceptance fostered the manufacture of bicycles, billiard tables, baseball and football equipment, sporting rifles, fishing rods and numerous other items. By 1880 the US Census Bureau listed 86 firms in the category of 'sporting goods' manufacture. Between 1879 and 1899 the growth in the value of products manufactured by the sporting and athletics goods industry increased from \$1,556,000 to \$3,628,000 or 133 per cent.[13] By the end of the nineteenth century several of the US sporting goods firms that were to dominate the twentieth century, such as Spalding, Reach, Rawlings, MacGregor and Hillerich & Son were thriving businesses. In addition, dozens of other sporting goods firms were actively in the market by the beginning of the twentieth century. Furthermore, department stores such as Macy's in New York City began carrying the manufactured sporting goods of these firms on a large scale during the 1880s. The 1895 Sears, Roebuck catalogue devoted 80 pages to sporting goods and equipment.

A former professional baseball player, Albert G. Spalding, opened his first sporting goods store in Chicago in 1876. Beginning with baseball equipment, he branched out into various sports, and by the end of the century his company had some 3,500 employees working in five manufacturing plants around the US. Spalding's influence in the sporting goods industry stretched throughout the world. Along the way the company bought out numerous competitors, further establishing its dominance in the sporting goods industry.[14] Despite expanding and diversifying his line of sporting goods, Spalding did not by any means have the industry to himself. In 1877, A.J. Reach, another former professional baseball player, founded the Reach Sporting Goods Company in Philadelphia.[15] The company was the first manufacturer of baseballs used by the Western League (the future American League). At the turn of the century, the Reach plant in Philadelphia was making an estimated 18,000 baseballs daily. Twenty brands of baseballs were cut and shaped by specially designed machinery. Although Spalding's firm acquired A.J. Reach's business in the late nineteenth century, Spalding operated it as a subsidiary, leaving the Reach name on products.[16]

Rawlings and Hillerich & Bradsby, two other sporting goods firms that were to have a major influence on the sporting goods industry throughout the twentieth century, also had their beginnings in the late nineteenth century. The Rawlings Brothers, George and Alfred, opened a retail sporting goods store in St Louis in 1887; within a few years, the company moved into manufacturing. In 1884 J. Frederich Hillerich, owner of a wood-turning shop making bedposts and handrails as well as well as tenpins and bowling balls, received a request from a professional baseball player to make him some new baseball bats. The player was so successful that Hillerich began to specialise with this product, and over the next two decades Hillerich & Son became famous for manufacturing baseball bats. As the company prospered, it manufactured bats for large sporting goods companies such as Rawlings Sporting Goods, Chicago Sporting Goods, Goldsmiths, C.C. Carr and Strall and Dean. In spite of its successes, even in 1907 Hillerich & Son was still a relatively small bat-manufacturing company. However, by 1923, Hillerich & Bradsby (the company name, Hillerich & Son, was changed to Hillerich & Bradsby in 1916) had become the number one bat manufacturer in America.[17]

Although Wilson Sporting Goods Company was not founded in the nineteenth century, because of its prominence in the sporting goods industry throughout most of the twentieth century, some mention of its origins seems appropriate. What ultimately became Wilson Sporting Goods was originally known as Ashland Manufacturing Company, a subsidiary of a meat-packing plant; it sold violin strings, surgical sutures and strings for tennis products, all of which are by-products of animal gut. In 1914 the company had a financial crisis and was taken over by New York bankers. The new firm was named Wilson and Company. It continues to be one of the leading sporting goods manufacturers, with a full line of products. During the 1990s, Wilson Sporting Goods had total sales amounting to 8.5 per cent of the world's sporting goods market, making it the largest such manufacturer in the world.[18]

With the rising popularity of numerous sports at the end of the nineteenth century, with advances in technology making possible the production of newer and better equipment and, finally, with improved manufacturing and distribution methods, sporting goods had become a multimillion-dollar-a-year industry. In the US, between 1900 and 1923, the average number of wage earners employed in sporting and athletics goods manufacturing increased 338 per cent. And the value of products manufactured in the sporting and athletic goods manufacturing industry increased 1,052 per cent.[19]

The sporting goods industry was unable to escape fluctuating economic conditions throughout the twentieth century. During periods of economic austerity, discretionary money became scarce, so the average citizen's participation in sport was reduced. Sporting organisations cut appropriations for equipment and professional teams often operated at a deficit because of reduced gate receipts. When the economy rallied, so did the sporting goods industry. During the Second World War, the supply of sporting goods for citizens was greatly reduced. In the US, a weekly business magazine reported that some 65 raw materials used to manufacture sporting goods equipment were under the control of the War Production Board. Furthermore, most sporting goods that were produced were sent to the armed services.[20] In the aftermath of the Second World War, commercial sport became a flourishing industry throughout the world and the sporting goods manufacturing industry experienced rapid and sustained growth. By the late 1960s, annual retail sales in the sporting goods industry in the US was near $4 billion. According to the Sporting Goods Manufacturers Association, by 1986 total manufacturer sales of sports apparel, equipment, and footwear had grown to $21.7 billion.[21]

Corporate mergers were epidemic in frequency from the 1970s through to the 1990s, and the sporting goods manufacturing industry was not immune to this trend. For example, Rawlings Sporting Goods was sold to Figgie International Holdings, Incorporated. A.G. Spalding was acquired by the Questor Corporation; PepsiCo bought Wilson Sporting Goods from LTV Corporation; Ben Hogan Golf Clubs was procured by AMF. In 1985 PepsiCo sold Wilson Sporting Goods to Wesray Capital Corporation.[22] In the 1990s the major sporting goods corporations in the industry were frequently components of corporate conglomerates engaged in a variety of business ventures. For example, Wilson Sporting Goods 'was owned by the Amer Group, a Finnish company that also manufactured paper envelopes and textbooks, as well as other products'.[23] Entering the twenty-first century, a few large corporations controlled a major portion of the sporting goods manufacturing industry.

The Global Economy

La Feber argues that globalisation 'is used to describe the spread of transnationals and technology across the globe'. According to the Organization of Economic Cooperation and Development (OECD), globalisation has its origins in the changing patterns of 'transborder operations of firms undertaken to organize their development, production, sourcing, marketing, and financing activities'. The global economy did not emerge suddenly in its present form. Although most people regard international commerce as a recent phenomenon, in fact trade across borders has taken place for centuries.[24]

The first foreign branch plant of an American manufacturing company appears to have been the London manufacturing plant set up by the Colt Patent Fire Arms Manufacturing Company of Hartford, Connecticut, in 1852. Three years after the foreign Colt factory was established, American partners in the firm of J. Ford and Company of New Brunswick, New Jersey, built a factory in Edinburgh, Scotland for the production of vulcanised rubber. This plant was US-financed, designed, equipped and managed. The factories of Colt and J. Ford and Company were the forerunners of the multinational corporations of the twentieth century.[25]

In the 1870s and 1880s many American companies built finishing assembly or manufacturing plants abroad to fill the needs of foreign markets. Examples are Babcock and Wilcox boilers, with manufacturing facilities in England, and Standard Oil of Ohio, with refineries in several countries. Between 1876 and 1887, 47 American branch, subsidiary or controlled affiliated manufacturers – mostly in the metal-working fields – were set up Canada. By 1900 many American enterprises were manufacturing or assembling their products abroad, but the size of US direct investment before the First World War was actually small – an estimated \$2.65 billion. Wilkins notes that American 'companies that could be called "multinational" were few in number'.[26]

Following the First World War, American corporations became more involved in a variety of foreign trade activities. Direct investment increased across a range of manufacturing industries. A 1929 list of US-owned multinational businesses contained more than two-and-a-half times the number of companies included on the 1914 list. In 1929 the book value of US direct investments abroad was slightly over seven per cent of the US gross national product.[27]

After the Second World War, manufacturers in most developed countries made huge foreign commitments. According to Wilkins, in 1957, '2,800 US businesses had stakes in some 10,000 direct investment enterprises abroad; 45 companies had foreign direct investments of over \$100 million'.[28] The OECD reported that for 1966, the book value of US direct investments abroad was greater than the book value of direct foreign investments of all the other major free world nations combined. In 1970 US direct investment abroad amounted to approximately \$70 billion.[29]

Manufacturing in the Global Economy

Although foreign commerce, even direct investment in other countries, has been a part of the national economies of industrialised countries for over a century, until about 30 years ago the production, distribution and consumption of most corporations' products and services took place within a country. Manufacturing corporations relied primarily on domestic labour, produced mostly industrial goods and were rooted almost entirely in the national market. A dramatic transformation began in the early 1970s with a transition involving, through mergers and acquisitions, the formation of giant transnational corporate empires integrated into worldwide business networks. This transformation is now commonly referred to as the global economy, and manufacturing is driving globalisation, as advanced capitalist and developing countries alike seek to increase their shares of the wealth of nations.[30]

There are now some 60,000 transnational corporations, which in turn control over 450,000 foreign affiliates worldwide; they account for about one-third of global production, while estimated sales by overseas affiliates are worth \$11 trillion. Economically, they exceed the size of many governments; indeed, of the world's hundred largest economies, 66 are transnational corporations and only 34 are nation states. Late-twentieth-century and early twenty-first-century transnational corporations also differ from earlier corporations involved in foreign commerce because the earlier firms largely employed domestic labour to produce their products, while contemporary transnational firms overwhelming make their products abroad and employ a foreign workforce.[31] In his State of the Union address in January, 2000, former American President Bill Clinton declared that 'globalisation is the central reality of our time'.

A key feature of the global economy is a capital system and division of labour known as the 'export processing system'. In this system, product research, development and design take place in developed countries while the labour-intensive assembly-line phases of product manufacture are relegated to developing countries. The finished product is then exported for distribution and consumption in the world's developed countries. The basic strategy employed by transnational firms involved in export-processing manufacture is to locate factories in countries where there is an authoritarian government, cheap land and labour, a non-union workforce, weak safety and environmental standards and favourable tax abatements from the foreign government.[32]

One of the consequences of this global export-processing system is the dramatic increase in revenues of transnational corporations from foreign export-processing subsidiaries. The dollar value of manufacturing exports from developing countries increased 168 per cent between 1982 and 1991. In the US, from the late 1970s to 1980, both exports and imports were in close balance and transnational corporations' revenues from imports and exports were closely balanced. But by the mid-1980s, over 80 per cent of US transnational corporate revenues were from overseas production, and less than 20 per cent were from exporting American-made goods to foreign countries, resulting in a growing national deficit reaching $141 billion in 1987. Because imported manufactured goods have risen sharply in the past 25 years, imported manufactured goods as a percentage of US manufacturing gross domestic product (GDP) soared from 10 per cent in 1970 to 55 per cent in 1996. Consequently, over one-third of the earnings of the 200 largest US transnational corporations are now from their export-processing operations.[33] Another consequence of the export-processing system is that transnational corporations have closed down factories in their own countries and exported jobs to people in developing countries throughout the world. In the US, the number of manufacturing jobs fell from a 1979 peak of 22 million to 18.3 million jobs in 1999, a drop of nearly 17 per cent. Between 1968 and 1998, the top ten US manufacturing corporations reduced their US employees by 33 per cent, from 3,355,888 to 2,258,100. Between 2000 and 2006, manufacturing jobs are projected to decline another two to three per cent.[34]

For workers in developed countries who have lost jobs to export-processing, the consequences have been grim: replacement jobs paying minimal wages, a variety of physical and mental afflictions related to the stress of unemployment and community disintegration linked to the global economy. Finally, median US hourly wages have fallen steadily as manufacturing jobs have declined and the economy has become more globalised.[35]

A third consequence of the export-processing system is that manufacturing exports now account for over half the foreign exchange earnings of the East Asian newly emerging countries, Mexico, the Philippines and Thailand. But accompanying this increase in exports are monumentally adverse consequences: long working hours, an absence of social welfare facilities, wages so low that workers cannot provide for their basic needs, unjust and inhuman working conditions, sexual exploitation, social disruption and distorted economic development.[36]

Furthermore, export-processing manufacture is being built on the backs of an exploited labour force composed largely of young women and children. Women not only make up the majority of the export-processing workforce; in certain industries, notably textiles, garment manufacturing and electronics assembly, women account for 90 per cent or more of the workers. Even worse, many children labour in the global economy. According to the International Labour Organisation, more than 250 million children between the ages of five and 14 are working in developing countries. The majority, 61 per cent, work in Asia.[37]

Governments in Asia and Latin America have restructured the labour sector to suppress radical activity in an effort to ensure political stability. Many have abolished trade-based labour unions and pushed the creation of company- or enterprise-based unions. In *The East Asian Miracle*, a World Bank team of economists hails the so-called 'high performing Asian economies' (HPAEs) and outlines how the suppression of workers' rights was a key component in their success. These World Bank economists then state that the principal benefit of wage suppression is 'higher profits' for private firms![38]

Today, transnational companies in dozens of industries roam the globe in search of cheap labour, generous packages of tax benefits and weak safety, health and environmental regulations. These are the conditions in developing countries where direct investment in export processing favour transnational corporate profit. The next, and final, section describes how the global economy is played out in the case of sporting goods manufacturing firms.[39]

Sporting Goods Manufacturing in the Global Economy

In this section two sporting goods manufacturing firms – Nike and Rawlings – are selected to illustrate how sporting goods firms have transferred their productive operations from the country in which they are incorporated to foreign export-processing operations in developing countries. The consequences of their actions for workers in developing nations are discussed. It is important to understand that Nike and Rawlings are just examples; there are hundreds of other sporting goods manufacturers whose productive operations have been relocated to developing countries. Sporting goods manufacturing is no different than other forms of global capitalist production; indeed, it is one of the most flourishing export-processing industries. Sporting goods manufacturers that produce all their products domestically are now a minority, because many of them have 'run away' to numerous low-wage export-processing countries across the world. According to SGMA, 72 per cent of sporting goods manufacturers now rely on some overseas production facilities and 30 per cent plan to move more production overseas. As a result, the total declared value of sporting goods imported into the US rose dramatically, from $4.95 billion in 1991 to $7.55 billion in 1999.

Manufacturing Nike Footwear

Athletic footwear is one of the most important segments of the sporting goods industry, and the market sales (at wholesale) of sporting footwear more than doubled between 1986 and 1998, increasing from $4.3 billion to $8.72 billion. Nike was the market leader in sporting footwear throughout the 1990s. The company is legally registered as an American corporation: its corporate headquarters are located in Beaverton, Oregon. However, none of Nike's footwear is currently manufactured within the US; everything is subcontracted out to suppliers, mostly Korean and Taiwanese manufacturers, who make Nike footwear in several Asian cheap-labour countries. Thus, Nike does not own its own factories in Asia; it contracts with these foreign manufacturers to make its sporting footwear.[40]

During the 1970s and early 1980s much of Nike footwear was made in American factories located in New Hampshire and Maine. Export-processing manufacture of Nike sporting footwear began in the late 1970s, when the company started contracting with manufacturers in South Korea and Taiwan to supply them with the shoes they wanted made. As the Asian factories became more efficient and profitable for Nike, its New England plants were closed in the mid-1980s. Then in the late 1980s a number of significant democratic reforms came to South Korea and Taiwan; wages increased dramatically and labour organisations gained the right to form independent unions and to strike. Also, in 1988 both South Korea and Taiwan lost their access to US markets under the General System of Preferences (GSP), which permits developing countries to export goods to the US without paying duties. Reacting to these developments, Nike began urging its Korean and Taiwanese suppliers to shift their footwear operations out of these two countries into politically autocratic, military-dominated countries like Indonesia, Thailand, China and, in 1995, Vietnam in a relentless drive for a favourable political climate and the lowest-cost labour.[41] By 1992, of Nike's seven top suppliers of sport shoes, three were operating in Indonesia, three were producing mainly in China and one was a Thai company. The value of athletic footwear exports in Indonesia rose from $4 million in 1988 to $1.5 billion in 1993. By 2000 some 40 per cent of all Nike shoe exports for the global market were produced in China, with Indonesia and Vietnam the other major Asian Nike footwear manufacturing countries.[42]

Reports on Nike's Footwear Factories

Nike employed between 350,000 and 530,000 workers in South-East Asia throughout the 1990s. Between 1991 and 1998 the factories that produced Nike footwear in Indonesia, China, and Vietnam were inspected by a number of academic, religious, labour, human rights and development organisations from various countries. Although the length of time collecting data, the expertise of the investigators and the methodology of data collection varied considerably, the investigations revealed similar patterns and conditions in Nike's Asian shoe factories. To summarise, approximately 75 to 80 per cent of Nike workers were women – mostly under the age of 24 – who routinely put in ten- to 13-hour days, six days a week, with forced overtime two to three times per week. A typical worker earned 13 to 20 cents (in US currency) an hour – between $1.60 and $2.20 per day, which was below the 'minimum physical needs' (MPN), the figure governments used as a subsistence level for a single adult worker in these countries. Several of the investigations found abuse of workers was widespread in factories supplying Nike. For example, Thuyen Nguyen, a Vietnamese-American businessman who investigated Nike's factories in Vietnam in 1997, found workers earning 20 cents an hour, forced into overtime and subjected to extreme corporal punishment, including have their mouths taped shut for stepping out of line, and being forced to run in circles in the sweltering sun.[43]

The reports on Nike's footwear suppliers uniformly found that the local laws requiring industrial safety were almost useless in practice in all these countries because Nike's contractors simply ignored the rules and regulations set out in the laws. Not surprisingly, the reports found that the results of cutting costs on the safety and health of the (mostly women) workers have been frightful. According to several reports, Nike's record on workers' rights in these countries has been deplorable. Independent unions have not been permitted in these factories. When these workers have attempted even the most minimal organising on behalf of their rights,

Nike's contractors have called in the police or military and workers have been arrested and subjected to torture and beatings. Such conditions existed because political officials in these countries were notoriously corrupt: they could be paid off and they, in turn, made sure police and military units maintained vigilance for signs of labour activism.[44]

The Nike Transnational Social Movement

A transnational social movement against Nike's Asian production operations began to form and mobilise in the early 1990s as global understanding and consciousness grew about Nike's Asian factories. It actually began with the workers in the factories. They initiated the struggle against the low wages, unsafe and unhealthy working conditions and abusive treatment. Worker complaints escalated to work stoppages and then to strikes against Nike contractors. The collective actions that initiated what ultimately became the Nike social movement was started by a worldwide coalition that included religious, labour, human rights and corporate monitoring organisations. Through a loose system of networking, the Nike social movement connected a multitude of initiatives which organised campaigns to address Nike's below-subsistence wages, abysmal working conditions, employment of very young girls, abuse of workers and anti-union practices. All of these conditions were highlighted to portray Nike as a repressive, abusive, unjust and inhuman corporation. This portrayal of Nike was a catalyst for the development of various campaigns against Nike's labour practices.

Despite the enormous diversity of individuals and organisations that made up the Nike network, very rapidly a nearly unanimous set of goals was agreed upon. They were: Nike should pay a living wage based on an eight-hour day, end forced overtime, stop using child labour, provide working conditions consistent with human dignity, permit independent unions and permit independent monitoring of factories. Nike's initial response to the reports about its Asian factories was to claim that it was just a buyer; that is, it merely contracted with suppliers, who actually manufactured the shoes, and therefore it could not control what went on in the factories. Nike's vice-president for production argued: 'We don't pay anybody at the factories and we don't set policy within the factories; it is their business to run.' This is, of course, absurd; Nike always had overall control of its productive operations. In 1992, Nike developed a code of conduct for its contractors as a response to the mounting critical reports of its Asian factories. Unfortunately for Nike workers, several investigations found that many workers did not even know about the code and that the code was flagrantly violated by Nike's contractors. Various interviews with Nike workers suggested that the code was mostly an instrument of damage control rather than a binding force for labour reform in its factories.

In 1994 Nike hired the accounting firm Ernst & Young to conduct audits of labour and environmental conditions inside its contractors' factories to determine whether they were in compliance with Nike's code of conduct. In early 1997 Nike commissioned former United Nations Ambassador Andrew Young and his Atlanta-based company to go to Asia and investigate its factory operations in Indonesia, China and Vietnam. In October 1997, Nike released a summary of a study of its Asian factories that had been done as a class project by a group of MBA students at the Dartmouth School of Business. Nike paid for all three reports; none of them were independent inspections of Nike factories. All three reports came under scathing criticism from international human rights, labour and religious organisations, as well as a number of journalists. Criticism centred around the lack of expertise of those conducting the investigations, the brevity of time spent collecting data, the studies' woefully inadequate methodology, the dependence on translators supplied by Nike officials, the inadequacy of worker interview protocols and the reports' silence on wages.[45]

One form of response by Nike to the reports about its factories and the Nike social movement was persistent: Why was Nike being singled out when productive operations in Asia of other sporting goods manufacturers are similar? The movement answered this question with several types of reply. First, it pointed out that Nike was the industry leader in moving its production jobs overseas, and complaints about its labour practices were the first to surface in the Asian sporting footwear industry. Second, it argued that Nike was far and away the market leader in the sporting footwear industry, with a 30 to 40 per cent share of the market during the 1990s. As the 'marquee firm' in the sporting footwear and apparel industry, other firms in the industry looked to Nike for leadership. Even Nike CEO Philip Knight acknowledged that 'Our competitors just follow our lead.'[46] A basic principle of collective labour actions is to go after the market leader. There was reason to believe that when Nike agreed to the demands of this movement network, other companies in that industry would swiftly follow. As Max White, an American human rights activist and founder of a Nike campaign called 'Justice. Do It Nike', put it: 'If Nike reforms, they will trumpet the change and other manufacturers will have to follow.'[47]

A third reason Nike was being targeted was what many of the Nike network organisations and supportive journalists considered to be arrogance and hypocrisy in Nike's management and corporate culture. As one leader of the Nike movement noted: 'The company and its founder have always had a reputation for being aggressive and unconventional, the "bad boys" of the shoe industry, built on an irreverence for the sporting establishment and for any authority which might cramp the individual's style.' Nike seemed to take pride in communicating a 'cool' in-your-face attitude and a win-at-all-cost image.

The Nike network was especially critical of what it considered the contradictions and hypocrisy of several Nike advertisements. For example, its ad 'If You Let Me Play' conveyed support for the empowerment of females through sport, but Nike employed girls as young as 14 years old in their Asian factories. The ad image of female power through play was created to sell shoes; meanwhile, disempowered females were making them. Nike also circulated a poster that proclaimed: 'Go Ahead – Demand a Raise. You Have Nothing to Lose.' But investigations of Nike's Asian factories found that they didn't pay workers a living wage; and in cases where workers had made wage demands they had been beaten and fired. By 1995, heightened conflict in Nike's Asian factories, a worldwide geographical extension of mobilisation and organisation, and Nike campaigns devoted to making the public aware of the company's labour practices, all contributed to producing new or transformed symbols, frames of meaning and a discourse to legitimise the Nike social movement. Over the next four years the Nike campaigns reached a peak of actions and influence.

Outcomes of the Nike Transnational Social Movement

The campaigns against Nike were instrumental in influencing governmental policies in several foreign countries. Their governments adopted new policies that permitted independent union organisation, the establishment of or increases in minimum wages, working condition standards and limitations on hours of work. Although Nike management denied that the Nike network had any effect, there is good evidence that the new national policies would not have been enacted without the pressure of the Nike campaigns. The Nike network was also instrumental in bringing their message about Nike's Asian factories to many American university campuses. Students organised and campaigned in a variety of ways in support of the Nike network. Inspired by the work of the Nike campaigns, in the fall of 1997 what became the United Students Against Sweatshops began to form at Duke University, and by the spring of 2000 more then 150 college campuses around the country had member chapters. Students at many colleges and universities were successful at having anti-sweatshop codes and institutional policies adopted by their university for products with the university name and logos. Students at Michigan, Wisconsin, Iowa, Arizona, the State University of New York at Albany and Georgetown University staged sit-ins at presidents' offices before anti-sweatshop agreements were reached. Demonstrations, sit-ins and rallies took place on dozens of other campuses between 1998 and 2000.[48] The Nike social movement damaged the Nike name and reputation for millions of people throughout the world. For many, the Nike swoosh became associated with sweatshops and the oppression of workers. Indeed, Philip Knight admitted this in a speech he gave in May 1998. 'The Nike product has become synonymous with slave wages, forced overtime and arbitrary abuse,' he said. 'I truly believe that the American consumer does not want to buy products made in abusive conditions.'[49] It seems likely that the Nike network campaigns played a role in the decline in Nike's earnings. Nike had a 49 per cent decline in its 1998 fiscal net income compared to 1997.

Finally, in 1998 Nike began to undertake a number of initiatives to directly address the demands of the Nike network. On 12 May 1998, Nike CEO Philip Knight announced plans for a substantially new course for the company. Speaking before the National Press Club luncheon in Washington, DC, Knight made public what he called 'new labour initiatives', which were Nike's plans for significant reforms in its labour practices. The most significant of the new initiatives were:

1. increasing the minimum age of footwear factory workers to 18, and the minimum age for all other light-manufacturing workers (apparel, accessories, equipment) to 16;
2. adopting US Occupational Safety and Health Administration (OSHA) indoor air-quality standards for all footwear factories;
3. expanding education programmes, for workers in all Nike footwear factories;
4. expanding its current monitoring programme.[50]

These initiatives were seen as a direct result of the four-year campaign to bring Nike's labour practices to world consumers' awareness. However, in its 'new labour initiatives' Nike did not commit itself to paying a living wage for a normal working week. This was a fundamental demand of the Nike network from its beginning, and many network organisations pledged to remain active against Nike until it committed itself on this issue. They also vowed to monitor Nike's labour practices to make sure the company delivered on its promises.[51] Thus closure is not yet achieved for the Nike social movement. Any attempt to assess its ultimate outcome is premature at this time, but its worldwide collective actions and campaigns led to a number of potential benefits not only for Nike workers but also for workers throughout the Third World.

Manufacturing Rawlings Baseballs

Rawlings Sporting Goods Co., headquartered in Fenton, Missouri, has manufactured the balls used in Major League Baseball since 1977. Although the yarn wound around the core of a baseball is made by machinery, the cover of the ball is still hand-stitched, mostly by women workers. It is tedious work requiring workers to run needles through the cover and jerk the threads so they tighten at the first draw. This must be done 108 times, the number of stitches there are in a baseball, to complete the job. Workers skilled at the task can stitch 35 to 40 balls during a day's work.[52] Until 1953, all Rawlings baseballs were manufactured in a plant in St Louis with unionised labour. In that year, to reduce labour costs, Rawlings shifted manufacturing to Licking, Missouri. At first, the Licking plant was non-union, but in 1956 the Amalgamated Clothing and Textile Workers Union organised it. The union immediately began efforts to improve wages and working conditions, and Rawlings began looking around for an offshore manufacturing site. In 1964, it moved its baseball manufacturing to Puerto Rico, where the Puerto Rican Economic Development Administration was promising 'higher productivity, lower wages and tax-free profits'.[53] But when the initial tax 'holidays' for foreign investors ran out and minimum wage laws were implemented in Puerto Rico, many companies left to exploit even cheaper labour in Haiti. Rawlings was one of the first to move. In 1969 it closed its Puerto Rican baseball plant and relocated in Haiti, the poorest country in the Western Hemisphere and one of the 25 poorest in the world.

In the 1980s Rawlings baseball manufacturing was the second largest assembly industry in Haiti, the ideal setting for offshore assembly operations. There were generous tax holidays, a franchise granting tariff exemption and the only legal trade unions were those operated by the government. Strikes were illegal and the minimum wage was so low that a majority of Haitians could not derive anything that might reasonably be called a 'living' from the assembly plants. Haitians who made baseballs for Rawlings were being paid 9 to 13 cents per ball – about $2.70 per day; weekly average wage was $18.[54]

In the later 1980s several human rights groups investigated reports of labour exploitation, denial of workers' rights, and appalling working conditions coming from past and present workers at the Rawlings plant. According to a report prepared by them, the following abuses were documented:

- Labour rights violations: discharges for union activity; threats and actual violence against union leaders; army intervention in labour disputes;
- Violations of minimum-wage laws: requiring an unreasonably high piece work rate in order to receive minimum wage; paying a sub-minimal wage during employees' probation period, then firing them when the probation period was over;
- Unhealthy working conditions: insufficient access to drinking water and toilets, only two 15-minute breaks per day and no lunch breaks;

- Wages of between $.09 to $.13 per ball, when materials are available, and no wages on days when materials are not available.[55]

In November 1990 Rawlings suddenly closed its plant in Haiti, claiming that the political climate in Haiti was unstable. All baseball manufacturing was moved to a plant in Costa Rica. In the spring of 2000 about 500 stitchers, most of them women, were formally employed in the Costa Rica facilities. The majority of workers are 'sewers'. They must stitch 30 to 35 baseballs per day to earn $9 to $12 a day. The working week is 48 hours long. There are reports that approximately 200 Costa Rican women also sew baseballs in their homes, earning 25 cents per ball. Trade union activity in Costa Rica is not well developed and workers who have attempted to organise a union have been fired, indirectly violating Costa Rican labour regulations.[56]

Concluding Comments

Today, sporting goods manufacturing companies roam the globe in search of the cheapest labour and the weakest safety and environmental regulations. By relocating their manufacturing in developing countries, transnational corporations are able to pay workers a fraction of what they would have to pay them in developed countries; they are able to work them longer hours under unsafe conditions; they are able to pollute the water, air and soil; they are allowed to dump toxic chemicals, banned pesticides and drugs that they are prevented from using in developed countries; and they are provided with tax abatements by both home and foreign countries. Thus while corporations are able to provide employment for many workers in developing countries, and extract enormous profits from the export-processing system, this system involves serious individual, social and environmental costs.

Over the past half-century the popularity of sport has grown as people have experienced the fun, excitement, fitness and improved quality of life that playing and watching sport affords. It is ironic that so much of the sporting goods and equipment that make sport enjoyable are now produced under conditions where workers are exploited and abused, using up their lives to support the indulgences of those involved in sport. The challenge for people throughout the world is to confront the transnational corporations and governments that protect them, forcing them to respect the human needs of workers, communities and entire nations.

NOTES

1. Sporting Goods Manufacturers Association, *State of the Industry Report 2002* (Palm Beach, FL: SGMA International, 2002).
2. Sporting Goods Manufacturers Association, *US Sporting Goods Market Outlook for 2000*, online at http://www.sgma.com/press/2002/press1018543821-25329.html.
3. S.L. Engerman and R.E. Gallman (eds), *The Cambridge Economic History of the United States: The Colonial Era*, Vol. 1 (New York: Cambridge University Press, 1996); M. Berg, 'Factories, Workshops and Industrial Organization', in R. Floud and D. McCloskey (eds), *The Economic History of Britain Since 1700, Vol. 1: 1700–1860*, 2nd edn (New York: Cambridge University Press, 1994), pp.123–50.
4. P. Le Blanc, *A Short History of the US Working Class: From Colonial Times to the Twenty-First Century* (Amherst, NY: Humanity Books, 1999); G.W. Marks, *Unions in Politics: Britain, Germany, and the United States in the Nineteenth and Early Twentieth Centuries* (Princeton, NJ: Princeton University Press, 1989).
5. Still, most nineteenth-century factories were extremely small by later standards. According to D. Nelson, *Managers and Workers: Origins of the Twentieth Century Factory System in the United States, 1880–1920*, 2nd edn (Madison, WI: University of Wisconsin Press, 1995) in the US 'only 67 of 2,500 Cincinnati industrial plants had 100 or more workers in the 1870s; only 49 of 919 Detroit plants employed 100 or more workers in 1889, and only seven employed more than 300' (pp.4–5); see also M. Josephson, *The Robber Barons: The Great American Capitalists, 1861–1901* (New York: Harcourt, Brace & World, 1962); W.G. Roy, *Socializing Capital: The Rise of the Large Industrial Corporation in America* (Princeton, NJ: Princeton University Press, 1997); and W. Licht, *Industrializing America: The Nineteenth Century* (Baltimore, MD: Johns Hopkins University Press, 1995).
6. Le Blanc, *Short History of the US Working Class*; Marks, *Unions in Politics*.
7. M.G. Blackford, *The Rise of Modern Business in Great Britain, the United States and Japan*, 2nd edn, revised and updated (Chapel Hill, NC: University of North Carolina Press, 1998) pp.176–234.
8. For detailed historical accounts of the rise of modern sport in several countries, see D. Brailsford, *British Sport: A Social History* (Cambridge: Lutterworth Press, 1992); D. Birley, *Land of Sport and Glory: Sport and British Society, 1887–1910* (Manchester: Manchester University Press, 1995); D. Birley, *Playing the Game: Sport and British Society, 1910–45* (Manchester: Manchester University Press, 1995); D. Morrow, M. Keyes, W. Simpson, F. Cosentino and R. Lappage, *A Concise History of Sport in Canada* (Toronto: Oxford University Press, 1989); B.G. Rader, *American Sports: From the Age of Folk Games to the Age of Television*, 2nd edn (Englewood Cliffs, NJ: Prentice-Hall, 1990); S.A. Riess, *Sport in Industrial America: 1850–1920* (Wheeling, IL: Harlan Davidson, 1995); and D.K. Wiggins (ed.), *Sport in America: From Wicked Amusement to National Obsession* (Champaign, IL: Human Kinetics, 1995).
9. See Brailsford, *British Sport*, pp.19–60, for a description of a variety of public sport and recreations in Britain before 1800; see also Birley, *Sport and the Making of Britain*, pp.49–149.
10. W. Vamplew, 'Sport and Industrialization: An Economic Interpretation of the Changes in Popular Sport in Nineteenth-Century England', in J.A. Mangan (ed.), *Pleasure, Profit, Proselytism: British Culture and Sport at Home and Abroad 1700–1914* (London: Frank Cass, 1988), p.13; see also D.J. Mrozek, *Sport and American Mentality, 1880–1910* (Knoxville, TN: University of Tennessee Press, 1983); Riess, *Sport in Industrial America*; Birley, *Land of Sport and Glory*; Birley, *Sport and the Making of Britain*.
11. B.G. Pitts, L.W. Fielding and L.K. Miller, 'Industry Segmentation Theory and the Sport Industry: Developing a Sport Industry Segment Model', *Sport Marketing Quarterly*, 3 (1994), pp.15–24.
12. The Edward K. Tryon Company of Philadelphia, Pennsylvania, published a book in 1936 titled *The History of the Oldest Sporting Good House in America, 1816–1936* (Philadelphia: By the Company, 1936). The contents of the book make it clear that the company focused primarily on guns, rifles, weapons accessories and fishing equipment. See also S. Hardy, 'Entrepreneurs, Organizations, and the Sport Marketplace: Subjects in Search of Historians', *Journal of Sport History*, 13, 1 (Spring 1986), pp.14–33; S. Hardy, '"Adopted by All the Leading Clubs": Sporting Goods and the Shaping of Leisure, 1800–1900', in R. Butsch (ed.), *For Fun and Profit: The Transformation of Leisure Into Consumption* (Philadelphia, PA: Temple University Press, 1990), pp.71–101.
13. E.E. Day and W. Thomas, *The Growth of Manufactures 1899 to 1923* (New York: Arno Press, 1976), p.175.

14. P. Levine, *A.G. Spalding and the Rise of Baseball: The Promise of American Sport* (New York: Oxford University Press, 1985); D.O. Whitten and B. Whitten, *Manufacturing: A Historiographical and Bibliographical Guide*, Vol. 1 (New York: Greenwood Press, 1990).
15. Some baseball historians claim that Reach was the first professional baseball player in the US.
16. Reach plant statistics in *Sporting Goods Dealer*, October 1899, pp.4–5; quoted in Hardy, 'Entrepreneurs, Organizations, and the Sport Marketplace', p.30.
17. L.K. Miller, L.W. Fielding and B.G. Pitts, 'The Rise of the Louisville Slugger in the Mass Market', *Sport Marketing Quarterly*, 2, 3 (1993), pp.8–16.
18. D.M. Sawinski and W. H Mason (eds), *Encyclopedia of Global Industries* (New York: Gale Research, 1996), pp.606–7; 'The History of Wilson Sporting Goods', online at http://www.wilsonsports.com/corporate/homepage.asp.
19. Day and Thomas, *The Growth of Manufactures*, pp.155, 175.
20. 'Ball and Bat Crisis', *Business Week*, 2 June 1945, pp.41–2.
21. 'The $4-Billion Market in Fun', *Business Week*, 8 February 1969, pp.82–4; Sporting Goods Manufacturers Association, *State of the Industry Report 2002*.
22. Whitten and Whitten, *Manufacturing*, pp.399–400. In 1994 Rawlings became a public company, and traded on the US NASDAQ stock exchange, symbol: RAWL.
23. Sawinski and Mason, *Encyclopedia of Global Industries*, p.605.
24. W. La Feber, *Michael Jordan and the New Global Capitalism* (New York: W.W. Norton, 1999), p.167; Organization for Economic Cooperation and Development (OECD), *Globalization of Industry: Overview and Sector Reports* (Paris, 1996), p.15. There are several interpretations of what globalisation is and what it means: see, for example, R.B. DuBoff and E.S. Herman, 'A Critique of Tabb on Globalization', *Monthly Review*, 49 (November 1997), pp.27–35; H. Magdoff, *Globalization to What End?* (New York: Monthly Review Press, 1992); D.C. Korten, *When Corporations Rule the World* (West Hartford, CT: Kumarian Press, 1995); or R. Robertson, *Globalization: Social Theory and Global Culture* (Newbury Park, CA: Sage, 1992). As Jameson, in F. Jameson and M. Miyoshi (eds), *The Cultures of Globalization* (Durham, NC: Duke University Press, 1998) notes, 'Globalization – even the term itself has been hotly contested' (p.xi).
25. M. Wilkins, *The Maturing of Multinational Enterprise: American Business Abroad From the Colonial Era to 1914* (Cambridge, MA: Harvard University Press, 1970), pp.29–30.
26. Ibid., pp.199–202; see also W. LaFeber, *The Cambridge History of American Foreign Relations, Vol. 2: The American Search For Opportunity, 1865–1913* (Cambridge: Cambridge University Press, 1993).
27. Wilkins, *The Emergence of Multinational Enterprise: American Business Abroad From 1914 to 1970* (Cambridge, MA: Harvard University Press, 1974), pp.3–129.
28. Ibid, p.374.
29. Blackford, *The Rise of Modern Business*, p.190. See also G. Jones, *The Evolution of International Business: An Introduction* (New York: Routledge, 1996), pp.127–45.
30. For good general discussions of the global economy, see W. Greider, *One World, Ready Or Not: The Manic Logic of Global Capitalism* (New York: Simon & Schuster, 1997); A. Hoogvelt, *Globalization and the Postcolonial World: The New Political Economy of Development* (Baltimore, MD: Johns Hopkins University Press, 1997; or J. Gray, *False Dawn: The Delusions of Global Capitalism* (New York: New Press, 1998).
31. D. Hale, 'A Second Chance', *Fortune*, 22 November 1999, pp.189–90; J. Madeley, *Big Business, Poor Peoples: The Impact of Transnational Corporations on the World's Poor* (New York: Zed Books, 1999); 'Corporate Cash: Few Nations Can Top It', *Campaign For Labor Rights Newsletter* (July/August, 1999), pp.6–7.
32. M.L. Blim, 'Introduction: The Emerging Global Factory and Anthropology', in F.A. Rothstein and M.L. Blim (eds), *Anthropology and the Global Economy: Studies of the New Industrialization in the Late Twentieth Century* (New York: Bergin & Garvey, 1991); P. Dicken, *Global Shift: Transforming the World Economy*, 3rd edn (New York: Guilford Press, 1998).
33. US Bureau of the Census, 'Futurework: Trends and Challenges for Work in the 21st Century', 26 November 1999, online at http: //www.dol.gov./dol/asp/public/futurework/report/chapter 6/table 6_1_text.htm/; C. Chase-Dunn, *Global Formation: Structures of the World Economy*, updated edition (New York: Rowman & Littlefield, 1998).
34. See S. Anderson and J. Cavanagh with T. Lee, *Field Guide to the Global Economy* (New York: New Press, 2000), p.56; S. Herzenberg, *New Rules for a New Economy: Employment and Opportunity in Postindustrial America* (Ithaca, NY: ILR Press, 1998); see also US Bureau of Labor Statistics, *Monthly Labor Review*, November 1999; Executive PayWatch, 'General Electric

CEO Jack Welch', online at http://adicio.org/paywatch/2ch_m1.htm. In the first five years after the NAFTA Treaty became law, the US Department of Labor certified over 200,000 workers as having lost their jobs as a result of that treaty.

35. See B. Bluestone and B. Harrison, *The Deindustrialization of America: Plant Closings, Community Abandonment, and the Dismantling of Basic Industry* (New York: Basic Books, 1992); K.M. Dudley, *The End of the Line: Lost Jobs, New Lives in Postindustrial America* (Chicago, IL: University of Chicago Press, 1997); and Madeley, *Big Business, Poor Peoples: The Impact of Transnational Corporations on the World's Poor* (New York: Zed Books, 1999).

36. See E.M. Wood, *Rising From the Ashes?: Labor in the Age of Global Capitalism* (New York: Monthly Review Press, 1998); see also A. Chan and R.A. Senser, 'China's Troubled Workers', *Foreign Affairs*, 76 (March/April, 1997), pp.104–17; and Madeley, *Big Business, Poor Peoples*.

37. See A. Fuentes and B. Ehrenreich, *Women in the Global Factory* (Boston, MA: South End Press, 1992); A. Howard, 'Labor History, and Sweatshops in the New Global Economy', in A. Ross (ed.) *No Sweat: Fashion, Free Trade, and the Rights of Garment Workers* (New York: Verso, 1997), pp.151–71. A summary of the ILO report is reported in its press release, 'Export processing zones growing steadily. Providing a major sources of job creation', online at http://www.ilo.org/public/english/235press/pr/1998/34.htm. Christian Aid Reports, 'A Sporting Chance, Tackling Child Labour in India's Sporting Goods Industry, 1999', online at http://www.christianaid.org.uk/reports/sporting.htm, pp.1–31; Foreign Policy In Focus press release: 'Child Labor in the Global Economy', online at www.foreignpolicy-infocus.org/media/releases/1998/childlab.html; Rothstein and Lim, *Anthropology and the Global Economy*, pp.12–13; R. Burbach, O. Núñez and B. Kagarlitsky, *Globalisation and its Discontents: The Rise of Postmodern Socialisms* (London: Pluto Press, 1997); Greider, *One World, Ready or Not;* K. Moody, *Workers in a Lean World: Unions in the International Economy*, (London and New York: Verso, 1997).

38. World Bank, *The East Asian Miracle* (New York: Oxford University Press, 1993), p.174.

39. W. Wolman and A. Colamosca, *The Judas Economy: The Triumph of Capital and the Betrayal of Work* (Reading, MA: Addison-Wesley, 1997); see also Anderson and Cavanagh, *A Field Guide.*

40. J. Ballinger, 'Introduction', in J. Ballinger and C. Olsson (eds), *Behind the Swoosh: The Struggle of Indonesians Making Nike Shoes* (Uppsala, Sweden: Global Publications Foundation, 1997), pp.6–24; D. Katz, *Just Do It: The Nike Spirit in the Corporate World* (New York: Random House, 1994).

41. B. Brookes and P. Madden, *The Globe Trotting Sports Shoe* (London: Christian Aid, 1995); H. Sender, 'Sprinting to the Forefront', *Far Eastern Economic Review*, 159 (1 August 1996), pp.50–1; J.B. Strasser and L. Becklund, *Swoosh, the Unauthorized Story of Nike and the Men Who Played There* (New York: Harcourt Brace Jovanovich, 1991).

42. R. Shaw, *Reclaiming America: Nike, Clean Air, and the New National Activism* (Berkeley, CA: University of California Press, 1999); see also UNITE! report, 'Sweatshops Behind the Swoosh', 25 April 2000), pp.1–11.

43. Some examples of reports about Nike factories are Associated Press, 'Nike's Workers in Third World Abused, Report Says', *The Arizona Republic*, 28 March 1997, p.A10; D.M. Boje, 'Nike, Greek Goddess of Victory or Cruelty? Women's Stories of Asian Factory Life', *Journal of Organizational Change*, 11 (1998), pp.461–80; CBS News, *48 Hours*, 'The Nike Story in Vietnam', 17 October 1996.

44. Asia Monitor Resource Centre and Hong Kong Christian Industrial Committee, 'Working Conditions in Sports Shoe Factories in China Making Shoes for Nike and Reebok', online at http://saigon.com/nike/NikeChina.htm (21 September 1997); Brookes and Madden, *The Globe Trotting Sports Shoe*, p.5; A. Chan, 'China Today: Boot Camp at a Shoe Factory', *Labor Notes*, January 1997, pp.8–9; ESPN, *Sportszone*, 'The American Sneaker Controversy', 2 April 1998.

45. D. O'Rouke, *Smoke From a Hired Gun: A Critique of Nike's Labor and Environmental Auditing in Vietnam as Performed by Ernst and Young* (San Francisco, CA: Transnational Resource and Action Center), online at http://www.corpwatch.org/trac/nike/news/Lewis.html (10 November 1997); B. Herbert, 'Mr. Young Gets It Wrong', *New York Times*, 27 June 1997, p.A29; Campaign For Labor Rights, 'Nike/Dartmouth Study Criticized', *Labor Alerts*, 15 January 1998, pp.1–5.

46. Katz, *Just Do It*, p.ix.

47. Quoted in Clean Clothes, 'Nike Case', online at http://www.cleanclothes.org/1/nike.htm (14 July 1998), p.1. The 'race to the bottom' refers to corporations from developed countries investing in developing countries where workers' wages, working conditions, environmental standards and social protections are the lowest, in the poorest and most desperate countries.

48. L. Featherstone, 'The New Student Movement', *The Nation*, 15 May 2000, pp.11–18; P. Street,

'The Anti-Sweatshop Movement', *Z Magazine*, 13 (May 2000), pp.20; National Labor Committee, 'Sweat-Free Student Movement: University Victories 1998–1999', online at http://www.org/student/usas9899.html (9 May 2000), pp.1–5.

49. Quoted in J.H. Cushman, Jr., 'Nike Pledges to End Child Labor and Apply US Rules Abroad', *New York Times*, 13 May 1998, pp.D1, D5.
50. *Nike Annual Report*, Beaverton, OR, 1998, pp.56–7.
51. See UNITE! Report, 'Sweatshops Behind the Swoosh'; this is a report on working conditions at Nike production facilities in Indonesia, China and other Asian locations. Inspectors found 'that Nike remains a sweatshop producer on a global scale'. During the summer of 2000 Nike's CEO Philip Knight, angered that US universities were joining the Worker Rights Consortium, a labor, student and human-rights-based factory monitoring consortium, terminated contracts with several universities.
52. A. Stamborski, 'Rawlings is Again Named Major League Ball Supplier', *St Louis Post-Dispatch*, 25 May 1999, p.C7; 'Executives Confirm Baseballs Are Hand-Stitched', *USA Today*, 23 May 2000, p.6C.
53. Fuentes and Ehrenreich, *Women in the Global Factory*, p.11.
54. A. Ebert-Miner, 'How Rawlings Use Haitian Women to Spin Profits Off US Baseball Sales', *Multinational Monitor*, 3, 8 (1982), pp.11–12; A. Ebert-Miner, 'Haitians Slave to Hatch Our Baseballs', *Business and Society Review*, Spring 1983, pp.12–13; J. DeWind and D.H. Kinley III, *Aiding Migration: The Impact of International Development Assistance on Haiti* (Boulder, CO: Westview Press, 1988).
55. P. Marshall, 'Report on Haitian Corporate Campaign and Interested Persons' sponsored by the International Labor Rights Working Group and the Washington Office on Haiti, (15 September 1988), pp.1–9; see also press release, 'Rawlings Plant closing seen as foul play for Haitian workers', *Pax Christi, USA* (3 December 1990), pp.1–2.
56. G. Mihoces, 'Behind-the-Seams Look', *USA Today*, 24 May 2000, pp.1C–2C.

3

Sports Globalisation, the State and the Problem of Governance

BARRIE HOULIHAN

The stimulus for the enthusiastic embrace of the concept of globalisation in the early 1990s was due less to the spread of particular cultural practices, or the recognition of the global commercial interests in major sports events such as the Olympics and the soccer World Cup, and more to the collapse of communism and the end of global political and economic bipolarity. The apparent triumph of capitalism, and the economic and social turbulence experienced by many former communist states, created a new social science agenda in which the concept of globalisation took centre stage. Political scientists,[1] economists[2] and international relations theorists[3] all perceived a need to frame their consideration of the post-Cold-War world in terms of, or at least with direct reference to, globalisation. Such was the enthusiastic embrace of the concept that Hirst and Thompson were moved to comment that 'globalisation has become the new grand narrative of the social sciences'.[4] Yet just at the time when globalisation was assuming paradigmatic status, unease began to be expressed about the utility of the concept, its descriptive accuracy and its explanatory potential – 'a fad word fast turning into a shibboleth'.[5]

Challenge and criticism came from a number of different quarters. For Hirst and Thompson the problem was the indiscriminate eclecticism of much of the globalisation research: '...this literature omnivorously gathers together the effects of often very different cultural, economic and social processes under the common concept of globalisation, treating them as instances of a wider phenomenon'.[6] They went on to suggest that 'there may be only instances and no phenomenon'.[7] For Bauman the weakness in much theorising of globalisation was that it concentrates on 'global *effects*, notoriously unintended and unanticipated, rather than … global *initiatives* and *undertakings*'.[8] In other words, the focus of theorising is on what is happening to us rather than what we do. For others the objection was to the overly rapid claim of the marginalisation of the state to the benefit of transnational corporations, which, buoyed by the unregulated and, supposedly, unregulatable movement of finance capital, now dominated the global economy. Yet, as Dearlove noted, 'nation-state policies are never a simple function of external constraints and so cannot be "read off" from the needs of footloose finance capital.'[9] He added that even if one accepts the political power of finance capital 'it cannot shape the policies of nation states directly in an unmediated way'.[10] In a similar vein, Weiss cautioned that 'Proponents of globalisation ... seriously underrate the variety and adaptability of state capacities.'[11] Others, such as Michie and Grieve-Smith[12] or Baker et al.,[13] argued that globalisation requires effective management and that such management can only be provided by the state. Thus 'global and national are not necessarily competing principles of organisation ... they can be – and indeed in many ways already are – complementary.'[14]

There is clearly a need to take stock of the utility of the concept as there is a risk that it will become degraded and exhausted through indiscriminate use and constant challenge from its critics, and consequently move to the 'back-burner' in social science. It is the intention within this chapter to use the current debate about the utility of the concept of globalisation to sharpen our understanding of the development of sport as it continues to move beyond the confines of national policy systems, and particularly the part played by the state in the process.

Globalisation, Internationalisation and Dimensions of Analysis

Most research on globalisation constructs a framework of analysis that gives priority either to economics or to culture. For those focusing on economic factors, evidence of globalisation is drawn from analyses of the behaviour of such commercial entities as Nike[15] or BSkyB,[16] which source sport products globally and seek to develop global markets. Economists emphasise the liberalisation of trade, as exemplified by the greater freedom of competition for television rights to domestic sport products such as the English soccer Premier League, and the greater freedom of movement of labour, such as that following the ruling of the European Court of Justice in the case of Jean-Marc Bosman, which allowed professional sports teams within the European Union (EU) to field an unlimited number of EU players. By contrast, those emphasising the cultural dimension of globalisation draw on an eclectic variety of evidence, including the number of countries participating in the Olympic Games; the marginalisation of regional or local sports and pastimes in preference for a largely western diet of Olympic sports; the close relationship between colonialism and the adoption of the sports of the imperial powers; and even the adoption of US-style presentation of commercially oriented televised sport. In addition to the economic or cultural emphases a third, but less commonly explored, dimension of globalisation is the development of a global organisational infrastructure for sport, evident in both the governmental and the non-governmental spheres.

Three interrelated problems present themselves when considering globalisation. The first problem is definitional and involves the establishment of a distinction between the process of globalisation and the particular features or configuration of international relationships that would constitute a globalised world. In other words, it is not always clear how we would recognise the arrival of a globalised world and avoid the conceptual elision of treating the process and the product as synonymous. The second, closely related, problem is the need to distinguish between a globalised and an internationalised world. A useful discussion is provided by Hirst and Thompson,[17] who have distinguished, in an ideal-typical fashion, between an international and a globalised economy, according to which the former is characterised by national economies as the principal entities in the international economy; national economies that are specialised and reflect an international division of labour; and multinational corporations that retain a clear basis in a national economy and that are subject to its regulation. In general, the international economy is one where there is a 'continued relative separation of the domestic and the international frameworks for policy-making and the management of economic affairs, and also a relative separation of economic effects'.[18] By contrast, in a globalised economy distinct national economies are subsumed within an economy that is 'autonomized and socially disembedded', thus making governance and the imposition of distinct patterns of domestic regulation 'fundamentally problematic'.[19] Stateless corporations exemplify the existence of genuinely rootless and fluid capital, which gains power at the expense of national governments in what is essentially a zero-sum game.

Hirst and Thompson's ideal type can be applied easily to commercial sport organisations, such as Nike, adidas, and products such as the Olympic Games or the soccer World Cup, and can be extended, without too much difficulty, to encompass change at the governmental level. It is at the level of culture that the greatest problems arise, largely because of the difficulty of identifying indicators and concepts equivalent to ownership, company registration and national currency within the economic sphere, or to sovereignty and citizenship in the political sphere. Although these indicators and concepts are far from unambiguous, they are arguably more concrete than those that might be claimed as indicators of cultural identity and differentiation, such as language, religion or sport.

The third problem is a consequence of attempts to produce ideal types to contrast a globalised and an internationalised world along economic, political and cultural dimensions, and concerns the daunting problem of identifying the relative importance of the economic, political and cultural dimensions of globalisation. Harvey,[20] the most significant of the Marxist analysts of globalisation, argues persuasively that the production of culture, including sport and sporting events, is increasingly tightly integrated into capitalist commodity production, leading to an exaggerated concern with style, rather than authenticity, and a celebration of the ephemeral. Harvey retains confidence in a 'base-superstructure' explanation of the relationship between the mode of production and culture. As Nash observes, postmodern culture is seen by Harvey as 'epiphenomenal, a by-product of a new stage of the capitalist mode of production dependent on the accelerated consumption of signs and services'.[21] Harvey's economic determinism denies that the cultural sphere or dimension of globalisation requires a new conceptual language for its analysis and, by implication, that political struggle located at the cultural level has transformative potential. Wallerstein,[22] in his world systems theory, is even more insistent on the priority of the economic sphere over both the political and, especially, the cultural sphere, which he simply dismisses as a mere ideological impediment to socialism.

Such Marxists are the exception among theorists of globalisation in arguing so strongly for the priority of one dimension of globalisation over others. It is more common for theorists to identify relatively distinct dimensions or spheres of globalisation, often with the intent of distinguishing the cultural from the economic and political as a way of asserting its particularity as a separate focus for analysis. Tomlinson, for example, argues that 'cultural practices lie at the heart of globalisation'[23] and, although he acknowledges the significance of politics and economics, he goes on to claim that 'the huge transformation processes of our time that globalisation describes cannot properly be understood until they are grasped through the conceptual vocabulary of culture'.[24] Taking a slightly different approach, Said provides a similar disaggregation and argues that 'practices, like the arts of description, communication and representation … have relative autonomy from the economic, social and political realms'.[25] Neither of these authors provides a convincing justification for either the disaggregation they suggest or the significance that they ascribe to culture as a dimension of globalisation. Indeed, a general weakness in much writing on global culture is the tendency to leap from case study to generalisation and to aggregate quite disparate phenomena as evidence of globalisation or even cultural homogenisation.

Two important problems remain at the heart of discussions on globalisation: first, the need to conceptualise the relationship between political, economic and social organisation, on the one hand, and culture on the other; and second, the need to distinguish between globalisation as a process and globalisation as a product. As regards the former, I suggest that, rather than attempt to distinguish between culture and other dimensions such as the political or economic, it is more persuasive to accept, provisionally at least, a threefold distinction between social, economic and political dimensions of society, and to recognise that each reflects and contributes to the overall constitution of culture, and that each is an important constituent in determining the cultural significance of sport in a community/nation. Table 3.1 distinguishes between prevailing patterns of social relations, the distribution of power and patterns of economic organisation, and suggests that each reflects the culture of a community at different degrees of intensity and stability. The core culture or deep structure of a community is the most impervious to change and is often reflected in taken-for-granted patterns of behaviour that rarely require codification. At a less permanent level are those patterns of behaviour and values that are frequently contested: these require state support, often in the form of legislation or regulation, to provide a degree of longevity. At the shallowest level are the fads, fashions and trends that are temporarily diverting.

While many studies of globalisation exhibit a quite proper concern with investigating the extent to which the deep structure of culture is affected by sports globalisation, too many focus on the shallower commercialisation of cultural commodities. However, they generally fail to give significant consideration to the role of the state or the role of international governmental organisations. All too often sports globalisation theory is

TABLE 3.1
CONSTITUTING GLOBALISATION: EXAMPLES OF DEPTH OF CHANGE

	Culture as		
Dimension:	deep structure	actions of the state	commodities
Social	relationships between genders and generations; attitudes to work and leisure, and also to the participation of women in sport and recreation	legislation/regulation concerning, for example, the protection of children involved in sport; doping; racist abuse at soccer matches; the retention of major sports events for terrestrial television	sports fashionwear; sports bars; individual sports, events and competitions
Political	commitment to democracy; limits on the power of the state and rights of the individual, e.g. the right of soccer supporters to travel abroad	administrative structures; degree of public participation, for example, in decisions over the use of lottery funding for sport, or the criteria for public subsidy for elite sport	political posturing, including the attendance of politicians at sports events and the vociferous defence of competitive sport in schools when there is little evidence of an attack
Economic	beliefs about property rights (access to the countryside for recreation) and profit	regulation of monopoly and competition, e.g. the limitation on the proportion of shares in a soccer club that a television company can own	club merchandise; web-based gambling; pay-per-view televising of sports events

'state-free' theory, with the state being treated as marginal to globalisation processes or at least ineffective in influencing the character of these processes. While media companies are given centre stage as the primary vehicles of globalisation, and international sports organisations such as the International Olympic Committee (IOC) are afforded an important secondary role, the state is rarely discussed. It is the central argument of this chapter that the achievement of globalisation, as opposed to internationalisation, is substantially shaped by the extent to which the state is marginal in affecting the development of modern commercial forms of sport and, consequently, that an analysis of the significance of the state in globalised sport is an essential prerequisite for an assessment of the extent and depth of globalisation.

Following Hirst and Thompson, it is possible to suggest a model of both globalised and internationalised sport that will provide a framework for

TABLE 3.2
GLOBALISED SPORT, INTERNATIONALISED SPORT AND THE STATE

Characteristic	Globalised sport	Internationalised sport
Nation as the defining unit of international sport, and nationality as the defining characteristic of sportsmen and sportswomen	Multinational/nationally ambiguous teams the norm, as in Formula One motor-racing or professional road cycling	Teams defined by their country of origin, as in the Olympic Games and international soccer club competitions
Extent of global diversity in sport	Diminishing diversity and/or the overlaying of regionally/ nationally distinctive sporting traditions with an increasingly uniform pattern of Olympic and major international team/individual sports	Maintenance of a vigorous national/regional sporting culture, which exists alongside or takes precedence over Olympic and major international team/individual sports
Extent of state patronage of elite sport	Minimal – sports are either financially self-sufficient or attract commercial patronage	Substantial – most Olympic and major international sports depend on state subsidy
Extent to which sports businesses and organisations operate within a national framework of regulation	Self-regulation by the industry or no regulation	National framework of regulation, e.g. licensing of clubs, coaches, sports venues and television broadcasting, or supranational framework of regulation, by, for example, the EU
Extent to which international sports federations and the IOC are subject to domestic control	Immune from domestic regulatory and legal systems or in countries where the legal system is 'protective' of corporate/organisational interests	Subject to legal challenge or state/supranational oversight

discussing the significance of the state in the process of globalisation – see Table 3.2. The first characteristic, which is by far the most controversial, concerns the place of the concept of nation and nationality in relation to the globalisation of sport. Maguire refers to the 'dislocation' of national identities as being 'connected to globalization processes'[26] and gives the examples of the 'European' teams that participate against the US in golf's Ryder Cup and alongside other national and continental teams, in the athletics World Championships. A further example of the increasing ambiguity or marginalisation of nation and nationality as reference points in sport is the number of track and field athletes who have switched nationality. For example, Fiona May, a British-born long-jumper, took Italian nationality and subsequently, in 1995, won a world title. However, four years later she lost her title to Niurka Montalvo, a former Cuban, but by then Spanish, athlete. There are also examples of Ethiopian-born athletes competing as naturalised Turks and Sudanese-born athletes competing as naturalised Qataris. Finally, Mohammed Mourhit, previously of Morocco, won bronze in the world 5000m cross-country championship in 2000 in Seville for Belgium and then posed wrapped in a Moroccan flag with his former team-mate Salah Hissou. Merged, blurred and ambiguous national identities would be expected in truly globalised sport. By contrast, under conditions of internationalised sport the nation would be protected as the defining unit of international sport. The status of the nation as an organising concept for sport is intimately linked to the significance of the state with which it has, in the vast majority of cases, a mutually dependent, if not symbiotic, relationship.[27]

A second characteristic is the extent of sports diversity throughout the world. Under conditions of globalised sport one might expect to find that local/regional sporting forms were retreating in the face of a largely European/North American diet of Olympic and major commercial sports. At the very least one would expect to find evidence of a 'third culture'[28] that overlays more localised sports cultures. In essence it would be the 'anational' holders of power, such as international federations or transnational sports businesses, that would provide the direction and momentum for change at the domestic level. By contrast, under conditions of internationalised sport the dynamics of change in sporting culture would be substantially national and while engagement with, and adoption of, non-traditional sports might be common it would be the result of choice rather than imposition or coercion.

Third, under conditions of globalised sport one would expect the role of the state as a patron of, and organisational focus for, elite sport to be slight, by comparison with commercial patrons, for example, thus minimising the influence of the state in determining the pattern of engagement with global sport. A situation where the state plays a central role in funding and organising elite sport reflects a situation where engagement with global sport is determined significantly by nationally set priorities.

A fourth characteristic is the extent to which commercial sporting organisations, such as soccer clubs, broadcasting companies and event organising bodies, operate within national frameworks of regulation. Globalised sport would be typified by minimal regulation or a pattern of self-regulation, while under conditions of internationalised sport national or regional (e.g. EU systems of licensing, certification and training would create a mosaic of distinctive regulatory systems and consequently of commercial sporting practices. The final characteristic is the degree to which international sports organisations, such as the IOC and the international federations (IFs), are subject to control by the domestic political/administrative/legal system. Under conditions of globalisation one would expect these engines of globalisation to be substantially immune from domestic systems of regulation, or to be located in countries traditionally protective of corporate interests, such as Switzerland and Monaco. Within an internationalised system IFs and the IOC would be open to legal challenge and interest-group lobbying and enjoy no privileges arising solely from their status as global sports organisations.

The central theme running through this ideal-typical duality is a challenge to the assumption that globalised sport is either beyond regulatory capacity of the state system or that the state system is of negligible significance to the trajectory and momentum of sports globalisation. I wish to argue that the globalising pressures affecting sport are located within a pattern of international governance where the state and international governmental organisations play a central, if not defining, role. However, it needs to be acknowledged that many definitions of global governance stress the significance of non-governmental organisations in establishing and maintaining effective patterns of governance, and such definitions are by no means wholly inappropriate. Over the past half-century what was once a weak, fragmented and politically insignificant infrastructure of global sport has changed almost beyond recognition. The range and frequency of international competition and the attendant commercial practices in all sports have increased apace. In soccer, for example, although FIFA was formed in 1904 it was almost 30 years before the first World Cup was organised. However, since the 1950s the growth of international soccer competitions has been rapid. UEFA was formed in 1955 and established the European Cup club competition in 1956, followed by the Fairs Cup/UEFA Cup competition in 1958 and the first European Championship between countries in 1960. Over the years the major competitions have been gradually expanded to incorporate more countries and clubs. Although slower to become established, women's soccer has followed a similar pattern of commercial development and is currently one of Europe's fastest-growing participation sports. Cricket has also expanded its range of international competitions for both men's and women's teams. Indeed, the women's game was the first to establish an international body, the International Women's Cricket Council, in 1958, and to establish a World Cup competition in 1973; the men's World Cup was first held in 1975. A similar pattern of international expansion can be found in (field) hockey, which featured in the Olympic Games as early as 1908, but more recently established its own World Cup – for men in 1971 and for women in 1974 – followed by the Champions Trophy (for the six leading nations) for men in 1978 and for women in 1987. The 1970s also saw the introduction of European national and club competitions.

For most major sports the early phase of development at international level took place in the last quarter of the nineteenth century and was followed by a prolonged period of slow growth of international fixtures, often limited to participation in Olympic competition. The problem of distance and the intervention of two world wars created obvious barriers to more rapid growth. The expansion of international competition was stimulated by the growth in reasonably cheap air travel, the spread of television, particularly live satellite broadcasts from the mid-1960s, and the Cold War. The growth in the number of international sports events and competitions was paralleled by the development of international organisational structures for sport, such as the General Assembly of International Sports Federations (GAISF), established in 1967; the Association of Winter Sports Federations (AWIF), established in 1970; or the Association of Summer Olympic Federations (ASOIF), formed in 1983. In addition to these organisations, whose primary concern was to protect the interests of the IFs in the face of the increasingly powerful Olympic movement, there was a large number of other bodies that were either specialist commissions or agencies of the IOC, such as the Medical Commission or Olympic Solidarity, or regional/continental groupings within the Olympic movement and the major IFs. The growth in organisational density involving sports bodies was complemented by a similar, though slower and less dramatic, growth in international governmental bodies/forums that either adopted an interest in sport, such as the Council of Europe or, more recently, the EU, or were established to deal with a specific aspect of sport, such as the various regional groupings of countries that have emerged to tackle problems of policy harmonisation on doping control.[29]

Rosenau's definition of global governance as 'governance without government ... regulatory mechanisms in a sphere of activity which function effectively even though they are not endowed with formal authority'[30] is particularly appropriate when considering the management and resolution of problems of collective action under conditions of sport globalisation. In an increasingly interconnected world, issues as diverse as human rights, environmental pollution and the transfer of mail between countries require the development of stable patterns of governance. Using terminology different from Rosenau's, but essentially referring to the same phenomenon, Krasner uses the concept of the international regime, which he defines as

> sets of implicit or explicit principles, norms, rules and decision-making procedures around which actors' expectations converge in a given area of international relations. Principles are beliefs of fact, causation or rectitude. Norms are standards of behavior defined in terms of rights and obligations. Rules are specific prescriptions or proscriptions for action. Decision-making procedures are prevailing practices for making and implementing collective choice.[31]

Krasner's definition is valuable, but it covers a potentially wide range of governance arrangements, from those where the only evidence of regime existence is a relatively stable pattern of behaviour to those with a clear organisational focus, such as the United Nations or the IOC. While the less formal governance regimes are significant in ordering international interaction, most regimes possess a greater degree of explicit organisation. Keohane et al. provide valuable insights into the character of regimes, and particularly the position within them of states, when they observe that they 'do not supersede or overshadow states. ... To be effective they must create networks over, around, and within states.'[32] Moreover, in keeping with the notion of governance as an intentional process, international institutions of governance are 'neither neutral reflections of exogenous environmental forces nor neutral arenas',[33] but are constraints on policy actors providing, or at least attempting to provide, a limit on what is permissible. Accordingly, the structuring of institutions is contested and reflects the concern of policy actors to shape institutions in order to gain strategic advantage and/or be able to control and regulate the behaviour of other policy actors.[34]

While some theorists of international governance[35] seek to balance the presumption of state centrality made by the realist school in international relations with an emphasis on the capacity of nongovernmental organisations, there is a broad consensus that the state has a key role to play in the establishment, operation and maintenance of governance regimes, based on the assumption that most international problems primarily require action by individual states for their successful resolution.

In summary, the marginalisation of the state in globalisation theory is a substantial weakness and one that is especially acute when analysing sport. In order to achieve an understanding of the process of globalisation, and to be able to distinguish between globalised and internationalised sport, it is important that more attention is paid to the capacity of states and supranational state bodies, such as the EU, to promote and protect their interests. The following section examines two recent issues in commercial sport as a basis for assessing the capacity of states to shape global sport.

Soccer: Player Transfers and Broadcasting Rights

One of the primary responsibilities of international sport federations is to establish the criteria according to which athletes may be deemed eligible to compete for their country and, in many team sports, for their club. Although at first sight the rules seem both straightforward and logical, they have proved to be a constant source of uncertainty, and of friction between FIFA, UEFA (FIFA's European regional federation) and member associations, as well as between FIFA and the EU.

Until the mid-1990s UEFA rules stated that for club competitions under its control clubs could field a maximum of three foreign players and two 'assimilated' players. 'Assimilated' players were defined as those who had played in a country for an uninterrupted period of five years, three of which had to have been at youth level. Defining foreign players in the context of the UK had always been problematic, as FIFA defined as eligible for national teams 'any player who is a naturalised citizen of a country in virtue of that country's laws' (Article 18 [UEFA, 2001]).[36] However, eligibility was only fixed when a player represented his country. Unfortunately, FIFA did not define 'country' and consequently posed a dilemma for footballers who were citizens of the UK. Until a UK player had represented his country he would remain eligible to play for two or even three countries within the UK, as each of the 'home countries' has its own governing body affiliated to FIFA and has its own 'national' team. For example, a player born in Wales with one parent from Northern Ireland retains his eligibility to play for more than one 'national' team. As Miller notes: 'Until he is actually included in a particular representative side, he will remain eligible to play for both, and cannot be classified as a foreigner [for club purposes]'.[37] What is significant for the present discussion is that this problem was resolved, partially at least, by FIFA creating a concept of dual nationality that covered players from the UK. Moreover, FIFA allowed the English FA to retain a rule that not only deemed players from the home countries to be exempt from UEFA's 'three foreigners' rule, but extended the exemption to allow players who were citizens of the Irish Republic to be similarly excluded. Although FIFA and UEFA were far from content with what they saw as an anomalous situation, they were willing to compromise and tolerate the peculiarities of the UK. The compromise over eligibility concluded between the soccer authorities and the UK football associations was built around the peculiarities of UK nationality law and culture, rather than requiring conformity to a global model.

Perhaps the most striking illustration of the continuing significance of national or regional conditions and requirements is the Bosman case. J.-M. Bosman, a Belgian national, was a player for the Belgian team RC Liège who, when he refused a new contract at a lower wage, was placed on the transfer list. Bosman wished to move to the French club Dunkerque, but RC Liège refused to release him because it claimed that Dunkerque did not have the resources to pay the fee. As both UEFA and the Belgian FA supported RC Liège, Bosman challenged the decision in the European Court of Justice. He eventually won his case in 1995. The judgment concluded that the case breached Article 48 of the EC Treaty, which concerns people's freedom of movement.[38] The consequences of the Bosman case are well known. It may be claimed, with some justification, that the judgment hastened the globalisation of soccer as it freed elite clubs from the constraints of nationality laws, thus allowing commercial brands such as Manchester United, Barcelona or Inter Milan to develop their global market positions more effectively. The argument presented by UEFA to the court – that 'the identification of spectators with the various teams is guaranteed only if those teams consist, at least as regards a majority of players, of nationals of the relevant member state'[39] – was rejected not just by the court but also by the elite clubs.

The national basis of international club competitions, long defended by FIFA and UEFA, was now overturned and, as Parrish commented, it was now 'the responsibility of FIFA and UEFA to find alternatives to the transfer system that would be compatible with EC law'.[40] However, FIFA's initial response was, as Sugden and Tomlinson noted, to announce 'its view that its own status as a global body placed it above the merely regional status of the European Union'.[41] Subsequently FIFA/UEFA sought to establish a standard player-club contract that would bind a player to a club for three years as a trainee and for a further three years as a professional. However, FIFA/UEFA were advised by the EU's Competition Commissioner that the contract was likely to be in breach of EU law. Attempts in individual countries to undo the perceived damage of the Bosman ruling, such as the Spanish FA's attempt to require a player to compensate his club for early release from his contract, have been subject to legal challenge and are likely to be deemed incompatible with EU law. Further undermining of the FIFA/UEFA position has resulted from a more recent case involving a Polish basketball player, Lilia Malaja, where the court ruled that sportsmen and -women from 23 associate member states of the EU who already work in the EU have the same, post-Bosman, rights as EU citizens.

Following intensive lobbying from UEFA, domestic football associations and some member governments, the EU began to reconsider its determination to treat sport as though it were like any other commercial activity. The addition of a declaration to the 1997 Treaty of Amsterdam that expressed the wish that the 'social significance' of sport be recognised began a process of review which led in 1999 to a report on sport being presented to the Helsinki meeting of the European Council. The report strongly defended the educational and social role of sport and considered the difficult issue of sport and EU competition policy. The theme of the paper was 'partnership', which on the one hand appeared to offer the prospect of a reinstatement of some of the autonomy lost by the international federations, but which on the other also legitimised the involvement of the EU in a much broader range of sporting issues. Evidence of the new attitude of the EU was reflected in two decisions – regarding the relocation of a soccer match across a national border and the multiple ownership of soccer clubs – where the EU supported UEFA's discretion, indicating the 'Commission's willingness to apply sporting criteria to cases rather than economic criteria'.[42] More recently, discussions between the French government, UEFA and the EU have led to the production of a draft protocol designed to enable sports authorities to limit the number of foreign players in a team, to six in the case of soccer. While this has been welcomed by some involved in soccer, many of the clubs in the English Premier League are, not surprisingly, opposed to any alteration of the current regulations.

Broadcasting is a second area where the EU and national governments have been involved in shaping policy in relation to international sport. The 1989 EU directive, 'Television Without Frontiers', represented 'a victory for the new commercial operators'[43] and embodied the deregulatory ethos dominant within the EU Commission. A review of the directive in 1994 saw a shift in the regulatory stance of the EU, with the new directive more concerned to ensure an adequate level of access for the public by allowing member states to draw up lists of major sports events which must be broadcast unencrypted. Parrish[44] identified a number of arguments that had been presented in support of the revision, including a recognition that action by the EU represented the most effective way for member states to protect sporting broadcasts and that, given the significance of sport to the success of television companies, member states may need to ensure unencrypted broadcasting of major sporting events in order to ensure the long-term survival of their national public service broadcasting.

At the national level there have been a number of recent cases which have emphasised the regulatory capacity of the state and the degree of variation in regulatory intent. In the UK the Monopolies and Mergers Commission (MMC) ruled that the proposed merger between BSkyB and Manchester United was against the public interest. According to Caiger, the 'MMC appears to have based its finding primarily on market considerations'[45] as they applied to the British broadcasting and football industries. A similarly strong economic perspective has been adopted by Dutch competition regulators who recently supported Feyenoord's challenge to the Dutch FA's claim that it could compel the collective selling of broadcasting rights. By contrast, German courts have allowed the collective selling of rights, although only within Germany, arguing that in all other situations broadcasting rights belong to clubs. Regulatory intervention in sport is increasing at both the national and EU levels. In particular, EU competition law is beginning to construct a distinctive regulatory framework for international sport that, according to Mario Monti, the Competition Commissioner, is designed 'to take account of the special characteristics of sport [for example, that sports organisations are not solely businesses] … to apply competition rules in a manner that does not question the regulatory authority of sporting organisations vis-à-vis genuine sporting rules, [and] to preserve the social and cultural functions of sport'.[46] There are currently over 60 sport-related cases lodged with the European Commission.

Outside the EU there is also considerable national variation in the treatment of broadcasting, much of which is designed to protect the character, social significance and commercial viability of national sport. In the US, for example, where the NFL has a $17.6 billion deal with CBS and the National Basketball Association has a $2.64 billion deal with NBC, the extent of state regulation is substantial. The most important element in the regulatory framework is the Sports and Broadcasting Act 1961, which granted sports leagues an exemption to anti-trust (monopoly) legislation such that leagues can restrict the freedom of individual clubs to sell broadcasting rights individually. Income from the collective sale of broadcasting rights is seen as an important way of protecting the weaker clubs and the overall viability of domestic leagues. Regulation is also significant in Australia, where the 1992 Broadcasting Services Act included an 'anti-siphoning' clause that gave the government power to specify sporting events that should be available free to the general public.

In the areas of employment of sportsmen and -women, their freedom of movement within the EU and sports broadcasting, sports clubs, leagues, federations and broadcasting companies have to operate within a complex framework of national and, within much of western Europe at least, supranational regulation. In soccer, for example, the particular balance of interest and advantage between elite clubs, domestic leagues, FIFA and media companies is the outcome of a process of bargaining that has states at its heart. The pattern of governance reflects the balance between the commercial interests of the global media and the brand marketing ambitions of elite clubs, on the one hand, and, on the other, the protection of the economic viability of domestic leagues and competitions, and of the social and cultural functions of sport. The extent to which the involvement of the state affects the trajectory of sports globalisation is difficult to assess, but it is probably fair to claim that, at the very least, state and/or EU intervention has slowed the pace of integration among commercial media entities and sports clubs, and may also play a central role, in conjunction with FIFA, in reversing the changes ushered in by the Bosman ruling.

Olympic Reform

The second example of the importance of states for an understanding of global sport is their role in the Olympic reform process. In December 1998 the Swiss IOC member, Marc Hodler, made a series of allegations of corruption in relation to the way in which decisions were made to select host cities for the Olympic Games. The subsequent internal enquiry conducted by the IOC, which focused particularly on Salt Lake City, resulted in the expulsion of six members, reprimands for ten and the resignation of four. If the IOC hoped that its prompt action would rapidly draw a line under the scandal, it was sadly disappointed, as further allegations soon emerged relating to the selection of Atlanta, Sydney and Nagano. As a result of the intensity of worldwide criticism of the Olympic movement, the IOC established an 80-strong reform commission, IOC 2000.

Far more worrying for the IOC than the wave of global criticism was the attitude of EU member states and the US government. Because two of the cities under investigation were in the United States, the US government launched its own investigation through a series of congressional hearings and also through the FBI. The IOC was acutely aware of the fact that 60 per cent of all its commercial revenue came from the United States, which provided nine of the 11 largest corporate sponsors and the bulk of broadcasting income. Consequently, threats by members of Congress to remove the IOC's tax-exempt status and make it subject to the Foreign Corrupt Practices Act were taken extremely seriously. Such was the influence of the US that Juan Antonio Samaranch, President of the IOC, agreed to give evidence before a congressional committee and to be interviewed by the FBI.

The report produced by IOC 2000 contained 50 recommendations, the most newsworthy of which was the prohibition on IOC members making official visits to bidding cities. In future members would make the choice of host city on the basis of a report by an IOC review team. Also significant were the changes made to the membership of the IOC. It was decided that its membership should be increased to 115, with 15 places each for athletes, presidents of international federations and presidents of national Olympic committees or continental associations, the remainder to be elected on an individual basis for eight-year renewable terms. The decision to ensure greater representation of athletes seems a positive step along the road to good organisational governance, although it is unclear how they will be elected and the fact that only athletes who have competed in the most recent

Olympic Games will be eligible will ensure a rapid turnover of members, and consequently little prospect of their accumulating sufficient knowledge and experience to make more than a modest contribution to committee deliberations. The token involvement of athletes is reinforced by the decision to include a representative, probably the chair, of the IOC Athletes' Commission on the IOC Executive Board. As the IOC President selects the chair of the Athletes' Commission, this change is likely to strengthen the president's control over the executive rather than challenge its current role as a legitimation device for presidential policy. The reform package also included a reduction in the age of retirement from 80 to 70, but as the ruling does not affect existing members it will take many years before there is any noticeable effect on composition.

Taken individually, the reform proposals do not amount to the radical shake-up of the Olympic movement that some had lobbied for, but collectively they do mark an important step towards a more orthodox pattern of corporate governance, and as such represent significant concessions to the pressure from the United States and the EU.

Discussion

As regards the role of the state, the two examples given in the previous section provide evidence of a substantial, and I would argue central, role for the state in determining the pattern, momentum and direction of the engagement between national and global sport, due to the dependence of almost all national sports systems on state funding and administrative support. However, the examples given also demonstrate the central role of the state in shaping the character of sport beyond national boundaries, where the resources of individual states have less value. Over the past ten years there has been a steady expansion in the extent and depth of cooperation between states over sporting issues.

Demonstrating the centrality of the state to the development of global sport, particularly in Europe, is relatively unproblematic: much more difficult is determining the effect of state involvement. In Table 3.2 a distinction was drawn between globalised and internationalised sport, and it was suggested that the pattern and character of state intervention are an important factor in determining the direction in which global sport would develop. Under conditions of globalised sport the concept of a hard-edged, clearly defined and recognised national identity would give way to a more fluid, ambiguous and malleable concept, according to which athletes and club teams would reflect multiple or nested identities that would, arguably, be more sympathetic to the commercial strategies of global media and business. To an extent the erosion of hard-edged national identity has, in western Europe and North America at least, been under way for some time and may be clearly seen in the willingness of athletes to seek alternative citizenship; the construction of English Premier League teams in which English players are in a minority; and, most recently, in the multi-ethnic French soccer team. While states have undoubtedly colluded in the dilution of national identity through their willingness to grant naturalisation or work permits to foreign athletes, there are signs of a reaction at least as far as team sports, and particularly soccer, are concerned. The reaction has its source not only in the national and international federations, but also in the EU and a number of member states, including Britain and France, all of which perceive a threat to the development of national talent and the integrity of domestic sport systems. However, the reaction should not be exaggerated. While there might be some tightening of the rules regarding the number of foreign players that can be fielded, this will be in the face of opposition from the major soccer teams, which service a global market. Moreover, it is also possible to argue that for an increasing proportion of the population in regions such as western Europe and North America nested, multiple or hyphenated identities are becoming the norm.

As regards the second characteristic, the extent of global sporting diversity, the vast majority of states undoubtedly play an important part in determining the range and variety of sports promoted in a country – first, through their control of the school curriculum and, second, through their provision of resources to support elite sport. Maguire[47] refers to the diminishing contrasts and increasing variety produced by globalisation. States have clearly contributed to this process, yet in a contradictory fashion, they are concerned at one and the same time to develop and maintain distinctive national identities, and also to participate in an increasingly uniform set of international activities and organisations, with the result that, paradoxically, countries use increasingly similar strategies to demonstrate their unique characters.

Concerning the remaining characteristics identified in Table 3.2, namely the extent of state patronage for elite sport, and the extent to which sports businesses and international sporting organisations operate within national systems of regulation, the evidence presented in this chapter demonstrates clearly the regulatory capacity of individual states and supranational bodies such as the EU. Not only is elite Olympic sport firmly and heavily dependent on state finance in almost all countries, but many countries exercise tight control over domestic sporting organisations and broadcasting media. Increasing state involvement in anti-doping policy and the sale of broadcasting rights is often justified in terms of objectives that extend beyond the purely commercial, and embrace the social and health-related. Even the relative immunity of the IFs and the IOC is beginning to be eroded as systems of governance are established that draw the IFs and the IOC into a framework of accountability and resource dependence, as illustrated by the example of IOC reform.

Drawing a firm conceptual distinction between globalised and internationalised sport is far from easy; demonstrating the existence of the distinction in practice is at least as difficult. However, there is a pressing need to refine the concept of sports globalisation and to give it a greater degree of precision, and thus allow the specification of the process and the criteria that have to be present before the identification of globalised sport is possible. While I acknowledge the problematic nature of the distinction encapsulated in Table 3.2, I suggest that, given the continuing significance of the state in shaping domestic engagement with international sport and the evidence of a strengthening capacity of states, both individually and collectively, to draw the IFs and the IOC into governance regimes, it is more accurate to talk of internationalised, rather than globalised, sport. Since the end of the Cold War the willingness of governments and intergovernmental organisations to be more assertive in setting political conditions for foreign aid in areas such as human rights[48] has begun to spill over into other areas of international interaction, including sport.

This conclusion endorses the suggestion that increased regulation is the most likely consequence of intensive globalisation. Vogel has argued persuasively that 'the rhetoric of globalisation ... serves only to obscure what is really going on'.[49] He suggests that 'liberalism requires reregulation', reports that 'I find stronger markets but not weaker governments' and concludes that globalisation has brought with it 'reregulation not deregulation'.[50] Rather than being treated as a residual category in the study of the commercialisation and globalisation of sport, the state needs to be seen as an integral part of the process. The extension of sport beyond national boundaries does not take place by bypassing the state but requires its active participation. It is therefore important that, at a time when the process of reregulation of internationalised sport is firmly under way, the centrality of the state is given full acknowledgement and weight in analysis.

NOTES

1. For example, D. Held, *Democracy and the Global Order: From the Modern State to Cosmopolitan Governance* (Cambridge: Polity Press, 1995).
2. For example, R. Stubbs and G.R.D. Underhill (eds), *Political Economy and the Changing Global Order* (London: Macmillan, 1994).
3. For example, S. Strange, 'Wake Up Krasner: The World *Has* Changed', *Review of International Political Economy*, 1 (1994); F. Halliday, *Rethinking International Relations* (London: Macmillan, 1994).
4. P. Hirst and G. Thompson, *Globalisation in Question*, 2nd edn (Cambridge: Polity Press, 1999), p.xiii.

5. Z. Bauman, *Globalization: The Human Consequences* (Cambridge: Polity Press, 2000), p.1.
6. Hirst and Thompson, *Globalisation*, p.xiii. A similar view is expressed by G. Morgan and L. Engwall, 'Regulation and Organisation: An Introduction', in G. Morgan and L. Engwall (eds), *Regulation and Organisation: International Perspectives* (London: Routledge, 1999).
7. Hirst and Thompson, *Globalisation*, p.xiii.
8. Bauman, *Globalization*, p.60; emphasis in the original.
9. J. Dearlove, 'Globalisation and the Study of British Politics', *Politics*, 20, 2 (2000), p.113.
10. Ibid., p.114.
11. L. Weiss, 'Globalization and the Myth of the Powerless State', *New Left Review*, old series 225 (1997).
12. J. Michie and J. Grieve-Smith (eds), *Global Instability: The Political Economy of World Economic Governance* (London: Routledge, 1999).
13. D. Baker, G. Epstein and R. Pollin (eds), *Globalisation and Progressive Economic Policy* (Cambridge: Cambridge University Press, 1999).
14. L. Weiss, 'Managed Openness: Beyond Neoliberal Globalism', *New Left Review*, old series 238 (1999), p.127.
15. D. Ashley, *History Without a Subject: The Post-Modern Condition* (Boulder, CO: Westview Press, 1997).
16. A. Brown, 'Sneaking in Through the Back Door? Media Company Interests and Dual Ownership of Clubs', in S. Hamil, J. Michie, C. Oughton and S. Warby (eds), *Football in the Digital Age: Whose Game Is It Anyway?* (London: Mainstream Publishing, 2000).
17. Hirst and Thompson, *Globalisation*.
18. Ibid., p.8.
19. Ibid., p.10.
20. D. Harvey, *The Condition of Postmodernity* (Oxford: Blackwell, 1989).
21. K. Nash, *Contemporary Political Sociology: Globalisation, Politics and Power* (Oxford: Blackwell, 2000), pp.60–1.
22. I. Wallerstein, 'Culture as the Ideological Battleground', in M. Featherstone (ed.), *Global Culture: Nationalism, Globalisation and Modernity* (London: Sage, 1990); I. Wallerstein, 'The National and the Universal: Can There Be Such a Thing as World Culture?', in A. King (ed.), *Culture, Globalisation and the World System* (London: Macmillan, 1991).
23. J. Tomlinson, *Globalisation and Culture* (Oxford: Polity Press, 1999), p.1.
24. Ibid, p.1.
25. E. Said, *Culture and Imperialism* (London: Chatto & Windus, 1993), p.xii.
26. J. Maguire, *Global Sport: Identities, Societies, Civilisations* (Oxford: Polity Press, 1999), p.202.
27. B. Houlihan, 'Sport, National Identity and Public Policy', *Nations and Nationalism*, 3, 1 (April 1997), pp.113–37.
28. M. Featherstone, 'Global Culture: An Introduction', in Featherstone, *Global Culture*, 1990 p.9.
29. B. Houlihan, *Sport and International Politics* (London: Harvester Wheatsheaf, 1994).
30. Quoted in A. McGrew, 'Democracy Beyond Borders', in A. McGrew (ed.), *The Transformation of Democracy? Globalization and Territorial Democracy* (Cambridge: Polity Press, 1997), p.15.
31. S. Krasner, 'Structural Causes and Regime Consequences: Regimes as Intervening Variables', in S. Krasner (ed.), *International Regimes* (Ithaca, NY: Cornell University Press, 1983), p.2.
32. R.O. Keohane, P.M. Haas and M.A. Levy, 'The Effectiveness of International Environmental Institutions', in P.M. Haas, R.O. Keohane and M.A. Levy (eds), *Institutions for the Earth: Sources of Effective International Environmental Protection* (Cambridge, MA: MIT Press, 1993), p.24.
33. J.G. March and J.P. Olsen, 'The New Institutionalism: Organisational Factors in Political Life', *American Political Science Review*, 78 (1984), p.742.
34. T.M. Moe, 'Political Institutions: The Neglected Side of the Story', *Journal of Law, Economics and Organisations*, 6 (1990).
35. For example, Keohane, Haas and Levy, 'The Effectiveness'; L. Ringius, 'Environmental NGOs and Regime Change: The Case of Ocean Dumping of Radioactivce Waste', *European Journal of International Relations*, 3 (1997), pp.61–104.
36. UEFA, *UEFA Statutes: Article 18* (Nyon: UEFA, 2001).
37. F.E. Miller, 'Profession: UK Footballer, Nationality: Unclear', *Sport and the Law Journal*, 2, 1 (1994), p.10.
38. S. Gardner, A. Felix, M. James, R. Welch and J. O'Leary, *Sports Law* (London: Cavendish Publishing, 1998).

39. Quoted in S. Greenfield and G. Osborn, *Contract and Control in Entertainment: Dancing on the Edge of Heaven* (Aldershot: Ashgate, 1998).
40. R. Parrish, 'The Bosman Case and European Competition Policy', *Sports Law Bulletin*, Sept. Oct 1998, p.12.
41. J. Sugden and A. Tomlinson, *FIFA and the Contest for World Football: Who Rules the Peoples' Game?* (Cambridge: Polity Press, 1998), p.50.
42. R. Parrish, 'The Helsinki Report on Sport: A Partnership Approach to Sport', *Sports Law Bulletin*, May/June 2000, p.17.
43. R. Parrish, 'The Broadcasting of Sport in Europe: The Television Without Frontiers Directive', *Sports Law Bulletin*, July/August 1998, p.12.
44. Ibid.
45. A. Caiger, 'Murdoch Loses Out in BSkyB/Manchester United Merger', *Sports Law Bulletin*, 2, 2 (1999), p.1.
46. Speech by Mario Monti, European Commissioner for Competition Policy, to the EU-organised Conference on Sport, Brussels, 17 April 2000.
47. Maguire, *Global Sport* (1999).
48. R. Thakur, 'Human Rights: Amnesty International and the UN', in P.F. Diehl (ed.), *The Politics of Global Governance: International Organizations in an Interdependent World* (Boulder, CO: Lynne Rienner Publishing, 1996).
49. S.K. Vogel, *Freer Markets, More Rules: Regulatory Reform in Advanced Industrial Countries* (Ithaca, NY: Cornell University Press, 1996), p.2.
50. Ibid., pp.2 and 3.

PART II:
THE PUBLIC SECTOR AND THE
COMMERCIALISATION OF SPORT

4

Government Subsidisation of Canadian Professional Sport Franchises: A Risky Business[1]

DAVID WHITSON, JEAN HARVEY
and MARC LAVOIE

Between 1997 and 2000 the future of 'major league' professional sports in Canada became the focus of political debate, to an extent that took many Canadians by surprise. In 1995 and 1996 Canada had seen the departure of two National Hockey League (NHL) teams, the Québec Nordiques and the Winnipeg Jets, to US cities that promised greater revenue potential as well as attractive public subsidies. The mid-1990s had also seen repeated threats by the majority owner of the Montreal Expos that without a new stadium in downtown Montreal, half of it financed by public funds, Canada's first Major League Baseball (MLB) franchise would ultimately be sold and moved to a US city. This was the context, then, in which a House of Commons sub-committee was formed, under the chairmanship of a Liberal MP, Dennis Mills (Broadview-Greenwood),[2] to study the funding of sport in Canada. The Mills sub-committee held hearings over the winter and spring of 1997–8, and heard arguments from many stakeholders in Canadian sports: amateur and professional sports organisations as well as multi-sport organisations such as the Canadian Olympic Association (COA) and the Canadian Intercollegiate Athletic Union (CIAU). The most urgent and controversial submissions, however, in terms of the 'problem' outlined above, came from Canada's major-league teams – in the NHL, in MLB and in the National Basketball Association (NBA) – and from these leagues themselves.[3] Their briefs argued that Canadian teams in the major leagues operate at a structural disadvantage compared to their US counterparts because of the lower value of the Canadian dollar and the higher levels of 'public costs', including taxes or rents charged for the use of public facilities, that are borne by Canadian owners. If Canadians wanted to hang on to their existing teams, NHL Commissioner Gary Bettman warned the sub-committee, their governments would have to start providing the same kinds of public subsidies and tax breaks to franchise owners that are now widespread in the United States.

The NHL's submission to Mills, like those from other major-league sports, pointed to the publicly funded facilities that many US cities have offered to sports operators virtually free of rent or other charges. It also pointed to features of the US tax system that benefit professional sport in other ways, permitting tax exemptions on municipal bonds used to fund sports facilities, for example, and lower rates of taxation for high-income professional athletes. It urged upon Canada's federal and provincial governments the position that professional sport is a significant industry in Canada:

> The National Hockey League estimates that the six professional hockey clubs generate 8,689 full-time and part-time jobs in Canada as well as 3,039 indirect jobs. In terms of annual wages, this represents $300.7 million directly and $100.3 million indirectly. The total impact ... of the National Hockey League, in terms of GDP, is estimated to be $437.6 million per year.[4]

Thus tax incentives and other 'reductions in public costs' ought not to be viewed as subsidies, let alone as giveaways to wealthy owners and players. Rather, they should be viewed as investments in job creation and prosperity, not unlike assistance programmes for the film and aerospace industries.

In November 1998 the Mills sub-committee reported to Parliament, recommending among other things a 'sport pact' involving other governments, the NHL and the NHL Players' Association. The proposed federal contribution to what was described as a 'Canadian professional sport stabilisation programme' outlined a package of tax measures that would have provided financial benefits to Canadian professional sports operators and athletes, as well as incentives to other businesses to subscribe to sports tickets or boxes. However, these proposed changes in Canadian tax regulations were made contingent upon reaching agreement with the other stakeholders on measures within their own domains (e.g. reductions in municipal and provincial taxes, revenue-sharing and salary containment measures) that would help to assure the future of the industry in Canada. In April 1999 the Canadian government rejected these recommendations. Nonetheless, the NHL continued to press its case, stressing the economic losses that Canada would incur if more franchises were to follow the Québec Nordiques and the Winnipeg Jets on the road south. By late 1999, it was being widely reported that the government was reconsidering its position, and in January 2000 the Minister of Industry, John Manley, did announce an aid package for professional sport, again subject to the participation of other stakeholders. Only three days later, however, after an unprecedented firestorm of public criticism, this offer was withdrawn.

This chapter briefly reviews these events, examines several changes in the continental economy of professional sport that have placed the future of

Canadian franchises in jeopardy, and considers the public policy issues that surround the question of government aid to professional sport. The first two sections outline the lobbying that shaped both the Mills Report and the Manley proposals, and summarise the arguments made by the industry and its supporters about the economic impact of professional sports: the business activity and jobs that are allegedly generated, and the taxes thereby generated for different levels of government. The next sections examine the economics of professional sport at the beginning of the twenty-first century, when the size and make-up of television audiences have become crucial, and publicly funded facilities have become the norm in the United States. These factors, together with the changing nature of inter-urban competition, have produced the now familiar phenomenon in which sports teams threaten to move and local governments compete for their business with increasingly generous financial inducements.[5] That this has become acceptable public policy in the US attests to the success of the sports industry in persuading many local politicians, as well as significant constituencies in US popular opinion, that, despite large subsidies, major-league sports teams do make significant net contributions to civic and regional economies.

It will be argued, however, that this is a misconception, and that the commissioned studies regularly trotted out by the industry and by local boosters are not corroborated by disinterested academic research. On the contrary, we argue, the consensus of independent research indicates that, although professional sports may redistribute spending patterns and business activity within a regional economy, there is rarely any *net* growth that can be discerned. In addition, although supporters claim that the presence of major-league sports plays a significant role in civic tourist industries, research suggests that the contributions of sport to urban tourism are difficult to quantify and are probably overstated. Thus, when the costs of public subsidies are factored in, as well as the 'opportunity costs' of spending public funds in this particular way, there are sound reasons to dismiss the economic rationale for public assistance to such sports.

Nevertheless, we also recognise that, even when the economic case for subsidy is judged to be weak, ice hockey subsidies, in particular, became a political issue in Canada because there remains an important constituency in the country for whom hockey – and indeed NHL hockey – is a defining feature of Canadian life. There are a great many Canadians who would experience the departure of more of their teams for greener US markets as an important national loss, and it was at least partly a political calculation that this was a sizeable constituency that produced Manley's subsidy proposals. However, there are also many people and interests who lose out when public money is allocated to professional sports rather than to other potential purposes (whether public services, tax cuts or debt reduction), raising issues of distributive justice and of political priorities that are too often obscured by the rhetoric of 'community' that surrounds professional sports. Finally, Canada changed, both demographically and in other important ways, during the latter part of the twentieth century, and we conclude that the public reaction to Manley demonstrates that NHL hockey no longer 'brings Canadians together' as it did in the post-war decades.

The Mills Report

Even though the Mills Report's agenda always had a lot to do with saving Canada's NHL teams, the sub-committee nonetheless invited input on a broad range of other issues and heard from a wide variety of stakeholders. The latter included, in addition to spokespersons for major professional sports already noted, representatives of the Canadian (Junior) Hockey League, the Canadian Football League and the Canadian Lacrosse Association. The sub-committee also heard from government organisations with responsibilities in amateur sport (Sport Canada, Sports-Québec), from NSOs (national sports organisations in the Olympic sports) and from umbrella groups representing minor sports, women in sport and the physical education profession. Finally, it heard from representatives of the media and sporting goods industries in Canada, and from Canadian economists and lawyers who have expertise on sports-related issues. Its report, *Sport in Canada: Everybody's Business*, tabled in late 1998, sought to respond at some level to this very broad range of interests and concerns. Its recommendations were couched as proposals for how sport in Canada – Olympic and community-level sport, as well as professional sport – might be assisted through public infrastructure provision and/or tax incentives and credits.

It must be noted that there was no attempt at critical analysis in the report, either of the specific claims made by professional (and Olympic) sports organisations, or of the larger and more general claim that sport is a 'public good' and thus deserving of public support. The enthusiastic claims of stakeholders about the social and economic benefits of sport at all levels were repeated as truisms, and used as justifications for recommending more funds and novel modes of funding. If all these recommendations had been implemented, there would have been something for almost every Canadian with any interest in sport. For those in the Olympic sports, there was a proposal for a 'high-performance sport tax credit' to assist athletes in meeting the expenses associated with the pursuit of sporting excellence; corporate sponsorship, meanwhile, would be encouraged by opportunities for a 150 per cent tax deduction. To assist grassroots sports, federal funding was proposed for community-level facilities, as were annual tax deductions for costs associated with 'taking coaching, officiating or first aid courses connected to amateur sport', as well as a 'child sport tax credit'.[6] Calculated on a progressive basis, the latter was intended to defray the now substantial costs of minor sports registration and children's sporting equipment. Finally, there were 'feel-good' recommendations that affirmed the importance of school and university sport, and of existing programmes to promote opportunities for women and for Canadians with disabilities, although no additional funds were proposed for these programmes.

The most contentious recommendations, however, were the proposals for a 'Canadian professional sport stabilisation programme' that offered tax assistance to Canadian sports franchises, even though federal assistance was conditional upon contributions being agreed by the leagues, players' associations and other levels of government. Among the measures proposed to assist Canadian franchises were changes to the Income Tax Act designed to allow private-sector owners of facilities such as the Corel Centre (in Ottawa) or the Air Canada Centre (Toronto) to accelerate their claims to capital cost allowances, or alternatively allow them tax credits of up to C\$5 million per year, based upon their revenues from sports operations.[7] Moreover, to assist in the sale of corporate seating, an essential 'revenue stream' in professional sports, it was also proposed to allow small businesses to deduct the full costs (rather than the current 50 per cent) of sports tickets or luxury boxes as business entertainment expenses. Finally, it was urged that the Canadian government negotiate with the US to harmonise taxes for professional athletes, with the aim of reducing the taxes paid by athletes on Canadian-based teams.[8] None of these measures was costed, even roughly.

Predictably, it was these proposals to 'stabilise' Canadian professional sport that attracted immediate criticism, both inside and outside the House of Commons. Each opposition party in the House attached qualifying or dissenting opinions to the sub-committee's final report. The Reform Party expressed reservations about industry-specific tax credits and subsidies whose likely costs (and likely success in achieving their stated objectives) remained matters of conjecture. The Progressive Conservative and New Democratic Parties gave broad support to those recommendations that promised assistance to parents, coaches, members of disadvantaged groups, and to amateur sport more generally. However, both parties explicitly opposed tax breaks for professional sport. The response of the Bloc Québecois offered the most detailed critique, opposing tax breaks for professional sports on both financial *and* social justice grounds, and noting that most states in western Europe do not offer any form of public subsidy to such sports. Within the government, moreover, there was also significant opposition. The Minister of Finance was concerned about the tax changes proposed, especially those that gave the sport industry special treatment: how could he justify revenue-based tax credits for professional sports operators, for example, or the acceleration of capital cost allowances, without also extending these opportunities to other, often equally beleaguered, industries? Other Liberals simply worried about the political optics, as well as the justice, of subsidising millionaire athletes while more pressing social needs were visibly going unmet.

Outside the Commons, arts advocates queried the logic of allowing full deductibility of business entertainment expenses for professional sports but not extending it to the arts. Others challenged the proposed 'child sport tax credit' as a regressive device that was likely to offer few benefits to poorer families.[9] Even in the sports media, although there was much predictable cheerleading, thoughtful observers of the economics of professional sport – such as Stephen Brunt and David Shoalts (*Globe & Mail*) or Jean Dion (*Le Devoir*) – argued that, even *with* public assistance, there was a good chance that teams in the smaller Canadian markets could not survive.

From many angles, then, it became clear that the Mills recommendations would be a hard political sell, and the government began to distance itself from a report that had not acknowledged, let alone tried seriously to answer, the difficult financial and political questions. In April 1999 came the official response that the Mills Report's tax recommendations 'have been considered, and no further action will be taken'. The Heritage Minister, Sheila Copps, explained: 'The government respects the objectives of the sub-committee in making these recommendations for improving sport in Canada. However, as stated by the government in the 1999 budget, tax reductions must benefit those who need them most – low- and middle-income Canadians.'[10]

The Manley Proposals

Nonetheless, within months discussions had resumed between representatives of the NHL and the Canadian government. In fact, perhaps anticipating that the Mills Report would carry little weight, the NHL had never stopped trying to press upon the government its case that its 'needs' were both unique and urgent (it is likely that NHL people felt that their case had suffered in the Mills process by being linked with claims made on behalf of other sports). Thus, in the spring of 1999 Rod Bryden, the owner of the Ottawa Senators, started to warn publicly that, in the absence of significant tax relief from federal and provincial governments, he would be 'forced' to sell his team, probably to buyers who would move the franchise to some US location. In this context, a meeting was convened in June 1999 that included representatives of the federal government, the NHL, the six Canadian teams, the four provinces concerned and the NHL Players' Association (NHLPA). Discussion was facilitated by the Public Policy

Forum, an Ottawa-based firm commissioned by the Minister of Industry, John Manley, to facilitate the negotiation of a mutually acceptable solution. It is important to recognise that the NHL was now talking to different people in government – specifically, to the Ministry of Industry, rather than Heritage – and that this represented a shift in strategy. The case for subsidy would henceforth be argued almost exclusively on economic grounds, stressing the economic impact of major-league sports on the cities in which teams were based and on the country. Subsidies or tax breaks could thus be depicted as industrial incentives, and compared with those offered to other industries, notably film and technology, as well as in US jurisdictions. Versions of this argument had been made before and indeed had been made to Mills. However, there was no longer any pretence of talk about ice hockey as Canadian heritage or about the importance of sport for Canadian youth. The argument was now about industrial fairness and the need to 'level the playing field' in relation to US-based competitors.

It was reported that government participants accepted the case that Canadian teams struggle to compete with those based in US cities, partly because of the strength of the US dollar but also because of the more favourable tax treatment that professional sport enjoys at every level of the US tax system. At this meeting no final agreement was reached on how these 'inequities' might be addressed. However, Manley said publicly afterwards that the federal government was now willing to 'be part of the solution' as long as the other stakeholders (the NHL, the NHLPA, and the relevant provinces and municipalities) agreed to contribute too.[11] This was immediately recognised by some parties – notably those in other sports, who were now being left out – as a shift in the federal position. However, as was also widely noted by critics and by Bryden himself, as long as the federal contribution depended upon commitments by all of the other parties, this remained a purely hypothetical solution. The NHL already had a 'Canadian Assistance Program' that offered modest annual support (C\$2–3 million per team) to the teams in the four smallest Canadian markets, contingent upon their meeting stipulated targets for the sale of season tickets, luxury boxes and advertising. However, several provinces were wary, at best, and the mayors of Toronto and Vancouver said bluntly that they could not forego municipal property taxes on professional sports venues. On the industry side, the NHLPA would make no commitments about containing salaries. Nonetheless, it was agreed that further meetings among the stakeholders would take place, with a view to negotiating a package that would address the needs of the Canadian-based teams. Over the summer months the Public Policy Forum continued to facilitate such discussions.

Still, difficult hurdles remained. The first concerned the form that tax assistance from the federal and provincial governments could take, without opening the doors to claimants from other industries. The federal government was acutely aware, from soundings taken after Mills reported, that any attempt to give special treatment to professional sport either on business entertainment deductions or on capital cost allowances would be very difficult to defend, logically or politically. Provinces that had their own entertainment taxes, notably Ontario, likewise found it hard to justify exempting professional sport while continuing to levy the tax on concerts and theatre. One way around this, suggested by the NHL, was that both levels of government pay licence fees based on the considerable revenues that they realise every year from sports-based lotteries, a large proportion of which, in Canada, comes from betting on NHL results. This got round the problem of other claimants for other kinds of tax breaks, even though it represented a departure from the NHL's longstanding policy of distancing itself from any connection with gambling. However, not unlike those many governments that have justified their growing reliance on gambling revenues when other forms of taxation have looked politically difficult, the NHL readily found ways of justifying its 'right' to a share of sports lottery proceeds.[12]

The political challenge was to find an acceptable formula and get all the relevant governments to agree. The federal government was sympathetic, and indeed offered in September 1999 to contribute some of the C$50 million it receives annually from the provinces in return for leaving the gambling business to them in the late 1970s, if the provinces would also give up a portion of their lottery revenues (perhaps as licence fees) to the leagues whose games were used. However, Ontario quickly rejected this, on the grounds that it would mean taking money for professional sports away from amateur sport, and from hospitals and schools. The difficulty highlighted here was that any solution involving lottery money had to win the agreement of all the provinces concerned, and the federal government had very little leverage. On 18 October the Public Policy Forum reported to the Ministry of Industry that, after more than 50 bilateral and multilateral consultations, no solution was in sight. A frustrated Manley was left announcing the appointment of yet another envoy who would continue to meet with the stakeholders in an effort to find a solution. Yet only a month later, in November 1999, it was announced that this process, too, had come to a dead end.

Almost immediately, however, Bryden stepped up the pressure, announcing on 2 December that the Ottawa Senators were up for sale, blaming high taxes and a lack of government support. This was followed less than a week later by the NHL's announcement that a renewal of its own Canadian Assistance Program for a further four years would be contingent upon federal tax relief for the four small-market Canadian teams. This served to put the pressure for action (and the blame, if nothing was done, and the Senators moved) squarely back on the federal government. At this point, indeed, the Senators appeared to have secured an important concession from the Ontario government, which agreed to allow municipalities, if they so chose, to reduce property taxes on sports venues. The region of Ottawa-Carleton had already agreed to do this (indeed it had helped to lobby for the change), promising savings of C$3.9 million per year to the team.[13] It was also reported that Ontario was prepared to permit relief from the provincial amusement tax to sports teams that restructured themselves as non-profit organisations, thus offering the Senators the prospect of a further C$3.5 million. This appeared to constitute some progress on the part of public sector partners, at least towards fulfilling Manley's condition that other stakeholders also contribute to any assistance package. In this context, it was rumoured through December and early January that the Liberal government was about to agree that Canada would, after all, contribute to the survival of the nation's NHL teams; and on 18 January 2000 Manley announced the aid plan that would be withdrawn only three days later, in the face of overwhelming public opposition.

It is important to recall that, despite the enthusiasm of Mills and the sympathy of some ministers for the objective of sustaining Canada's representation in the NHL, the federal government was always wary of opposition to what could readily be construed as subsidies to wealthy owners and players. Thus, the package that Manley announced had carefully capped the proposed federal contribution at a maximum of C$3 million annually per team until the year 2004. The precise amounts for each team, moreover, were to be tied to the contributions agreed by the respective provinces and municipalities, as well as those forthcoming through the NHL Assistance Program, with the federal contribution further limited to 25 per cent of the total aid made available to each team. This was intended to put some pressure on the teams to continue their efforts to maximise the contributions they got from other stakeholders, while also opening up the prospect that packages could be negotiated for some teams (likely to be Ottawa and the two Alberta teams) even in the event that other governments (British Columbia, Québec and Toronto) ultimately refused to participate. Equally importantly, Manley's proposal was intended to share the political responsibility for turning public opinion around, or, in the worst case, for taking the flak, with those provinces and municipalities that the federal government believed had also agreed, in principle, to provide aid. In the event, of course, it appears that many politicians, at every level, had seriously misjudged public opinion on this issue. However, it was the federal government that was left exposed. It is clear that Manley believed that Ontario and Alberta had agreed to the principle of assistance; yet as public protest mounted, both Ontario's Premier, Mike Harris, and Alberta's Treasurer, Stockwell Day (who later in the year became the national leader of the new right-wing federal party, the Canadian Alliance) quickly came out against the plan. Thus Manley was left to announce, only three days later, 'It is now clear that the very stakeholders who implied they might be receptive to negotiating are not prepared to do so.'[14] More than a year's political effort by the industry and some ministers in the federal government to find a 'shared solution' appeared dead.

The Business of Professional Sport in North America

It is worth remembering that the events described here represent only the latest phase in an ongoing struggle to attract, and then keep, National Hockey League teams in Canada. Canadian fans recall very clearly the relocations in 1995 and 1996 of the Québec Nordiques and the Winnipeg Jets, each after prolonged campaigns by their Canadian owners and sectors of the local business communities to get new arenas built at public expense. In Winnipeg the Jets' departure had been delayed for several years by an agreement between the owners, the city and the province whereby the public-sector partners had covered the team's operating losses while the funding prospects for a new arena were explored.[15] Over the same time period, too, Edmonton Oilers' owner Peter Pocklington had extracted arena renovations, rent concessions and rights to ancillary revenues from the publicly-owned Northlands Coliseum (ultimately at the expense of the city of Edmonton) by threats that without such assistance he would move the team to a succession of rumoured locations (including Hamilton, Minneapolis and Houston). In the end, the Oilers' owner was contractually bound to sell the team to a local consortium. However, it is fair to say that the continued existence of NHL franchises in Edmonton and Calgary owes itself to federal infrastructure grants in the mid-1990s that funded arena renovations that included luxury seating, and to management contracts with the respective cities that give the teams virtually all of the revenues (and none of the costs) generated by these publicly-funded buildings. The public sector, in other words, is already a big part of the 'solution' in these cities.

At this juncture several comments are warranted on the nature of the 'major' leagues, and the construction of 'major league' sport as a business. First, the major leagues in all North American professional sports have long operated as cartels, whose approach to 'the good of the game' has always had less to do with national or civic traditions than with the promotion of their collective business. It should further be recognised that professional sport in North America has been a continental business since the 1920s and that Canadian interests in ice hockey have repeatedly been subordinated to the growth opportunities available in larger US markets. Indeed, the establishment of the NHL's monopoly over 'major league' hockey was achieved in 1926, when the Western Hockey League (with teams in western Canada and on the Pacific coast) folded, and the Patrick brothers sold their player contracts and their expertise as hockey businessmen to new NHL teams based in much larger US cities.[16] Later, in the era of post-war expansions, it is important to recognise that 'franchising' in professional sports involved the same dynamic of corporate expansion as in other businesses: namely, selling the rights to offer a national product and brand-name (e.g. NHL hockey, or NBA basketball) in a new market area. Indeed expansion in 'major league' sports coincided in the 1960s with a dramatic growth in franchising as a business strategy and with increasing market domination by national brands. What is unique about sports is that the franchisers, as national monopolies in their respective sports, have been able to limit access to a widely desired resource: major-league sports. It is this monopoly position that has enabled US owners to extract generous public subsidies (including state-of-the art venues built at public expense) from many cities competing for the few available places.[17]

It is significant that the Mills Committee heard from Appleton & Assoc., a law firm with some experience in NAFTA (North American Free Trade Association) disputes, that there could be some prospect of a successful NAFTA challenge against these subsidies.[18] Certainly, American municipal and county governments now assist the professional sports industry with tax breaks and free facilities. This was not always the norm; indeed the Pittsburgh Civic Centre remains an example of a facility where the team has been charged something like a market rent, with the result that the Penguins were in bankruptcy courts through much of 1999. Thus the struggle to survive in a small market is not a problem confined to Canada. However, team owners have found many US counties and cities willing to provide them with new facilities at public expense, as well as management contracts that enable them to generate lucrative revenues from advertising and catering and from marketing the facility for other events – all with little or no return to the public purse in the form of rents or taxes. Additional forms of public subsidy have included development opportunities on adjacent lands (in Tampa and Denver), and even substantial cash grants (in Nashville). Indeed the major leagues actively encourage such deals because, over the last 20 years, innovative forms of subsidy that initially benefited one owner have become bargaining chips in other negotiations, and ultimately industry standards.[19] It is precisely for this reason, it can be suggested, that Canadian sports owners have *not* urged the Canadian government (as have other Canadian industries) to pursue a NAFTA challenge, and may well have come under pressure from their US partners not to. For the 'level playing field' that Canadian owners and the major leagues seek is not one where the public subsidies that are now common in the US are deemed illegal – an outcome that would appal US owners, the major leagues, and indeed players' associations. It is, rather, one where Canadian owners are granted access to similar kinds and levels of subsidy. Only this outcome, the one sought from both Mills and Manley, is consistent with sustaining the publicly-subsidised profitability currently enjoyed by the successful US franchises and (it should also be noted) the current salary levels of major league players.

It may be necessary to ask, in these circumstances, whether Canadian provincial cities can afford to be in the major leagues any longer.[20] The most obvious issue here is whether player costs can be contained through some sort of salary cap. Average NHL salaries tripled between 1989 and 1994, from US$180,000 to just over US$500,000, and they have more than doubled again since then.[21] This means that whereas teams based in Edmonton and Calgary could win the Stanley Cup in the late 1980s with total player budgets of less than US$4 million, in 2000 they spent in excess of US$20 million and still struggled to make the playoffs. Teams in the US metropolitan markets (and Toronto) have payrolls that are more than double this figure, and teams that cannot compete with these salaries regularly lose players in the free-agent market. The effects of this are registered in Canadian teams' loss of many players, from Wayne Gretzky to journeyman defenders, and in a gradual decline in the success of most Canadian-based teams through the 1990s. Canadian owners have sought to depict the problem, as we have seen, as a product of high 'public costs' (taxes, rents etc.), and to claim that the solution lies in 'levelling the playing field' in this respect with their American counterparts. However, as Brunt and others have pointed out, unless the league and the players agree to contain the growth in salaries that has characterised the past ten years, reducing public costs can only temporarily delay the time when franchises based in the smaller Canadian cities can no longer afford to be competitive.

The other side of this equation, of course, concerns revenues: in particular, whether teams based in smaller Canadian markets like Edmonton or Calgary can ever generate from ice hockey the levels of revenue (now in the order of US$30–40 million) required to compete with 'large market' franchises in the US and Toronto. The designations of 'large' and 'small' markets have become so widely (and loosely) used in the whole debate about sports subsidies that it bears remarking that they now refer, effectively, to the total money-making potential of a franchise based in a particular market area. While this once equated primarily with the numbers of ordinary fans in a city who were committed enough to regularly buy tickets (i.e. on 'live gates'), it now depends much more on other 'revenue streams' – from television, advertising and corporate seating – and on the size of a metropolitan drawing area. Originally, sports market rankings were derived from rankings developed for the US television industry of the potential value of the audiences that advertisers could reach in different local/regional markets. For these purposes the Dallas or Boston markets, for example, included not just those cities themselves but the much larger regional populations (in Texas or New England) that regularly watch TV stations based there. Potential viewers, of course, need to be translated into actual audiences; and the NHL's US television ratings in the 1960s were very disappointing. However, in the 1980s, when sports television was booming (both on the networks and in the new format of speciality channels), industry optimism held that effective marketing could 'sell' new sports in places where they had no historical roots. Thus, the television audiences of Florida and the San Francisco Bay area represented enormous untapped potential, for both the hockey and television industries. If even small proportions of these audiences could be induced to take some interest in ice hockey, they were worth more to national (US) advertisers and, in turn, to media outlets and to teams, than the entire Canadian west.

The size of a team's regional television market has now assumed even greater importance with the growth of specialty channels and regional cable networks, and this is especially true in ice hockey, which gets far less money from US national network contracts than do any of the other 'major league' sports. While the NFL and (to a lesser extent) the NBA divide enormous revenues from the national broadcast networks equally among member teams, thereby allowing teams in places like Green Bay, Indianapolis and Portland to thrive, in hockey and baseball the network revenues are far smaller, with the result that teams rely heavily on the revenues they get from local media. This affords enormous competitive advantages to teams in major metropolitan markets (e.g. New York, Los Angeles, Boston, Toronto) as well as to teams (like the Atlanta Braves and the Mighty Ducks of Anaheim) that are owned by global media entertainment conglomerates. In both situations the advertising revenues generated by cable television and other media platforms, and the revenues that flow through to the teams, reflect the size and spending power of the audiences they reach. In addition, regular television exposure adds to the income that these teams can realise from rink-board and ice surface advertising and from the marketing of star players. This is why assets like Wayne Gretzky and Eric Lindros – and sports television 'properties' like major-league sports franchises – have been able to generate more income in large American markets than in smaller Canadian ones. Professional sports are now part of 'circuits of promotion' that can be exploited more fully and lucratively in large markets.[22]

The other important factor in the 'small market' equation has to do with the size and nature of the local corporate sector. One of the most important revenue sources in the new economy of professional sports follows from the growth in corporate seating: the luxury boxes and 'club' seats that have become a ubiquitous feature of arenas and stadiums (like the SkyDome) built in the past 15 years. Corporate seating brings in much more revenue than the cheaper seating it replaces, which explains why older facilities have been replaced throughout professional sports, and why the Calgary Flames demanded that what was a showcase Olympic facility in 1988 be renovated at public expense, less than ten years later, to include luxury boxes. However, this changes the nature of the audience, and it means that the amount and kind of wealth in a city have become more important than the number of loyal hockey fans. The willingness of the local corporate sector to invest in this form of public relations is now a necessary condition of survival in the NHL. This is why team owners in Ottawa, Calgary and Edmonton have all been heard in recent years urging the business communities in their respective cities to increase their purchases of boxes and club seats,[23] and why the teams in Calgary and Ottawa, with their burgeoning corporate sectors, may yet stand a better chance of survival than those in Edmonton, Winnipeg or Québec. Nevertheless, the size and nature of the corporate sector in such cities as Chicago and Dallas will always mean that more boxes can be sold, and at higher prices, than is likely to be the case in any Canadian cities other than Toronto.

Amid all the debate about whether Canadian governments, federal and/or provincial *should* subsidise professional sport, this discussion serves to remind us that they already do so in a significant way, through the tax deductions available to corporations for half the costs of seats and luxury boxes. Consider this analysis offered by Ken Dryden in 1994, before he became president of the Toronto Maple Leafs:

> Revenue Canada and the IRS say that, appearances to the contrary, when a corporate employee is sitting in a corporate seat looking like a fan he is really there only to be with clients, to talk business, to make more money. The money his company spends for this opportunity is … [like other business expenses] a cost of its business which then gets subtracted from … the profits on which the company pays taxes.

The result is that

> for every dollar paid for these expenses, 50 cents doesn't get paid into taxes, which means 50 cents less available for what taxes can buy: more government services, lower deficits, etc. … It also means that for every dollar spent on football tickets, the company pays 50 cents and the taxpayers, *us,* who would like nothing more than to sit in those seats but can't afford them, pay the other 50 cents. Pretty nice of us.[24]

Although tax deductibility has since been reduced by half, with the result that corporations pay more and the taxpayer now subsidises only 25 per cent of these costs, the principle remains the same.

Two issues follow from this. First, it is clear that one effect of replacing cheaper seats with seats intended for corporate entertaining has been to move ticket prices increasingly beyond the reach of individual fans who pay with their own (after-tax) money. This may offer some insight into why fewer Canadians apparently cared about saving 'their' teams than might once have been the case. Second, as long as this form of corporate entertaining remains even partially tax-deductible, the Canadian public is contributing to the very explosion in salaries and franchise values that threatens the survival of its small-market teams. The annual amount of the subsidy to professional hockey that occurs through lost federal taxes has been estimated at roughly C\$20 million a year, and that amount can be increased by at least another C\$10 million to take into account lost provincial taxes.[25] Yet although this total may not seem a large price to pay to save a popular national institution, it might be suggested that without tax deductibility, subscriptions to luxury boxes would likely collapse, and the whole inflated economy of major-league sports (including franchise values as well as salaries) might be in jeopardy. Indeed, before he became president of the Maple Leafs, Dryden himself suggested: "Make the corporate fan pay like the real fan, for seats and the corporate boxes ... and many won't pay. Then watch what happens ... it is the false market Revenue Canada and the IRS have created that has been the underpinning of [sport's] growth.'[26] Today, of course, Dryden has other interests to defend. However, the analysis he put forward in 1994 of the role of tax-deductibility in professional sports' salary explosion remains hard to fault, so that Mills' proposal that sports entertainment expenses be again 100 per cent deductible should be seen as a retrogressive step, whose primary beneficiaries would be wealthy owners and players.

The other important subsidy to professional sports in Canada, of course, comes in the form of sports venues that have been built at significant public expense. The most expensive and well-known of these are the SkyDome in Toronto and the Olympic Stadium in Montreal, both facilities that have resulted in enormous costs to the public purse in their respective provinces.[27] However, we cannot forget the Saddledome in Calgary or the Skyreach Center (and Commonwealth Stadium) in Edmonton, each facilities that, like the Olympic Stadium in Montreal, were funded out of allocations for international games but were always intended to serve afterwards as venues for professional sports.[28] Although the Oilers and the Flames originally contracted to pay market rents for the use of these civic facilities, their financial difficulties in the 1990s (and, in the case of the Oilers, the threats to leave described above) produced renegotiations, the outcome of which is that both teams now conduct their business virtually rent-free, amounting to a continuing municipal subsidy. Both facilities were also renovated in the mid-1990s with allocations from the federal infrastructure programme, another considerable public investment.

Subsidies – or Investments in Urban Prosperity?

In what follows we critically examine the major arguments that professional sports teams are appropriate candidates for public subsidies. In this section we look at the economic arguments that sports teams contribute in significant ways to the economies of cities and regions. This economic rationale for subsidy was, as noted above, central to the NHL's campaign to win support from the Canadian Ministry of Industry. The league urged upon the government the view that ice hockey was an important industry in Canada, and it argued that the Canadian government should invest in keeping the industry, and the jobs associated with it, in Canada, just as it invests in other 'growth' industries. This will lead into consideration of the 'world class' cities arguments, in which professional sports are important not only for their own economic contributions (which, as we shall see, are comparatively small), but also for what their presence adds to efforts to attract tourism and other kinds of 'new economy' business to a city. Here the prestige and visibility associated with being in the major leagues are seen by civic boosters as important in efforts to promote their cities as 'world class' destinations, for tourism and other kinds of urban economic development.[29]

We noted above that central to the NHL's submission to the Mills Committee were figures that purported to depict the economic impact of NHL hockey in Canada (C$437.6 million, annually). We also observed that the figures provided by the NHL were simply reported by Mills without critical analysis, as were similar calculations provided by the Toronto Blue Jays, the Montreal Expos and the Vancouver Grizzlies. The original sources of the figures, in each case, were economic-impact studies prepared by consulting firms under contract to the teams. Typically, these studies (and similar studies conducted in earlier years on behalf of the Jets, the Nordiques and the Blue Jays) tally team revenues (from gate receipts, concessions, advertising, media etc.) and team expenditures (on salaries and wages, transportation, supplies and maintenance), and multiply this total by a multiplier intended to capture the effects of its re-circulation in the local economy. However, a recent volume published by the Brookings Institution concludes that these consultants' studies are systematically biased by their clients' interests in demonstrating that sports teams have positive and substantial economic impacts, and that they are laden with methodological difficulties:

> First, they often confuse new spending with spending that is diverted from other local activities. Second, they attribute all spending by out-of-town visitors to the sports team, regardless of the motive for the visit. Third, they overstate the multiple by ignoring crucial characteristics of sports spending. Fourth, they apply this multiplier to gross spending, rather than local value added. Fifth, they omit the

negative affects from the taxation that is used to finance construction and operating deficits of sports facilities.[30]

Independent or academic analysis, the editors proceed to suggest, reaches conclusions about economic impact and job creation that are very different from those found in studies commissioned by the industry.

Mills attempts to minimise the force of this argument by suggesting that care should be taken in extrapolating to Canada the results of American studies.[31] However, we want to argue that the commissioned studies produced by Canadian sports teams or by civic boosters and development authorities in support of claims for the economic impact of professional sports are every bit as optimistic and as methodologically flawed as those reviewed by the authors in the Brookings volume. One recent example is a November 1999 report by the Ottawa Economic Development Corporation on 'The Economic Impact of the Ottawa Senators Hockey Team'. This document states that the team would contribute, nationally, from C$1.2 to C$1.4 billion in economic activity, including C$420 to C$460 million in taxes, over a ten-year period. Locally, the tax contributions of the team were estimated at between C$117 and C$120 million over the same period. If the team were to leave Ottawa, the report warned, between C$400 and C$500 million in regional economic activity would be lost. Finally, the report trumpeted the contribution of the team to Ottawa's 'brand recognition', using indices like the number of mentions of the team in web pages (11,000) and in US newspapers (4,000), to support a claim that the Senators brought attention to the city that equated to C$66 million per game in advertising value. Such figures are indeed impressive, but they are unsubstantiated and, indeed, unsubstantiable, leading University of British Columbia Commerce Professor Paul Kedrosky to observe that 'the report's numbers are ephemeral, unsupportable and up there with string theory in their unfalsifiable airiness'.[32]

We agree broadly that the claims characteristic of these studies are unsupportable. Yet we would further propose that if professional sport *has* major impacts in local and regional economies, one should find these reflected in the standard measures of urban economic activity: property prices, employment growth, business start-ups and failures and consumer spending (and the sales taxes collected on this). The overwhelming consensus of academic opinion, however, in the studies reported in the Brookings volume and elsewhere, is that the long-term economic effects of major-league sports franchises are statistically insignificant. As an industry, professional sport is actually much smaller than its cultural visibility (and its own publicity) would suggest, making up a statistically tiny part of any metropolitan economy. 'In Jacksonville, for example, the gross revenues of its NFL team account for 0.4 per cent of metropolitan area effective buying income (EBI), or total disposable income; in St. Louis the figure is 0.2 per cent of EBI; and in New York 0.02 per cent.'[33] Thus a sports team is less important in the urban economy, the authors observe, than many much lower-profile enterprises, in both the private and public sectors. A major university, for example, would take in more revenues (in grants and tuition), employ more staff, spend more on supplies and services, and generate more local economic activity than any professional sports franchise.[34] Likewise, in the private sector, the semiconductor and software industries created many more value-added jobs and much more business activity in the Ottawa region than the Senators will ever create. Moreover, the majority of the output of such companies is sold abroad, thereby bringing new money into the greater Ottawa region (and into Canada) rather than simply recirculating money already there.[35] Similarly, in Vancouver and Calgary, expansions in the communications and biotech industries mean much more to the growth and future of these regional economies than do their professional sports franchises. There are examples, thus, on both sides of the border, that support the conclusion that industry-funded studies have systematically overstated the impact of what is a comparatively small industry.

Two of the current authors have addressed some of the methodological flaws in these studies, at the Mills hearings and elsewhere.[36] We discuss the error of treating the gross revenues reported by sports teams as an injection of new money into the local economy, or conversely as a loss of business from the local economy if a team departs. Indeed it is demonstrable that when teams do leave (e.g. the Nordiques and the Jets), most of the money that local people once spent on hockey generally remains in the local economy, directly benefiting other local leisure and entertainment businesses (skiing and other sports, restaurants, theatre and music) and with at least as many indirect beneficiaries. We further argue that team-commissioned studies routinely fail to consider the 'leakage' that occurs when income that has been earned locally and spent by local residents on professional sport leaves the community in the form of players' incomes. The issue here is that team expenditures on player salaries are treated in these studies (just like wages paid to arena staff) as money that is normally re-spent locally. However, unlike waged employees, most professional athletes today do not reside in the communities where they play; thus the (abnormally high) salaries they make are not re-circulated in the local economy in the ways that the standard economic model assumes. This was even more the case in small cities like Winnipeg and (especially) Québec, cities where players not from these communities very rarely made their homes. Indeed, professional sport may actually have constituted some drain on the economies of these cities, in the form of both public and private spending turned into player salaries that were subsequently repatriated and invested elsewhere. At the very least, there is no evidence that the departure of NHL franchises from Winnipeg and Québec has led to economic downturns in either city, in terms of any of the normal measures of economic health identified above.

It is also necessary, we would submit, to take into account the 'opportunity costs' that follow from spending public money on professional sport for the purposes of job creation. Although professional sport undoubtedly provides some employment, commissioned studies overstated the job losses that would follow the departure of the Nordiques and the Jets. Moreover, there is evidence that, outside perhaps 30 or 40 playing and managerial jobs, most of the jobs associated with professional sport are part-time and seasonal service jobs, while the costs associated with creating these jobs (i.e. the public money invested in keeping the team in the city) are relatively high.[37] This is not to imply that governments should not invest in job creation in the service sector. However, if job creation is to be the primary rationale for public expenditures, governments can realise greater returns on these investments by offering incentives to other kinds of businesses – businesses where substantial internal growth can be expected, where most workers will be employed in skilled and well-paying jobs and whose presence might attract other private investment into the region – precisely the kinds of businesses, it might be observed, that Industry Canada's Technology Partnership Program is designed to assist.

Sports advocates and some politicians try to argue that even though the predicted economic disasters did not materialise in Winnipeg and Québec, these cities have still suffered in intangible ways from the loss of major-league entertainment that 'put them on the map'. This brings us to the second rationale for sports subsidies prefigured above, in which professional sports franchises are believed to contribute to the local economy by making the city a more attractive destination for leisure and consumption – for tourists and residents alike. Here Noll and Zimbalist suggest that there is a plausible case that professional sports do contribute what they call 'consumption benefits', defined as amenities that residents enjoy as consumers, even though they may cost them money as taxpayers. Some literature proposes that 'world class' consumer amenities can yield significant economic benefits if they attract visitors to a city. However, even though out-of-town fans undoubtedly attend major-league games, Noll and Zimbalist argue that today professional sport is much less likely to be the primary reason for a tourist visit than was the case 40 years ago, when many fewer cities had major-league teams. Today the 'tourists' who appear in team statistics are more likely to have come to a city for other reasons (business, family or conventions) and to have taken in a game while there. Another kind of visitor is the rural fan who may drive into Edmonton or Winnipeg for sports events from nearby farm communities; in Winnipeg, such fans were thought to constitute about seven per cent of the Jets' attendance. However, this 'rubber tire trade' typically returns home after the game without spending much money outside the venue itself. Thus, as in the case of family visitors, it is misleading to represent them as tourists in calculations of economic impact. Yet too many studies of the impact of pro sports have credited *all* non-resident fans with the spending patterns of the 'average' tourist (i.e. on hotels, meals and other attractions), and have depicted all this hypothetical spending as money that sports bring into the city. When this figure is compounded again, as it often is, by a 'regional tourism multiplier', the result is to exaggerate the very modest contribution that sports do make to a civic economy.[38]

There are, in any event, good reasons to question the investments that many US and Canadian cities have made in recent years in growth strategies emphasising tourism. In many American cities, attracting tourism has been a prominent theme in the rationales for new sports stadia and arenas as well as other kinds of cultural and consumer venues designed to draw both holiday visitors and conventioneers. In Canada, too, part of the discourse justifying bids for hallmark events (Olympic and Commonwealth Games, World's Fairs) has stressed putting cities on show to the world, in order to develop urban tourism industries. There is now much research that questions the returns on these kinds of investment, but we will limit ourselves here to a recent evaluation by economist Marc Levine of several decades of strategic efforts by Montreal and Baltimore to construct themselves as tourist destinations.[39] The deficits and debt load incurred in conjunction with the Olympics and the Olympic Stadium are well known, but Levine also notes that the Palais des Congrès and Montreal's 'scientific attractions' have required substantial public subsidies, as of course have the Expos.[40] Moreover, despite numerous consultants' studies that claim large *retombées économiques* (economic fallouts) from the tourism associated with these attractions, Levine observes that *even if one ignores their methodological flaws* (and he identifies flaws very similar to those found in the sports-related studies cited above), the 'figures suggest surprisingly modest "retombées" so far … in light of the enormous public subsidy involved'.[41]

The urban tourism market is a highly competitive one in which, as Levine and others have noted, each innovative stadium or harbour development or theme park is quickly imitated elsewhere, so that initial increases in tourist visits are rarely if ever sustained. Moreover, the quality of tourism-related jobs is low, and Levine cites statistics that show incomes in tourist occupations in Montreal actually declining between 1990 and 1995. Indeed, tourism has not grown significantly since 1980 as a proportion of the Montreal economy, and it remains a relatively small component of that city's economy. Levine's conclusion is that in both Baltimore and Montreal tourist attractions have been created and sustained at enormous public expense. However, even though he considers both cities 'winners', relatively speaking, in the competitive North American tourist market, 'In neither city … has world-class tourism been the engine of prosperity its advocates would propose'.[42]

Yet even when tourism revenues prove disappointing, advocates of a leisure-and-consumption growth strategy often argue that the same kinds of lifestyle and entertainment attractions can help to attract 'new economy' business to a city. The availability of 'world class' entertainment, this argument runs, is among the factors that influence corporate decisions about where to locate management and technical staff. The suggestion is that executive and professional people want access to major-league sports, as well as to the other attractions that often come to major-league venues. Thus the presence of a major-league franchise can help 'sell' a city to companies that could bring hundreds, even thousands, of value-added jobs. Noll and Zimbalist remark, though, that what research there is on corporate location decisions indicates that other factors – costs, the quality of the local labour force and the availability of quality education and health care – are all more likely to influence such decisions than is the availability of professional sport. They propose, moreover, that the relevant question here is not whether professional sports make a city attractive to corporate decision-makers. It is whether, if attracting high-tech businesses is the ultimate goal, subsidising professional sport is a *better* way of achieving this than building research parks, offering tax incentives to *these* kinds of businesses, upgrading computers in local schools, or providing better funding to engineering and science faculties.[43] Certainly it appears to have been the skills available in the local labour force (and behind this, the quality of Ontario engineering and computer science schools), much more than the presence of NHL hockey, that have attracted Cisco Systems and other global technology firms to the Ottawa region's 'Silicon Valley North'.[44]

Concluding Remarks

If the economic arguments for subsidising professional sport are thus deemed to be weak, as is the consensus of academic opinion, and the role of sport in attracting tourism and new business to a city is judged 'unproven' at best, we are then returned to the somewhat older question of whether Canada should subsidise major league sports – NHL hockey, in particular – because of the league's established place in Canadian popular culture. Certainly, hockey remains popular in Canada, and many Canadians take pride in their historical prowess in the game. There is thus an argument that subsidies that kept Canadian representation in the NHL at its current levels would yield 'consumption benefits' (following Noll and Zimbalist above) that many Canadians would value strongly, albeit in ways that would be difficult to quantify. However, it must also be noted that outside Toronto, there are now empty seats, often thousands of them, to be found in every NHL rink in Canada, even in Montreal. This may be attributable to weaker teams, as well as to ticket prices that have risen beyond what many fans can afford. Yet if hockey is to be supported for its 'consumption benefits' out of public funds, it would then seem imperative to make these benefits accessible to the many hockey fans who will never be occupants of corporate boxes.[45] It would also appear imperative, given the history of cost escalation in the NHL, to find some way of quantifying how *much* Canadians are willing to pay from their taxes to keep teams in Canada, so that the commitment is not open-ended.

This raises the further question of the circumstances in which professional sports teams can be deemed 'public goods', where these are defined as institutions that provide benefits (or positive externalities, in the jargon of economists) to the entire community, whether or not an individual chooses to pay for them. If the presence of sports teams confers a benefit upon all citizens, whether or not they attend games, it may be legitimate for local governments to subsidise their operations out of tax revenues. However, if the benefits of professional sports accrue primarily to the paying customers, or to those who make money by doing business with the team, then public funding amounts to an ongoing and generous subsidy to the industry and to that relatively small (and already privileged) subsection of the community who can afford to attend. Among several different categories of public goods, Burton goes on to define as 'merit goods' a variety of elective goods and services that are taken advantage of by individuals and are of interest only to some individuals, but which communities decide to subsidise because their presence makes that community 'a better place'. Societies must always make difficult choices among many candidates for such subsidies (extracurricular activities in schools? community recreation facilities? 'world class' spectator facilities for the performance arts and sports?), and arguments based on principle are always heard from advocates for different kinds of 'merit goods'. However, as Burton observes, the ultimate test is what public opinion will support.[46]

Historically, professional sports teams have occupied a unique position in popular culture, as commercial businesses but also communal institutions which many fans used to feel belonged to them. Even in America, where commercial logic began to reshape professional sports long before it did in Europe, the practice whereby popular local institutions could be moved to other cities simply for business advantages became commonplace only in the 1980s. Yet although fans in the cities left behind have regularly called for public subsidies that would keep 'their' teams in town, and for a time it was hard to find politicians who would stand firm against what they believed to be popular support for professional sports, it has become more common in the 1990s to find that, when sports subsidies have been put to public votes (in referenda, for example, or as taxation questions on state or local ballots), they have been defeated.[47] Clearly, the public outcry that greeted the Manley subsidy proposals challenges any complacent assumption that support for hockey subsidies is automatic in Canada. Some Canadians objected to the various ways in which hockey has become commercialised and Americanised, others to the high player salaries and the lack of 'loyalty' to fans and communities that is encouraged by free agency. Some simply objected to spending money on sport while urgent social needs went unmet. What was crystal clear was that although many Canadians still profess to care about ice hockey, they no longer care in the ways that earlier generations once did about the NHL.

Should this surprise us? If it can be agreed that ice hockey still carries very special meanings for many men who grew up in the post-war decades, when most homes did not get sports channels and hockey was the normal winter recreation for most Canadian boys, it should also be recognised that in recent decades, young Canadians have grown up in a multi-channel universe where ice hockey competes for their interest and attention with basketball, NFL football and many other televised sports, as well as MTV and the internet. In major Canadian cities, moreover, they are now more likely to participate in football (soccer for North Americans) or basketball than in hockey. Today, ice hockey is an individual (and family) choice, and one among many, rather than the ritual of Canadian winter so fondly recalled among men of the post-war generations.

It should further be recognised that hockey (and, more generally, professional sport) are often the source of very different kinds of meanings for women. Varda Burstyn has proposed, for example, that in the struggles over housework and child-rearing responsibilities that have divided millions of couples over the last half of the twentieth century, 'what was often at stake in these arguments was men's right to spend time away from mate and family … to be "with the boys", playing sports or watching the game at the local bar or at home, while women tend to laundry, cleaning, shopping and childcare'.[48] In these circumstances many women may be less inclined than men to support massive public subsidies for 'men's cultural centres',[49] and it may also be that as more women move into influential positions in public life, the assumption that professional sport is so important in our lives that it must be saved at any cost is likely to be increasingly challenged. Indeed, arguably, an under-reported subtext in the public outcry after the Manley announcement is simply how badly many middle-aged men who were formed in the 1950s and 1960s misread how other Canadians feel about the game. Obviously, the level of public anger surprised the politicians who had supported the idea of aid, and it doubtless surprised the NHL, too.

In this context, then, when both professional sport and Canada have clearly changed profoundly, is there any basis for considering Canada's NHL teams as 'merit goods'? On the one hand, both the game and the NHL remain objects of keen interest for a great many Canadians, and it may yet be that politically palatable ways can be found to assist Canada's NHL teams. However, it is also clear that professional ice hockey is no longer regarded by most Canadians as a 'priceless' part of their heritage, to be saved at any cost. Today they want to know the costs, and also the 'opportunity costs' – the other public goods and services that are likely to remain underfunded if public money is spent subsidising NHL hockey. The public reaction to the federal government's proposals in January 2000 demonstrated that there is no longer the almost automatic popular support that might once have been expected for subsidies to professional sports. In this (rare) respect, it might finally be proposed, Canada may be moving away from US norms and closer to European ones.

NOTES

1. This chapter is an amended version of one first published as 'The Mills Report, the Manley Subsidy Proposals, and the Business of Professional Sport', *Canadian Public Administration*, 43, 2 (2000). The Institute of Public Administration has given permission to reprint this material and owns the copyright. We acknowledge the financial support of the Social Sciences and Humanities Council of Canada.
2. This was a subcommittee of the Standing Committee on Canadian Heritage, chaired by Clifford Lincoln, MP (Liberal, Lachine-Lac Saint Louis).
3. It should be noted, however, that the officials of the NBA did not ask for public funds.
4. *Sport in Canada: Everybody's Business*, Report of the Sub-Committee on the Study of Sport in Canada (House of Commons, November 1998), p.25.
5. See Charles Euchner, *Playing the Field: Why Sports Teams Move and Cities Fight to Keep Them* (Baltimore, MD: Johns Hopkins University Press, 1992).
6. *Sport in Canada*, pp.78–80.
7. Marc Lavoie, 'Les équipes sportives professionnelles n'ont pas d'impact significatif: le cas des Expos', *Avante*, 6, 1 (2000), p.76, provides a quick assessment of the amounts involved. Accelerated depreciation for each major facility would have been equivalent to a cash subsidy of about C$35 million.
8. *Sport in Canada*, pp.101–5.
9. See Jean Harvey, 'La vision du rapport Mills s'appuie sous de fausses prémisses', *La Presse*, 8 Dec. 1998, p.B3.
10. Graham Fraser, 'Ottawa Dismisses Mills Report', *Globe & Mail*, 29 April 1999, pp.S1, S2.
11. David Shoalts, 'Optimism Abounds in NHL Aid Talks', *Globe & Mail*, 29 June 1999, pp.S1, S2.
12. 'As one high-placed NHL official told a *Globe & Mail* reporter, "Why should that money go to hospitals? It's not like anyone is betting on the patients".' Stephen Brunt, *Globe & Mail*, 29 June 1999, p.S1.
13. It is worth noting that although the Ontario government's 'permission' to municipalities to offer relief on property taxes also made significant savings available, in principle, to the Toronto teams, Mayor Mel Lastman indicated that Toronto could not afford to lose the tax revenues it receives from the Air Canada Centre and the SkyDome. Outside Ontario, the two Alberta teams already play in publicly owned arenas, so that property taxes are not an issue, while Vancouver and Montreal have consistently refused to make concessions on this front. On 1 December 1999 the Ottawa-Carleton region kept this promise by reducing the Corel Center taxes by 85 per cent.

14. Mark MacKinnon, 'Public Outcry Leads Manley to Pull the Plug on Hockey Aid', *Globe & Mail*, 22 Jan. 2000, pp.A1, A4.
15. See Jim Silver, *Thin Ice: Money, Politics, and the Demise of an NHL Franchise* (Halifax, NS: Fernwood Books, 1996).
16. For a fuller discussion of these events, see Richard Gruneau and David Whitson, *Hockey Night in Canada: Sport, Identities, and Cultural Politics* (Toronto: Garamond, 1993), pp.97–101.
17. See Euchner, *Playing the Field*; Mark Rosentraub, *Major League Losers: The Real Cost of Sport and Who's Paying For It* (New York: HarperCollins, 1997).
18. See *Sport in Canada*, pp.95–8.
19. George Sage, 'Stealing Home: Political, Economic, and Media Power and a Publicly Funded Baseball Stadium in Denver', *Journal of Sport and Social Issues*, 17 (1992), pp.110–24. See also James Quirk and Rodney Fort, *Hard Ball: The Abuse of Power in Pro Team Sports* (Princeton, NJ: Princeton University Press, 1999).
20. S. Brunt, 'New NHL Strategy: Subsidy by Stealth', *Globe & Mail*, 27 March 1999.
21. In 1988–9 the average salary was US$180,000; in 1999–2000, this had risen to US$1,350,000. For more details on these rises see Marc Lavoie, *Avantage numérique, l'argent, et la Ligue nationale de hockey* (Hull, PQ: Vents d'Ouest, 1997), pp.186–90.
22. David Whitson, 'Circuits of Promotion: Media, Marketing, and the Globalization of Sport', in Larry Wenner (ed.), *MediaSport* (New York: Routledge, 1998), pp.57–72. The concept of 'circuits of promotion' is adapted from Andrew Wernick, *Promotional Culture* (London: Sage, 1991).
23. See 'Senators Extend Ticket Campaign Another 10 Days', *Globe & Mail*, 12 Feb. 2000, p.S2; 'Flames Embark on Tough Selling Job', *Globe & Mail*, 19 May 2000, p.S6.
24. Ken Dryden, 'Ownership, Identity at Heart of Sports Battle', *Montreal Gazette*, 6 Nov. 1994, p.C5, reprinted in Peter Donnelly (ed.), *Taking Sport Seriously: Social Issues in Canadian Sport* (Toronto: Thompson, 1997), pp.279–85.
25. See Marc Lavoie, 'Les dépenses fiscales du gouvernement fédéral en faveur des équipes canadiennes de la Ligue nationale de hockey (LNH), 1998–1999', working paper, Jan. 2000.
26. Dryden, 'Ownership, Identity at Heart of Sports Battle'.
27. See Bruce Kidd, 'Toronto's SkyDome: The World's Greatest Entertainment Centre', in J. Bale and O. Moen (eds), *The Stadium and the City* (Leicester: Leicester University Press, 1995); Nick Auf der Mer, *The Billion Dollar Game: Jean Drapeau and the 1976 Olympics,* Toronto: James Lorimer, 1976).
28. See D. Whitson and D. Macintosh, 'Becoming a "World Class" City: Hallmark Events and Sports Franchises in the Growth Strategies of Western Canadian Cities', *Sociology of Sport Journal*, 10, 3 (1993), pp.221–40.
29. D. Whitson and R. Gruneau, 'The (Real) Integrated Circus: Political Economy, Popular Culture, and the Business of Major League Sport', in W. Clement, *Understanding Canada: Building on the New Political Economy* (Montreal/Kingston: McGill-Queen's University Press, 1997), pp. 359–85; see also Marc Levine, 'Tourism, Urban Development, and the "World-Class" City: The Cases of Baltimore and Montreal', in Caroline Andrew, Pat Armstrong and Andre Lapierre (eds), *World Class Cities: Can Canada Play?* (Ottawa: University of Ottawa Press, 1999), pp.421–50.
30. Roger Noll and Andrew Zimbalist, 'Sports, Jobs, and Taxes: The Real Connection', in R. Noll and A. Zimbalist (eds), *Sports, Jobs, and Taxes: The Economic Impact of Sports Teams and Stadiums* (Washington, DC: The Brookings Institution, 1997), pp.496–7.
31. *Sport in Canada*, pp.94–5.
32. Paul Kedrosky, 'Taxpayers Score in Their Own Net!', *National Post Online*, 6 Nov. 1999. Online at http://www.nationalpost.com/story.asp?f=991106/120248.html (9 Nov. 1999).
33. R. Noll and A. Zimbalist, 'The Economic Impact of Sports Teams and Facilities', in Noll and Zimbalist, *Sports, Jobs, and Taxes*, pp.56–7. For other influential treatments, see Mark Rosentraub, *Major League Losers*; and Robert Baade, 'Professional Sports as Catalysts for Metropolitan Economic Development', *Journal of Urban Affairs*, 18, 1 (1996), pp.1–17.
34. Noll and Zimbalist, , 'The Economic Impact', p.57. The authors note that Stanford University collected US$258 million in tuition in 1995–6.
35. Marc Lavoie, 'Les subventions à la LNH: Le coeur et la raison', *Le Droit*, 1 Feb. 2000, p.15. See also Robert Baade and Allen Sanderson, 'The Employment Effect of Teams and Sports Facilities', in Noll and Zimbalist, *Sports, Jobs, and Taxes*.
36. See, for example, Jean Harvey, Marc Lavoie and Maurice Saint-Germain, 'Le sport au Canada: poids, impact économique et rôle du gouvernement', Mémoire soumis au Sous-Comité sur l'Étude du sport au Canada, 27 Jan. 1998, online at http://strategis.ic.gc.ca/SSGF/sg03425f.html.

See also Harvey and Lavoie, 'Les subventions au sport professionnel ou la socialisation du risque d'enterprise', *Themes canadiennes/Canadian Issues*, 21, 2 (1999), pp.10–11; Lavoie, 'Les équipes sportives professionnelles'.

37. Baade and Sanderson, 'The Employment Effect of Teams and Sports Facilities', pp.99–102. See also Ian Hudson, 'Bright Lights, Big City: Do Professional Sports Teams Increase Employment?', *Journal of Urban Affairs*, 21, 4 (1999), pp.397–407.
38. Noll and Zimbalist, 'The Economic Impact', pp.68–70.
39. Levine, 'Tourism, Urban Redevelopment, and the "World Class" City'. For other discussions, see Maurice Roche, 'Mega-Events and Urban Policy', *Annals of Tourism Research*, 21, pp.1–19; Dennis Judd and Susan Fainstein (eds), *Places to Play: The Remaking of Cities for Tourists* (New Haven, CT: Yale University Press, 1999).
40. Levine goes on to note, indeed, that despite polls showing Quebec opinion to be solidly against contributing public funds towards the construction of a new downtown baseball stadium, the Quebec government has now committed itself to grant up to C$8 million per year, 'on the undocumented grounds that the Expos helped "promote" Montreal as a tourist centre'. Levine, 'Tourism, Urban Development, and the "World-Class" City', p.440.
41. Ibid., p.439.
42. Ibid., p.443.
43. Noll and Zimbalist, 'The Economic Impact', p.73.
44. S. Tuck, 'Cisco to Create up to 2400 Jobs in Kanata', *Globe & Mail*, 28 Feb. 2000, p.B3.
45. A survey done in Winnipeg in 1994, on behalf of a citizen coalition that opposed public funding for the Jets, indicated that only among men earning over C$60,000 per year was there clear majority support for spending tax dollars to keep the team in Winnipeg. See J. Silver, *Thin Ice*.
46. Tim Burton, 'Merit Goods, Public Recreation, and the Enabling Authority of the State', in P. Faid (ed.), *Reshaping the Public Good: People, Places, Parks* (City of Edmonton, 1999), pp.109–19.
47. See Rodney Fort, 'Direct Democracy and the Stadium Mess', in Noll and Zimbalist, *Sports, Jobs, and Taxes*.
48. Varda Burstyn, *The Rites of Men: Manhood, Politics, and the Culture of Sport* (Toronto: University of Toronto Press, 1999), p.129. See, for an illustration, 'Hockey Night in Canada' (by Gwen Frank), on the cover of Gruneau and Whitson, *Hockey Night in Canada*.
49. Bruce Kidd, 'The Men's Cultural Centre: Sports and the Dynamic of Women's Oppression/Men's Repression', in M. Messner and D. Sabo (eds), *Sport, Men, and the Gender Order* (Champaign, IL: Human Kinetics, 1990).

5

Private Control of a Civic Asset: The Winners and Losers from North America's Experience with Four Major Leagues for Professional Team Sport

MARK ROSENTRAUB

Over the past two decades, as the world has experienced a more integrated economic framework and the role of tourism in several economies has expanded, sport has become an important commercial vehicle for establishing a nation or region's image as a destination for visitors.[1] Nations and cities now desire to be the home to professional sports teams and to host national and international events, to underscore both their elevated roles in the international economy and their popularity as a tourist destination.[2] In the past few years China, South Africa, Cuba, Israel and the Palestinian Authority have each sought to host international sporting events to underscore their identities and to help build a tourism economy.[3] At the local level community leaders now seem completely convinced that hosting a team is essential to establish their city's identity and reputation as a leading centre of civic and commercial life.[4]

The importance placed on hosting teams and mega-events necessarily raises the issue of how the supply of these assets will be distributed in response to the demands and the goals of different cities and countries. An interesting dilemma of sorts exists with regard to the distribution. On the one hand, cities and nations resent when their applications to host a team or event are rejected by a sport's governing body. This resentment usually includes a call for the leagues or sanctioning bodies to have less authority. On the other hand, part of the value of hosting a team or event lies in its exclusivity. In other words, if every city that wanted a premier level-team or to host a world championship or Olympics had their demand satisfied, the value of being home to a team or event would diminish. Juxtaposed with this notion that part of the value of hosting a team or event comes from its scarcity and the unsatisfied demand of other communities, is that control of the supply of teams or events does create an opportunity to auction rights to the highest bidders and enjoy excessive profits or economic rent. In addition, without sufficient oversight and controls, rampant bribery results. How is the supply of teams and large-scale events to be managed?

The increasing population and expanding wealth in several countries has raised anew the issue of the supply of teams and how franchises in a league should be managed to address the expressed demand and the often-conflicting interests of fans, players, team owners, the media and other stakeholders. Elsewhere in this volume, the role of international organisations and the allocation of these events are addressed. This chapter expands the discussion of the management of the supply and demand for franchises within a nation through an assessment of the 'American system' of governing major professional sports leagues. The evolution of the 'American system' and the effects of its structure on regional and local governments and their residents will then be identified in an effort to propose alternative governance models that can balance the many conflicting interests of fans, franchise holders and players.

The Roots of the 'American System'

Four very powerful leagues have unfettered control of the supply of franchises and the location of teams in the United States and Canada. However, when these four leagues were initially formed, no one would have imagined that they would become significant and powerful institutions that would lead to higher taxes in many cities. The history of professional football, basketball and ice hockey in North America is littered with teams that went bankrupt or repeatedly relocated in search of a profitable market. For example, in 1949 the National Basketball Association (NBA) was created from competing leagues that struggled to establish an identity and a profitable environment. The NBA began with 17 teams, but only nine teams completed the 1954–55 season. The National Hockey League (NHL) was formed with four teams in 1917, and before the Second World War the league had only six members, including just two of the original four franchises. Expansion and an increase in league members would not occur until the 1980s with the formation of the World Hockey League and its eventual merger with the NHL.

The early years of the National Football League (NFL) were no more robust. The precursor to the NFL, the American Profession Football Association was founded in 1920 and just three of its teams survived to become members of the NFL. Between 1926 and 1949 four other professional football leagues would emerge and compete to be the leading organisation for American football. Only one team from these fledgling organisations – the New York Giants – would survive to join the NFL. Challenges to the supremacy of the NFL would continue into more recent times, notably with the formation of the American Football League in 1960. Each of the original teams in this league eventually joined the NFL when the two leagues merged in 1966. In the 1980s the World Football League attempted to compete with the NFL, but it went bankrupt and none of its teams survived to become a member of the NFL. Recently plans were announced to form another football league and this effort received some limited support from one major television network. However, this league failed after one season.

By comparison, Major League Baseball (MLB) had a far more stable early history. The National League was founded in 1876. Four of the eight teams in this initial league failed, but the eight teams that existed in 1892 are still members of MLB. The American League was created in 1901, and each of its original eight teams is still a part of MLB.

In summary, the early history of the four major sports leagues was characterised by teams and leagues struggling to find adequate markets and to survive. Many teams in three of the leagues were forced to declare bankruptcy and some leagues even ceased operations. Baseball had the lowest failure rate, but even there some teams did declare bankruptcy and several of the original franchises moved to find more profitable venues. On balance, however, the failure rates in terms of teams and leagues may have not been any larger than normally would be anticipated for any new business venture. Professional team sports did not emerge as a business until the 1870s (for baseball). The other leagues were creations of the twentieth century. Initial failures, struggling operations and instability are frequent characteristics of new industries, and when the failure rate in sports is compared with other business ventures little difference is found. For example, Scully noted that from 1876 until 1900 approximately one team failed each year.[5] This yields a 3 per cent business failure rate, given the number of teams in the leagues at the time, which is comparable to rates in other sectors of the economy.

Those leagues that did survive established three goals. First, each league attempted to routinise play through the establishment of rules and regularised competition. To attract fans to games a 'visiting' team was needed and this team had to play the game according to accepted rules that did not vary when home teams went to other cities. The establishment of a schedule to be played across a season, with competitions designed to produce a league champion, was also needed to raise and maintain fans' interests in pennant and cup races. Second, each league attempted to ensure financial stability and profitability through the establishment of territorial 'rights'. These rights were designed to provide each team with a sufficient market of fans to permit profits to be earned. Further, each league member agreed not to move into the market area of another team and not to play matches or games with non-league teams that could, if successful, move into the market areas of other league members. In this manner, each owner's franchise or market area was protected. Third, the leagues also tried to attract new owners who would establish teams to ensure that there was both a pool of competitors and a sufficiently large number of different teams to attract fans to games in their home cities. If there were too few teams, fans might not want to attend as many games as when there was a variety of teams playing a 'home' team. It was correctly assumed that fans would be less interested in repeated attendance at games involving the same small set of franchises.

At a time when teams and leagues were struggling, few would probably have objected to these powers. For at least three of the four leagues (the NFL, the NBA and the NHL), financial instability and struggles to survive dominated their earliest years. Only MLB achieved a degree of financial stability and profitability early in the twentieth century, as baseball became the favourite sport for the expanding immigrant and working classes of the United States. Being or becoming an American was tantamount to being a baseball fan. As the owners had considerable ability to control labour costs, baseball players were bound to each team through a 'reserve clause'. Owning a MLB team became a valuable and profitable commercial enterprise.

The Evolution of the 'American System' and the Emergence of Cartels

How did the four major sports leagues emerge as powerful commercial entities, given their rather modest beginnings and early history? The roots of what would become a powerful cartel system, dominating the supply and location of professional team sports, lie in a 1922 US Supreme Court ruling that pertained only to baseball. Other actions by the US Congress and other federal courts secured the cartel power of the other sports leagues.

As noted, MLB had its beginnings with the National League, formed in 1876, and referred to today as the 'senior circuit'. For the 1901 season the National League left Cleveland without a team. The seventh largest city in the US, with 381,768 residents at the time, Cleveland attracted the interest of a minor league, the Western League. Franchise owners of Western League teams wanted to create a second major league to compete with the National League. The opportunity to place a team in Cleveland gave the upstart league a powerful position from which to launch its new initiative. Other teams in major cities were soon added and the league changed its name to the American League to compete with the National League. Franchise owners in the American League packaged their teams to appeal to the immigrant population and were soon attracting sufficient fans and revenues to enable them to recruit players from the more established National League. The new 'upstart' league was so successful that in less than two years team owners from the 'senior circuit' were willing to accept a merger in an effort to control labour costs. In 1903 Major League Baseball was formed, comprising the National and American Leagues.

In 1913 a different set of investors formed the Federal League, and in 1914 a new eight-team league emerged as a competitor for MLB. Its popularity by 1915 permitted teams located in Newark (a relocation from Indianapolis), Brooklyn, Baltimore, Buffalo, Chicago, Kansas City, Pittsburgh and St Louis to compete for players employed by MLB teams. As with the formation of the American League, the Federal League enjoyed sufficient economic success to permit team owners to bid for players from the older 'Major League'. Just as player salaries had increased when the American League challenged the National League, now the Federal League was increasing the costs of owning a team for franchise owners in MLB. Conflicts over players and other issues between the two leagues eventually led to lawsuits and, at the urging of a federal court judge, an out-of-court settlement was reached. The owners of the Chicago and St Louis franchises in the Federal League were permitted to buy franchises in MLB (the Cubs and Browns, respectively) and the owners of the other Federal League teams received money in exchange for the sale of their franchises to MLB. Each of the teams sold to MLB was dissolved, with the players dispersed among franchises. Many of the owners who were compensated for the loss of their teams made sufficient profits to be pleased with the proposed settlement. However, the owners of the Baltimore franchise in the Federal League were not willing to accept the settlement and sued MLB, arguing the forced buyout represented an abusive trade practice by a monopoly. In 1922, the US Supreme Court ruled that MLB was beyond the reach of US anti-trust laws.[6]

The effect of the 1922 decision was to establish MLB as a monopoly with unfettered control of the supply of franchises and the location of teams without interference from any level of government. The 16 teams that existed in 1922 remained unchanged until the 1960s, when MLB would finally expand rather than face the possibility of the creation of another league. Teams would continue to move, but until the City of New York threatened to anchor the Continental League in 1960 in response to the movement of the Brooklyn Dodgers to Los Angeles and the New York Giants to San Francisco, MLB was content to retain tight control over the supply of teams despite the growth of the US population. In 1922, a population of approximately 110 million Americans supported 16 MLB baseball teams. However, since there were no teams west of St Louis, the 16 teams actually had a fan base of just 63.7 million. The smallest city with a team in 1922, Cincinnati, had a population of 402,000. By 1960 the population of the US had increased to 179.3 million and Kansas City, with a population of 475,539, was the smallest with a major league team. However, in 1960 there were 11 cities with populations larger than Kansas City's that did not have a team. Many of these cities would eventually get a team in MLB or another major sport attesting to their interest in hosting a franchise. However, MLB had established itself as a cartel controlling the supply of teams to meet its objectives and placing a team in some of those other cities was not a priority for the league in the 1950s and 1960s.

Subsequent Supreme Court and federal court cases dealing with professional sports have recognised that the logic used to grant MLB an exemption from anti-trust laws was misguided.[7] However, rather than reversing itself, the Supreme Court was content to advise or argue that it was Congress's responsibility to amend the anti-trust laws to include baseball and other sports. Observing that Congress has seen fit not to change the law, the Supreme Court has continued to give MLB limited protection from the anti-trust laws, interpreting a lack of action by Congress as a decision to support the Court's initial, if irrational, decision. However, subsequent justices of the Supreme Courts have not been interested in extending the exemption given to MLB to the other sports leagues. As a result, when these leagues have wanted to restrain markets and enhance their control of the supply of teams, they have needed Congressional or judicial action. The request for protection from anti-trust laws has rarely been opposed.

For example, in 1966 the NFL and the upstart American Football League (AFL), founded in 1960, sought permission to merge. As a result of its success in markets without an NFL team, the AFL was able to offer players lucrative contracts to join the new league. Just as the American League had challenged the National League in MLB and raised the cost of operating a team, the new football league was making it increasingly expensive for NFL team owners to retain and attract the best players. Players' salaries continued to rise as the AFL secured itself in several key markets and by the 1960s owners in both leagues wanted a merger. Eliminating the competition for players between the established NFL and the AFL could have been interpreted as the establishment of a trust or cartel and thus in violation of US laws. In addition, the presence of one instead of two leagues could also have meant that other cities that wanted teams would stand less of an opportunity if one league controlled the supply of teams. To ensure that no legal challenges could be filed, the two leagues sought Congressional approval of their proposed merger.

During the Congressional hearings held to discuss an anti-trust exemption for a single football league, questions were raised over the implications for cities if one league had complete control over the supply of professional football franchises. Representatives of the NFL and AFL made two commitments to reduce this concern and eliminate opposition to the

proposed merger. First, the leagues pledged to add several teams across the next few years. Second, owners from both leagues pledged to keep teams in their existing markets. Some members of Congress were concerned that without the existence of a competing league a community that lost a team would have no option but to pursue an existing team. Owners assured Congress that they would not move their teams.[8] Bob Dole, then a member of the House of Representatives and a co-author of the proposed legislation, reported that he too had received a guarantee that the existing teams would stay in their present locations: 'According to their testimony, professional football operations will be preserved in the 23 cities and 25 stadiums where such operations are presently conducted.'[9]

In terms of honouring these two commitments, the NFL would add but one team to its ranks across the ten years from 1967 to 1976. However, between 1976 and 2000 the NFL would add five more teams and a sixth team began play in 2002. The NFL was also unable to honour its commitment not to move teams. Since 1967 five teams have moved to other cities; two of these teams moved twice, yielding a total of seven franchise relocations since the NFL/AFL merger.

The National Basketball Association (NBA) and the competing American Basketball Association (ABA) also received permission from a federal court to merge. Fearing that a merger between the two competing leagues would lead to lower player salaries, several athletes sued in an effort to use anti-trust laws to block a merger that would suppress wage levels. Eventually the players and the leagues owners compromised on a compensation plan and the court permitted the NBA and ABA to merge. Similar logic was used to authorise the merger of the National Hockey League (NHL) and its competitor, the World Hockey Association (WIIA).

At the conclusion of the mergers, each of the four major team sports was organised into a cartel that controlled the supply and location of teams. The issue of the costs or burdens that these organisational structures create in the 'American system' must be examined in relation to the performance of the leagues. For example, if the four organisations were operated in such a manner as to include the interests of all of the stakeholders interested in sports, then the mere existence of cartels would not necessarily imply that there are any negative consequences. On the other hand, if the interests of players, fans, taxpayers or cities are not being represented, then the behaviour of the cartels may well be abusive and designed merely to ensure commercial gain.

The Cartels and the Interests of Stakeholders

Sports are unlike any other business in that to succeed teams or athletes need other teams or individuals to stage competitions. Teams are organised into leagues or groups for the staging of games. This is in sharp contrast to virtually any other business, where a single firm can exist without the presence of a competitor. Sports teams are linked to each other in an element of competition and cooperation.[10] However, the fact that a group of teams unify within a league structure and then execute certain powers does not necessarily mean that the interests of consumers are being harmed. Indeed, one could argue that without a league or cartel the quality of competition would be less and fans would be worse off. As a result, in terms of classifying the effects of a league on a sport and whether or not the cartel is abusing the interests of any stakeholder, a careful analysis is required of the major organisational elements of a league's structure. In these assessments the central question or issue is whether or not the cartel represents the interests of all its stakeholders or if an alternative structure could better serve these needs.

Who are the stakeholders with interests in the structure of team sports, and who stands to benefit or lose from alternative organisational frameworks? In any sport the stakeholders consist of owners, players, fans, community leaders and taxpayers. Owners can often be characterised as seeking to maximise commercial gain, but numerous franchise holders often focus on other benefits (welfare maximisation), including contributing to the image and recreation available in a particular community or the enjoyment that comes from owning a winning team.[11] Some owners are even willing to 'lose' or invest money to build a winning team. A winning team sometimes permits an owner to maximise his or her welfare instead of profits.

Players' interests generally involve a similar framework. On one level they seek to earn as much as possible, but they too may seek to maximise their welfare through playing for a certain team (a likely champion or a team near their preferred home community). Fans want as many teams as there are quality athletes to support. With quality held constant, fans also want as many competitive games as possible with the price of tickets held to the lowest possible level. Community leaders want a sufficient number of teams to exist so that they can secure the name recognition and civic identity conferred by a team's location. However, this is a double-edged sword: if there are too many teams, then the distinctiveness created by having a team is reduced. However, if there are too few teams, many communities will not be able to enjoy the benefit of having a home team. Taxpayers would prefer to spend as little as possible to procure the benefits of having a home team. In North America, at least, this has become a major issue as state and local governments have repeatedly provided extraordinary subsidies to attract and retain teams.[12]

How have the four North American leagues or cartels performed relative to the interests of stakeholders? With regard to owners, the available evidence would suggest their commercial interests have been well protected. Across

the past decade, when teams have been placed on the market for sale, there has been no shortage of bidders, and the prices paid continue to escalate. Four NFL franchises have been sold since 1998 and each cost in excess of $500 million. The new Houston franchise cost its owner $700 million, and the New York Jets were sold in 1999 for $635 million despite the requirement that the team must play in an older facility for several more years. Since then three MLB teams have been sold for more than $250 million each, and in early 2000 the New York Islanders of the NHL were sold for $190 million The value of franchises has soared because the leagues have restrained the supply of these valuable assets. Further, while player salaries have risen in the NFL, and for many franchises in other sports leagues, the costs of ownership have not risen to the point where economic returns, however measured by those desiring teams, have deteriorated. There is some evidence that some teams in MLB and some in the NHL are not profitable and, if sold, would not command the prices secured for NFL teams andother franchises in MLB, the NBA or the NHL. However, where unprofitable teams exist it is usually a result of the failure of the leagues to share revenues or local mismanagement.

TABLE 5.1
MLB TEAM PAYROLLS, 1990–99

Season	Team payrolls in millions of dollars				Annual change (%)
	Average	*Total*	*Lowest*	*Highest*	
1990	17.3	450.2	8.1	23.6	
1991	26.2	680.9	12.1	39.2	51.2
1992	35.2	915.9	10.1	59.3	34.5
1993	35.8	1,003.2	12.2	56.2	1.7
1994	29.9	836.2	11.1	47.3	−16.6
1995	31.2	872.2	12.1	50.5	4.3
1996	35.4	992.2	17.5	63.0	13.8
1997	37.6	1,053.3	11.6	65.5	6.2
1998	41.1	1,232.4	8.3	71.9	19.5
1999	48.6	1,456.5	14.7	92.0	13.8
2000	59.3	1,780.1	15.7	114.4	22.2

The existing system has also provided important benefits for players as their salaries have continued to rise. In MLB, for example, the total amount of money paid to players is increasing by ten per cent per year across the past seasons and by 22 per cent from 1999 to 2000 (see Table 5.1). While superstars earn more than other players and the median salary has actually declined across the last few years,[13] the proportion of players earning in excess of $4 million increased from 10.7 to 13.9 per cent in just two seasons, while the proportion of players earning between $300,001 and $500,000 also increased, from 7.6 to 10.5 per cent. There were also

TABLE 5.2
MLB SALARIES IN 1998 AND 1999 – A RISING TIDE CARRYING ALL SHIPS

Salary level	Percentage of all MLB players by salary level	
	1998 season	*1999 season*
$200,000 or less	28.1	11.4
$200,001 to $300,000	17.3	26.0
$300,001 to $500,000	7.6	10.5
$500,001 to $1,000,000	11.7	12.3
$1,000,001 to $2,000,000	11.7	11.6
$2,000,001 to $4,000,000	13.0	14.2
More than $4,000,001	10.7	13.9

increases in the percentage of MLB players earning in excess of $1 million (see Table 5.2).

Players and owners in the NBA recently agreed to a new six-year contract that places a cap on the money any one player can earn: $14 million per season after ten years of service. However, the players were guaranteed that not less than 48 per cent of agreed components of gross revenues would be dedicated to player salaries. This established $34 million as the cap for each team for the 1999–2000 season. With between 12 to 15 players on each team, the potential exists for every key player to earn around $3 million every season. This guarantee was given to the players in exchange for a salary cap on the money earned by the sport's leading celebrities. The NBA players association saw this concession as meeting or satisfying the interests of their members.

Players in the NFL have had a similar contract with team owners, guaranteeing that their salaries would equal 63 per cent of all broadcast revenues and ticket sales. The owners retain 100 per cent of all other revenues, and the salary cap was extended to 64 per cent in 2002. In addition there is also a salary floor that dictates a minimum overall salary level for each team. In this way the players are guaranteed that they will receive a substantial pool of revenue for salaries and that no owner can attempt to pay less than the 'floor' level. In the NHL only the salaries of rookies are capped in exchange for a restrictive free-agency policy that permits smaller market teams to retain their stars for several seasons. The players have accepted this provision and their collective bargaining agreement extends through to the 2003–4 season. There is little doubt that the cartel system adequately protects the interests of players, although the possibility does exist for a labour battle in MLB.

The objectives of fans, community leaders and taxpayers can be grouped together as their interests involve (1) the existence of an adequate supply of teams able to compete effectively for championships; (2) the lowest possible ticket prices for competitive games; (3) the absence of subsidies from the public sector; and (4) the presence of a team in each community that wants one to maintain its civic identity and culture. This last goal includes the benefits stemming from the prestige associated with hosting a major or premier-league team, the intangible benefits generated by a team's presence, and the small economic benefits from a team's presence.[14] The issues that must be addressed, then, are to what extent have the cartels (1) created an adequate number of teams relative to the demand of sports fans and cities for franchises; (2) ensured that all teams have the opportunity to earn sufficient revenues to remain competitive; and (3) minimised the use of subsidies for their operations.

The ability of any community to support a team is a function of the size and wealth of its population. Preferences for different sports also are quite important. In 1995, the *New York Times* performed an analysis of the number of baseball teams that could be supported in the United States. This examination focused on four criteria enumerated for each metropolitan area: the number of men between the ages of 18 and 54; per capita incomes; population growth; and the potential for the sale of luxury suites (the number of firms and wealthy households in an area). The *Times* found nine areas without MLB teams that could definitely support a team, five areas that could possibly support a team and as many as five other areas with teams that could support at least one *more* team. With 28 teams based in the United States, the analysis by the *New York Times* would suggest MLB should have at least 37 teams and possibly as many as 47.[15]

If one focused only on the increased population of the US, there would also appear to be too few teams. There are nine metropolitan areas with populations larger than the smallest area with a MLB baseball team. If one focused on the number of large corporations in an area as a measure of the financial viability of a region to support a franchise, additional teams should exist in Northern Virginia, the Austin/San Antonio area, Portland, Oregon, and in the San Bernardino area. The current US population and the distribution of large businesses are sufficiently robust to support 33 or 34 major-league baseball teams. In the NFL, Buffalo is the smallest market team, but 13 other metropolitan areas with larger populations are without teams. As many as 42 NFL teams could be supported if population and local wealth were the factors determining supply and demand; however, the NFL had only 32 in 2002. Other analyses have identified several markets without NBA or NHL teams that could support either a major-league hockey or basketball team.[16] Using wealth and the size of the population in a region as critical variables indicates that too few teams exist with regard to demand. In a free market setting it is reasonable to expect that there would be more teams and that cartels have restricted the supply of teams.

The distribution of revenue is critical to the integrity of athletic competition in a league. If teams have very different levels of income, then high-income teams will have a greater potential to attract and retain the best players. If this occurs, a group of teams can dominate a league and effectively eliminate competition.[17] A measure of the extent to which the leagues represent the interests of the fans is the extent to which revenues are shared between high- and low-revenue teams and the extent to which the race for pennants and cups is truly competitive.

As described in Table 5.1, team payrolls in MLB varied from a high of more than $92 million to a low of approximately $15 million. Disparities of this nature destroy the competitiveness of the sport and this led Sandy Alderman, a member of the staff of the Commissioner of MLB to conclude that 'small market teams are no longer in the business of competitive baseball – they're in the business of entertainment – because their knowledgeable fans know that these teams can't compete'.[18]

In MLB the time when a small market team could win the World Series may have passed. Of the final four teams that played for league pennants in 1998, only the San Diego Padres had a payroll below $60 million, while the league average was $41.1 million. In 1999 the Braves, Mets, Yankees and Red Sox were MLB's final four, and no team had a payroll below $71.5 million, while the average team salary was $48.6 million. In 2000, baseball's final four each had a player payroll in excess of $53 million and the two finalists each had payrolls of approximately $100 million In the NBA since 1980 only four teams from market areas with fewer than three million people have made the NBA finals. The Portland Trail Blazers have appeared twice (in a market area of 2.6 million people), the Orlando Magic (2.7 million residents in their market area) and the Utah Jazz (in a regional market of 2.2 million people) have each made one unsuccessful appearance in the finals. In 1999 the San Antonio Spurs, playing in a market area of less than 2 million (3.2 million if the Austin area is added) won the NBA title. However, the team threatened to leave the area if a new subsidised arena was not built. Voters approved the subsidy even though the team's current home, the Alamodome, is only seven years old. In contrast, between 1980 and 2000, the Los Angeles Lakers have been in the NBA finals ten times, the Boston Celtics and Chicago Bulls five times, the Houston Rockets four times and the Detroit Pistons, New York Knicks and Philadelphia 76ers three times each. None of these markets have fewer than 4.6 million residents.

The NFL, with the most robust revenue-sharing programme of the four North American leagues, does tend to produce more champions from smaller markets. Since 1997, the NFL champion has come from Denver, Green Bay and St Louis. None of these markets has more than 3.2 million residents. However, prior to the victories by the Packers, Broncos and Rams, the last time a team from a region with fewer than three million residents won the Super Bowl was in 1980 (the Pittsburgh Steelers). In

addition, after the Packers and Broncos won their titles, both teams needed to raise additional revenue. The Packers sold additional stock that has no real market value, and the Broncos renewed their demands for a publicly subsidised stadium. Under a threat that the Broncos would move if a new stadium was not built, voters agreed in November 1998 to subsidise a new facility for the team. In early 2000 the Packers also sought a public subsidy to remodel their ageing stadium. The Wisconsin state legislature approved enabling legislation and by the end of the year the local residents of the NFL's smallest market voted to use tax money to ensure that the team would remain competitive. The Rams, who relocated to St Louis from the Los Angeles/Orange County region, play their home games in a publicly subsidised stadium and receive one of the largest annual subsidies of any team in the NFL. As a result, even with extensive revenue-sharing, NFL teams in small markets seem to be able to compete for championships only if the local community provides a substantial subsidy.

While Scully and others have shown that there is a statistical association between revenues and winning, recent cases underscore that revenues create winners. For more than two decades, the Cleveland Indians languished at the bottom of the American League. The team's revenues have increased dramatically since the heavily subsidised Jacobs Field opened. In 1990 the team earned $34.8 million; in 1997, the team's earnings had increased to $134.2 million for a real increase of 214 per cent. In the same period, the team's payroll increased from $19.1 million to $66.9 million for a real increase of 250 per cent. In 1990, player salaries accounted for 44.3 per cent of total revenues; this figure increased to 49.3 per cent in 1997.

The team's increased expenditures for players and revenues have matched their increased winning percentages. From 1993 to 1994, the Indians increased player salaries by 30 per cent and the team had a winning season in 1994 for the first time in more than a decade. Since increasing salaries, the team has never had a losing season. In 1997, they won the American League pennant and in 1998 lost in the final rounds of the playoffs. Increased revenues and expenditures for players have changed Cleveland from a two-decade loser to an annual competitor for the American League title.

The importance of revenues for a winning team does not imply that managerial talent does not matter. Some teams in large markets have consistently done poorly and have also failed to win division titles and championships, despite a willingness to spend dollars to attract the best playing talent. The Yankees had several poor seasons in the 1980s and early 1990s, as did the Mets, the Chicago White Sox, the Dallas Cowboys, and the Los Angeles Lakers. Philadelphia's sports teams each enjoy the ability to market their sports in a very large region but they have consistently failed to offer sports fans a winning franchise.

The Implications of the American Model for Managing Sports

Despite functioning in an economy described as market-driven, professional team sports in North America are managed by four cartels. The justification for this seeming contradiction has been the peculiar nature of sport as a business. Each team's financing success is dependent on the existence of other teams to attract fans to competitive games. The leagues, then, exist to ensure that competitive games attract fans. How well have the leagues performed their task?

If success is measured by the wealth attracted to the games through attendance and media contracts, the leagues have indeed been quite successful. Player salaries, once unfairly depressed by owners, have now soared. At the same time franchises continue to escalate in value, generating substantial returns on every owner's investment. These two stakeholders then have clearly gained commercial benefits from the cartel structure of sports. Other constituencies may not have fared as well.

For example, by manipulating the supply of teams, the four major leagues have been able to receive lavish subsidies from communities that want teams. Essentially, teams have been able to make excessive demands for public subsidies and threaten to move to a more pliable community if their requests are not met. Between 1985 and 1997, more than $7 billion in public debt was negotiated to build new facilities for teams.[19] Across the next several years it is anticipated that the total state and local debt for sports facilities will climb to $15 billion.[20] This $15 billion is produced by the levy of special sales or excise taxes, or the deflection of property, income and sales taxes from state and local governments to repay the bonds used to pay for the facilities used by teams. It represents one of the costs of the cartel system to North American taxpayers and sports fans. The other costs involve the absence of teams in communities that want one and the potentially higher price of tickets to games caused by the artificial scarcity of teams.

Fans are also being 'short-changed' by this system in that the very essence of competition is being undermined. Despite increasing ticket prices, the competitiveness of the leagues is being undermined by a failure to share revenues. In baseball, where only the highest-revenue teams win championships, ticket prices have increased by 92.9 per cent since 1991 while the consumer price index has risen by just 25.9 per cent. The NFL's average ticket price rose by 81 per cent while the NBA's ticket prices have increased by 81.3 per cent.[21] Winning has been dominated by larger-market teams in the NBA, while those smaller-market teams that have won championships in the NFL all demand large subsidies from local communities to augment their revenues. If these communities fail to offer the subsidy demanded, teams leave for other areas. The NHL's roots are to be found in Canada, but recently teams in smaller Canadian cities have moved to the greener pastures of the US, just as smaller US cities have lost their teams to larger areas.

The cartels do not protect the interests of fans, who are paying more for less competitive teams. Those communities that ultimately pay subsidies simply raise the cost of sport for all residents. Some residents may well see this as an appropriate investment, but the actions of the cartels raise the costs of sport and some leagues are failing to ensure a competitive environment for all teams. As a result, taxpayers and fans are spending more money, and championships are being won by large-market teams. Some have argued that if the current patterns continue and fans are truly dissatisfied with the structure of the sport they will eventually decide not to attend games. The ensuing economic losses will then force the owners to address each of their sports' problems. While there is certainly a degree of validity to this position, equally if not more valid would be the position that if cartels, created and sanctioned by a government, fail to address the needs of stakeholders, then reforms should be implemented that return more market competition to the industry. Further, if cartels fail to meet the needs of fans it is unlikely that they would make the needed responses without the exercise of political pressure. Sport is an important part of every society, and if the structures developed and encouraged fail to meet the needs of fans, the structures need to be changed so that fans can articulate their demands through an unfettered market place. How could this be achieved? What sort of public policies and laws could be considered?

The simplest and most direct measure would be to retain the structures of leagues, but have more than one league competing to attract fans to games. As each of the four existing leagues was the product of mergers, the existing unions could be broken into their component parts. Two leagues (such as the American and National in MLB) could still schedule a championship between the best teams in each league, but attractive markets without teams would have a greater opportunity to secure a franchise, as each league would fear that the other would enter, and secure income from, a potentially profitable market. The existence of competing leagues could mean more teams in more markets.

The largest markets, New York and Los Angeles, could also become areas where existing leagues would want to place another team to preclude the existence of a second team from the other league. Each of the four cartels has a very powerful incentive to keep at least one viable market without a team. The availability of a potentially profitable market for a team creates pressure on other cities to meet their team's demands. If those demands are not met the team could always move to the city without a team. But if there were two or more leagues in each of the four professional sports, each would want to capture the profits possible in a market without a team before another league did.

Creating competitive leagues and using market forces to establish the number of teams that should exist is but one response that could be made to end the cartel control of professional team sports. Another could involve a more proactive role for government. For example, currently only the leagues can award franchises giving the owners control over the supply of teams. This responsibility could be extended to include local governments in the process of establishing new teams. How could such a system work? It could be modelled after the system used by the NFL to place expansion franchises in such cities as Cleveland and Houston.

To establish a new Cleveland Browns football team (to replace the one that had moved to Baltimore), the NFL held an auction. After bids were submitted, an ownership group acceptable to the NFL was granted a new franchise. The city agreed to build a new stadium, and the NFL helped the new owners finance their share or contribution to the facility's capital costs. The NFL gave the new franchise the first draft pick in 1999 and gave the new owners an equal share of all pooled revenues. The winning bid was $535 million and the revenues were then divided among the existing owners.

This system could easily be adapted to fit any sport and permit a larger role for local governments in the creation of franchises. Any city that wished to be home to a new team in a league could apply for a franchise and the league would then be required to hold an auction to find a suitable owner. The bids received would reflect the present value of access to the league's pool of shared revenues and local profit potential. If the existing owners shared the franchise fee, as they did in the NFL's expansion into Cleveland, then no existing team owner would suffer a loss in the value of its franchise. With more franchises, there would be more jobs and more teams to bid for players, so they too would gain. To protect the interests of existing owners, a minimum bid level equal to the median value of league franchises could be established. A minimum bid level would also ensure that markets too small to produce an adequate return would not attract investors.

Would such a system mean that there would be hundreds of teams in each of the sports? The experience of numerous American cities with gaming enterprises illustrates that a bidding procedure is quite efficient. The first cities that award franchises for casinos are generally successful. But when too many franchises are awarded, the market shares required for each to be profitable are constrained and franchise auctions fail to attract bidders.[22] In this regard, some cities may want teams, but when an auction is held it is possible that no acceptable bids are received. If the public sector could require that an auction be held to determine if there are acceptable investors, areas could acquire the teams they want. In addition, larger metropolitan areas might be able to get an additional team if investors had interests in taking that risk.

These are just two public policies that can be considered to change the cartel structure of sport in North America without jeopardising the property rights of owners and the ability of players to earn high incomes. Existing laws and the cartel structure of the four major sports leagues have created excessive costs for taxpayers and fans. A return to a framework with competitive leagues would reduce the need to subsidise teams. Requiring the leagues to hold auctions for expansion teams would also eliminate the subsidy wars between cities. Allowing the current system to continue, however, will simply mean that the subsidies will continue. The US is a nation that prides itself on the existence and maintenance of competitive markets. It is time to instil this level of competition in the governance structure of professional sports to reduce the costs paid by taxpayers and fans.

NOTES

1. D. Judd and S. Fainstein (eds), *The Tourist City* (New Haven, CT: Yale University Press, 1999).
2. C.C. Euchhner, 'Tourism and Sports: The Serious Competitive for Play', in Judd and Fainstein, *The Tourist City*.
3. P. Kotler, D. Haider and I Rein, *Marketing Places* (New York: The Free Press, 1993).
4. M.W. Danielson, *Home Team: Professional Sports and the State* (Princeton, NJ: Princeton University Press, 1997).
5. G.W. Scully, *The Business of Major League Baseball* (Chicago, IL: University of Chicago Press, 1989).
6. *Federal Baseball Club of Baltimore v National League of Professional Baseball Clubs*, 259 US 200, 1922.
7. M.S. Rosentraub, 'Are Public Policies Needed To Level The Playing Field Between Cities and Teams?' *Journal of Urban Affairs*, 21 (1999), pp.377–95.
8. US House of Representatives, Professional Football League Merger, Subcommittee Number 5 of the Committee of the Judiciary, 1966.
9. Ibid., p.106.
10. B. Costas, *Fair Ball: A Fan's Case For Baseball* (New York: Broadway Books, 2000).
11. P.J. Sloane, 'The Economics of Professional Football: The Football Club As A Utility Maximizer', *Scottish Journal of Political Economy*, 17 (1971), pp.121–45.
12. R. Noll and A. Zimbalist, *Sports, Jobs, and Taxes: The Economic Impact of Sports Teams and Stadiums* (Washington, DC: The Brookings Institution, 1997); J. Cagan and N. deMause, *Field of Schemes: How the Great Stadium Swindle Turns Public Money into Private Profit* (Monroe, ME: Common Courage 1998).
13. B. Costas, *Fair Ball*; J. Weiner, *Stadium Games: Fifty Years of Big League Greed and Bush League Boondonggles* (Minneapolis, MN: University of Minnesota Press, 2000).
14. D.S. Swindell and M.S. Rosentraub, 'Who Benefits from the Presence of Professional Sports Teams? The Implications for Public Funding of Stadiums and Arenas', *Public Administration Review*, 58 (1998), pp.11–19.
15. T. Ahmad-Taylor, 'Who is Major Enough for the Major Leagues', *New York Times*, 2 April 1995, p.E5.

16. *Sport Business Journal* (2000).
17. R. Hughes, 'Manchester Displays its Wealth of Talent', *International Herald Tribune*, 17 March 2000, p.22.
18. Costas, *Fair Ball*, pp.58–9.
19. Noll and Zimbalist, *Sports, Jobs, and Taxes*.
20. Cagan and DeMause, *Field of Schemes*; D. Zimmerman, 'Public Subsidy of Stadiums', *NTA Forum, The Newsletter of the National Tax Association* (Columbus, OH, 1998).
21. CNNSI, 'The Cost of Sitting: New Ballparks Lead Wave of Higher Ticket Prices', 4 April 2000. Online at www.cnnsi.com.
22. D. Felsenstein, L. Littlepage and D. Klacik, 'Casino Gambling as Local Growth Generation: Playing the Economic Development Game in Reverse?', *Journal of Urban Affairs*, 21 (2000), pp.409–22.

6

Partnerships between Local Government Sport and Leisure Departments and the Commercial Sector: Changes, Complexities and Consequences

LUCIE THIBAULT, LISA M. KIKULIS
and WENDY FRISBY

Public-sector organisations have a mandate to achieve essential social missions, including provision in education, employment, health-care and other areas that are not adequately provided for by the private sector. The role of the public sector is also a compensatory one because its policies, programmes and services provide remedies for the social problems created by market failures, and therefore contribute to the 'public good' by focusing on disadvantaged groups whose needs are not met in the marketplace.[1] Like other local government services that ensure safety and basic living requirements (such as water, sewerage, police and fire services or waste management), departments responsible for the provision of sport and leisure provide local governments with direct and positive links to citizens. As advocates for active participation in community sport and leisure, the services offered by these departments are believed to enhance quality of life by contributing to physical, psychological and social health, and serve as the main avenue for mass participation.[2] The mission of sport and leisure departments in local government is therefore a social one, to provide sport and leisure opportunities to all citizens in order to improve quality of life.[3] Through the provision of facilities such as parks, fields, swimming pools, ice rinks and community centres, and the delivery of programmes at no or minimal charge, sport and leisure departments in local governments have been able to fulfil their social mission by providing recreation, fitness, sport and skill-development opportunities for the community at large, regardless of ability, age, race, class or gender.

The provision of sport and leisure opportunities by local governments has been facilitated by a long and successful history of partnerships with public-sector and non-profit agencies, such as schools, school boards or local non-profit sport and leisure organisations. These partnerships have been based on the shared values of contributing to the social good and ensuring access to services for community citizens. More recently, however, sport and leisure departments have developed partnerships with organisations in the commercial sector as a means of providing programmes, facilities, equipment and/or resources.[4] Crompton states that this development is a strategic shift involving the adoption of an 'entrepreneurial mindset [that] has led to increased interest in cooperating with commercial enterprises'.[5] He also suggests that commercial partners are attractive because they have the ability to raise capital expeditiously to take advantage of market opportunities; they can respond more quickly to change and they can also provide specialised expertise that can help to minimise labour costs.[6] In contrast to partnerships developed with other public agencies or non-profit organisations, those developed with commercial organisations require local governments to change and adapt their thinking and operations to accommodate commercial goals and involvement. The tension between values underpinning the traditional social mission of the public sector and business-oriented values raises a number of concerns and challenges for the development and management of public-commercial partnerships. There has, however, been little discussion or debate regarding the potential opportunities, challenges and consequences that public-commercial partnerships bring to the delivery of local sport and leisure services. The purpose of this chapter, therefore, is to address this gap by considering the following questions:

• What changes in public management have enabled the development of public-commercial partnerships?
• What are the complexities of public-commercial partnerships in the delivery of sport and leisure services at the local level?
• What are the consequences of public-commercial partnerships for key stakeholders?

In the following section we set the context for public-commercial partnerships by discussing 'New Public Management' as an ideology and policy approach that has enabled the public sector to place increasing confidence in partnerships with the commercial sector. In the second section we identify the key stakeholders in the provision of sport and leisure at the local level. We discuss the complexity of the environment in which public-commercial partnerships are embedded. In the third section we discuss the consequences of public-commercial partnerships. This is where we consider why local government sport and leisure departments and commercial organisations want to partner with each other. We also discuss the impact of such partnerships on each of the key stakeholders. In the concluding section, we consider the implications of public-commercial partnerships for the future of local sport and leisure services.

New Public Management and Public-Commercial Partnerships for Sport and Leisure Departments in Local Government

In this section we focus on the role of New Public Management (NPM) and its relevance for the development of the enabler role and public-commercial partnerships in local government more generally, and in sport and leisure services in local government more specifically.

Significant changes in the roles, responsibilities, structures and management of local governments have been enabled and constrained by a number of economic, social and political shifts.[7] The emphasis of national governments on deficit and debt reduction during the 1990s meant severe cutbacks to public spending and services and the offloading of responsibilities onto other levels of government (e.g. county, state, provincial, local). Consequently, with reduced budgets and increased responsibilities, local governments have put more emphasis on cost reduction initiatives and have given priority to revenue-generating services. Second, while the public sector continues to struggle with these fiscal constraints, it has also faced increasing pressures for high-quality social services and public policies that meet the needs of the increasingly pluralistic communities they serve. Finally, the political climate favouring 'pro-business' policies[8] and less government has meant that local governments have adopted policies of no or limited increases in property and business taxation and have increased their support for local economic growth and development.

Together these economic, social and political shifts have provided a context for the adoption of a new public-service ideology in Western democracies known as NPM.[9] While there is no one definition of NPM, most definitions refer to the adoption of private sector, market-driven practices so that governments are more entrepreneurial, client-centred, service-oriented and results-focused.[10] As Aucoin states, 'enhancing cost-consciousness, doing more with less and achieving value for money [have become] the objectives of this finance-centred perspective on public management reform'.[11] Consequently, public services and the investment in these services are now evaluated not only on the traditional functions and obligations of fulfilling a social mission and serving the public interest, but also on their efficiency, cost-consciousness and, most importantly, their support for market growth serving private interests. Murdock suggests local governments are shaping their role and are being shaped by more privatised or commercial criteria when he states:

> They are under increasing pressure to demonstrate their efficiency and 'value for money' by adopting managerial practices and philosophies developed by private enterprise. They come to be evaluated, and to

judge themselves, by the same criteria as commercial companies.
They increasingly see their role as competing for consumers in a
competitive marketplace rather than meeting the needs of citizens.
Measures of quantity are eagerly developed – how many users are
attracted to spend time with the services, how quickly are they
processed. Qualities that cannot be easily calibrated disappear from
managerial rhetoric. The commitment to contribute to the common
good is displaced by the injection to square demands of clients –
individually and in aggregate – with the pressures generated by an
increasingly privatised operating environment.[12]

An illustration of this point is the decision by city councillors in the city of
Edmonton in Canada who voted 8–4 in favour of closing down a free public
wading pool for three weeks during the 2001 World Athletics
Championships and turning it into an upscale café selling snacks, beer and
wine to generate revenues for the city.[13]

One aspect of NPM that has been adopted by local governments as a
way of managing the tensions between fiscal restraint, revenue generation
and demands for quality services that serve the public's interests is the
broadening of the institutional role of local governments from direct-service
provider to 'service enabler', where the aim is to specify and support the
provision of services through alternative service delivery strategies.[14]
Adopting an enabling role means that local government councillors and
civil servants are looking to the network of private agencies and
organisations that are part of the local community as partners to assist with
service delivery. For example, the local government might provide cheap
land or waive taxes to encourage commercial investment in sport and
leisure facilities. Other types of partnership involve joint ventures where the
commercial partner provides the capital, equipment or expertise and the
local government sport and leisure department provide facilities. It is
important to note that the cultural, social, political and historical conditions
of a particular local government will influence what type of enabling role
and what public-commercial partnerships are developed.

While the virtues of an efficient government are difficult to ignore, the
adoption of public policies that promote efficiency and economic growth
has meant that there is a real danger that economic criteria will become the
sole standard used by local governments for determining service,
programme and partnership decisions. The result will be that many of the
community's social welfare needs, such as the equitable provision of
quality services that respond to the public interest, will not be met.[15] Rather,
a business orientation in local government will intensify inequalities by
focusing on 'target markets' that are cost-efficient or revenue generators, at
the expense of ensuring the provision of services that benefit all citizens.

With efficiency and economic growth guiding local government policy, and with the role of government changing towards enabler, the emergence of public-commercial partnerships that reflect an increased emphasis on market-driven values has gained the interest of many local government managers, city councillors and corporations. Will this ideological shift be able to balance the opposing goals of social policy and economic growth? Will the interests of the public be compromised to advance the interests of the commercial sector? Will public-commercial partnerships change values with regard to the role of local government sport and leisure departments, so that the priorities of local government are determined by commercial rather than public interests? It is these types of question that need to be at the forefront of discussions and debate when considering public-commercial partnerships. In the next section we examine the complexities of local government and the diversity of stakeholders, their roles and their interests in the provision of sport and leisure at the local level. We discuss these roles in an effort to explain the dynamics of public-commercial partnerships that have become an important part of sport and leisure provision in local communities.

The Complexities of Public-Commercial Partnerships

As discussed above, the changes taking place in local government have meant that sport and leisure departments have developed a growing interest in partnerships. While public-commercial partnerships have become more prominent as local government sport and leisure departments have joined with commercial organisations to ensure that facilities are built and maintained, access to services and programmes is increased or maintained, and income is generated, these partnerships are embedded in a larger network of stakeholders that have an interest in the provision of sport and leisure at the local level. Hutt, Stafford, Walker and Reingen suggest that, although partnerships are usually depicted as dyadic relationships, both partners usually have a plethora of partners or stakeholders enmeshed in their social networks that will be affected by, and could react to, each new partnership arrangement.[16] Managers of sport and leisure departments have to deal with stakeholders that have different mandates, ways of operating, values and interests, and resources. These differences are not always compatible with the values and interests of local governments or the public they serve. The capacity of local governments to cope with these different stakeholders is critical to the success of these partnerships. In the context of local sport and leisure, there are numerous stakeholders that could be identified. We have focused on five key stakeholders: (1) local government sport and leisure department employees; (2) elected politicians; (3) citizens (sport and leisure participants and non-participants); (4) traditional public and non-profit partners; and (5) commercial partners.

Local Government Sport and Leisure Department Employees

Traditionally sport and leisure department employees were considered to be in the best position to understand the needs and expectations of the public because of their regular communication and contact with citizens through direct programme provision. In addition, their expertise and training as sport and leisure professionals were premised on the value of developing policies and programmes that serve the sport and leisure needs of all citizens. As the mandates of the departments in which these employees work have broadened from direct service delivery to include collaborative programmes, services and ventures with agencies, these employees have had to develop new management capabilities that enable them to develop, manage, maintain and evaluate these partnerships to ensure accountability.

Elected Government Officials

Elected government officials within local governments are representatives of their ward, neighbourhood or region and possess the ultimate decision-making authority in the local government structure. Politicians who are elected by the public have the important task of debating policies and initiatives that are introduced by local government employees, members of the business community, their constituents and other levels of government. They play an important role in decision-making and in the strategic orientation of local governments. Local elections in Canada and the US are non-partisan – that is, the focus is issue-specific. Nevertheless, the political ideology of more 'business-like' government has underpinned many recent policy and service decisions.

Citizens (Current Sport and Leisure Participants and Non-participants)

Citizens elect government officials who they feel best represent their community interests and are also those who benefit from the services provided by local governments. However, the cultural, social, economic and political plurality of communities means that serving its citizens is an increasingly challenging endeavour for local governments. In addition, when costs or economic growth underpin local government decisions, some citizen groups have less voice and influence. For sport and leisure departments, the tensions between economic goals and community plurality has meant that community associations have become an important tool for lobbying government and identifying sport and leisure needs.

Traditional Public and Non-profit Partners

In the management of their operations, sport and leisure departments interact with other local government departments. For example, the maintenance of facilities (e.g. parks, fields, swimming pools, ice arenas) may be the responsibility of a 'public works' department. To ensure services are offered in a safe environment, there needs to be direct communication between the sport and leisure department that provides programming and the 'public works' department that maintains facilities. Similarly, programmes aimed at providing leisure for youth have been developed in collaboration with police departments, social services and other levels of government responsible for justice. In addition, sport and leisure departments also interact with non-profit organisations that run leagues and clubs for both competitive and 'learn to' sport and leisure opportunities. Drawing on the expertise of volunteers, coaches and instructors within these settings, managers in sport and leisure departments have been able to offer a wider range of sport and leisure programmes to the public. Schools and school boards have also been long-standing partners of local governments. Through reciprocal agreements, schools have been able to use local government facilities during the day for their physical education programmes while local governments are able to use school fields and facilities during the evenings and weekends, thereby maximising the use of sport and leisure facilities in many communities.

Commercial Partners

The newest stakeholder in the local provision of sport and leisure is the commercial sector. With local government interest in economic growth and development coupled with pressures for more efficient government, commercial organisations have played an increasingly important role as key partners in the provision of services. Commercial organisations have developed partnerships with local sport and leisure departments that have facilitated greater access to, and provision of, equipment, expertise and facilities. In exchange, local governments have contributed to the business objectives of their commercial partners by providing land at low cost, tax breaks and enhanced visibility and credibility as 'community citizens'.

While each stakeholder described above may have established a partnership of some type with the local government sport and leisure department, our focus is on public-commercial partnerships developed as strategic initiatives by managers in local government sport and leisure departments and commercial organisations as a result of the policy interests of elected government officials. It is clear, however, that any partnership has an impact on relations in the broader network of stakeholders. This complexity has often created tensions among and between these stakeholders that is particularly evident when we consider public-commercial partnerships. Consequently, the pace at which local governments have adopted public-commercial partnerships for the provision of sport and leisure services, the comprehensiveness of such partnerships as part of service delivery and the type of services provided through these partnerships have varied within and between local governments. Leach, Stewart and Walsh argue that the outcome of such differences 'will reflect the relative strength of bargaining power of the two [or more] participants which will itself be partly dependent on the views and concerns of the politicians. In one [local government] the outcomes may go one way, in another quite the opposite way'.[17]

The economic, social and political shifts that have allowed the adoption of an NPM ideology and provided the context for an increased emphasis on the enabling role have meant that some local government sport and leisure departments have embraced the enabling role and the opportunity it has provided for the development of public-commercial partnerships. By contrast, a decline in financial resources available to local government sport and leisure services and/or policy or strategic changes in the responsibilities of local governments may result in public-commercial partnerships being developed out of necessity rather than shared values, leading to tensions and problems. Other tensions arise when city councillors and/or city employees feel it is the responsibility of local government to provide certain services to ensure access for all citizens, while certain commercial organisations view the service as an entrepreneurial opportunity to make a profit. Under these circumstances, there may be resistance by local government to developing a partnership.

It is also important to recognise the interests and power of stakeholders in maintaining or enhancing their access to, or distribution of, resources that enable or hinder public-commercial partnerships. Hardy and Phillips identify three aspects of power that are particularly relevant to understanding public-commercial partnerships for the provision of sport and leisure. They state that the power dynamics underpinning partnerships are understood 'by asking who has formal authority, who controls key resources, and who is able to manage legitimacy discursively'.[18] The formal authority, or the holding of legitimate positions of power to make decisions, is demonstrated by elected officials who pass or repeal by-laws and make decisions that support or hinder commercial interests. The second aspect of power, the capacity to control access to, or distribution of, scarce or critical resources, such as money, expertise, facilities or information, has shifted from the public to the commercial sector. Faced with declining budgets, local government sport and leisure departments have looked to the commercial sector as a resource pool, enabling commercial organisations to pick and choose what services they will support. Finally, discursive legitimacy is the ability of an organisation or agency to influence others because it is socially accepted that they speak on behalf of those who have an interest in the issue. City council or community advocacy groups often have discursive legitimacy and are able to influence the development of public-commercial partnerships. Thus while some groups may not have authority or resources to exchange, their values regarding the appropriateness of a specific public-commercial partnership may be particularly important if their voices are loud enough to be heard. For example, a public-commercial partnership that involves the corporate sponsorship of facilities may raise concern from residents when they see the fences in their park covered with corporate signs. The same citizens however may be very supportive of a public-commercial partnership where the commercial partner offsets the maintenance costs of a local park in exchange for corporate signage on ball-field fences. In still other communities, corporate signage may only be tolerated in arenas and indoor facilities.

The existence of both social and business goals within these partnerships clearly adds to the complexity of sport and leisure provision. The discourses, training and practices of the professionals who are coming together to negotiate these partnerships differ widely, increasing the potential for conflict, power imbalances and inter-organisational miscommunication, possibly jeopardising the intended impact of these inter-organisational alliances. Mackintosh describes the tensions created by public-commercial partners as a transformation model of partnership, whereby

> each partner in a joint venture is not merely trying to work with the other and find common ground for mutual benefit. Each is also trying to move the objectives and culture of the other more towards their own ideas. This struggle for mutual transformation is only partly overt, rarely openly debated and within schemes, but emerges quite clearly in exchanges.[19]

In the next section we explore these issues in more detail when we discuss the consequences of public-commercial partnerships.

Consequences of Public-Commercial Partnerships for Stakeholders

There are a variety of consequences associated with the growth of public-commercial partnerships in local sport and leisure that need to be carefully considered. In this section several consequences will be described and the relevance to the major stakeholders will be discussed. We have identified seven key consequences for public-commercial partnerships: (1) achieving a social mission; (2) achieving a business mission; (3) improving efficiency; (4) loss of autonomy; (5) increasing legitimacy; (6) increased access to improved sport and leisure services; and (7) accountability. It is important to note, however, that this list is not exhaustive and not all consequences are equally relevant for each key stakeholder. In addition, the consequences should not be viewed in binary terms as being simply negative or positive and they will undoubtedly change over the tenure of public-commercial partnerships. While we present and discuss them independently, it is clear that consequences are interdependent, again increasing the complexity of public-commercial partnerships. It is also important to consider the consequences for all major stakeholders because they do not benefit equally from public-commercial partnerships and some will overtly resist these alliances if their interests have not been adequately taken into account.

Achieving a Social Mission

While sport and leisure services are sometimes viewed as a marginal form of social service, because housing, medical care, education and other services are deemed more essential,[20] the traditional rationale for government involvement has been that sport and leisure services perform a socially integrative function that contributes to a sense of community solidarity while counteracting social and economic inequalities.[21] More recently, efforts have been made to document the numerous personal, social, economic and environmental benefits of participation in local sport and leisure programmes to justify the need for this so-called 'soft or intangible' social service.[22] In addition, involvement in sport and leisure is increasingly being viewed as an effective form of physical and mental health promotion and disease prevention that is an alternative to the treatment-oriented modality of the traditional health care system. As such, participation has been shown to reduce health care costs.[23]

As discussed in the previous sections of this chapter, the dwindling resource base available to local governments, the shift towards more business-like operations in the public sector and the diverse and often conflicting demands of the various stakeholders have meant that local governments have looked to other sectors and agencies to assist them in achieving this social mission. Coupled with the interest of local governments in economic growth and development, 'synergy' has become the 'public face of partnerships'[24] as politicians, sport and leisure professionals, businesses and public interest groups work together for mutual benefit and to control environmental uncertainty. Logsdon elaborates on the potential role of public-commercial partnerships in ameliorating social problems:

The formation of cross-sectoral collaboration for social problem-solving will become more common in the future if organizations see the solution of social problems as consistent with their fundamental interests in efficiency, stability, and legitimacy, and as dependent on their participation with other parties in solving these problems. Developing a community of interests may be the only method for solving many social problems in this period of government cutbacks, and their decentralized approach may yield more social experiments and perhaps more effective remedies than does traditional reliance on large-scale government programs.[25]

Kanter supports this view when she states that creative partnerships can be forged to tackle complex social problems in a way that has positive consequences for both the public and the commercial sectors.[26] Even though public-commercial partnerships may ensure or improve access to the benefits of participation in local sport or leisure, these partnerships raise suspicion when commercial interests encroach on areas traditionally controlled by government. The danger occurs when the public sector fails to deal with the problems associated with this complexity, and instead relinquishes its socially-oriented values by uncritically adopting the market-driven values and practices of its commercial partners. As a consequence, social missions are undermined when business values redefine the public as 'consumers' or 'markets', programmes as 'commodities' or 'products', and performance indicators as 'cost recovery', 'efficiency' and 'the bottom line'.[27]

The lines between public and commercial forms of service provision become blurred in this case, as pricing policies are changed through fee increases in order to make joint ventures financially viable for commercial partners. To justify fee increases and to attract segments of the public who are able and willing to pay, many local sport and leisure departments are striving to offer the latest trends in programmes and equipment, with professionally trained instructors, modern facilities and manicured open spaces. Like their commercial partners, the public sector is then catering to the middle and upper classes, and essentially making their services inaccessible to those who are least able to pay.[28] As a result, the ability of local sport and leisure departments to achieve the principle of equal opportunity for everyone to participate, in line with their social mission, is increasingly being compromised.

We agree that, in light of the changes occurring in local government and the complexity of the network of stakeholders in which sport and leisure are provided, local sport and leisure departments should offer popular programmes such as youth sport programmes or adult fitness programmes to generate revenue. This should, however, be seen as primarily a strategy for subsidising activities that are socially desirable but not revenue-generating (e.g. programmes for persons on low incomes, for persons with disabilities, for recent immigrants and for seniors), thus enabling the achievement of the social mission.[29]

While practitioners and academics have advocated the development of public-commercial partnerships to offset the pressures governments are facing, making it possible for them to achieve their social missions, we concur with Smale and Reid, who contend that although local sport and leisure professionals have been quick to respond to new economic realities, they have lost their vision of contributing to the 'public good' by doing so.[30] Our argument is that the social mission traditionally pursued by these departments is threatened when an overemphasis is placed on entrepreneurialism and the pursuit of commercial partners. For public-commercial partnerships to succeed, each sector must maintain its respective social and business missions, but both parties must come to understand each other's expectations, strengths and limitations.[31]

Achieving a Business Mission

While we have argued that the public sector has increasingly developed more 'business-like' objectives, we focus here on the business mission of the commercial sector. In an era of downsizing and highly competitive markets, businesses are no longer partnering with the public sector for philanthropic reasons. Rather their goal is 'to capitalize on market opportunities to realize profits for owners and investors'.[32] For most businesses, mass-marketing campaigns are increasingly ineffective,[33] so they are seeking opportunities to build relationships more directly with specific target markets. The local sport and leisure department is an attractive partner because of its existing and trusted relationship with citizens.

Kanter argues that another reason why the commercial sector is seeking partnerships with the public sector is that it provides opportunities for research and development where new ideas, technologies and markets can be developed. She sees this as a shift from *corporate social responsibility* to *corporate social innovation* where

> companies have discovered that social problems are economic problems, whether it is the need for a trained workforce or the search for new markets in neglected parts of cities. They have learned that applying their energies to solving the chronic problems of the social sector powerfully stimulates their own business development.[34]

According to Compton, there are four primary benefits sought by businesses when they enter into partnerships with local sport and leisure departments. These include increased product awareness, product trial or sales opportunities, image enhancement and hospitality opportunities. Crompton focused primarily on sponsors, ranging from local businesses to multinationals, that are interested in associating their products with community-based programmes or special events.[35] Sponsorship, however, is not the only type of public-commercial partnership in which businesses are involved. The sport and leisure departments of local governments have entered into joint-venture agreements with developers to build new facilities and are outsourcing to commercial organisations to deliver programmes they are not capable of offering due to limited resources.

Developers achieve their business missions when they are able to lease scarce land at a nominal cost over the long term to develop sport and leisure facilities as domestic or tourist attractions in residential or commercial areas. In return for sharing the cost and risk associated with large capital projects, developers often seek to leverage their involvement by operating programmes and ancillary services directly, or by negotiating profit-sharing arrangements once the facility is completed (e.g. for programme fees, concessions, merchandising). While developers lose some autonomy through these partnerships, they often have considerable power, especially when their capital contributions outweigh the amount contributed by the public sector.

The consequence of public-commercial partnerships in local sport and leisure for commercial organisations is that their business mission has not been compromised. In fact, the interest of local governments in economic growth and development has meant that this mission has often guided partnership development.

Improving Efficiency

Local sport and leisure departments, commercial partners, elected government officials and current participants are the major stakeholders who stand to gain the most through improved efficiencies in service provision. Rather than working from the traditional 'silo model' where public service organisations act as autonomous self-sufficient units heavily reliant on government funding, the shift towards the NPM ideology discussed earlier suggests that the quantity and quality of services can be more efficient by partnering with the commercial sector.[36] The argument is that new capacities are created by leveraging resources, including the skills, knowledge, finances and social networks of partners, to develop innovative solutions that cannot be created by a single entity acting on its own.[37] Politicians also benefit from these arrangements when they can provide evidence to the public that tax-based dollars are being spent wisely and tax increases are not necessary.[38]

Citizens who are current participants also benefit through greater access to quality programmes and instructors when efficiencies are the focus of public-commercial partnerships. Citizens who are not current participants, typically the majority of community residents, do not benefit from local governments that adopt efficiency-based service provision where 'bottom-line' performance indicators are linked to increased fees for services. Thus when public-commercial partnerships result in new facilities that are cost-intensive, such as ice arenas, in response to current users who are demanding more facility time, access is increased for those who can pay but remains beyond the reach for most community citizens.

There have, however, been attempts to link efficiency and social outcomes. For example, citizens in a low-income neighbourhood of a large Canadian municipality received considerable media attention when they attempted to block a public-commercial partnership between Nike and the sport and leisure department that involved the resurfacing of an outdoor basketball court in exchange for recognition. While the sport and leisure department stood to benefit through the reduction of facility upgrading costs and ensuring facility access in a low-income neighbourhood, Nike was looking for increased exposure to advance its business mission by reinforcing its 'inner city' image. Citizens were outraged and questioned the legitimacy of this initiative. They cited the high cost of Nike footwear and apparel as being incongruent with the impoverished living conditions in their neighbourhood and also commented on their distaste for the practices of Nike's suppliers in Third World countries. As a consequence, while the legitimacy of the partnership was threatened by negative media exposure, Nike did agree to cover the cost (C$50,000) of the court resurfacing and agreed that its 'swoosh' logo would not be used on signage or advertising at the facility.[39] While the partnership went ahead, and both partners essentially achieved their goals of access and publicity, it is clearly an indication that local governments have placed a high priority on efficiency.

It is debatable whether the traditional public and non-profit partners benefit from the rhetoric surrounding the efficiencies of public-commercial partnerships. Local sporting groups may simply become conduits for generating revenue, while the access of schools and other community associations, which have a limited ability to pay, may be confined to 'non-prime time' facility usage.

Service duplication is often identified when local governments establish 'outsourcing' partnerships with commercial organisations to improve efficiencies. These types of partnerships also support the business mission of commercial partners. An example of this approach was seen when a local sport and leisure department in Canada formed an alliance with several small outdoor adventure companies to provide hiking, kayaking, rock climbing and other outdoor programmes to the public. The department achieved considerable cost savings by not having to buy equipment, hire specialised staff or assume liability insurance costs by outsourcing to these small independent companies, rather than duplicating programmes that were already in existence. The outdoor adventure operators benefited by partnering with the department and having their services widely advertised at no cost in brochures regularly distributed to every household in the community.

Public-commercial partnerships however, do not always result in reduced duplication in services. For example, if sport and leisure departments partner with fitness equipment suppliers and developers to construct new fitness facilities, they can become direct competitors for commercial organisations offering similar services. Once again, the distinction between the public and the commercial sector becomes blurred because of similar services targeted at the same upper- and middle-class markets with the objective of revenue generation.

The consequence of efficiency-based public-commercial partnerships is explained by Kernaghan. As he notes, 'The use of partnerships has evolved from an ad hoc response to particular problems to a general approach to problem-solving and to improving the efficiency, effectiveness and responsiveness of public organizations. In some instances, the concept has been adopted as a key element of an organization's strategic planning.'[40] The concern is that efficiency has become the end by which public services are evaluated. Critics argue that in reality partnerships have become a strategy for government to offload responsibility for service provision. Wharf elaborates on this point when he argues that 'In contrast to previous decades where the state sought to resolve social problems by sponsoring community development projects, governments, and particularly those of a neo-conservative bent, are now interested in community only as a way of offloading responsibility for social issues.'[41]

A Loss of Autonomy

Oliver contends that a loss of organisational autonomy, 'an organization's freedom to make its own decisions about the use and allocation of its internal resources without reference or regard to the demands or expectations of potential linkage partners',[42] is one of the most significant consequences of establishing inter-organisational relationships. Both local sport and leisure departments and commercial partners stand to lose autonomy when they establish a partnership. When entering into a public-commercial partnership, local sport and leisure departments must divert resources, including staff time and energy, into joint activities, while at the same time losing power and control over how decisions are made. This issue of human resources is an important one because partnerships need to be managed and monitored, but public-sector employees often do not have the time, training or infrastructure support required for these additional responsibilities. As a result, a partnership may show a short-term gain in the 'savings' column but a long-term loss of autonomy may occur due to a weak investment in human resources from the public sector.

For public organisations, relinquishing control is a political risk because they are accountable to the public for the use of public resources in the best interests of the community. Roberts and Bradley argue that collaboration in the development of innovative public policy requires the involvement of competing and diverse stakeholder interests in an interactive process that is both reflexive and self-critical.[43] Barriers to such open collaboration include asymmetrical power distribution among stakeholders, disparate political cultures and the technical complexity of the issue negotiated.[44] The consequence is a public-commercial partnership where the inclusiveness of interests is reduced and the democratic process is restricted.

Increasing Legitimacy

Public-commercial partnerships can increase or decrease the legitimacy of not only the primary partners (local sport and leisure departments and commercial organisations) but also elected politicians. When these partnerships threaten the ability of local governments to meet their traditional social mission, questions of legitimacy are raised. Drawing on institutional theory to explain how legitimacy is a consequence of partnerships, Oliver states that

> institutional environments impose pressures on organizations to justify their activities or outputs. These pressures motivate organizations to increase their legitimacy in order to appear in agreement with the prevailing norms, rules, beliefs, or expectations of external stakeholders. The establishment of [partnerships] for purposes of increasing legitimacy can originate from an organization's motives to demonstrate or improve its reputation, image, prestige, or congruence with prevailing norms in its institutional environment.[45]

Claims of unfair competitive advantage also threaten the legitimacy of public-commercial partnerships when tax benefits or cheap land are provided by the public sector. When access to facilities is limited to those who can pay the fees, the concern of citizens is that they have already contributed through their tax assessments and thus additional fees are unfair. These concerns are often ignored when the programming responsibility is outsourced to a commercial organisation.

Anti-development sentiments are also running high in many communities because of concerns over environmental degradation and unlimited growth when public-commercial partnerships are established for facility development. Developers can increase their legitimacy and overcome negative public reactions and media exposure by partnering with the public sector and gaining political approval for their ventures.

Sagawa and Segal warn that local governments risk losing their tax-based status and their legitimacy in the eyes of the public if they adopt market-driven values and an overemphasis on fiscal responsibility that 'leaves those hardest to serve with nowhere to turn'.[46] However, in the examples of Edmonton City Council voting in favour of closing a public wading pool and opening an upscale café during the city's hosting of the 2001 World Athletics Championships and of the Nike-local sport and leisure department facility upgrading partnership, both went forward even though citizens were vocal in their position against these arrangements. Consequently, what is seen to be 'legitimate' in the eyes of the public and those directly involved in the partnerships may be very different. Legitimacy may be more closely linked to the ability of public and commercial partners to discount the 'discursive legitimacy' of the public in favour of their own voice which is argued to represent the 'silent majority'.[47]

Increasing Access to Improved Services

It is those currently participating in sport and leisure programmes, rather than non-participants, who are most likely to have increased access to improved services as a result of public-commercial partnerships. Participants have power because they are already contributing to revenues and departments want to retain them as repeat customers. They are also in a better position to influence decision-making because they 'understand the system' and are in regular contact with staff. In contrast, there are a number of barriers to participation for many community citizens. For example, Hoffman contends that in Canada only 15 per cent of the entire female population over ten years of age engages in physical activity frequently enough to derive physical health benefits.[48] Kidd also notes that despite the myth of 'sport the great equalizer', participation in modern forms of physical activity in consumer-oriented societies remains heavily dependent upon financial resources, cultural capital and other prerequisites of participation.[49]

Frisby, Crawford and Dorer illustrate this point by demonstrating how the culture of grassroots participation in local sport and leisure is predominantly youth-oriented, skill oriented, middle class and highly masculinised. Women in their study, who were single mothers living below the poverty line, reported that having to 'prove poverty' to receive fee subsidies, not having the 'right' clothing, equipment, body type or skill level created significant barriers to participation that were compounded by structural problems like poor transportation, inadequate childcare and unsafe neighbourhoods. Local sport and leisure departments rarely tackle personal and structural barriers to participation, especially when their reward system is based on improving the bottom line and their attention diverted towards attracting commercial partners.[50]

While local governments recognise many of their citizens' low participation rates, the typical strategy has been to place the responsibility for getting involved on the individual. Well-educated middle-class sport and leisure professionals typically make programming and marketing decisions with little or no consultation with non-participants and then expect all members of their community to 'show up' at predetermined times and locations. If minimum numbers are not achieved, programmes are cancelled because of a lack of interest. Traditional marketing strategies have, however, proved unsuccessful in reaching many community citizens, and a lack of consultation has resulted in programme offerings that exacerbate rather than alleviate barriers to participation.[51] In other instances, well-intentioned front-line workers engaged in community development with disadvantaged segments of the population encounter oppositional discourses when they deal with middle managers and politicians who espouse the bottom line as the performance measure of services, making meaningful and systemic social change and broader-based access more difficult.

While public-commercial partnerships have the potential to increase access to improved services if both partners champion this goal, more often than not it is efficiency or revenue generation that characterises these partnerships. Consequently, if partnerships with traditional partners (e.g. schools, public health units, social services, advocacy groups) that work directly with disadvantaged populations are not maintained, it is likely that the majority of citizens in a community will continue to have limited or no access to programmes and services.

Improving Accountability

Throughout this chapter we have implied that depending on the prevailing values and norms of local government, accountability can be framed in a variety of ways. If the 'social remit' becomes less of a priority or is defined in a narrow manner such as short-term economic gain, attendance numbers and financial indicators such as cost savings, cost recovery rates and profit levels are used to demonstrate accountability. By contrast, when local government is focused on achieving longer-term social goals aimed at ensuring access and opportunities for all citizens, increased participation rates, particularly among disadvantaged groups, coupled with relevant qualitative and quantitative measures of the benefits of participation are used to demonstrate accountability.[52]

Obviously, given the changes that have taken place in the public sector, and the variety of stakeholders that need to be considered when developing and assessing the consequences of public-commercial partnerships, the challenge for sport and leisure departments and elected officials is to demonstrate accountability of resources and social problem solving. Marshall, Wray, Epstein and Grifel suggest this may be achieved if more emphasis is placed on developing partnerships with citizens where they become the co-producers and evaluators of public services as well as the catalysts for community action. If efficiency measures of performance are viewed as a means of achieving the end of more participatory and responsive services to the public, several benefits will result, including increased public confidence in local government.[53]

In order to demonstrate accountability fully, process indicators as well as the outputs of public-commercial partnerships need to be assessed.[54] According to Frisby, accountability of process could be assessed in terms of the steps taken to reach disadvantaged groups and build partnerships, as well as the development of structures and decision-making processes that empower citizens rather than reinforce existing hierarchical power structures.[55] There is no doubt that pressures will continue to be placed on local governments to demonstrate results and that the survival of sport and leisure departments will depend on their ability to juggle the complex issues surrounding accountability.

Conclusions

While academics and practitioners have advocated the advantages of partnerships and alliances, considerable challenges and issues surface when public and commercial organisations choose to cooperate in order to fulfil their mandates. As emphasised in this chapter, public-commercial partnerships are challenging, particularly when one looks beyond the initial development of the partnership and considers the complexities of managing and maintaining a partnership that brings together agencies and organisations that have very different goals. However, we have suggested that with the shift in public goals towards improved efficiency and economic growth, goal incompatibility has not seemed to be a problem for these partners. Rather it is many of the other stakeholders that have considered the seemingly contradictory nature of their goals.

While many positive outcomes are achieved when local governments work with other agencies to deliver services, it is important for leaders and managers to consider the notion that negative outcomes may also ensue. Partnerships are complex and the conditions under which public-commercial partnerships can have a positive or negative impact need to be considered.

Before embracing public-commercial partnerships, the public, politicians and local government employees must anticipate and address the potential negative outcomes of these arrangements. It is clear that the presence of commercial organisations in community centres, swimming pools, ice rinks and open spaces has generated a great deal of interest and concern from the public, local government councillors and city managers. Local governments that uncritically adopt public-commercial partnerships, without addressing the potential negative consequences for the public and other stakeholders such as those discussed in this chapter, are less likely to retain and achieve their traditional social missions of providing equal access to opportunities for all citizens. When public-commercial partnerships are focused on economic gain, it is citizens who do not actively participate in sport and leisure programmes – the majority of the population in most communities – as well as the traditional partners that have the least to gain. Thus, the extent to which the social mission of local governments has shifted, and the extent to which public-commercial partnerships can be scrutinised by the public and other stakeholders in the community, both need to be addressed.

Future research on the topic of public-commercial partnerships should focus on the strategies undertaken to reconcile the differences in values and interests between public and commercial organisations. The under-management of these partnerships, due to weak investment in human resources and methods of evaluating the success of partnerships, also needs to be addressed. Uncovering what is required of leaders, managers and employees to manage partnerships successfully is important in ensuring their longevity. The overall concern should be for the impact that changes in the public sector towards an NPM ideology are having, particularly on the social mission of public agencies responsible for sport and leisure provision.

NOTES

1. S. Sagawa and E. Segal, 'Common Interest, Common Good: Creating Value Through Business and Social Sector Partnerships', *California Management Review,* 42, 2 (2000), pp.105–22; B.J.A. Smale and D.G. Reid, 'Public Policy on Recreation and Leisure in Urban Canada', in E.P. Fowler and D. Siegel (eds), *Urban Policy Issues: Canadian Perspectives* (Toronto: Oxford University Press, 2002), pp.172–91.
2. See Canadian Parks and Recreation Association, *Benefits of Parks and Recreation Catalogue* (Ottawa: Canadian Parks and Recreation Association, 1997).
3. M.S. Searle and R.E. Brayley, *Leisure Services in Canada: An Introduction* (State College, PA: Venture Publishing, 2000).
4. See J.L. Crompton, 'Partnering: The Complementary Assets of Business and Park and Recreation Agencies', *Journal of Park and Recreation Administration* 16, 4 (1998), pp.73–94; L. Thibault and J. Harvey, 'Fostering Interorganizational Linkages in the Canadian Sport Delivery System', *Journal of Sport Management,* 11, 1 (1997), pp.45–68; L. Thibault, W. Frisby, and L.M. Kikulis, 'Interorganizational Linkages in the Delivery of Local Leisure Services in Canada: Responding to Economic, Political and Social Pressures, *Managing Leisure: An International Journal,* 4, 3 (1999), pp.125–41.
5. J.L. Crompton, 'A Taxonomy of Public-Commercial Joint Ventures', *Loisir et société/Society and Leisure,* 12 (1989), p.119.

6. Crompton, 'Partnering'.
7. See S. Leach, J. Stewart and K. Walsh, *The Changing Organisation and Management of Local Government* (London: Macmillan, 1994); P. Aucoin, *The New Public Management: Canada in Comparative Perspective* (Montreal: Institute for Research on Public Policy, 1995); Thibault, Frisby and Kikulis, 'Interorganizational Linkages'; C.R. Tindal and S.N. Tindal, *Local Government in Canada* (Scarborough, ON: Nelson, 2000).
8. M. Dobbin, *The Myth of the Good Corporate Citizen: Democracy under the Rule of Big Business* (Toronto: Stoddart Publishing, 1998); P. Hoggett, 'New Modes of Control in the Public Service', *Public Administration*, 74, 1 (1996), pp.9–32; Tindal and Tindal, *Local Government in Canada*.
9. Aucoin, *The New Public Management*.
10. Ibid.; N.C. Bardouille, 'The Transformation of Governance Paradigms and Modalities: Insights into the Marketization of the Public Service in Response to Globalization', *The Round Table*, 353 (2000), pp.81–106; D. Farnham and S. Horton, 'Public Service Managerialism: A Review and Evaluation', in D. Farnham and S. Horton (eds), *Managing the New Public Services* (London: Macmillan, 1996), pp.259–276.
11. Aucoin, *The New Public Management*, p.9.
12. G. Murdock, 'New Times/Hard Times: Leisure, Participation and the Common Good', *Leisure Studies*, 13, 4 (1994), p.241.
13. See B. Mah, 'It's Final: The Café Stays, the Pool Closes', *Edmonton Journal*, 13 June 2001, online at http://www.edmontonjournal.com/city/stories/010613/5026924.html
14. See T.D. Glover and T.L. Burton, 'A Model of Alternative Forms of Public Leisure Services Delivery', in M.F. Collins and L.S. Cooper (eds), *Leisure Management: Issues and Applications* (Oxford: CAB International, 1998), pp.139–55; Leach, Stewart, and Walsh, *The Changing Organisation and Management of Local Government*; R. Leach and N Barnett, 'The New Public Management and the Local Government Review', in S. Leach (ed.), *Local Government Reorganisation: The Review and its Aftermath* (London and Portland, OR: Frank Cass, 1998).
15. See Dobbin, *The Myth of the Good Corporate Citizen*; Bardouille, 'The Transformation of Governance Paradigms and Modalities'.
16. M.D. Hutt, E.R. Stafford, B.A. Walker and P.H. Reingen, 'Case Study: Defining the Social Network of a Strategic Alliance', *Sloan Management Review*, 41, 2 (2000), pp.51–62.
17. Leach, Stewart and Walsh, *The Changing Organisation and Management of Local Government*, p.10.
18. C. Hardy and N. Phillips, 'Strategies of Engagement: Lessons from the Critical Examination of Collaboration and Conflict in an Interorganizational Domain', *Organization Science*, 9, 2 (1998), p.227.
19. M. Mackintosh, 'Partnership: Issues of Policy and Negotiation', *Local Economy*, 7 (1992), p.216.
20. A. Clarke, 'Leisure and the New Managerialism', in J. Clarke, A. Cochrane and E. McLaughlin (eds), *Managing Social Policy* (London: Sage, 1994), pp.163–81.
21. F. Coalter, 'The Mixed Economy of Leisure', in I. Henry (ed.), *Management and Planning in the Leisure Industries* (London: Macmillan, 1990), pp.3–32.
22. Canadian Parks and Recreation Association, *Benefits of Parks and Recreation Catalogue*.
23. C.J. Frankish, D. Milligan and C. Reid, *Active Living and Mental Health: Their Relations in the Context of Life Circumstances and Determinants of Health* (Report by the Institute of Health Promotion Research, University of British Columbia for the Canadian Fitness and Lifestyle Research Institute and Health Canada, 1996); J.F. Sallis and N. Owen, *Physical Activity and Behavioral Medicine* (Thousand Oaks, CA: Sage, 1999).
24. M. Mackintosh, 'Partnership'.
25. J.M. Logsdon, 'Interests and Interdependence in the Formation of Social Problem-Solving Collaborations', *Journal of Applied Behavioral Science*, 27, 1 (1991), p.36.
26. R.M. Kanter, 'From Spare Change to Real Change: The Social Sector as Beta Site for Business Innovation', *Harvard Business Review*, 77, 3 (1999), pp.122–32.
27. See Clarke, 'Leisure and the New Managerialism'; W. Frisby, 'Broadening Perspectives on Leisure Service Management and Research: What Does Organization Theory Offer?', *Journal of Park and Recreation Administration*, 13 (1995), pp.58–72.
28. W. Frisby, S. Crawford and T. Dorer, 'Reflections on Participatory Action Research: The Case of Low-Income Women Accessing Local Physical Activity Services', *Journal of Sport Management*, 11, 1 (1997), pp.8–28.
29. Smale and Reid, 'Public Policy on Recreation and Leisure in Urban Canada'.

30. Ibid.
31. Sagawa and Segal, 'Common Interest, Common Good'.
32. Ibid., p.110.
33. See R. Copeland, W. Frisby and R. McCarville, 'Understanding the Sport Sponsorship Process from a Corporate Perspective', *Journal of Sport Management*, 10, 1 (1996), pp.32–48.
34. Kanter, 'From Spare Change to Real Change', p.124.
35. J.L. Crompton, 'Partnering with Business: What's in it for Them?', *Journal of Park and Recreation Administration*, 15, 4 (1997), pp.38–60.
36. See Crompton, 'Partnering'; and J.L. Crompton, 'Programs that Work: Forces Underlying the Emergence of Privatization in Parks and Recreation', *Journal of Park and Recreation Administration*, 16, 2 (1998), pp.88–101.
37. See Hutt, Stafford, Walker and Reingen, 'Case Study'; Sagawa and Segal, 'Common Interest, Common Good'; J. Storck and P.A. Hill, 'Knowledge Diffusion Through Strategic Communities', *Sloan Management Review*, 41, 2 (2000), pp.63–74.
38. K. Kernaghan, 'Partnership and Public Administration: Conceptual and Practical Considerations', *Canadian Public Administration*, 36, 1 (1993), pp.57–76.
39. See B. Aird, 'Corporation Puts its Marks on B.C. Basketball', *Vancouver Sun*, 11 May 1996, pp.A1 and A6; R. Goldman and S. Papson, *Nike Culture* (London: Sage, 1998).
40. Kernaghan, 'Partnership and Public Administration', p.59.
41. B. Wharf, 'Editorial Introduction: Community Development in Canada', *Community Development Journal*, 34, 4 (1999), p.267.
42. C. Oliver, 'Network Relations and Loss of Organizational Autonomy', *Human Relations*, 44, 9 (1991), p.944.
43. N.C. Roberts and R.T. Bradley, 'Stakeholder Collaboration and Innovation: A Study of Public Policy at the State Level', *Journal of Applied Behavioral Science*, 27, 2 (1991), pp.209–27.
44. B. Gray, *Collaborating: Finding Common Ground for Multiparty Problems* (San Francisco, CA: Jossey-Bass Publishers, 1989); Hardy and Phillips, 'Strategies of Engagement'.
45. C. Oliver, 'Determinants of Interorganizational Relationships: Integration and Future Directions', *Academy of Management Review*, 15, 2 (1990), pp.241–65.
46. Sagawa and Segal, 'Common Interest, Common Good', p.113
47. See Hardy and Phillips, 'Strategies of Engagement'; Mah, 'It's Final: The Café Stays, the Pool Closes'.
48. A. Hoffman, 'Women's Access to Sport and Physical Activity', *Avante*, 1, 1 (1995), pp.77–92.
49. B. Kidd, 'Confronting Inequality in Sport and Physical Activity', *Avante*, 1, 1 (1995), pp.1–19.
50. Frisby, Crawford and Dorer, 'Reflections on Participatory Action Research'; W. Frisby and J. Fenton, *Leisure Access: Enhancing Opportunities for Those Living in Poverty* (Vancouver: BC Health Research Foundation, 1998).
51. Frisby and Fenton, *Leisure Access*.
52. Ibid.
53. M. Marshall, L. Wray, P. Epstein and S. Grifel, '21st Century Community Focus: Better Results by Linking Citizens, Government, and Performance Measurement', *Public Management*, 81, 10 (1999), p.14
54. M. Mayo, 'Partnerships for Regeneration and Community Development', *Critical Social Policy*, 17, 3 (1997), pp. 3–26; B. Ettorre, 'Alliances Multiply, but Most Fail to Deliver', *Management Review*, 89, 1 (2000), p.7; Sagawa and Segal, 'Common Interest, Common Good'; W. Frisby, 'From Organizational Effectiveness to Empowerment Evaluation: A Personal Journey in Sport Management Research', paper presented at the North American Society for Sport Management Conference, Colorado Springs, 2 June 2000.
55. Frisby, 'From Organizational Effectiveness to Empowerment Evaluation'.

PART III:
THE COMMERCIALISATION OF
'AMATEUR' SPORT

7

Piercing the Veil of Amateurism: Commercialisation, Corruption and US College Sports

ELLEN J. STAUROWSKY

> The best definition of amateur is one who can get away with it and not be nicked with the goods.
>
> Grantland Rice[1]

In 1999 D. Stanley Eitzen suggested that sport presents a variety of paradoxes comprised of elements characterised as either fair or foul.[2] In the case of US college sport, the fair side can inspire people to extol the accomplishments of college kids who play for the 'love of the game', relate to shared passions for the excitement of championships and be moved by the sheer youth, beauty and excellence of the performers. All this is done, purportedly, for the education of athletes and the generation of a positive community identity around which campus constituencies rally.[3] Former United States Democratic presidential candidate Bill Bradley, who played basketball at Princeton University before becoming a Rhodes Scholar, professional athlete and politician, captures the essence of this connection between sport and the things we hold most dear when he wrote, 'In a world full of unrealized dreams and baffling entanglements, basketball seems pure' and provides a clear example of 'virtue rewarded'.[4]

However fair the perception of college sport, whatever its perceived potential to promote the virtuous, there is also ample evidence to demonstrate just how foul college sport can be. The contemporary practice of targeting 12-year-old male basketball players by college recruiters and representatives of athletic shoe companies like Nike and Adidas and viewing them as 'the best billboards money can buy' is a sobering reality that reveals the pervasive corporate quest for profit associated with US college sport.[5]

The duality posed by the fair/foul framework is reflective of the dualistic logics that are believed to shape college sport and its place within higher education in the US. Theoretically, the ideal around which college sport is built embraces the fair poles of related dualisms – amateurism, education and not-for-profit status. Conversely, the failings of college sport are typically identified as occurring at those junctures where the 'foul' poles impinge on the 'fair', when the enterprise appears too professional, too entertainment-oriented, too geared towards a profit motive.

Historically, the college sport reform movements of the past hundred years, initiated by such esteemed academic institutions as the Carnegie Foundation, the American Council on Education and the Knight Foundation shared a common assumption about the source of the problems they attempted to remedy.[6] They believed that the problems plaguing college sport arose from these impingements or ambiguities and, if reconciled, would allow the 'fair' to flourish and the 'foul' to disappear. Notably calls for intercollegiate athletic reform throughout the twentieth century have proven, for the most part, to be unsuccessful.

The most recent institutional plan for college sport reform, embodied in a 1991 report entitled *Keeping Faith With The Student-Athlete: A New Model for Intercollegiate Athletics*, outlined the necessity for a regulatory process grounded in the 'primacy of academic values' and in efforts to insure that 'those on the field are students as well as athletes'. The authors of the report rejected outright any argument that favoured a reduction or elimination of responsibilities that students are expected to assume in response to the demands of the athlete role. In their words, 'Such a scheme has nothing to do with education, the purpose for which colleges and universities exist. … American higher education has the ability to devise a better solution to the problems of intercollegiate athletics than making professionals out of the players.'[7]

The remarkable resistance college sport has shown to change suggests that the ambiguities reformers have so conscientiously attempted to rein in may, in fact, be duplicities that mask its corporate underpinnings. Just as David Andrews argues earlier in this book that, at one time, 'sport may have possessed a degree of autonomy from profit-driven rhythms and regimes' and that 'misty-eyed nostalgia exaggerates the extent of this long lost independence', the time is long since past when college sport could be thought of as educational, amateur and non-profit-oriented, if it ever was those things to begin with.[8] If the educational premise to which reformers often adhere is abandoned in favour of returning to the site of the origin of college sport in 1852, one discovers that commercialism and professionalism are the principles upon which college sport was founded. In that fateful year James Elkins, the superintendent of the Boston, Concord, and Montreal Railroad, proposed to Yale oarsman James Whiton: 'If you get up a regatta on the Lake between Yale and Harvard, I will pay all the bills.'[9] Thus, on the waters of Lake Winnipesaukee in New Hampshire an all-expense-paid eight-day excursion for the contestants, replete with abundant beverages and lavish prizes, culminated in Harvard registering the first of many sought-after victories over their future rival. As historian Ron Smith notes, 'in the years between 1852 and the initial meeting of the National Collegiate Athletic Association in 1905, the basis for the highly commercial and professional sports in colleges was established'.[10]

By conceptualising college sport as a corporate entity, governed from the outset by classic principles of advancing capitalism, the source of the perennial problems afflicting college sports, like suspect graduation rates, academic fraud, questionable admissions practices, the intrusion of agents and gambling influences and inappropriate compensation of athletes become easier to locate. In many ways, the economic evolution of college sport conforms closely to the prophetic advice of the economist John Maynard Keynes. Writing during the late 1920s and 1930s, he speculated that future generations might live in a world where everyone shared the wealth and where poverty and deprivation were non-existent. However, to achieve such an end there would need to be a span of time in which 'we must pretend to ourselves and to everyone that fair is foul and foul is fair; for foul is useful and fair is not. Avarice and usury and precaution must be our gods for a little longer still. For only they can lead us out of the tunnel of economic necessity into daylight.'[11]

The remainder of this chapter will focus on the ways in which the National Collegiate Athletic Association (NCAA), Division I conferences, institutions of higher learning and the mass media have behaved as if avarice and usury rather than student welfare were the 'gods' they revere the most in shaping big-time college sport.[12] An argument will be made that institutions of higher education, in collusion with the NCAA, have been separated from their academic moorings when it comes to big-time college sport, functioning instead as the booking agents for mass-mediated spectacle while relying on an invisible and unnamed workforce.

Piercing the Veil of Amateurism

In cases of blatant and wilful corporate wrongdoing, a judicial process occasionally used to hold decision-makers accountable for their actions is called 'piercing the corporate veil'.[13] The notion of a corporate veil derives from institutional structure. The corporation itself, as an organic structure, provides the basis for a distinction between action taken by the corporal body in contrast to actions taken by officers who work for the corporation. When a corporate veil is in place, actions emanate from a company, firm or enterprise, not an individual employee, manager, chief executive officer or even board of directors. As long as a corporate veil remains intact, the source of accountability when something goes awry is traced to the amorphous entity of the corporation rather than those most directly responsible for what has occurred. To pierce the veil is to penetrate the protective fortress afforded by the 'corporation'.

In college sport the ideology of amateurism constructs a surface reality that denies the existence of a corporate veil while at the same time serving as one. As a consequence, big-time college sport has been protected by a veil on top of a veil. Through this ideological sleight of hand the NCAA assumes an amorphous mantle, positioning itself as a hybrid education association/amateur sport governing body rather than an athletic corporation/cartel. The NCAA's veil of amateurism functions to obscure the corporate foundations at the core of college sport while simultaneously putting forward a fiction that college sport is about students and education. Piercing the amateurism veil that surrounds big-time college sport reveals a complex corporate entity in the mature stages of capitalist expansion, an entity scholar Murray Sperber so aptly calls 'College Sport Inc.'.[14]

This gap between the principles of the academy and the marketplace presents rich territory for the 'fair is foul and foul is fair' ethos of college sport to operate. Those who work within the college sport system are well aware of its hold. In a 1997 survey of college presidents, conference commissioners and athletics directors, they expressed consensus about the need for reforms designed to protect the integrity of higher education while also indicating a collective 'unwillingness to do so at the sacrifice of their financial interests'.

The seismic upheavals in Division I conference alignments during the mid-1990s are symptomatic of the pressures associated with revenue generation, the maintenance of a big-time profile and winning that takes precedence over institutional relationships among academic peers. As Eugene Trani, president of Virginia Commonwealth University (VCU), explained following the successful move on the part of the Metropolitan College Athletic Conference in 1995 to expel VCU and another institution from the conference because neither institution was situated in a prime television market, 'the athletic conferences representing members of the NCAA's Division I are aligning not around regional or institutional similarities but around the potential for earnings from contracts to televise football and men's basketball games'.[15] Efforts to federate the NCAA, with the resultant separation of Division I powers into football- and non-football-playing institutions and Division I-A and I-AA schools along with the exclusion of the 'minor' Division II and III programmes from the power structure, were driven by similar economic interests.[16] The class structure of the NCAA, which will be discussed in greater detail later in this chapter, reveals that Division I uses the lower divisions in order to sustain the veil of amateurism. Under that veil they then proceed to engage in largely unregulated business practices for the purpose of generating more revenue while regulating in turn, their workforce.

The Fiction of the 'Student-Athlete' Woven into the Veil of Amateurism

Amateurism as it is promoted and marketed so widely and effectively by the NCAA may, in fact, be one of the most illusory corporate veils ever conceived. As represented by the NCAA, amateurism contradicts the very essence of what a corporation is and does. Consider the principle of amateurism (Article 2.9) as published in the *1998-1999 NCAA Manual*: 'Student-athletes shall be amateur in an intercollegiate sport, and their participation should be motivated primarily by education. ... Student participation in intercollegiate athletics is an avocation, and student-athletes should be protected from exploitation by professional and commercial enterprises.'[17]

Theoretically, based on this definition, corporate America is where big business, not big-time college sport, occurs. Corporate America is where the exploitative practices of professionalism and commercialism take root. Corporate America is where people are paid a real wage for performing serious work, not where student-athletes receive scholarships for playing inconsequential games. Corporate America is where people with real jobs, vocations as it were, devote their time, not where college athletes with avocational preferences wile away their youth. Corporate America is where professional sport is housed, not where sport that teaches life's lessons is fostered. Corporate America is where profit motives, not educational motives, have primacy. In summary, corporate America is clearly no place for amateurs. In turn, college sport is no place for corporate America and clearly no place for the professionalism and commercialism that goes along with it. Or so it seems.

A closer examination of the context out of which the 'amateur' language so often associated with college sport emerges, however, reveals a great deal about the underlying corporate and professional foundations in which intercollegiate athletics is grounded. The genesis of the term 'student-athlete' confirms this point. Contrary to the popular supposition that the expression 'student-athlete' is an extension or permutation on the Greek ideal of mind/body integration, or in other words just another way of saying 'scholar-athlete', the term is a legal invention. It was created in 1953 as a tool for obfuscating the employee-employer relationship that had been established when athletic scholarships (or grants-in-aid) were awarded to college athletes for their services on the playing field or court.

Until 1953 a college athlete was eligible for financial assistance on the basis of academic performance and financial need. This significant shift in the criteria used in the awarding of financial aid from one based on academic performance and need to one based on athletic performance reshaped the relationship between college athletes and educational institutions. Athletic administrators engaged in the discussion were aware that they were potentially establishing a compensation scheme for services rendered, as reflected in their characterisation of the grant-in-aid system as 'pay for play'. As the director of athletics at Arizona State, Donald R. VanPatten, pointed out at that time to Walter Byers, the first full time executive director of the NCAA, 'I think this is wrong. Regardless of what anyone says this is a contract and it is a two way street.'[18]

Following the NCAA's decision to award athletic scholarships, courts and labour commissions heard a series of worker compensation cases wherein athletes who had lost their scholarships after being injured 'on the job' sought benefits available to other classes of workers. To undermine the argument that college athletes were paid and were therefore employees, Walter Byers recalls that 'We crafted the term *student-athlete*, and soon it was embedded in all NCAA rules and interpretations as a mandated substitute for such words as players and athletes. We told college publicists to speak of "college teams", not football or basketball "clubs", a word common to the pros.'[19]

Similar sophistry is found in the language used to define those things that the association is most intent on prohibiting, namely 'professionals', 'pay' and even the appearance of athletes being 'special' in relationship to other students on their campuses. Scrutiny of its by-laws and principles reveals that the NCAA and member institutions are not fundamentally opposed to professionalism but to professionalism they cannot regulate. This is reflected in the substance of the bylaws pertaining to amateurism. For example, in by-law 12.02.3, a 'professional athlete' is 'one who receives any kind of payment, directly or indirectly, for athletics participation *except* as permitted by the *governing legislation of the Association*'. Pay, as defined in by-law 12.02.2, is the 'receipt of funds, awards or benefits *not permitted* by the governing legislation of the Association for participation in athletics'.[20] (Emphases have been added.)

This qualification in the association's feigned opposition to things professional is evidenced in cases involving seven male college basketball players (Erick Barkley and others) who were suspended during the 1999–2000 season when it was determined they had received 'improper benefits' in the form of financial assistance from a variety of benefactors (ranging in amounts from $1,200 to $20,000).[21] The issue was not that these young men received benefits or even the timing of the acquisition of the benefits. The issue, as defined by the NCAA, was that these young men received benefits over which the NCAA did not have control.

The issue of control is clearly demonstrated in the construction of the 'athletic scholarship' or 'grant-in-aid'. Those who argue that the NCAA is not a cartel and that its practices do not result in the exploitation of an unrecognised class of workers often observe that an athletic scholarship is sufficient compensation for student-athletes because it represents a 'free ride'. As the Knight Commission wrote in 1991: 'Scholarship athletes are already paid in the most meaningful way possible: with a free education. The idea of intercollegiate athletics is that the teams represent their institutions as true members of the student body, not as hired hands.'[22] In the spring of 2000, Kenneth Shropshire, a member of the NCAA's Working Group to Study Basketball Issues and professor at the Wharton School of Business, expressed the viewpoint that college athletes who believed they should be paid should 'go to the professionals'.[23]

These sentiments would offer engaging rhetoric but for the dizzying logic at the root of the argument that scholarship funds serve as 'free' education and that athletes are 'true members' of the student body. The very fact that the scholarship is perceived to be adequate compensation by itself demonstrates that the awarders understand that a quid pro quo exists.[24] Allen Sack, professor of sport management at the University of New Haven, argues that the athletic scholarship is the 'linchpin' that allows institutions of higher education, under the guise of amateurism, to manipulate a workforce in service to its own interests while violating the rights of college athletes.[25]

The strength of Sack's argument is reinforced when the irreconcilable contradictions that circulate within the concept of the athletic scholarship are examined. In a very real sense, the purpose of a scholarship within academe is to facilitate intellectual scholarship rather than athletic participation or revenue generation. To accept that an athletics scholarship is appropriate and ample 'compensation' for playing a sport, one must ask the question – compensation for what? For being a student, a scholar, a pupil? Or for being an athlete, a potential draft pick, a good revenue producer?

The answer to this question is based on the standard terms and conditions of athletic scholarships, which vest in coaches the right to review the eligibility of an athlete for a scholarship on a yearly basis, much like supervisors of at-will employees. In effect, the athlete serves at the will of the coach, being subject to termination for any or no reason at all. Thus athletes, whether encumbered by the demands of their education at the expense of their athletic performance, a bad season or an injury, are not guaranteed a 'free education' but are required to earn their keep each year or be gone from the programme and, inevitably, gone from the institution.

Thus, the depiction of athletes as 'true' or 'normal' members of the student body is suspect. Those familiar with higher education have a refined sense that there really is no such thing as a generic student body. 'The student body' is as much an illusion as 'the student-athlete'. Student bodies consist of an array of formations and subcultures created by the converging forces of intellectual ability, academic majors, career interests, class status, socio-economic backgrounds, lifestyles and student status (full-time, part-time). As economist Andrew Zimbalist and politician Tom McMillan have noted, the term 'student-athlete' is a complete anomaly on college campuses.[26] 'If student athletes were normal university students, then either the term would not be necessary or it would be joined by other terms like student-musician, student-artist, or student-engineer.'[27] Tellingly, the one category of student that does approximate the 'student-athlete' is the 'student-worker' established by federal work-study programmes.

Despite the lack of an extant generic student body, the NCAA relies on it to connect student-athletes to their academic institutions. To pause and peer too deeply into this relationship between student-athlete and student body is to begin uncovering the fallacy that student-athletes are 'just like' other students. Presumably, what qualifies student-athletes for membership in the student body is not their athleticism but their role as students. And yet, what distinguishes them from other students is neither their athleticism per se nor the fact that their 'play' might be construed as 'work' (other students work as well). What disqualifies them as integral members of 'the student body' is their special status as 'student-athletes', a status conferred or imposed on them by, and achieved through, the regulatory practices of the NCAA.

The 'Student-Athlete' Welfare State

To confront the illusion of the 'student-athlete' leads to an understanding that higher educational institutions, in collusion with the NCAA, participate in the regulation of a class of workers that simply cannot be found anywhere else within the ranks of the student population. The fate of no other class of students rests on their performance in mass-mediated public spectacle with the legislated expectation that their performance will result in the generation of significant revenue for their institution while parallel legislation regulates the lives of scholarship athletes before, during, and after their college careers.

When the litany of regulations governing college athletes is interpreted from the standpoint of the 'workplace' rather than the 'school environment', the rights of athletes to exert their own will and to act in accordance with their own volition are severely impaired. These impediments to college athlete freedom can be conceptualised as occurring at four separate junctures. At pre-entry, before an athlete applies to college, s/he is confronted with freshman academic requirements monitored by the association's Initial Eligibility Clearinghouse along with recruiting regulations, the National Letter of Intent, the limit set on number of scholarships available and prohibitions with regard to what kind of payment athletes may receive while still in youth or high-school sports. Within what will become their existing workplace, the college sport environment, the conditions for retaining a scholarship and the regulation of their 'work week', which is technically set at 20 hours in season, along with the regulation of their earning power, serve to restrict their prospects, opportunities and even behavioural options. For athletes who desire to move upward into professional sport, or laterally to another institution, obstacles are presented in the form of regulations applying to professional drafts, agents, special benefits and the process of transferring to another school.

These practices, steeped as they are in the verbiage of 'student welfare', delimit the lives of athletes academically, socially and financially and create in the process something akin to a 'student-athlete welfare state'. As one example, the falsity of the claim that athletes are treated like all other students is seen in the impact the National Letter of Intent (NLI) and transfer rules have on restricting the athlete's opportunity to review other situations. The National Letter of Intent obliges an athlete to attend one institution after reaching an agreement regarding an athletics scholarship for one year and the subsequent agreement of all other institutions not to recruit that student after the signing has occurred. In turn, the athlete 'who does not fulfil his/her one academic year at the institution with which he/she signed would have to serve two years of residence at any other institution that participates in the NLI program and lose two seasons of competition to that institution'.[28] An athlete is then prohibited from enquiring about transferring to another institution unless and until officials at their current institution give them permission to do so. At a superficial level, the NLI is presented as a safeguard for athletes against excessive and aggressive recruiting, but in reality it intentionally hampers or discourages athletes from exploring programmes that might be more favourable to their interests by publicly monitoring their activities and, in some cases, withholding from them permission to pursue such a course of action. As a result, athletes assume substantial risk when they attempt to consider alternatives, potentially attracting the disfavour of their present coach and jeopardising their prospects for retaining their scholarship as a result of the inquiry.[29]

The NCAA's intrusion into the earning power of athletes is seen in the funds created to distribute back to them roughly $25 million out of $287 million in a convoluted and fragmented process that has been likened to a 'money-laundering' scheme that sustains a 'plantation system'.[30] It is not a coincidence that in the wake of the establishment of the $1 billion television deal for the men's basketball championship (and other championship events) in 1988, the NCAA developed the Special Assistance Fund, the Catastrophic Insurance Program, the Academic Enhancement Fund and the Exceptional Student-Athlete Disability Insurance Fund, all funds that mete out 'benefits' to the athletes whose performances constitute the product marketed by the NCAA and Division I conferences.

With a $10 million appropriation in 1991, the NCAA started the Special Assistance Fund in response to well-publicised stories of athletes who were receiving a 'free education' and yet did not have the financial wherewithal to purchase a suit of clothes, to attend a family funeral or to go home for a holiday because the conditions of athletic scholarships dictated that the athlete earn only a limited amount of money in a given fiscal year and not work for a wage during the academic year, a circumstance that changed only this year. Notably, not all college athletes are eligible to receive benefits from the fund – only those from Division I who are 'Pell Grant eligible or who have demonstrated financial need'.[31]

In effect, only the poorest Division I athletes are eligible for the fund. The restrictions on summer earnings and other work opportunities outside their sport during the school year virtually guarantee that economically disadvantaged athletes will remain economically disadvantaged throughout the duration of their college athletic careers. Thus, the 'special assistance' available to athletes in the form of a $500 clothes allowance, course supplies and emergency expenses render athletes almost totally economically dependent on the system while being subject, at the same time, to termination at the will of the coach who assesses their value to the system.[32]

Offering assistance to 'needy student-athletes' while insuring that those same individuals remain dependent is also at the heart of the insurance programmes developed by the association. Because the association cannot provide worker's compensation benefits to athletes without an admission that an employee/employer relationship exists, the Catastrophic Injury Insurance Program covers medical expenses associated with serious injuries that demand long-term medical attention after other insurance policy benefits are exhausted. This coverage does not replace the benefits available through worker's compensation but coverage for catastrophic injuries, which are provided to athletes across all divisions, defuses the number of cases that would be brought forward to challenge the failure of college sport to recognise their 'revenue-producing' athletes as workers.[33]

The Exceptional Student-Athlete Disability Insurance Program was designed in 1990 to offer coverage to those athletes who are in a position to protect against future earnings losses as professional athletes, as determined by the programme administrator. As the 'value' of the 'student-athlete' continues to rise exponentially with each succeeding billion-dollar and multi-billion-dollar television deal (in 1988 the NCAA's deal with CBS was worth $1 billion; that contract was renegotiated for $6 billion, effective in August 2002), the association searches for ever more creative ways to mediate the relationship between athletes and the corporate enterprise of college sport without having to afford athletes rights as workers. Thus the NCAA has been careful not to fund the insurance policy for professional-calibre athletes, but has brokered it. The association initiated the programme through American Specialty Underwriters and then arranged for athletes approved for the programme to qualify automatically for loans through the Mercantile Bank in Kansas City.[34] If this kind of deal had been brokered for an athlete by an agent or booster, the act would have been illegal. Because the NCAA developed the deal, the act is legal and the athlete remains amateur.

Whereas the previous three funds parcel out payments or loans in the form of 'benefits' to select athletes, the Academic Enhancement Program Fund was created in response to charges that big-time college programmes were not consistently graduating those 'amateur' athletes who were receiving ample compensation to play in exchange for a 'free education'. According to the 1999 NCAA Graduation-Rates Summary, 58 per cent of scholarship athletes who enrolled in 1992 completed their degrees within six years, a rate that has been relatively steady over an eight-year period and is on a par with or slightly lower than graduation rates for all students nationwide.[35] However, in the sports of football, men's basketball and women's basketball, the rate of graduation was the lowest recorded since 1985. In an analysis of the relationship between graduation rates and revenue generation conducted by researchers at the University of Arkansas-Fayetteville, an inverse relationship was found: in programmes with higher rates of revenue generation, lower graduation rates are evidenced.[36]

In combination with an NCAA mandate that all Division I programmes offer academic support and tutoring services to athletes (by-law 16.3.1), the Academic Enhancement Fund Program dispenses $50,000 per year to each Division I athletic programme.[37] The result has been the ignition of yet another athletic department 'cottage industry'.[38] According to the National Association of Academic Advisors for Athletics (N4A), there were fewer than ten full-time academic advisors providing services specifically to college athletes existed in 1975. As of 1997, membership in N4A had reached over 500 dues-paying members representing all 50 states, with most of this growth happening in the 1990s.[39]

Across Division I a growing number of examples of this kind of 'special' investment in athletes has emerged. At Arizona State University, 'all 500 student-athletes are assigned to coordinators' after it was reported that only 17 per cent of football players graduated in 1991.[40] For the academic year 1999–2000 the University of Nebraska allocated $900,000 for academic programmes and support services for athletes, while the University of Oklahoma spent about $1 million, with approximately $200,000 of that being used for tutorial services.[41]

Although these overtures generate positive publicity, the fact remains that the industry is such that these services are necessary to create an impression that the academic aspects of the student experience are being maintained, while also raising questions as to how successful other undergraduates would be if afforded similar individualised support. It is the case that even as these programmes have been implemented throughout Division I with enormous investments of capital and human resources, as seen in the allocation of roughly six to ten academic counsellors and undisclosed numbers of tutors for 800 athletes on average, academic fraud scandals have erupted at the University of Tennessee, the University of Minnesota, the University of Nebraska and even the usually sacrosanct University of Notre Dame, during the same period.[42]

Despite the NCAA's contention that these funds and programmes are motivated by benevolence, the truth of the matter is that these funds demonstrate that the association is operating a welfare state for college athletes, designed to sate the most immediate financial needs of students and public relations crises of the industry while keeping athletes beholden to the very system for which they generate revenue. Replicating other exploitative class systems, athletes in the highly stratified world of college sport are by far the least powerful. Although not exclusively so, the athletes affected are often black and poor, and they are the ones who bear the greatest burden when not selected for a professional career if they also fail to earn a degree. Such is the price and the power of the veil of amateurism.

The Corporate Power Structure behind the Veil of Amateurism

In response to criticisms that the practices associated with intercollegiate athletics are petty, absurd, overly intrusive or unfair, NCAA officials are quick to point out that these practices are the manifestation of deliberations made by representatives of higher education. The explanation that the association acts merely on the wishes of its voluntary membership base, comprised of 1,257 dues-paying entities in all, with 972 colleges and universities along with 91 conferences having voting privileges, implies that there is equity across the membership with regard to voicing perspectives and having those perspectives heard.[43] An examination of the NCAA's decision-making structure reveals, however, a closed system that reinforces the power of certain constituencies while marginalising the influence of the membership at large. Particularly in the aftermath of the 1996 restructuring process, in which the NCAA adopted a federated organisational structure, the decision-making power for the association has been localised primarily with the representatives of eight Division I conferences.[44] As a result, the association does not actually represent the views or perspectives of the higher education community. Instead, it reflects the preferences, predispositions and predilections of those Division I presidents, conference commissioners and athletics directors who are most occupied and preoccupied with the business of college sport.

Power and prominence within the association is directly related to the involvement an institution has in the generation of revenue through its athletics programmes or their affiliations through conferences with institutions that are similarly positioned and inclined. Thus, although Division I institutions comprise only 33 per cent of the overall membership, they nevertheless wield the greatest amount of power in the area of decision-making by virtue of their revenue-producing capacity. From a financial perspective, of the $287-million-dollar operating budget for the 1999–2000 fiscal year, approximately $181 million was distributed in accordance with established revenue-distribution formulas to Division I institutions (318). The percentage of revenue distributed to the 'lower' divisions is legislated as well, with Division II (261 institutions) allotted a guarantee of 4.37 per cent each year while Division III with 393 institutions receives a 3.18 per cent guarantee. This translates into less than 8 per cent of the NCAA operating budget being distributed to over 67 per cent of the membership.[45]

However, the presence of the lower divisions lends credibility to the claims of amateurism and commitment to education espoused by the association. In point of fact, the small Division III institutions provide the seed of truth that has allowed the veil of amateurism to exist. One might argue that the Division III schools have been bought off much too cheaply if viewed from that perspective. The philosophical relationship between divisions sheds light on the commercial interests that drive the association. As John Biddiscombe, chair of the Division III Management Council, observed before the January 2000 NCAA Convention, 'Since the NCAA restructuring, the Division III Convention agenda has become more educational in nature, with a focus on student-athlete welfare.'[46] Student-athlete welfare takes on an entirely different meaning within a philosophical context that embraces the idea that athletics is for athletes and not spectators and the athletics department is expected to be funded in a manner consistent with all other departments on campus. Not a word about revenue generation can be found in the Division III philosophy and yet the substance of the Division I philosophy statement deals with those matters almost exclusively after a perfunctory nod to 'high standards of academic quality'.[47] At a philosophical level, Division I establishes national excellence as the goal of intercollegiate athletics and a dual objective to serve the college community and general public while specifically promoting 'spectator-oriented sports', namely the income-producing sports of football and basketball with the expressed intent of paying for programmes through the revenue generated.[48] One need not search any further than the philosophy statement to understand that the business of Division I athletics programmes is the promotion of mass entertainment and spectacle, not student education.

The financial picture of college sport can be examined from a couple of different perspectives to gain an appreciation of the magnitude of the corporate enterprise under consideration. On the one hand, it would appear that college sport is a relative lightweight when compared to other professional sport entities. Whereas *Street & Smith's SportsBusiness Journal* projected the telecast rights for the 'Big Four' professional leagues (the National Football League, Major League Baseball, the National Basketball Association and National Hockey League) at $8.87 billion and collegiate telecasts at $987 million in December 1999, the revised television deal with the NCAA has clearly put college sport into the billion-dollar range, certainly short of the 'Big Four' but definitely a player nonetheless.[49] Further, the overture from International Sports and Leisure (ISL), the second largest sport marketing firm in the world in 1999, to promote a playoff for college football to the tune of $3 billion, may be a portent of deals to come despite the fact that it was declined. ISL was undeterred in its pursuit of the college sports market, coming back in the year 2000 to outbid incumbent sales agency Host Communications, Inc. to pick up the rights to market NCAA sponsorships for $800–$850 million until 2013.[50]

College sport finances are baffling, however. The revenues are substantial and yet the industry cries poor, not unlike its 'professional' major-league counterparts. According to updated data from the NCAA, fewer than 80 Division I institutions operate their programmes at a profit.[51] This figure is open to dispute, depending on whether each programme ignores administrative expenses involved in the operation of their programme or includes them within their financial accounting procedure. In 1996, economist Richard Sheehan applied this analysis to Division IA football schools in the early 1990s and determined that of the 85 programmes reporting that they made money, only 54 could have reported the same result if they had included administrative expenses.[52]

Trying to get a handle on college sport profit/loss figures becomes even more problematic when three other factors are considered. First, college sport as an industry has not been held to a strict standard of accountability with regard to financial reporting and is as prone, it would appear, to 'creative accounting' as are professional franchises. As the National Association of College and University Business Officers noted in 1993, there are areas of indirect expenditure associated with athletics that often are not accounted for within athletic department reports.[53] In a recent discussion of how the newfound wealth of the NCAA will be distributed, recognition was given to the fact that 'even when funds are earmarked, some NCAA constituent groups are not certain the money is well-spent'. There is also a 'trust gap', meaning that there is a perception that certain decision-makers will use targeted NCAA payments for 'other parts of the athletics budget and not what is intended'.[54]

Second, as Art Padilla and David Baumer pointed out in their economic analysis of college sport, 'some institutions with [athletic] profits may attempt to spend most of the revenue generated'.[55] This appears to be a contradiction unless considered within the context of the spending ethic fostered by the 'non-profit' status of the industry. Despite the much-touted contributions programmes like Notre Dame's make to their institutions' general funds (approximately $5 million in 1999), the many programmes that might otherwise report a profit spend the money on what have been described as excesses.

Third, for all the conversation that surrounds the financial circumstances of the NCAA, it is largely a conversation prompted by the revenue generated from the sport of basketball only. The association does not realise any funding from the college football bowl games, and the revenue distributed to Division I members is nearly as much as that which is generated by basketball. For the 1998–9 fiscal year, post-season football bowl games accounted for close to $142 million distributed to Division I-A and I-AA institutions and conferences.[56] Not surprisingly, the football powers have threatened on more than one occasion to leave the association and strike out on their own.

Over the years the veil of amateurism has obfuscated the need for consistent and accurate methods of financial reporting while allowing the evolution of a college sport system of haves and have-nots to emerge, not just between big-time programmes and athletes, Division I programmes and Division III programmes, but between Division I-A and I-AA institutions as well. Predictably, the elite programmes have been getting richer while the smaller programmes struggle mightily and often unsuccessfully under the pressure to keep up.[57] Within this framework, the notion that a common ideology of amateurism can be uniformly applied to all schools across all divisions is frankly naive. As Richard Sheehan noted after ranking the University of Michigan, the University of Florida and the University of Notre Dame among the 25 most valuable athletic franchises, 'the Gators – and the Wolverines and Fighting Irish – are the financial equals of virtually any pro team.'[58]

Conclusion

The imperfections of the human condition guarantee that there will be shortfalls between expressed ideals and the efforts made by people and organisations to live up to them. Systemic and individual tolerance or intolerance for these shortfalls is dependent on their frequency and severity.

Breaking points occur when the symptoms of serious shortfalls, such as corruption and hypocrisy, become rampant and remain unchecked. The tenuous balance that institutions have attempted to strike between the profit-seeking practices of highly commercialised, professionalised sport and the educational objectives of higher learning might be thought of as an attempt to avert such a breaking point by minimising the shortfall. However, the promotion of professionalised sport intentionally misrepresented as amateurism is a shortfall wholly unbefitting of academic institutions because of the 'fair is foul, foul is fair' ethos required to sustain the charade.

With ever-increasing levels of commercialisation, there is growing evidence that the strain of maintaining the veil of amateurism is producing fissures in the foundation of higher education, signalling serious structural damage due to the stresses of big-time college sport. A poignant lesson illustrating how much the economic interests of college sport are in conflict with the ideals of higher education is found in the story of Indiana University and its former basketball coach, Bob Knight.[59]

Knight has had a long history of abuse towards players, officials, fans and the media.[60] One of the most recent incidents occurred in the spring of 2000 when Neil Reed, a former player, reported he had been physically attacked by Knight during a practice and the university initially failed to fully investigate Reed's allegation. Only after a media outlet produced physical evidence in the form of a videotape of the incident did the university consider a serious review of the charge. In the highly publicised investigation, conducted by the board of trustees, it was revealed that Knight had also physically threatened an administrative assistant in the athletics department and the athletics director, Knight's immediate supervisor. For an employee of an academic institution, this kind of charge ordinarily warrants dismissal, particularly given Knight's history of physical violence. The university, however, chose to give Knight another chance. Indiana University President Myles Brand instituted a zero-tolerance policy, which would subject Knight to instant dismissal if he were to slip up again. In September 2000 Knight got into an altercation with a freshman student and on 10 September he was fired from his job.

Several aspects of the Knight story are germane to this discussion. The university's tolerance for the manner in which students, athletes, fans and officials were treated by a professional member of the staff is quite telling. Professors and coaches, as educators working within higher education, are charged with a sacred duty to protect the welfare of their students. The notion that an employee of a university community could exhibit a history of this kind of behaviour over a span of three decades was a gross violation of what the academy is supposed to stand for.

One of the most revealing of the outcomes from the Knight story is what happened to Murray Sperber, a professor at the university who has written critically about intercollegiate athletics. Following the Reed allegations, Sperber was sought out by the press for his perspective. As a result of observing that the university simply would not have tolerated this kind of abuse if a member of the faculty had treated a student in such a manner, Sperber received threats of physical harm resulting in his announcement that he would take an unpaid leave of absence in the fall of 2000 because he feared for the safety of his family, his teaching assistant and his students. This case should serve as a signal that the breaking point has arrived. The experience of Sperber is similar to that of other faculty who have attempted to take on the corrupting influence of athletics on college campuses. Linda Bensel-Myers, head of the writing programme at the University of Tennessee, has also received threats from fans and was given reason to believe that her office had been broken into because of her attempts to persuade the university to act on academic fraud perpetrated through the athletic academic support unit for men's athletics. Faculty members such as Jan Kemp from the University of Georgia have actually been dismissed for broaching the topic of athletic corruption on their campuses, while other faculty remain silent, intimidated due to fear of reprisal.[61] There can be no doubt that higher education is in not just a compromised but an irredeemable position when abusive coaches inspire mild rebuke and little disfavour while faculty seeking to protect and defend the integrity of higher education become the targets of hate.

Despite the record of failed reforms, there are those who argue that reform must happen. The Drake Group, a newly formed collective of college sport reformers who are faculty members, has advocated the eradication of the term 'student-athlete' from the language of sport as a small but necessary step in piercing the veil of amateurism and defusing the power of the fictions that form its fabric. In concert with calling athletes what they are, the group's platform recommends the elimination of athletic scholarships, which would convert athletics participation back to an avocation rather than a vocation.[62]

For the growing number of critics of college sport agitating for substantive change rather than mere tinkering, there is a perception that if one concedes that big-time college sport is professional, there is an obligation to professionalise the big-time football and basketball programmes on college campuses, separating them from the amateur programmes. My colleague Allen Sack and I have argued that there are mechanisms already in place within the economic and organisational structure of universities, referred to as auxiliary services or businesses unrelated to the central educational mission of the institution, that exist and prosper. Traditional versions of auxiliary services include bookstores, conference centres, summer camp programmes and campus television and radio stations. The designation of athletics departments as auxiliary services is not an unheard-of concept. At Penn State, the athletic programme is so designated although it continues to operate, even with that designation, as an 'amateur' enterprise. What is distinctive in this plan is that the big-time programmes would actually run as businesses with the remaining athletic teams operating as amateur, educational enterprises.[63]

One of the central purposes of the academy is to serve as the 'moral antennae' of our society. As long as the veil of amateurism is permitted to remain in place, institutions of higher education in the United States that participate in the NCAA at any level will be tainted by its practices and inhibited in asserting their moral authority with any genuine force because of their collusive participation in the maintenance of college sport in its present state. It is widely acknowledged that the intercollegiate athletic community has a 'trust' problem. In a culture where fair is foul and foul is fair, where usury and avarice have visited abuses upon athletes and faculty, how could trust survive? William D. Dowling, Professor of English at Rutgers University, has eloquently argued that the corrupting force of college sport on college campuses is a cancer that must be eradicated if the soul of the academy is to be restored.[64] His observation delivers us to the heart of the issue, because institutions of higher education do not need either amateurism or athletics for that matter. What they absolutely do need, however, is their integrity. So long as the veil of amateurism remains intact, there remains a fundamental disconnection between higher education and its soul. Let the restoration, and the redemption that would come from it, begin.

NOTES

1. C. Fountain, *Sportswriter: The Life and Times of Grantland Rice* (New York: Oxford University Press, 1993), p.128.
2. D. Stanley Eitzen, *Fair and Foul: Beyond the Myths and Paradoxes of Sport* (Lanham, MD: Rowman & Littlefield, 1999), pp.105–30.
3. Thad Williamson, 'Bad As They Want To Be', *The Nation*, 10 August 1998, pp.38–42; John Feinstein, *A March to Madness: The View From the Floor in the Atlantic Coast Conference* (Boston, MA.: Back Bay Books, Little Brown & Company, 1999); Jack McCallum, 'Sweet 'n' Low', *Sports Illustrated*, 22 March 1999.
4. Bill Bradley, *Values of the Game* (New York: Artisan, 1998), p.4.
5. Dan Wetzel and Don Yeager, *Sole Influence: Basketball, Corporate Greed, and the Corruption of America's Youth* (New York: Warner Books, 2000), p.214; 'Recruiters Bend Rules to Target Younger Athletes', *USA Today*, 12 November 1999, p.A14; Darcy Frey, *The Last Shot: City Streets, Basketball Dreams* (New York: Touchstone Books, 1994).
6. Donald Chu, Jeffrey O. Segrave and Beverly J. Becker, *Sport and Higher Education* (Champaign, IL: Human Kinetics, 1985), pp.36–56; William C. Friday and Theodore M. Hesburgh, *Keeping Faith With the Student-Athlete: A New Model for Intercollegiate Athletics* (Charlotte, NC: Knight Foundation Commission on Intercollegiate Athletics); Allen L. Sack and Ellen J. Staurowsky, *College Athletes For Hire: The Evolution and Legacy of the NCAA Amateur Myth* (Westport, CT: Praeger, 1998), pp.11–50; Murray Sperber, 'In Praise of 'Student-Athletes': The NCAA Is Haunted By Its Past', *Chronicle of Higher Education*, Opinion & Arts, 8 January 1999; Murray

Sperber, *Onward to Victory: The Crises That Shaped College Sports* (New York: Henry Holt, 1998).

7. Friday and Hesburgh, *Keeping Faith With The Student-Athlete*, p.11.

8. See David Andrews' essay in this collection.

9. Ronald A. Smith, *Sports and Freedom: The Rise of Big-Time College Athletics* (New York: Oxford University Press, 1988), p.3.

10. Ibid., p.4.

11. Ernst F. Schumacher, *Small is Beautiful: Economics as if People Mattered* (San Bernardino, CA: Borgo Press, 1991), p.22.

12. Many people are not aware that within the Division I philosophy statement emphasis is placed on sponsoring 'at the highest feasible level of intercollegiate competition one or both of the traditional spectator-oriented, income-producing sports of football and basketball'. This can be found in Vanessa L. Abell (ed.), *The 1998–1999 Division I NCAA Manual* (Overland Park, KS: NCAA, 1998), p.342 (The NCAA has since moved to Indianapolis, IN.)

13. The concept of a corporate veil is described in Henry Campbell Black (author) with Joseph R. Nolan and Jacqueline M. Nolan-Haley (eds), *Black's Law Dictionary*, 6th edn (St Paul, MN: West Group, 1990), pp.1147–8. The complexities of piercing a corporate veil and the benefits of doing so are elaborated in the story of the Buffalo Creek Disaster. See Gerald M. Stern, *The Buffalo Creek Disaster: How the Survivors of One of the Worst Disasters in Coal-Mining History Brought Suit Against the Coal Company–And Won* (New York, NY: Vintage Books, 1977).

14. Murray Sperber, *'College Sports Inc.: The Athletic Department vs. The University'*(New York: Henry Holt, 1990).

15. Eugene P. Trani, 'The Distorted Landscape of Intercollegiate Sports', *Chronicle of Higher Education*, 17 March 1995, p.B1–B2.

16. *The NCAA News, 91st Convention Issue*, 'An Association in Transition: New-Look NCAA To Emerge With New Structure', 13 January 1997, p.1.

17. Abell, *The NCAA Manual*, p.9.

18. Sack and Staurowsky, *College Athletes for Hire*, p.83; Allen L. Sack and Ellen J. Staurowsky, 'A Rejoinder to Timothy Smith, Intercollegiate Athletics in the Next Millennium: A Framework for Evaluating Proposals', *Marquette Sports Law Journal*, Fall 1999, pp.117–22.

19. Walter Byers (with Charles Hammer), *Unsportsmanlike Conduct: Exploiting College Athletes* (Ann Arbor, MI: University of Michigan Press, 1996), p.69.

20. Abell, *The NCAA Manual*, p.71.

21. Welch Suggs, 'NCAA Faces Wave of Criticism Over Crackdown on Payments to Players While They Were in High School', *Chronicle of Higher Education*, 17 March 2000, A5S.

22. Friday and Hesburgh, *Keeping Faith With The Student-Athlete*, p.11.

23. Jay Weiner, 'Putting on a Happy Face: Strip Away The Hoopla of the NCAA Tournament and You'll Find College Basketball Struggling To Find Ways for Big Business and Academic to Coexist', *Minneapolis Star Tribune*, 15 March 2000, p.1C.

24. Ellen J. Staurowsky, 'Another Perspective on the Payment of Student-Athlete Debate', *NCAA News*, 28 June 1995, pp.4–5.

25. Sack and Staurowsky, *College Athletes For Hire*, pp.1–8.

26. Andrew Zimbalist, *Unpaid Professionals: Commercialism and Conflict in Big-Time College Sports* (Princeton, NJ: Princeton University Press, 1999); Tom McMillen (with Paul Coggins), *Out of Bounds: How the American Sports Establishment is Being Driven By Greed and Hypocrisy – and What Needs to be Done* (New York, NY: Simon & Schuster, 1992).

27. Zimbalist, *Unpaid Professionals*, p.37.

28. Quoted from the National Letter of Intent. Copies can be obtained from the National Letter of Intent office at 2201 Richard Arrington, Jr. Blvd. N., Birmingham, AL 35203-1103. Materials can also be accessed via the Internet at www.national_letter.org.

29. For details regarding regulations governing transfer, see Abell, *The 1998–1999 Division I NCAA Manual*, pp.91–8.

30. Walter Byers, *Unpaid Professionals*.

31. Allocations for this and the other funds discussed were confirmed through an examination of materials on the NCAA website (http://www.ncaa.org) such as the 1999–2000 NCAA Revenue Distribution Plan as well as sources such as Gary Brown, 'The Money Pie: NCAA Leaders work to balance campus Association-wide needs', *The NCAA News*, 3 July 2000, News & Features, p.1, and specific materials pertaining to each of the funds. Further, I spoke with Beth Alstadt, an NCAA legislative services assistant, on 27 June 2000. For a history of the Special Assistance

Fund, see Josheph M. Camille, 'Special Questions May Result From Special Assistance Fund', *NCAA News*, 1 September 1997, and 'Athletes Gain Greater Access To Assistance Fund', *NCAA News*, 13 May 1996.

32. Ibid.
33. Ibid.
34. See 'Exceptional Student-Athlete Disability Insurance Program Summary', online at http://www.ncaa.org/insurance/exceptional.html.
35. See '1999 NCAA Graduation-Rates Summary – Division I', online at http://www.ncaa.org/grad_rates/.
36. Erik Lords, 'Colleges' Basketball Success Relates Inversely to Graduation Rates, Study Finds', *Chronicle of Higher Education*, 3 April 2000, p.A53.
37. See http://www.ncaa.org/enhancement/.
38. The reference to the concept of the athletic academic support arm of intercollegiate athletics creating 'another' cottage industry is based on the observation that athletics has an entire infrastructure that supports its enterprise. Other examples of the impact increased professionalisation of intercollegiate athletics has had on staffing include athletic training/sports medicine, strength training, marketing, media relations, specialisation and growth of coaching staff and compliance officers. Several years ago, there was discussion that higher education was prone to a condition referred to as 'administrative bloat'. It appears that this same condition either applies to college sport or may have got its origins in college sport.
39. See 'History of N4A' at http://www.aad.berkeley.edu/UGA/OED/ASC/N4A.html. This is the website for the National Association of Academic Advisors for Athletics.
40. Paola Boivin, 'ASU Emphasizes Speed, Eligibility', *Arizona Republic*, 20 October 1999, p.C1.
41. Erik Brady, 'College Help To Make The Grade With Athletes, Not For Them', *USA Today*, 19 October 1999, p.3C.
42. Erik Lords and Welch Suggs, 'NCAA Places Notre Dame and 2 Other Universities on Probation', *Chronicle of Higher Education*, 14 January 2000, p.A54; Welch Suggs, 'University of Minnesota Ousts 4 Top Athletics Officials in Academic-Fraud Scandal', *Chronicle of Higher Education*, 3 December 1999, p.A52; Welch Suggs, 'University of Tennessee Restructures Tutoring Program for Athletes', *Chronicle of Higher Education*, 14 June 2000, p.A51; Welch Suggs, 'Scandals Force Colleges To Reassess Roles of Academic Advisors for Athletes', *Chronicle of Higher Education*, 3 December 1999, p.A51.
43. See 'NCAA Membership Link' at http://www.ncaa.org/membership for details.
44. There will be some who will argue that the association is representative of all members because they 'approved' of the restructuring plan. There has long been a major power struggle within the NCAA. The activities of the association are overseen by an executive committee. Out of a 20-member committee, 12 represent Division I, two represent Division II and two represent Division III. The remaining four members are ex officio (the executive director being one and the chairs of the three divisional management councils filling the other three slots).
45. Analysis based on the breakdown of membership by division and financial data reported in the 1999–2000 budget. The most recent figures for this are found in Brown, 'The Money Pie', and the 1999–2000 NCAA Revenue Distribution Plan as reported at http://www.ncaa.org/financial/revenue_distribution/.
46. 'Diversity, Amateurism Among Discussion Topics In Division III', *NCAA News*, 3 January 2000.
47. See philosophy statement for Division I and III in Abell, *The NCAA Manual*.
48. Ibid.
49. David Broughton, Jennifer Lee and Ross Nethery, 'The Question: How Big is the US Sports Industry. The Answer: $213 Billion', *Street & Smith's SportsBusiness Journal*, 20–6 December 1999, pp.23–30.
50. Andy Bernstein and Langdon Brockinton, 'ISL In Line For NCAA Sponsorship Rights', *Street & Smith's SportsBusiness Journal*, 12–18 June 2000, pp.1, 51. ISL subsequently went bankrupt.
51. Brown, 'The Money Pie'.
52. Richard G. Sheehan, *Keeping Score: The Economics of Big-Time Sports* (South Bend, IN: Diamond Communications, 1996), p.277.
53. National Association of College and University Business Officers, *The Financial Management of Intercollegiate Athletics Programs* (Washington, DC: NACUBO, 1993).
54. Brown, 'The Money Pie'.
55. Arthur Padilla and David Baumer, 'Big-Time College Sports: Management and Economic Issues', *Journal of Sport & Social Issues*, May 1994, pp.123–43.

56. See 'Financial Results of 1998–1999 NCAA Certified Postseason Football Bowl Games', online at http://www.ncaa.org/financial/bowl_distribution.html.
57. Trani, 'The Distorted Landscape of Intercollegiate Sports'; Welch Suggs, 'Football's Have-Nots Contemplate Their Place In The NCAA', *Chronicle of Higher Education*, 30 June 2000, p.A47; 'Sidelines: Survey Shows SEC Has Highest-Paid Commissioner and Finds Widening Gap Between Conference "Haves" and "Have-Nots"', *Chronicle of Higher Education*, 7 January 2000, p.A54.
58. Sheehan, *Keeping Score,* p.316.
59. Phil Berger, *Knight Fall: Bobby Knight – The Truth Behind America's Most Controversial Coach* (New York: Pinnacle Books, 2000); Mike Tharp, 'Knight Goes, But Not Gently', *US News & World Report*, 25 September 2000; Welch Suggs, 'Ouster at Indiana', *Chronicle of Higher Education*, 22 September 2000; Murray Sperber, 'My Life and Times with Bob Knight', *Chronicle of Higher Education*, 26 May 2000; Alexander Wolf, 'Knight Fall: Bob Knight's Controversial 29-year Reign at Indiana Came to an Ironic End When He Gave a Student an Unmannerly Lesson in Manners', *Sports Illustrated*, 18 September 2000.
60. See http://members.aol.com/rmkgeneral for a list of Knight's outbursts.
61. Sidelines, 'Georgia Dogged By Concerns About Academic Standards', *Chronicle of Higher Education*, 7 August 1991, p.A51.
62. Tom Witosky, 'New Group Will Press For Reform', *DesMoines Register*, 23 October 1999, p.35; Jay Weiner, 'College Athlete Reformers Find It's a Daunting Task', *Minneapolis Star Tribune*, 23 October 1999; Erik Lords, 'Professors' Group Seeks to Reform College Sports', *Chronicle of Higher Education*, 7 April 2000, p.A53
63. Sack and Staurowsky, *College Athletes for Hire*, pp.129–39.
64. William C. Dowling, 'To Cleanse Colleges of Sports Corruption End Recruiting Based on Physical Skills', *Chronicle of Higher Education*, 9 July 1999, pp.B9–10. This article presents an overview of Dowling's position on intercollegiate athletes. The specific remarks noted in the text were voiced at the March 2000 meeting of the Drake Group in DesMoines, IA.

8

Strategic Responses to Institutional Pressures for Commercialisation: A Case Study of an English Rugby Union Club

DANNY O'BRIEN and TREVOR SLACK

Until recently, rugby union football was one of the few international sports that had withstood commercial pressures and strictly adhered to the ideals of amateurism. The roots of the game's amateur principles can be traced back to 1886, when the Rugby Football Union (RFU), the governing body of the sport in England, enacted legislation that forbade payment of any kind to players for loss of earnings incurred through playing the game. The International Rugby Football Board (IRFB), also established in 1886, similarly ruled that the principles of amateur competition were to be applied worldwide. For nearly 100 years, this amateur ideal remained central to the sport.

However, in the 1970s and 1980s, mounting commercial pressures began to challenge the dominance of amateurism as a way of organising. These pressures arose from the increasing global televising of the game and the institution of a quadrennial Rugby World Cup in 1987. The game became so popular as a result of these initiatives that in June 1995 the South African, New Zealand and Australian Rugby Unions (SANZAR Ltd) and the media conglomerate News Corporation signed an unprecedented US$555 television contract. Significantly, the Australian Rugby Union (ARU) passed on 95 per cent of its share of the revenue from this contract to its national team players. When the South African and New Zealand Rugby Unions followed this example, pressure increased on the IRFB to abandon its amateur stance.

On 25 August 1995, the IRFB held a meeting in Paris that led to the announcement that the amateur principles upon which the game had been founded were to be repealed. In what became known as the Paris Declaration, the IRFB stated that participation in the game of rugby union football should be bound by the principles of an 'open game', in which players could receive financial remuneration for playing.[1] This announcement was greeted with astonishment in England, where amateurism remained firmly ingrained and the game was largely insulated from the growing commercial pressures in other parts of the world. At the time of the Paris Declaration, elite level rugby union in England was organised around a multi-divisional club structure. All clubs were operated on strictly amateur values, with volunteers fulfilling all administrative and technical roles. As many of the top clubs were established in the late nineteenth century, these amateur values and ways of operating had, over time, become heavily entrenched and taken for granted. When values, such as amateurism, and their related operating procedures are validated through the force of habit, history and tradition, they become unquestioningly accepted and thereby institutionalised.[2]

However, the Paris Declaration caused unprecedented turmoil in the institutional environment of senior English rugby union. The institutional environment encompasses social forces such as norms, standards and expectations common to all an organisation's relevant constituents.[3] Pressures from the institutional environment influence managers to incorporate institutionally favoured characteristics in the hope that their organisation will be judged as appropriate and legitimate, hence improving their access to valuable resources. In senior English rugby union, the Paris Declaration led to unprecedented institutional pressures for a more commercially based form of organisation.

How clubs strategically responded to these pressures was crucial to their survival in the new commercial era. As clubs increasingly chose to commercialise, they were faced with more than simply paying players. There were other more complex factors to be dealt with in the changes that these formerly amateur, volunteer-led organisations were confronting. Indeed, with long histories of organisation and competition founded upon amateur values and volunteer decision-making, many clubs had parochial support communities that went back several generations. This meant that, due to the unknown prospect that commercialisation represented, some organisational actors had a vested interest in resisting these institutional pressures. Using a case study approach, this chapter provides an empirical analysis of the roles of organisational actors and the strategic behaviours they employed in responding to institutional pressures to adopt a more commercial form of organisation.

Theoretical Background

A basic tenet of institutional theory is that organisations are pressured to increase their probability of survival by conforming to institutionally prescribed expectations of appropriate organisational arrangements.[4] In an effort to increase legitimacy and secure access to resources, decision-makers structure organisational arrangements and coordinate behaviours to conform to these pressures.[5] The institutional environment encompasses social forces such as norms, standards and expectations common to all of an organisation's relevant constituents.[6] Institutional constituents include interest groups, regulatory bodies, suppliers, state and professional associations, customers and the general public.[7]

Some theorists have criticised the institutional perspective for its determinism and assumptions of organisational passivity.[8] In response to this criticism, Oliver offered a typology of strategic responses that organisations might engage in as a result of institutional pressures.[9] These strategies ranged from passive conformity to compromise, avoidance, defiance and finally, proactive manipulation. She hypothesised that certain institutional antecedents could be used to predict the occurrence of the proposed strategies and the degree of organisational conformity or resistance to institutional pressures. These factors included: the *cause* of the institutional pressures for conformity; the *constituents* affected by these pressures; the actual *content* of the pressures; the inherent institutional *control* mechanisms; and finally, the environmental *context* within which the pressures become manifest.

Oliver's approach was particularly appropriate for this study. As discussed earlier, the institutional environment of senior English rugby union became increasingly turbulent following the Paris Declaration. As a consequence, pressure grew for clubs to adopt a more commercially oriented form of organisation. Analysing the salient features of the pressures themselves can help develop a deeper understanding of the rationale underpinning organisational actors' strategic responses to them. Each of the institutional antecedents proposed by Oliver and the related strategic responses are discussed below.

Cause is concerned with the underlying rationale, expectations or intended objectives of the institutional pressures for conformity. Oliver[10] suggested that the factors leading external actors to exert pressures for conformity are essentially founded upon the pursuit of social and/or economic fitness. Thus, the lower the degree of social legitimacy or economic gain forecast to be attainable from conformity to institutional pressures, the greater the likelihood of organisational resistance to them. Here, actors employ strategies and tactics designed to avoid, defy or manipulate the pressures exerted on them. However, legitimacy may be perceived to be enhanced by conformity. In this case, organisational decision-makers are pragmatic in acquiescing to pressures for conformity as they employ tactics such as compliance or imitation.

Institutional *constituents* may impose a variety of laws, regulations and normative expectations that effectively define an organisation's social reality.[11] With a variety of institutional constituents, organisations confront pressures from multiple and sometimes conflicting sources. Oliver referred to this situation as multiplicity, 'the degree of multiple, conflicting constituent expectations exerted on an organisation'.[12] Bartunek proposed that when institutional pressures are exerted from multiple sources, change is effected through a dialectical process among constituents.[13] Her contention was that old and new ways of understanding interact, finally resulting in a synthesis of interests. In Oliver's terms, it would be expected that in such situations, compromise strategies would prevail with tactics that balance or pacify the concerns of institutional constituents.[14]

Oliver posited that two dimensions of the *content* of institutional pressures help predict the likelihood of organisational resistance. The first is related to the consistency of organisational goals with institutional pressures; and the second pertains to the degree of discretionary constraint that compliance imposes on the organisation. Organisations are more likely to resist institutional pressures if conformity carries with it requirements or norms that are inconsistent with organisational goals. Therefore, when consistency between conformity and organisational goals is low, defiance and manipulation strategies are likely. When there is moderate consistency, organisations will be more willing to employ compromise and avoidance strategies; and finally, only when contextual pressures or expectations are accordant with internal organisational goals, are acquiescent strategies more probable.

Oliver also suggested that the likelihood of resistance to institutional pressures is heightened when conformity impedes an organisation's decision-making autonomy. As such, the level of resistance within an organisation to institutional pressures for conformity will vary in accordance with its associated loss of independence in decision-making. Alternatively, when compliance to institutional pressures involves little or no constraints on organisational decision-making, the employment of acquiescent strategies is likely.

Two singular processes constitute institutional *control*: legal coercion and voluntary diffusion. Both processes pertain to how institutional pressures are imposed on organisations or the mechanisms through which institutional rules are administered.[15] When the law mandates compliance to institutional pressures, the penalties for non-compliant strategies may be punitive and rigidly enforced, making non-compliance an unlikely option. Thus, when legal coercion is high, acquiescent strategies will best advance organisational interests. When sanctions for nonconformity are more modest, organisations will be more inclined to seek concessions on the extent and/or temporal scale of compliance. When the degree of voluntary diffusion of an organisational practice in an institutional environment is high, organisations will be likely to succumb to pressures to adopt these practices. Conversely, under conditions of only moderate or low levels of diffusion, organisations will tend to be more sceptical and therefore hesitant to conform, particularly when values and practices have not been institutionally validated through extensive mimicry.[16]

The last of Oliver's predictors pertains to the environmental *context* within which institutional pressures are exerted. She hypothesised that two significant contextual dimensions affect organisations' conformity or resistance to institutional demands. The first is environmental uncertainty; the second is the level of interconnectedness between organisations in an institutional environment.

The uncertainty that often characterises institutional environments demonstrates that they are not always coherent or uniform.[17] Indeed, Scott argued that institutional forces alone do not influence organisational action, but a variety of market-led and other exogenous forces 'compete for the loyalties of any organisation'.[18] Similarly, Oliver noted that in periods of high competition, task environment pressures might take precedence over institutional pressures.[19]

In addition to the level of environmental uncertainty, Oliver contended that strategic activity is affected by the level of interconnectedness between organisations in an institutional context.[20] Miner, Amburgey and Stearns proposed that one way organisations strategically respond to environmental uncertainty is to create 'resource buffers' through the establishment of inter-organisational linkages.[21] They contended that these linkages, particularly in periods of significant organisational change, provide crucial resources that create a 'transformational shield' that reduces the risk of organisational failure.

Further to the notion of inter-organisational linkages as resource buffers, theorists have cited the interconnectedness of institutional environments as facilitating the voluntary diffusion of norms, values and collective information.[22] Oliver contended that in highly fragmented, loosely coupled institutional environments, the likelihood of resistance to institutional pressures for conformity increases.[23] However, high interdependence among organisational units may also lead to the employment of resistant strategies as organisations negotiate the conditions of exchange.[24] When this negotiation involves a loss of discretionary power, decision-makers may attempt to decouple intra-organisational processes from the influence of external relationships through compromise and avoidance strategies. Conversely, these conditions of high organisational interconnectedness may also actually increase pressures for organisational conformity.[25] Acquiescent strategies may be employed as the strategies of other organisations provide a benchmark for a focal organisation to measure performance.

The central message of Oliver's work is that organisational responses to institutional processes cannot be theoretically predefined as either passive or active, conforming or resistant.[26] She called for a less deterministic approach that focused on the predictive characteristics of the pressures being exerted. Thus, the implication is that conformity to institutional processes is neither inevitable nor necessarily essential to organisational survival. Moreover, as institutional environments are not always uniformly coherent, the pressures inherent to them may be prone to shift.[27] In these periods of uncertainty, Goodrick and Salancik suggested that organisational vested interests may frame strategic choices.[28]

Inherent in Oliver's arguments is the fact that habitually followed and taken-for-granted norms do indeed impact strategic decisions in organisations.[29] However, as uncertainty is common in institutional environments, decision-makers also make rational, pragmatic decisions based on organisational interests to either accept or resist institutional pressure for conformity. Therefore, what is *im*plicit in this perspective is that strategic responses to diverse institutional pressures are less likely to be singular isolated decisions, but will more often involve a crucial temporal dimension that operates through different organisational levels. One way of uncovering how this process becomes manifest in an empirical setting is to examine one organisation's strategic responses to the institutional processes taking place in its field. Indeed, Dacin argued that 'local level analyses offer fine-grained insights not available at the population level and allow for a potential examination of the extent to which institutional and competitive forces drive selection at multiple levels of analysis'.[30] Our focus here, therefore, is on a 'fine-grained analysis' of the institutional factors that influenced the extent to which members of a senior English rugby union club conformed to or resisted institutional pressures for commercialisation.

Method

The club chosen as the focus of this case study, Maclean[31] Rugby Union Football Club (RUFC), was founded in 1885. This meant that when the IRFB declared the game 'open' in August 1995, Maclean had 110 years of organisation, competition and culture based on amateur values. As a consequence, its 600 members formed an extremely parochial community. Amateur values were heavily institutionalised in this community through not only the club's playing history, but also its structures, rites, rituals, myths and culture.

Both primary and secondary data were collected in order to construct the case. Primary data came from 23 interviews conducted over a three-year period from November 1996 to December 1999. Interviews were carried out with individuals who represented the respective commercial and volunteer/amateur interests inherent in the club and its institutional environment.

Interview questions were guided by Oliver's typology of strategic responses to institutional pressures and centred around five key areas: (1) why the club was being pressured to conform to institutional rules or expectations (cause); (2) who was exerting institutional pressures on the club (constituents); (3) to what norms or requirements was the club being pressured to conform (content); (4) how or by what means were the pressures being exerted (control); and (5) what was the environmental context within which the institutional pressures were imposed (context).[32] Collection of secondary data was also ongoing throughout the period of the investigation and consisted of press coverage from local and national newspapers; the club's website; past and present game-day programmes; and informal discussions with club members, players and officials.

Primary and secondary data were scanned and categorised according to codes that were based on Oliver's typology of strategic responses. The results of this case study and a discussion of the pertinent theoretical issues are presented in the ensuing Results and Discussion section.

Results and Discussion

Despite the SANZAR-News Corporation deal announced in June 1995, the amateur ethos of rugby union remained strongly institutionalised in England.[33] This meant that the institutional context for Maclean RUFC remained extremely stable. Indeed, most RFU and club administrators in England dismissed the deal as merely an aberration to the amateur status quo.[34] However, three senior members of the Maclean RUFC management committee foresaw that the deal could eventually lead to the commercialisation of the world game. The members of this small coalition were local professionals and former players for Maclean, or 'the Kings', as supporters knew the club. As a result, they were well respected for their knowledge of the game and dedication to the club. The coalition believed that the eventual commercialisation of rugby union in England would increase demands for financial efficiency and accountability, thus necessitating major structural and strategic changes to the club.

Overcoming Paradigm Stasis through Agency

In July 1995 the coalition began private discussions on a plan to rationalise the club's unwieldy volunteer committees, believing that a more commercially focused operation would require more centralised decision-making structures. However, given the institutionalised nature of the amateur ethos, it recognised that overly ambitious attempts at strategic or structural change would be met with strong resistance. So the coalition embarked on a carefully planned agenda of proposals that it introduced to the rest of the management committee in a piecemeal fashion. As one coalition member explained,

> It was change by stealth. We had it in our minds what we wanted to do. We were trying to bring along acceptance of streamlining from *within* the committee. But we would just put one contentious issue on the table at a time, as opposed to hitting them with it all at once. ... It wasn't easy because people who'd been doing a job for 20 years or whatever and had always done it that way were feeling pushed out. But what they were doing just wasn't the way forward any more.

Although amateur values and elaborate volunteer committee-based structures remained heavily institutionalised in the club, the coalition set about the task of reshaping these values. Specifically, it sought to deinstitutionalise[35] the amateur content of members' normative expectations by manipulating the structures that represented them, the volunteer committees.

Despite the SANZAR-News Corporation deal and fundamental shifts evolving in Maclean's institutional environment, the deeply entrenched nature of the amateur ethos mired the club in inertial forces, or 'paradigm stasis'.[36] However, the Paris Declaration, and the RFU's subsequent acceptance of it, vindicated the views held by the coalition, which began more openly to discuss the possibility of the club's eventual commercialisation. Crucially, within two months of the Paris Declaration, despite the RFU's imposition of a moratorium on change, five senior clubs had been restructured as commercial enterprises and had signed top players to lucrative, multi-year contracts. Clubs like Maclean RUFC that, due to paradigm stasis, were slower to react to fundamental changes in their institutional environment, continued to have players 'poached' by the clubs that had commercialised. Indeed, by March 1996 the coalition's intensive lobbying of management committee members had created a receptivity to the idea that if Maclean was to stay among the country's elite clubs, it would also have to adopt a more commercial form of operation and employ professional players. However, commercialisation would involve far more than a decision to pay players. It also involved organisational restructuring and strategic planning as to how the club would raise crucial financial resources. Underpinning these issues, however, was the task of deinstitutionalising amateurism and galvanising the support of the management committee and club membership for change.

A major source of organisational resistance to change, as Greenwood and Hinings pointed out, derives from the normative embeddedness of an organisation within its institutional context.[37] However, as the RFU had failed to impose sanctions on clubs that defied its one-year moratorium on commercialisation, its legitimacy as an effective mechanism of institutional control was weakened. The resultant multiplicity of pressures increased uncertainty in Maclean's institutional environment. The certainty of the club's institutional context prior to the Paris Declaration was therefore fragmented by the unprecedented events that followed it, and this created the potential for extensive organisational change.

Influencing Turkeys to Vote for Christmas

The continued deinstitutionalisation of the club's amateur ethos was hastened by the RFU's inability to state unequivocally its position on the issue of commercialisation, let alone to recommend strategic guidelines to clubs that chose to pay players. The first clubs to commercialise therefore enlisted the financial help of wealthy benefactors. These benefactors used the resulting 'discretion', as Goodrick and Salancik described such periods of uncertainty, to 'pursue their particularistic and strategic interests'.[38] As uncertainty is a potent force that encourages imitation,[39] the coalition mounted its own search for a benefactor. Significantly, this search was carried out *before* the coalition had formally approached the management committee for a vote on commercialisation. This strategic decision by the coalition involved controlling information in order to decrease the multiplicity of pressures exerted by constituents opposed to this move. By employing what Oliver (1991) referred to as 'influence tactics', the coalition hoped to delegitimise the club's institutionalised amateur practices by creating a cogent scheme for commercialisation. However, the search for a benefactor initially yielded little result until ironically, in May 1996, one coalition member was contacted by David Hole,[40] a sports promoter and part-owner of a European media conglomerate, Continental Media Associates (CMA). Hole proposed that CMA would finance Maclean's transition by effectively buying the club and appointing a board of directors to replace the volunteer management committee. Though the coalition accepted that the club needed CMA's financial resources, when the content of institutional pressures imposes discretionary constraints on an organisation in this way, the likely organisational response will be one of resistance.[41]

Predictably, the coalition refused Hole's original proposal, knowing that such an obvious loss of organisational discretion would be unacceptable to the management committee. As one coalition member suggested, 'turkeys aren't going to vote for Christmas!' Consequently, the coalition sought a compromise deal with CMA that would provide access to its resources, but also leave the club some modicum of autonomy. Clearly, both parties needed the involvement of the other, while neither wished to cede control of the relationship. For CMA, and Hole in particular, the interest shown in Maclean was strictly commercial as it provided an opportunity to enter a burgeoning professional sport at 'ground level'.

After two-and-a-half months of clandestine negotiation, the outline of a deal was finally agreed. However, supporting Oliver's contention that organisations may use cooptation tactics to lessen institutional opposition,[42] in the renegotiated deal, a new company called Maclean Rugby was formed, ostensibly as a 50–50 partnership between Maclean RUFC and CMA. The board of Maclean Rugby would consist of three representatives from CMA and three elected members from Maclean RUFC, one of whom would have chairmanship of the board. Crucially, however, a newly appointed chief executive, who would be one of CMA's three board members, would have the deciding vote. In return, CMA would contribute between £300,000 and £400,000 per year over five years to finance the club. Although under the terms of the agreement the new company would be a 50–50 partnership, CMA was clearly the dominant partner as it held the casting vote in board decisions. These controlling tactics employed by CMA were to prove pivotal in the long term.

In July 1996, the coalition presented the proposed deal to the management committee. With task environment pressures high and the beginning of the season one month away, uncertainty within the club had soared. Although the proposal's inherent loss of privilege for committee members raised inertial pressures, the ramifications of the decision before the committee were clear. As one committee member described,

> One of the things we had to do was vote ourselves out of office. There was no way we could embrace this commercial era, go into a 50–50 partnership with [CMA] and still retain our management committee and the structures underneath it. So the big decision we had before us before we went to the membership was that we had to be prepared to vote ourselves out of office. … A lot of people were reluctant to do that. People who had given a lot of service to the club. … I wouldn't say we did it happily, but we did vote unanimously to do it.

By agreeing to the terms of the partnership, Maclean RUFC would become almost completely dependent on the financial support of CMA to maintain legitimacy in the new era. When dependence is high on a constituent imposing institutional pressures in this way, Oliver hypothesised that acquiescent strategies are a likely option.[43] However, many directors held that they could coopt, rather than conform completely, to the controlling tactics of CMA.

Following the unanimous management committee vote in favour of the deal, the proposal was presented to the membership. Of the club's 600 members, over 400 attended the special general meeting. All but one of the members in attendance voted in favour of the deal. The membership's support for change was somewhat surprising given the vociferous elements that had earlier opposed commercialisation. However, numerous clubs had followed the lead of the high-profile clubs. When the strategies of powerful actors in a field become legitimised through intensive mimicry and diffusion in this way, isomorphic pressures increase for the adoption of these particular strategies.[44] Moreover, with the RFU's inability to enforce its moratorium, the field's traditional mechanism of institutional control, legal coercion, was substantially weakened. Thus, the coalition and Hole were strategic in taking advantage of this uncertainty in the institutional order that they sought to alter. As Hoffman so accurately posited, although entrepreneurs cannot construct the institutional order, 'they can influence its ultimate design through participation in the institutional negotiation process'.[45] This combination of an uncertain institutional context and the persuasive vision provided by the coalition, and particularly, by Hole, convinced members that decreased organisational discretion was a price worth paying if it meant legitimacy and 'catching up with the money clubs'.

Strategic Responses and Institutional Consequences

Following the membership vote, the process of restructuring Maclean RUFC to create Maclean Rugby began. A senior management committee member explained the initial impact of commercialisation on the club. He noted:

> I think it's fair to say that when the 'old' club members saw the opportunity with [CMA], they didn't really understand what they were letting themselves in for. ... The changes that had to be made were considerable. Not just on the playing side, but in the whole infrastructure of the club. It moved from a small venture run by volunteers to a commercial business run by professionals.

As part of the content of the institutional pressures for commercialisation, this imposition of discretional constraints on club members proved extremely difficult for volunteers to accept. Nevertheless, compliance with institutional pressures often involves an admission of limited autonomy and the requisite loss of organisational freedom.[46] This became apparent when, to enhance communication between Maclean RUFC members (the 'old' club) and the partnership board, a streamlining of the club's elaborate committee structures was undertaken. Thus, although Maclean RUFC still maintained its own management committee, it was reduced from 24 members to only six, with just three of these, the original coalition, on the partnership board. In addition, when CMA employed professional administrators and support staff, many of the subcommittees and volunteer positions were made obsolete.

Thibault, Slack and Hinings argued that when professionals are employed by a formerly volunteer organisation, because of their training they 'pose a challenge to the indispensable nature of the volunteer in running some of the central tasks of the organisation'.[47] Such an erosion of decision-making power for volunteers has been highlighted as problematic in the professionalisation of formerly volunteer sport organisations.[48] In this case, the erosion of organisational discretion prompted the rise of inertial forces and, subsequently, members' resistance to the controlling tactics of CMA.

Clearly, the basis of CMA's power was its material resources, specifically money. However, determinants of power may also include normative resources such as control of information, media and communication networks.[49] In December 1996 and January 1997, a number of Maclean RUFC directors who felt marginalised by the new regime 'leaked' sensitive club information to local reporters. These attacking tactics resulted in several damning articles appearing in Maclean's regional newspapers. The articles were about issues such as the club being served writs over non-payment of bills to local merchants,[50] disclosure of Hole's past legal problems relating to company ownership, chronically late payment of wages to administrative and technical staff and CMA's 'secret talks' to build a leisure complex on the club's home ground.

At this time, CMA had invested more than double the first year's promised £400,000. Thus, in February 1997 Hole moved that he should replace the chairman of the board of directors, who was from the amateur club, and should also be given the casting vote in board decisions. He was forthright in explaining his reasoning; as he explained, 'I want to keep a closer eye on my money. … All the detrimental publicity will stop and there'll be no more leaks to the press for starters.' Predictably, with the casting vote at that time resting with the CMA-employed chief executive, Hole's proposals were passed. In rationalising the move, CMA's group solicitor explained that 'the structure of the partnership was drawn up specifically to allow Mr [Hole] to take an active interest'. Clearly, CMA had anticipated resistance from the former regime and had strategically structured the partnership so as to manipulate this resistance if and when it materialised. Therefore, Hole's 'active interest', or what Oliver referred to as controlling tactics,[51] enabled him to overpower and dominate the sources of institutional resistance.

Hole leveraged this dominance in May 1997, when he proposed to the board that CMA would only continue its higher-than-agreed level of investment if its stake in Maclean Rugby was increased from 50 per cent to 90 per cent. Given CMA's control of the decision-making process, the proposal was passed by the board of directors. Clearly, both Maclean RUFC and CMA aspired to on-field success, and both parties saw continued investment in technical staff and club infrastructure as crucial to achieving this. With this level of consistency in organisational goals, the employment of acquiescent strategies in response to institutional pressures is likely.[52]

Thus, although their organisational discretion was to be even further eroded, the directors from the members' club complied with Hole's proposal.

Interestingly, however, Oliver also hypothesised that resistance is likely when conformity imposes a high degree of discretional constraints on an organisation.[53] Although the potential for multiple strategic responses is left unaddressed by Oliver,[54] in this study, different strategic responses emanated from different parts of the organisation. Significantly, the three Maclean RUFC directors who acquiesced to CMA's restructured arrangement were the same coalition members that had initially devised the partnership with CMA. Since their election to the board, resistance to their pro-CMA decisions had grown, and the membership became increasingly opposed to ceding ever more control to professional staff. However, the only form of resistance left to the disenfranchised and powerless members was non-attendance at Maclean's home games.

By the end of the 1996–97 season, the average weekly attendance was only 2,300 people, a figure insufficient to support the players' yearly wage bill of £1.3m. As a consequence, Maclean Rugby returned an overall loss in excess of £500,000 on the season. The following season proved even more financially difficult for Maclean Rugby as it returned a deficit of £1.8m. Despite the team's unprecedented on-field success, the average weekly attendance in 1997–8 was still only 2,400 people, far short of the club's projected figure of between 5,000 and 6,000. So although it retained only 10 per cent control of the partnership, the membership was, as the prime consumer of Maclean Rugby's products, the club's most important institutional constituent. Certainly, the collective impact of the members 'staying away in droves' was a defiance of CMA's controlling tactics. One member of the club's professional staff, who was forced to resign after prolonged non-payment of wages, pointed out CMA's failure to recognise the importance of gaining the support and social approbation of its key institutional constituent. She explained that

> At the end of the day, there is nobody bigger than the club. You have to remember that support. You can put in as much money as you want, but if you don't have the support of the fans and the money coming in through the gate, then eventually, you run out of money and you don't *have* a club. It surprised me that they [CMA] never seemed to quite grasp that.

Far from acceding to the interests of members, in May 1998 CMA employed avoidance tactics and coerced Maclean Borough Council to approve plans to build corporate hospitality facilities at the club. By creating a revenue stream from corporate hospitality and reducing the extent to which it relied on gate receipts, CMA sought to decrease uncertainty by buffering itself from the membership's desire for increased control. Employing buffering tactics, as Oliver suggested, 'may serve the organisation's interests, especially in terms of maintaining autonomy, minimising external intervention, and maximising efficiency'.[55]

To continue the club's high standard of technical performance in the 1998–9 season, it was therefore imperative for CMA to secure more reliable access to financial resources. Indeed, as CMA had invested heavily in players thought capable of performing at this level, strategically, corporate hospitality was seen as a 'transformational shield'[56] to insulate the club from the probability of failure. Hole warned that if borough council approval was not forthcoming within an eight-week period, he would move the club elsewhere. As he stated, CMA 'has already put £2.5m into the club. That has gone, and we shall never see that again. … It is time for the council to show us that they really want us to stay in [Maclean].' Though building plans were approved in the specified eight-week period, Hole continued to pressure institutional constituents to show more support for the club or risk losing it to another city. With the antagonistic relationship he had developed with the local press, his demands received widespread coverage.

Compounding the problems Maclean Rugby had in establishing institutional support, in July 1998, it was revealed that Hole had grave legal problems that had resulted in authorities freezing his assets in the United Kingdom. Despite initially denying he was in legal and financial difficulty, Hole was indeed the defendant in two long-running high-profile court cases. As a result his assets, including CMA and Maclean Rugby, were indefinitely frozen. With the 1998–99 season about to commence, and Hole's case the object of great media interest, potential sponsors became hesitant to associate their respective corporate images with Maclean Rugby. With its legitimacy and transformational shield shattered, the continued poor levels of attendance and decreased revenue from sponsorship meant that the club was unable to meet its monthly wage bill of £150,000. However, when questioned on his legal problems, Hole responded by vehemently denouncing Maclean's local businesses for their lack of support.

With the club's ongoing financial difficulties, players and administrative staff became frustrated at the pay disputes that resurfaced every month. Several, therefore, accepted offers from Premiership competitors. In light of this exodus of key staff and players, the partnership between Maclean RUFC and CMA grew increasingly acrimonious throughout 1998. In October that year a consortium of members mounted a community-based campaign to buy CMA's 90 per cent stake. The consortium aimed to oust CMA from Maclean. One consortium member explained that, by doing so, Maclean Rugby would 'become a club again' and be returned to the control of its members.

After one of the cases pending against Hole was finally resolved in mid-January 1999, divestiture of the ongoing expense of Maclean Rugby became a priority for CMA. Hole offered the consortium CMA's 90 per cent stake in the club for the sum of £1, provided the consortium took responsibility for the club's debts that totalled £500,000. Three consortium members offered to contribute £250,000, and approached local businesses to raise the other £250,000. However, with the club's poor public image, there was an indifferent response and the plan was aborted. Importantly however, the consortium used its £250,000 to start a 'development fund', which was used for the upkeep of basic club infrastructure. Therefore, constituents' dependency for resources shifted away from CMA and towards the consortium, which further eroded CMA's legitimacy in the partnership arrangement.

The Strategic Non-compliance to Institutional Pressures

In April 1999, Harold Horsley and Michael Groom, who represented a London-based company, Waterton Boyd International (WBI),[57] made contact with three disenfranchised former members of the amateur club's management committee.[58] These individuals subsequently arranged for Horsley to meet privately with Hole, with a view to buying CMA's 90 per cent stake in Maclean Rugby. By approaching Hole through former committee members, Horsley convinced Hole that the membership approved the transfer. However, the members who introduced Horsley to Hole decided to keep their activities confidential, and thus, failed to inform the membership of the impending change in the club's major partner.

When the sale was completed, Horsley immediately installed himself as chief executive of Maclean Rugby. Subsequently, rather than have members' democratically elect their representatives onto the partnership board of directors as was the norm, he gave directorships to the three members who had earlier introduced him to Hole. Thus, without the knowledge of the club's membership, WBI bought CMA's 90 per cent stake for the sum of £1, and completely replaced the leadership of Maclean Rugby. As Hole had before them, Horsley and Groom had anticipated potential resistance to the sale and had coopted individual club members who had a vested interest in seeking the privilege of board directorship. This 'opportunistic use of institutional links'[59] effectively neutralised institutional opposition from Maclean RUFC. Ultimately however, it did little to enhance the legitimacy of WBI as the club's major partner.

Indeed, the manipulative tactics used by WBI caused great consternation among members. Despite Horsley's hand-picked members' 'representatives' on the partnership board, the membership still held annual elections for its management committee. Consequently, the three founding members of the consortium that initiated the development fund in January 1999 were elected. The members that Horsley had coopted onto the partnership board were ostracised by the membership for what constituents saw as their duplicity in allowing WBI to assume its 90 per cent stake in the partnership. The membership refused to recognise the legitimacy of the new board members, who were seen as ambitious and self-serving. Instead, its election of the consortium, whose militancy and aim of returning the club to members' control was well known, was a clear act of defiance. What further eroded the new leadership's legitimacy was the fact that, even with the change in ownership, staff were still not paid on time, and sometimes were not paid at all. As was the case when CMA was the major partner, this lack of consistency in the normative expectations between the club's professional leadership and its institutional constituents caused increasing social pressure for change. Consequently, in June and again in July 1999, the members' management committee unanimously recommended that Horsley sell WBI's share in the club to a consortium member who had offered him £100,000. Despite having paid only £1 for WBI's 90 per cent stake merely three months earlier, Horsley refused on both occasions.

The crisis deepened in mid-August 1999, when, as the minor partner in Maclean Rugby, Maclean RUFC was served notice by the United Kingdom Department of Customs and Excise that charges were pending against Michael Groom for cocaine smuggling. As the major shareholder of WBI, Groom was also the major shareholder of Maclean Rugby. The notice stipulated that Maclean RUFC, as the 10 per cent partner of Maclean Rugby, was barred from 'disposing of, or diminishing the value of, [Groom's] assets'. Clearly, these revelations explained why Horsley had repeatedly declined to sell WBI's 90 per cent stake in the club. Supporting Dacin's point that institutional forces can sometimes accelerate the effects of other political and economic pressures,[60] WBI's further loss of legitimacy resulted in sponsors cancelling agreements for the forthcoming season. Thus, what little remaining confidence that existed in the club's professional leadership evaporated, and eight of Maclean Rugby's administrative staff resigned when their demands for payment of wages were not met.

Moreover, as WBI had consistently failed to support the club financially, constituents had again been forced to decrease their dependence on the 90 per cent partner. In turn, some of the club's basic financial commitments, such as the wages of one of its two remaining administrators, were being met from the development fund. When the degree of external dependence on pressuring constituents is lessened, Oliver suggested that the likelihood of organisational resistance to institutional pressures increases.[61] Accordingly, the consortium intensified its political activity by pressuring WBI to forfeit its 90 per cent stake and return decision-making autonomy to the membership.

By the end of September 1999, despite the charges pending against him, Groom had been given permission from Customs and Excise to sell WBI's 90 per cent stake in Maclean Rugby. However, rather than offering WBI's stake to the consortium, in early October 1999, Groom announced that he had sold it to a Second Division club. For this to happen, however, the sale had to be sanctioned by England Rugby Partnership (ERP), a coalition of the RFU, English Second Division Rugby (ESDR) and the body that, since commercialisation, had become the primary mechanism of institutional control in the First Division, English First Division Rugby (EFDR). Obviously, such disruptive events have a dramatic impact on the process of change in an organisation.[62] Within one day of the announcement, the consortium that had earlier initiated the development fund mounted a campaign called the 'Save the Kings Appeal', which drew over 2,000 concerned members and citizens to an emergency meeting to decide on ways to stop the proposed sale. One of the consortium members described the urgency of the situation. As he explained,

> We started a development fund twelve months ago. But it didn't get going with sufficient support, not in the same way it did when [Groom] wanted to sell the club. ... There was a stark reality. You either put your hand in your pocket to support the club or there wouldn't be a club to support!

Thus, the consortium focused on gathering social and financial support while simultaneously exerting pressure on ERP to oppose the sale. Although one of the prime aims of the appeal was to raise financial resources, Beamish noted that normative resources such as the media and informal communication networks can also be mobilised to influence processes of change.[63] Indeed, the support of local newspapers, radio and television stations was integral to generating support for the appeal. This social pressure proved particularly effective. Board members of EFDR, the major shareholder in ERP and the main regulatory body pertaining to the Premiership, had become sensitive to the negative publicity caused by the exit of a number of high-profile benefactors from the field. The withdrawal of these benefactors resulted in the subsequent bankruptcy and forced amalgamation of the Premiership clubs they supported. Accordingly, EFDR, and by proxy, ERP, was unwilling to risk further negative publicity that the 'death' of another Premiership club, such as Maclean Rugby, would cause. Finally, in mid-October, the ERP board announced that the proposed sale of Maclean Rugby was 'not in the best interests' of the Premiership, and the transaction was therefore declined.

With the sale blocked, the appeal organisers turned their attention to constructing a plan to oust Groom. Consortium members devised budgets and business plans based on revenue generated from the appeal, and subsequently, approached ERP to demonstrate the financial viability of their plan to return the club to members' control. By establishing institutional relations with key constituents such as supporters and ERP, Maclean RUFC was able to 'mobilise cultural support for its goals and activities and to demonstrate its social validity and conformity with institutional rules, norms, and regulations'.[64]

Groom finally relinquished WBI's stake in Maclean Rugby in exchange for what one club negotiator described as 'minimal legal expenses'. Groom also assumed the club's debts, estimated to be in excess of £500,000. One of the club's chief negotiators explained that 'I believe Mr [Groom] wanted out and realised that we were his only hope. When he tried to make other deals, he found no one showed up.' As a consequence of the widespread social, cultural and financial support generated, the 'Save the Kings Appeal' generated a total of £515,000. This resulted in ERP's approval of the consortium's plans for restructuring, which featured mechanisms to limit the influence of professional staff in decision-making. Volunteer directors were elected based upon the number of shares they bought in the club. Crucially, structures were established that placed an upper limit on the number of shares any individual could hold, and members were given rights of veto that included the prevention of the club being moved away from Maclean.

Conclusion

This chapter has borne out the accuracy of Oliver's predictive dimensions, particularly with reference to the employment of manipulative strategies to shape social perceptions. From this perspective, Maclean RUFC's strategic responses to institutional pressures for commercialisation had inherent temporal, political and processual dimensions that evolved at multiple organisational levels; issues not explicitly dealt with by Oliver. Initially, the club succumbed to the pressures for commercialisation and willingly exchanged organisational discretion for the financial resources deemed necessary to do this. Constituents' subsequently used resistant strategies when the return on their forfeiture of organisational discretion fell short of expectations. This demonstrated that, in choosing levels of compliance with institutional demands, actors behaved strategically and responded according to their interests. This supports the contentions of theorists who have argued for a less deterministic approach to analysing strategic responses to institutional processes.[65]

Certainly, volunteer decision-making was a manifestation of the club's traditional amateur values. Thus, with professionals employed but with volunteers remaining at the pinnacle of the organisation, with complete control over strategic decision-making, Maclean's strategic response to the institutional pressures for commercialisation was ultimately more of a compromise. Clearly, the strategic decision to move to a more commercially-oriented organisational structure was strongly influenced by agency-infused actors. However, the findings of this study demonstrated that the excessive use of influence tactics by these actors resulted in a lack of organisation-wide consultation and involvement in the decision process. This lack of transparency and inclusion in the club's strategic development was completely at odds with its traditional institutionalised forms of volunteer self-governance. As a consequence, key constituents were left marginalised and unwilling to support commercialisation, making the success of any related strategic responses problematic. Thus, while the content of the dominant institutional pressures dictated that commercialisation would enhance legitimacy, conformity to these pressures failed to eliminate uncertainty. Under such circumstances, as Goodrick and Salancik noted, 'norms must develop around the remaining uncertainties and are affected by actors' interests if these interests are consistent with the institutional framework'.[66] Therefore, the norms that eventually framed Maclean RUFC's strategic responses were founded upon the interests of its key constituency – the membership. With new mechanisms of institutional control established, the norms and interests of the club's membership were finally legitimised as being consistent with the Premiership's new commercial institutional framework. Thus, the active agency of 'strategic non-compliance'[67] mobilised the sufficient material and normative resources to secure the club's ultimate organisational and, crucially, *commercial* survival.

NOTES

1. Rugby Football Union, *RFU Commission Report* (1995).
2. P.J. DiMaggio and W.W. Powell, 'The Iron Cage Revisited: Institutional Isomorphism and Collective Rationality in Organisational Fields', *American Sociological Review*, 48 (1983), pp.147–60; J.W. Meyer and B. Rowan, 'Institutionalized Organizations: Formal Structure as Myth and Ceremony', *American Journal of Sociology*, 83 (1977), pp.340–63; C. Oliver, 'The Antecedents of Deinstitutionalization', *Organization Studies*, 13 (1992), pp.563–88.
3. DiMaggio and Powell, 'The Iron Cage Revisited'.
4. Ibid.; Meyer and Rowan, 'Institutionalized Organizations'; L. Zucker, 'The Role of Institutionalization in Cultural Persistence', *American Sociological Review*, 42 (1977), pp.726–43.
5. C.R. Hinings and R. Greenwood, *The Dynamics of Strategic Change* (Oxford: Basil Blackwell, 1988).
6. DiMaggio and Powell, 'The Iron Cage Revisited'.
7. C. Oliver, 'Strategic Responses to Institutional Processes', *Academy of Management Review*, 16 (1991), pp.145–79; C. Oliver, 'The Influence of Institutional and Task Environment Relationships on Organisational Performance: The Canadian Construction Industry', *Journal of Management Studies,* 34 (1997), pp.99–124; L. Kikulis, T. Slack and C.R. Hinings, 'Towards an Understanding of the Role of Agency and Choice in the Changing Structure of Canada's National Sport Organizations', *Journal of Sport Management*, 9 (1995), pp.135–52; A.J. Hoffman, 'Institutional Evolution and Change: Environmentalism and the US Chemical Industry', *Academy of Management Journal*, 42 (1999), pp.351–71.

9

Commercialisation of the Modern Olympics

TARA MAGDALINSKI and JOHN NAURIGHT

From the very beginning of the Olympic movement, civic leaders and entrepreneurs have recognised the political and economic benefits of hosting the Olympic Games, while sponsors have aligned their products with the philosophies of Olympism in the pursuit of ever greater market share. Despite the close relationship between the Olympics and commerce, it has only been over the last two decades that the Olympic movement has capitalised on its global reach and sought to intensively commodify its product. Before the 1980s, the Olympics were supported largely by local business, sponsors and governmental funding, despite the tenets of the 'amateur spirit' which demanded that the Games remain 'pure' and free from the evils of commercial ventures. Companies such as Kodak and Coca-Cola have been associated with the Olympics since 1896 and the 1920s respectively, and more recently, The Olympic Program (TOP) has provided sponsors with exclusive arrangements designed to showcase their products to a cumulative audience of around eight billion people.

As most spectators only ever witness a mediated version of the Games, to fully deliver its potential to marketers, the Olympic movement has broadened opportunities for viewers to 'participate' personally in the Olympic Games by licensing its product and associated symbols. Today, spectators can relish their Olympic experience by drinking official Olympic beer, nibbling on official Olympic mascot cheese shapes, wearing official Olympic clothing, sitting on official Olympic rugs, clutching official Olympic toys while talking to friends on official Olympic telecommunications devices. The Olympic logo and rings are everywhere and are particularly directed at the consumer who insists on Olympic 'authenticity'. To reach this global network of consumers, the Olympic movement relies on the sale of its television broadcasts to the highest bidder, a figure that for the Sydney 2000 Games generated over one billion dollars. To say that the Olympics are a thoroughly commercialised event would be a gross understatement; however, given the movement's promotion of its moralistic philosophy of Olympism, the historical antecedents and contemporary realities of this assertion are not always apparent.

While it is a popular contemporary pastime to lament the recent commercialisation of the Olympic Games, the relationship between commerce and the Olympics has been recognised, and criticised, since the early twentieth century. In 1910 the USA's first Olympic gold medallist James Connolly accused the American Amateur Union of succumbing to commercial pressures, suggesting that sporting goods manufacturer A.G. Spalding's power had become such that he determined the composition of the US Olympic team. Connolly further charged that Amateur Athletic Union (AAU) athletes had simply become 'another advertising agent' for the corporate interests aligned with American Olympic sport.[1] Several decades later, the then International Olympic Committee (IOC) President Avery Brundage expressed his disappointment that the Games had become 'a huge business enterprise instead of another sports event' and suggested that the Olympics were in danger of becoming simply a 'commercial carnival'.[2] Despite this early cognisance of the commercial nature of the movement, proponents of Olympic amateurism have maintained that the Olympics have, 'in the past', been free from commercial influence. These traditionalists insist that each generation heralds the 'beginning of the end' for the movement, as its philosophical basis is undermined by a relentless assault by commercial interests. The Los Angeles 1984 Olympic Organizing Committee (LAOOC), for example, was told in 1980 by an IOC member: 'You represent the ugly face of capitalism and its attempts to take over the Olympic Movement and commercialise the Olympic Games'.[3] The LAOOC was also charged with commodifying the Olympic torch relay, insisting that community organisations, businesses or individuals pay $3,000 for the honour of carrying the Olympic flame. The Greek National Olympic Committee (NOC) objected strongly, accusing the LAOOC of using the torch relay 'as a tool for collection of money for athletic resources'.[4] LAOOC chair Peter Ueberroth found these objections ironic, given that the economy of Olympia was and remains dependent on the flame's commercialisation, with its Olympic Flame Hotel and shops that sell plastic Olympic torches and other Olympic memorabilia.[5] The commodification of the Olympic movement has thus been a highly contentious issue over the past century and requires careful analysis.

In this chapter we examine the commercialisation of the Olympic movement throughout the twentieth century, with particular focus on the progressive development of the games from an idealistic vision of the 1890s to the largest corporatised multi-sport event. In the process, the Olympic Games have become the most significant sporting commodity and global spectacle, an important product for television companies and multinational sponsors, as well as a driving force behind civic, economic and nationalist boosterist strategies and urban development. This chapter clearly cannot be exhaustive, so we have elected to concentrate on the emergence of the

Olympics as a desirable political and economic commodity for host cities and local business, as well as the contemporary manifestations of the Games as a brand and product that are 'sold' to consumers through sponsors' advertising, licensed products and Olympic education.

Emerging Nationalism, Training and Enterprise

Begun in the late nineteenth century as the idealistic project of French nobleman Baron Pierre de Coubertin, the modern Olympic movement was by the end of the twentieth century the most significant multi-sport event, incorporating around 200 'nations'. Coubertin, an ardent French nationalist, believed that reviving the ancient games as a quadrennial event to bring together the youth of the world would enhance international understanding, though his promotion of the Olympics also had other more nationalistic aims. In the aftermath of the Franco-Prussian War (1870–71), Coubertin saw a demoralised French nation, a people emasculated by defeat and in need of moral and physical revival. Bruce Kidd points out that Coubertin was 'particularly concerned about the immiserisation and exploitation that characterised rapid industrialisation and urbanisation, and the resulting class conflict, poverty, disease and despair'.[6] Coubertin believed the answer lay in educational reform and travelled extensively throughout the western world observing and studying physical education programmes.[7] He was extremely impressed with the organisation of sports and games in the British public schools and attempted to have these incorporated in the French educational system. He believed that adhering to a moral or character code would reinvigorate the defeated French youth and advance 'French political and cultural primacy'.[8]

While Coubertin advocated physical activity and organised a plethora of sporting events, he also recognised the universality of 'festivity' and included banquets and musical interludes that helped court politicians and other bureaucrats who might help advance his educational agenda. At one such event in 1892, Coubertin first promoted the re-establishment of the Olympic Games of ancient Greece as an international event,[9] though it was not until the Sorbonne Congress in 1894 that he began formally organising a committee to oversee preparations for the inaugural Games. Despite Coubertin's initial preference for the first Games to be staged in 1900 in Paris to coincide with the Paris Exposition, at the International Athletic Congress in 1894, Athens was selected as the site of the first Games, though London also enjoyed strong support.[10] Staging any international event was, of course, a costly undertaking and despite the trappings of amateurism, the Olympic movement relied on the financial support of local entrepreneurs as well as national and civic leaders. In 1896 the support of the Greek royal family, particularly Prince Constantine, provided the impetus to attract large donations from wealthy expatriate Greeks, while Olympic commodities, such as commemorative medallions and postage stamps, were sold to raise the necessary funds.[11]

By the late nineteenth century, world fairs had become 'the focal point for western civilisation's celebrations of science and social engineering, modern progress and prosperity'.[12] These events provided a number of indicators that allowed nations to compare their political stability and economic prosperity on a global scale as they exhibited national achievements in a range of fields, from engineering feats to physical abilities. Thus, as Mandell suggests: 'It was only natural that modern, high-performance sport would be eventually included among the great cultural manifestations of the later nineteenth century'.[13] The Olympic Games in 1900 and 1904 were both staged in conjunction with international expositions, while the 1908 London Games were linked to the Anglo-French exhibition.[14] These world expositions hosted international meetings of scholars from a range of subdisciplinary fields. Coubertin planned such a congress in physical education for 1900, alongside demonstrations of, and competitions in, athletic activities.[15] Such a meeting, Coubertin hoped, would inspire the French authorities to adopt the British model of school-based physical education[16] and provide an international stage upon which to display a revitalised France.

Despite the boost to international reputations that these events augured, initially competitors made their own way to Athens and often came as nominees of individual sporting clubs, such as the London Athletic Club, while the American contingent were primarily from the ranks of Ivy League varsity athletes. Participants were admitted as individuals and the strict national affiliation, now an undisputed aspect of the event, was still several years away. This is not to say, however, that no national significance was derived from victories at international sporting events. By the late nineteenth century, international sporting competitions had already become sites where nations could measure themselves against others, draw conclusions about their relative political strength and economic success, and generate international exposure. Nationalism thus became a strong factor in the organisation of the Games and was quickly incorporated by the IOC through formal recognition of national teams by 1912.

Olympic teams had originally travelled to the Games under their own financial steam; however, governments increasingly understood the need for more formal funding arrangements. Most national associations that selected Olympic teams in the early 1900s relied on voluntary funding and resisted government control and interference in sporting matters.[17] As sporting contact became further entrenched in nationalist promotion, governments began allocating funds for the preparation of Olympic teams.

In Sweden the government had direct financial involvement in the preparation of their team for the 1912 Stockholm Games,[18] while Sir Arthur Conan Doyle argued that, as other countries used the Games a political tool, then a grant of £100,000 should be raised for the preparation of the 1916 British team. While international success could be viewed as a symbol of a nation's progress and efficiency, the fusion of sport and nationalism worked in the opposite direction as well, and poor results spawned fears that the 'racial virility' of a nation was under threat.[19] In England, King George V himself was so concerned about the performance of the British athletics team at the 1912 Stockholm Games that he urged the British Olympic Committee to raise funds to hire a national coach to prepare for the next Olympics. The Germans went one step further and provided money for professional coaches and scientific research in 1914, while in Coubertin's homeland athletes were brought together in training camps before the First World War.[20]

Across the Atlantic in the USA, and powered by a press that had started to regard international sporting victories as evidence of national superiority, moves were already taking place by the second Games in Paris in 1900 to consolidate the national organisation of Olympic teams. American leaders believed that there was a significant link between national success, national prowess and economic achievement, and that athletic success was linked to the dynamism of the American economy.[21] By 1900 economic and nationalist sporting interests were closely entwined, to the extent that the corporate world and amateur sport were often comprised of the same people. Executives and owners of sporting goods companies were regularly elected to governing bodies of national sports organisations and, in the case of Albert G. Spalding, dictated the nature and style of a range of sports by publishing 'official' rule books, which in turn advertised his sporting goods. Spalding's relationship to US amateur and Olympic sport guaranteed further exposure for his manufactured products, particularly as he orchestrated their selection as 'official' equipment for the 1904 Olympics in St Louis. Other members of Spalding's company, James Sullivan and Julian W. Curtiss, were heavily involved in the administration of amateur sport in the US, and by the turn of the century, there was little separation between the Spalding company and the AAU. As a result, Spalding exercised a significant influence over the US Olympic teams, to the extent that at the 1900 Games, Spalding was the director of sport for the US team and Sullivan was his assistant. While in Paris, however, Spalding not only supervised the activities of the American athletes, but also had sufficient time to oversee the exhibition of his prize-winning sports equipment at the trade show.[22]

The relationship between amateur sport, civic boosterism, local entrepreneurs and nationalist aims is well summarised by the debates surrounding the location of the first Olympic Games on US soil. Coubertin quickly recognised that the USA would eventually play a potent role in the emerging Olympic movement. As a relatively young nation, with an eagerness to prove itself on the world stage, the USA represented the ideal Olympic contender. After the Paris Games, Coubertin and the IOC decided that the 1904 Games should be awarded to the USA and five American cities expressed interest. Chicago emerged as the leading candidate, and raised over one million dollars to lobby the IOC.[23] The Chicago committee produced a number of strategies to ensure their successful selection, but most significantly, they devised a financial agreement that guaranteed most of the profits generated by the event would revert to the IOC.[24] The presumption that the Olympics might be regarded as a profitable venture for the city was thus already entrenched in the minds of civic boosters early in the twentieth century.

Chicago eventually lost the Games to St Louis, and the Olympics were held in conjunction with the Louisiana Purchase Exposition. With Sullivan as chair of the physical culture department for the World Fair, it is of little surprise that the Spalding Company was closely associated with the preparations for the 1904 Games. Peter Levine reveals that in St Louis 'A.G. Spalding and Brothers designed the stadium, organised the track-and-field competition, provided the necessary athletic equipment, and once again won awards for the quality of its products'.[25] Spalding utilised his close relationship with the Olympic Games, suggesting in promotional materials that his equipment had been selected for 'exclusive official use …because of their acknowledged superiority, reliability, and official standing'.[26] Sponsors have thus sought out the Olympic Games as a means of promoting their products since the first decade of the twentieth century.

While the pre-First World War Olympic Games had contributed to the political and economic capital of the respective host cities and their local business people, following the war cities recognised great potential in staging the Olympic Games for urban development and civic promotion. Officials in Antwerp, Belgium, began to lobby for their city to host the Olympics as early as 1913, but the First World War interrupted their initial discussions. In 1920, the first post-war Olympics were hastily organised as Antwerp leaders remained interested and viewed hosting the games as a likely stimulus to local economic development in the aftermath of war. Once they had been awarded to Antwerp in 1919, sporting clubs explored revenue streams to develop their facilities. Members of the Beerschot Athletic Club, for example, used the Olympics as rationale 'to get their stadium rebuilt, complete with an access road, gas, water and electricity installations, all paid for by public funds'.[27] Yet, tensions have always existed between those who have regarded the Olympics as a means of generating greater investment in, and an international reputation for, the host city, and those who have looked to the ideals of Coubertin as a basis for their commitment to the Olympic movement.

For example, the organisation of the 1956 Melbourne Olympic Games, according to Graeme Davison, was characterised by the 'entrepreneurial, futuristic and international' civic and business leaders and the 'official guardians' of Olympism who were 'more militaristic, traditional and imperial in outlook'.[28] The traditionalists, however, had to rely on the business acumen and financial backing of leading Melbourne entrepreneurs in order to secure the Games. Frank Beaurepaire, a leading Melbourne businessman, former Lord Mayor of Melbourne and former Olympic swimmer, led the city's bid and regarded the games as an impetus not simply for local amateur sport but also for 'business confidence and civic pride'. At the same time, the Melbourne Chamber of Commerce 'hailed the games as a boost to tourism and investment'.[29] Despite their commitment to Olympic philosophies, amateur athletes in Melbourne were keen to use the forthcoming Games as a means of securing their own facilities.

While these examples illustrate that the IOC has always depended on local economic and political elites for the games to succeed, other relationships between the corporate world and the Olympic movement have developed since 1896. By 2000, the most explicit expression of the articulation between capital and the Olympic movement was embodied in the plethora of commercial sponsors and partners eager to align their goods and services with the movement.

The Rise of Sponsors and Commercial Partnerships

As civic boosters relied on improving and promoting a city's international reputation and image on a global scale, at the commercial level advertisers have long understood the significant economic gains and heightened corporate awareness that can be achieved by supporting the Olympic movement. From Spalding in the early 1900s and Frank Beaurepaire in the 1950s through to Horst Dassler in the 1970s, entrepreneurs have eagerly associated themselves with the glittering prize of the Olympics. In the early part of the movement, corporate interests, amateur athletics and Olympic organisers were often one and the same people, while today the reliance on sponsors' funds means that the IOC remains beholden to corporate interests.

While many reminisce about the 'old days' of Olympic competition, where sport was played for sport's sake and commercial interests took a back seat to the athletes, the relationship between advertising and the Games extends back to the beginning, when Kodak placed advertisements in the 1896 Olympic programme. Since then the relationship has strengthened. Official licensing of products at the Olympics began in 1912,[30] while at the 1924 games in Paris advertising appeared for the first and only time inside an Olympic stadium. The IOC was outraged as a result and implemented a policy stating that 'Commercial installations and advertising signs shall not be allowed in the stadia, nor in the other sports grounds'.[31] This policy had little effect on the emerging commercial strategies that were developed in the following Olympics, however. In 1928 in Amsterdam, local organisers raised money by selling on-site concessions, one of which was bought by the Coca-Cola company. While Coca-Cola became one of the earliest companies involved in the Olympics in 1928, it was the next games, held in the movie capital of the world, that took commercialism and the Olympics to a new level. Los Angeles capitalised on the Olympic Games by promoting itself as a desirable holiday destination, with advertisements appearing in *Country Life* magazine across the USA. The Games had strong support from oil companies Standard Oil of California and Union 76 in their advertisements, while the media in general promoted the Games as a 'depression buster'. A number of other companies joined the Olympic advertising bandwagon; the Piggly Wiggly supermarket chain, for example, sold Olympic emblems to support the US Olympic team.[32] By the 1936 Olympics in Berlin, the Olympics had become a venue for corporate entertaining and deal-making as companies such as Coca-Cola invited large entourages to attend the Olympics.[33]

Although these initial efforts are noteworthy, the commercial relationships that engulfed the Olympics increased exponentially after the Second World War with the introduction of television and the enhanced possibilities for sponsors to communicate their corporate messages to a global Olympic audience. Some Olympic events received television coverage in 1936; however, it was not until the late 1950s that televised sport began to reach mass audiences. With the Cold War in full swing, the Olympics became a site for heightened drama in the global struggle for ideological supremacy, and Olympic sponsors fuelled this 'war by other means', photographing Soviet athletes drinking Coke, that ultimate symbol of Western consumerism.[34]

In the US, television networks by the 1960s paid for the rights to air broadcasts of the Olympics. From a meagre $394,000 paid by CBS in 1960 to the nearly one billion paid by NBC to host the games through to 2008, there has been a consistent and rapid rise in revenue generated from the sale of television broadcasting rights.[35] In a series of articles, Stephen Wenn has outlined the politics and economics behind the sale of television rights and the role of television in the games from 1956 onwards.[36] Suffice it to say here that the sale of television rights enabled the IOC and the Olympics to operate on a larger scale, thereby enhancing its potential audience, much to the delight of sponsors whose 'potential profits were tied to the increasing size and visibility of the Games'.[37] With increased exposure through television, sporting goods and other companies sought commercial benefits from associating their name and products with the Olympic movement. Horst Dassler, the founder and head of adidas, was one of the first entrepreneurs to recognise the transformation of the games from an amateurish affair to a grand televisual spectacle and the benefits that sponsors could derive from increased exposure and renewed public interest. Television, combined with the escalation of the Cold War, meant that the international ideological conflict between Western and Soviet nations was a narrative well suited to the antagonistic structure of elite sport. This additional dramatic tension delivered a large audience to sponsors willing to exploit the commercial possibilities of the Olympic Games. And while the IOC forbade advertising in the stadium, the athletes themselves became walking billboards by the mid-1950s, when, at the Melbourne Games, Dassler provided track and field athletes with his shoes to wear in competition.[38]

Despite the breadth of appeal and the willingness of sponsors to be involved in the Games, sporting organisations such as the IOC did not maximise their earning potential and indeed did not seem to appreciate the level of revenue that could be generated through sponsorship. The IOC only slowly realised the financial benefits yielded by television coverage, though during the mid-twentieth century, there were some moves to secure and improve the organisation's finances. As early as 1955, Avery Brundage, IOC President from 1952 to 1972, cautioned against overspending by the IOC as outgoings were significantly greater than revenue. With the rapid expansion of the number of national affiliated Olympic committees and the concomitant globalising of the movement, the IOC began to feel financial pressure. By 1974 the IOC became concerned with its long-term financial situation as costs continued to rise, even though from 1972 the IOC had negotiated to receive one-third of the proceeds from the sale of television rights, which it then partly distributed to national Olympic committees and international sporting federations.[39] With an extremely limited product increasingly in global demand, the IOC should have been in a strong economic position. However, by the late 1970s the IOC had a minimal net worth and was desperately seeking alternative revenue streams.[40] But it was not until an alliance was formed with International Sports and Leisure (ISL), which was brokered by Dassler, that the IOC began to reap any financial rewards.[41]

As the Cold War began to fade during the 1980s, and following on the heels of the highly profitable, privately-run Los Angeles Games of 1984, the IOC, under its new President Juan Antonio Samaranch, with the assistance of Dassler, supported escalating the commercialisation of the Olympic brand. Under Samaranch the IOC progressed from what many saw as an organisation clinging to hopelessly outdated ideas to a more streamlined transnational giant that adopted a business-like approach to the management of Olympic events and properties. Some argue that as a result the Olympics have moved from ritual to entertainment and in the process have become 'de-ideologised';[42] thus the IOC has worked carefully with sponsors and its own marketers to recapture its mystique, an image that distinguishes the movement from other global sporting spectacles. While Olympism remains the stated foundation of the movement, under Samaranch the Olympics have become massively commercialised, bureaucratised and spectaclised. In 1983 Samaranch announced that Swiss-based ISL would manage the IOC's new fund-raising programme, TOP,[43] a strategy modelled on LAOOC's fund-raising principle of assuring sponsors of global exclusivity in each product category. This programme reduced commercial clutter by targeting fewer sponsors, who would pay a large sum to be an exclusive Olympic partner. In this way, each sponsorship would increase in value and, more importantly, each sponsor would provide advertising for the Olympics, for which the IOC incurred no additional financial liabilities.[44]

Commercial Saturation: Atlanta, Sydney and Beyond

The sponsorship programs established in the 1980s flourished to such an extent that the Olympics became a thoroughly saturated commercial venture by the end of the twentieth century. From the slick bid campaigns to the marketing of associated merchandise, the 1996 Atlanta and 2000 Sydney Games have embodied more than any other the commercial exploitation of the Olympics. The sheer cost of staging the games now requires a dedicated commitment from sponsors and governments alike, while the withdrawal of one sponsor can seriously damage an organising committee's budget. Yet throughout the 1980s, the IOC kept close control on the financing of the Games, retaining the right to license the exclusive use of Olympic insignia, taking a percentage of sponsorship and broadcast revenues raised by organising committees while remaining removed from the everyday financing of the games themselves. These programmes have been enormously successful, with the IOC generating nearly $15 billion through its marketing and licensing programmes from 1980 to the end of the century.[45]

While the IOC remains in control of Olympic logos and associated brands, the committee is not required to finance the games themselves. Instead, local hosts must raise the funds necessary to stage this massive event. And yet, since the successful 1984 Los Angeles Olympics, where organisers turned a substantial profit ($215 million) for the first (and last) time, civic boosters have fallen over themselves seeking to adorn their cities with the five rings. Large sums of money are spent on marketing the merits of a potential host in a bid process that lasts around a year. While the bids themselves are often funded with private money, the actual event demands a massive capital injection by local, provincial and national governments.

Throughout the 1990s, a succession of reports and inquiries revealed that the Olympic bid process was corrupt, with IOC members receiving excessive gifts and 'hospitality' from candidate cities, resulting in the expulsion of several of IOC members and a reformation of the movement.[46] These 'reforms' eventuated after major sponsors threatened to withdraw their financial support from the movement,[47] though nearly all Olympic sponsors eventually expressed their support for the IOC and congratulated the committee on its decisive actions.[48] The power of the sponsors to elicit reforms from a movement as opaque as the Olympics demonstrates the degree to which corporate interests have become germane to the central working of the Olympic movement.

Olympic sponsors are committed to retaining a positive association with the Olympics and seek to link their products and services with the philosophies of Olympism. Sponsors have successfully constructed their interest in the Olympics as purely altruistic; reference to them as 'partners', 'supporters' or 'members' of the Olympic family or, as in the case of Sydney 2000, 'Team Millennium' creates an aura of patronage rather than commercial interest. The success of these linguistic contortions is evident. In a recent report on the environmental policies of some Sydney 2000 sponsors, Greenpeace inadvertently revealed that they too have succumbed to the propaganda that insists Olympic corporate partners are philanthropic. In its document *Green Olympics, Dirty Sponsors*, Greenpeace states with some incredulity that 'McDonald's and Coca-Cola are exploiting their sponsorship of the Olympic Games to increase sales and profits'.[49] That a generally radical organisation such as Greenpeace seemingly buys into the mythology of a supposed altruistic Olympic sponsorship confirms the success of Olympic marketing.

Despite missives that advocate Olympism over commercialism, with sponsors' tie-ins through children's competitions, the artificial construction of the 'new sport' of pin collecting as well as the promotional activities of mascots, the corporate influence permeates every Olympic encounter. Both Alan Bryman and Ellen Seiter argue that in late modernity, social identities derive not from an individual's profession but from their consumption practices, such that 'all members of modern developed societies depend heavily on commodity consumption, not just for survival but for participation – inclusion – in social networks'.[50] The purchasing of Olympiana means that consumers can participate individually in an event that is advertised for all. Just as the Olympic torch relay serves to concretise an imagined community and allow participants and spectators alike to appreciate their inclusion in a greater social network, Olympic memorabilia and licensed products entitle purchasers to secure their position as avid participants in the global Olympic community. Indeed, to experience the Olympics these days, it is essential to purchase commodities that are appropriately and legally stamped with bona fide insignia. From pins to clothing, dinnerware to jewellery, stamps to coffee cups, every possible surface on every possible product has been printed, embossed, engraved or soldered with an Olympic logo, allowing the public to 'own [their] own piece of the Olympic Games'.[51] The significance of purchasing 'authentic' Olympic consumables is ratified by the use of DNA to mark products as legitimate. The genetic material of (in)famous Australian swimmer Dawn Fraser was incorporated into the labelling of Olympic merchandise that was sold before the Sydney 2000 Olympics. This genetic 'stamp' reassures consumers that what they are purchasing are authentic goods, the sole purveyors of the 'real' Olympic experience. Such is the devotion to buying only genuine Olympiana that customers can inform authorities of the illegitimate use of Olympic insignia. If consumers are in doubt about the validity of a product, they are provided with opportunities to report 'brand violations' to the appropriate authorities.[52] As such, Olympic consumers are made proudly complicit in the preservation of the sanctity of the movement.

Despite the array of products available for purchase outside the main gates, the IOC still insists that the corporate hand does not extend into the stadium, arguing that despite the over-commercialisation of the games, the Olympic stadia themselves remain free from influential advertising. It is clear, however, that the 'clean' arena has a further economic imperative. Television stations are able to 'on-sell' advertising to rival sponsors, who would not appreciate their message being diluted by the presence of the banners and placards of their competitors.[53] Despite this, Olympic broadcasters must give first right of refusal of on-air advertising to official Olympic sponsors, an opportunity that greater numbers of sponsors are taking up. Indeed, the removal of commercial 'clutter' from telecasts comes at a premium and means that broadcasters can 'generate more revenue from fewer sponsors', while sponsors are able to 'achieve their business objectives by fully leveraging their Olympic involvement through comprehensive, uncluttered advertising campaigns'.[54]

While Olympic sponsors are guaranteed access to a cumulative global audience of several billion, the sheer saturation of the market with Olympic-related advertising means that corporations must work hard to distinguish themselves and their products from competitors. In recent years, ambush marketing has led consumers to identify 'official' Olympic sponsors incorrectly; thus other mechanisms have been employed to ensure that a current and a future market audience learn to link the correct sponsors with the Olympics. Children are thus targeted as important consumers of Olympiana, and, as a result, have become the focus for a range of 'educational' campaigns, co-developed with official sponsors and designed to increase market profile among a captured group of future consumers.

Olympic 'Education' and Mascots in the Commercialisation Process

Since the 1980s the Olympic movement has increasingly relied on coopting children into the business of attracting and selling the games. Children's competitions are run, encouraging young people to either artistically design or best exemplify the themes of Olympism; winning entries are displayed on a range of Olympic merchandise from coffee mugs to stamps, as well in the corporate advertising of the sponsoring company; and sponsors focus on families and children as a way of disseminating their corporate message. Indeed, the Sydney 2000 bid has become something of a model of how to incorporate children into the marketing of potential host cities. Throughout the bid process an 'Olympic Schools Strategy' was implemented, which paired schools throughout New South Wales with individual IOC members,[55] while a schoolgirl was used as a 'secret weapon' in the final bid presentation in 1993. Most significant, however, has been corporate intrusion into the classroom under the guise of 'educating' children about the Olympic movement.

The IOC has long regarded education as key to its promotional activities. Coubertin was convinced that an antidote to the social ills of the late nineteenth century lay in educational reform and his dedication to sport as a means for reform underpinned his philosophy of Olympism. More recently, Coubertin's firm belief in the primacy of culture and education has been revived by the IOC's Commission for Culture and Olympic Education, which seeks to disseminate Olympism. The movement arranges international Olympic academies and other venues for the discussion and promotion of Olympism among young people, athletes and administrators. Bruce Kidd notes that the bulk of Olympic educational activities are 'technical in nature, aimed at improving the athletic performance or administration, or directed at schoolchildren, potential spectators, and others'.[56] Thus those 'educational' efforts not focused on performance target children as the next generation of Olympic consumers. In essence, these programmes, particularly the school-based curriculum guides produced by Olympic organising committees, are fundamentally corporate advertising vehicles, aimed at raising Olympic awareness which, supported by the plethora of advertising-based activities, equates with brand awareness in the minds of young Olympic consumers. According to Erika Shaker, the school setting provides the most conducive advertising environment, 'an environment of trust and familiarity' that can target 'future consumers' by 'ensuring that vital messages can be delivered where they may most effectively change behaviour or attitudes'.[57] On the one hand, advertisers are able to enhance their corporate image by invoking a more altruistic motivation, while the school, an 'uncluttered' advertising environment in which a company's message will 'stand out', provides a quasi-endorsement of the products advertised on its grounds.[58] Given that the Olympic education kits are 'literally framed by corporate logos' and activities include collecting images of athletes in order to identify corporate logos,[59] it is clear that the objectives of such kits have less to do with education and more to do with developing a consumer base and raising the profile of corporations.

Throughout the 1970s, at a time when public confidence in large companies was declining, corporate leaders waged campaigns to counter their public image as 'greedy' and 'uninterested in the public good'.[60] As a result, 'corporations dropped extra hundreds of millions of dollars into public relations advertising designed to promote corporate images and ideological dispositions'.[61] The Olympic movement participated in this process and sought to link its product and brand further with the ethos of Olympism that was designed to elicit consent for a movement that was becoming increasingly reliant on corporate funds for its operation. It is thus no coincidence that as corporations began basing their advertising campaigns on cute characters designed to appeal to children, the Olympic movement adopted mascots as a way of accessing a youthful target market by 'conveying a message and fostering a mood'.[62]

Mascots have been part of the Olympic movement since 1972, when Waldi the Dachshund was incorporated into the Munich Olympics marketing programme. Since then, every Olympics has adopted a totem, usually derived from the indigenous fauna and often linked to national stereotypes and political agenda (the German Dachshund, the great Russian bear, the American Bald Eagle). They have ranged in success from Mischa the Bear (Moscow 1980) to Izzy the 'Whatizit' (Atlanta 1996), and are used extensively in marketing campaigns primarily directed at children. To increase the range of products that bear the images of mascots, more recently Olympic organising committees have increased the number of mascots – Nagano 1998 employed the services of four, essentially identical, 'Snowlets' while the Sydney 2000 Games used three native Australian animals, named Syd, Millie and Olly. Salt Lake City 2002 replicated this system and developed three animal mascots, each of which is designed to represent simultaneously an aspect of the surrounding landscape and the Olympic motto.

Mascots are designed almost explicitly with children in mind. Cute cartoon characters, easily transformed into plush toys, are regarded as an important tool to introduce children to the Olympic movement. President and CEO of the Salt Lake Organizing Committee (SLOC) Mitt Romney explicitly stated that 'SLOC's mascots give children a link to the Games. They are cute, lovable characters'. In response to the unveiling of Sydney's mascots, leading Olympic officials commended the selection arguing that 'While they will appeal to people of all ages, I expect children will really fall in love with them', while Australian IOC member Kevan Gosper concurred: 'Above all, a mascot should be attractive to children – and these three are favourites that the children of Australia and the world will love.'[63] Mascots serve to reinforce children's awareness of the Olympics, and Games sponsors have employed them in the targeting of youthful consumers of the event.

The 'Kids' pages on the Sydney 2000 website, supported by Australian financial institution Westpac, presented a plethora of activity sheets for teachers to use in the classroom, in which the official mascots were the central characters around which children ostensibly learned skills such as counting, hand-eye coordination and sharing. Other activities included teaching the children to recognise, sort and group Olympic insignia, but above all the main aim of these sheets was for children to learn to recognise and appreciate the official mascots that appeared on a glut of licensed merchandise. Syd, Millie and Olly were expected to generate $150 million in merchandise related sales, with their images appearing on 'everything from pens to bed linen'.[64] According to a note in the *Journal of Olympic History*, the Sydney Olympics organisers approached the producers of TV shows, theatre performances, internet sites and CD-ROMs to fully saturate the children's market.[65]

Most importantly, mascots are deemed to be a 'communication' tool, designed to tell the story of the Olympics and 'come alive' for children and families around the world. Of course all 'living' things exist in context, and so an attendant mythology was developed for the mascots, explaining their selection and role in the Olympics. The Olympic Mascot Legend, an invented 'dreaming' story, provides the trio with a kind of historical authenticity, one that is rooted in a pseudo-indigenous heritage. Branding the Olympic insignia, mascots and ceremonies with an Aboriginal 'theme' was a deliberate strategy on the part of the organisers, who were looking for 'something with Aboriginality' in the design concepts to distinguish Australia's bid and Games from its competitors and to provide an authentic and distinct image that would represent 'Australia'.[66] The SLOC adopted elements of indigenous branding and developed a set of mascots that try to incorporate elements of an invented native American mythology to 'reflect American West and Tradition of Storytelling'.[67] Romney linked the mascots to the indigenous culture of the region explaining that:

We are thrilled to present these three mascots for the 2002 Games as representatives of the land and culture of Utah and the American West. Their stories are a wonderful translation of a Native American legend into the symbolism of the Olympic movement. The theme of swifter, higher, stronger crosses the boundaries of time.

As a result, the Sydney and Salt Lake Olympic Games have been 'branded' with indigenous authenticity, although, as in recent Canadian examples, images were 'selectively constructed to fit within the naturalised, dominant images already existent … which portray Native cultures in a static "pre-history"'.[68] The reliance on indigenous culture is crucial for the presentation of a city as unique in the global community.

The Olympics and the Creation of 'World Class' Cities

In a global marketplace where cities are increasingly indistinguishable by their architecture or commodities, the Olympics and other mega-events provide opportune moments for cities to differentiate themselves and to attract the international tourist and investment dollar. Cities rely on staging bigger and better spectacles to engender greater global recognition and develop a competitive advantage over other similarly sized and resourced cities.[69] Cities are repackaged and reconfigured to appeal to both national and international audiences, enticing both capital and tourists. The Olympics have a balance to achieve between remaining essentially the same 'product' each time, while being packaged differently to fit the national and regional specifics of the host city.

   As Helen Wilson points out, cities that pretend to the prefix 'world class' rely on investing in and developing a range of investment and touristic strategies that seek to confirm that city's place in regional and global hierarchies.[70] One of the most common and successful strategies by the late twentieth century has been to rely on hosting 'hallmark' or 'mega' events, in order to drive tourism as well as public investment in infrastructure. The Olympics, with its image of wholesome sport contested between nations in a friendly atmosphere of 'fair play' is the jewel in the global crown of hallmark sporting events and since the mid-1980s cities have spent millions of dollars in the hopes of hosting the quadrennial festival. Indeed as many as 12 American cities lined up before the year 2000 in efforts to win the right from the USOC to be the American bid city for 2012.

   David Whitson and Don Macintosh argue that mega-events such as the Olympic Games rely on a split discourse that emphasises 'hospitality and international friendship', while at the same time stressing the 'opportunities for commercial gain and for civic and national self-promotion'.[71]

Throughout the 1980s and 1990s first-world cities shifted focus from resource-based heavy industries to the promotion of prestige projects and urban mega-projects to promote urban regeneration and to attract outside expenditure to urban centres.[72] As a result, urban spaces were redesigned and city centres were regenerated with new facilities such as trendy shopping precincts, casinos, convention centres and sports arenas and stadia, though these were often built at the expense of economically disadvantaged residents who were forcibly relocated.[73]

The attraction of major sporting events became a key battleground between aspiring global cities with the Olympics as the ultimate prize to put a city on the so-called global map. After Los Angeles succeeded in raising a substantial profit, the IOC was eager to ensure that future Games were also well run, but that it would receive a large portion of the proceeds. Conversely, it did not want to be saddled with any potential debt caused by local funding problems, as had been the case with Montreal in 1976. The IOC therefore requires that host cities provide assurances that losses will be covered while prohibiting private control of organising. With cities lining up to bid after 1984 and its limited product in high demand, the IOC was able to set strict conditions for the hosting of the games while city after city from almost every continent tried to gain exposure from hosting the Olympics, or at the least the extra media attention that an Olympic bid might bring. From early on in the modern Olympics, civic boosters and corporate officials sought to align themselves with the games. With the global potential so great in the television and Internet age, the possible returns lead many local business elites to gamble with public money in the hopes of gaining the biggest multi-sport prize.

Conclusion

From the beginning of the modern Olympic Games in 1896, commercial interests have remained central to the organisation of Olympic events, despite the fact that commercialisation was actively resisted for much of the twentieth century. Without the financial support of local and national leaders as well as the business community, the Olympic movement would not have developed into the global media spectacle that it is today. As a result, the IOC has relied on business and government leaders for the successful funding, infrastructure and promotion of the Olympic Games, despite its initial commitment to the philosophies of amateurism that eschewed the crass commercial exploitation of Olympic insignia. While governments, and thus taxpayers, are obliged to underwrite the cost of an Olympic Games, multinational organisations are able to profit well from the massive global audience generated by the event. Entrepreneurs have always been a crucial part of Olympic organisation, and corporate leaders, such as Spalding, Beaurepaire and Dassler in the past, successfully integrated their personal business interests into the Olympic movement, forever securing the relationship between corporations and Olympic sport. These associations have been further cemented by the development of exclusive sponsorship arrangements that are so revered that host nations are compelled to implement legislation protecting the rights of those who have paid to endorse the Olympics.

The attraction of the Olympic movement for sponsors was made possible by increased mass communications technologies that emerged after the Second World War. Television, along with the narrative of Cold War competition, reshaped the Olympics into a large, desirable commodity for sponsors eager to reach a global audience. These Olympic 'partners' have also sought alternative means of appealing to consumers, and through competitions and curriculum packages aimed at children have opened up another avenue of advertising that coalesces with the promotion of Olympism. Under the presidency of Juan Antonio Samaranch in the last two decades of the twentieth century, the Olympics became the hottest global sporting product for cities wishing to promote a reinvigorated image to potential investors and tourists. At the same time, host cities are able to fast-track infrastructural developments designed to leave a 'legacy' for future generations.

The Olympics are recognised as a glittering prize in global urban presentation and development, in the generation of revenue-raising tourism and in the promotion of the national image both at home and abroad. At the same time, the IOC and other Olympic organisations and sponsors embrace the movement's mythical status as the harbinger of pure, clean, wholesome sport in the creation of brand loyalty among consumers. Accordingly, it is crucial to acknowledge that the Olympic Games are a commodity, the commercial outcome of an ongoing process that began when Coubertin first mooted the idea of organising an international sporting festival.

NOTES

1. P. Levine, *A.G. Spalding and the Rise of Baseball: The Promise of American Sport* (New York: Oxford University Press, 1985), p.138.
2. R. Gruneau and H. Cantelon, 'Capitalism, Commercialism, and the Olympics', in J.O. Segrave and D. Chu (eds), *The Olympic Games in Transition* (Champaign, IL: Human Kinetics, 1988), p.361.
3. P. Ueberroth, *Made in America: His Own Story* (New York: William Morrow, 1985), p.72.
4. Ueberroth, *Made in America*, p.165.
5. Ibid.
6. B. Kidd, 'Taking the Rhetoric Seriously: Proposals for Olympic Education', *Quest*, 48 (1996), p.83.
7. R. Mandell, *Sport: A Cultural History* (New York: Columbia University Press, 1984).
8. Ibid.
9. Ibid.
10. D. Young, 'Demetrios Vikelas: First President of the IOC', *Stadion*, 14, 1 (1988), pp.85–102.

11. W. Baker, *Sports in the Western World* (Urbana and Chicago, IL: University of Illinois Press, 1988); T.I. Philemon, 'Olympic Games – Athens 1896', *Olympic Review*, 154 (1980), pp.447–58.
12. M. Dyreson, 'America's Athletic Missionaries: Political Performance, Olympic Spectacle and the Quest for an American National Culture, 1896–1912', *OLYMPIKA*, 1 (1992), pp.70–91.
13. Mandell, *Sport: A Cultural History*, p.199.
14. Gruneau and Cantelon, 'Capitalism, Commercialism, and the Olympics'; Mandell, *Sport: A Cultural History*.
15. Mandell, *Sport: A Cultural History*.
16. T. Chandler, '*Le regime Arnoldian* and its influence on Baron Pierre de Coubertin', unpublished paper presented to the North American Society for Sport History Conference, Auburn, AL, May 1996.
17. P. Beck, *Scoring for Britain: International Football and International Politics, 1900–1939* (London: Frank Cass, 1999); M. Dyreson, *Making the American Team: Sport, Culture, and the Olympic Experience* (Champaign, IL: University of Illinois Press, 1998).
18. A. Krüger, 'The origins of Pierre de Coubertin's *religio athletae*', *OLYMPIKA*, 2 (1993), pp.91–102.
19. R. Holt, *Sport and the British* (London: Oxford University Press, 1989).
20. Krüger, 'The origins of Pierre de Coubertin's *religio athletae*'; A. Krüger, '"Buying Victories is Positively Degrading": The Beginning of Government Intervention to Achieve National Prestige Through Elite Sports', *International Journal of the History of Sport*, 12, 2 (1993), pp.183–200.
21. Dyreson, *Making the American Team*.
22. Levine, *A.G. Spalding and the Rise of Baseball*.
23. Dyreson, *Making the American Team*.
24. R. Barney, 'Born from Dilemma: America Awakens to the Modern Olympic Games, 1901–1903', *OLYMPIKA*, 1 (1992), pp.92–135.
25. Levine, *A.G. Spalding and the Rise of Baseball*, p.88.
26. Ibid.
27. R. Renson and M. den Hollander, 'Sport and Business in the City: The Antwerp Olympic Games of 1920 and the Urban Elite', *OLYMPIKA*, 6 (1997), p.73.
28. G. Davison, 'Welcoming the World: The 1956 Melbourne Olympic Games and the Re-presentation of Melbourne', *Australian Historical Studies*, 28 (1997), p.66.
29. Davison, 'Welcoming the World', pp.67 and 69.
30. C. Hill, *Olympic Politics: Athens to Atlanta 1896–1996*, 2nd edn (Manchester: Manchester University Press, 1996).
31. S. Rozin, 'Olympic Partnership: How Corporate Sponsors Support the Atlanta Games', *Sports Illustrated*, 24 July 1995, p.10.
32. M. Dyreson, 'Marketing National Identity: The Olympic Games of 1932 and American Culture', *OLYMPIKA*, 1 (1992), pp.23–48.
33. M. Pendergrast, *For God, Country and Coca-Cola: The Unauthorized History of the World's Most Popular Soft Drink* (London: Weidenfeld & Nicolson, 1993).
34. Ibid.
35. A. Senn, *Power, Politics, and the Olympic Games: A History of the Power Brokers, Events, and Controversies that Shaped the Games* (Champaign, IL: Human Kinetics, 1999).
36. S. Wenn, 'Lights! Camera! Little Action: Television, Avery Brundage and the 1956 Melbourne Olympics', *Sporting Traditions*, 10, 1 (1993), pp.436–41; S. Wenn, 'An Olympian Squabble: The Distribution of Olympic Television Revenue, 1960–1966', *OLYMPIKA*, 3 (1994), pp.27–48; S. Wenn, 'Growing Pains: The Olympic Movement and Television, 1966–1972', *OLYMPIKA*, 4 (1995), pp.1–22.
37. Gruneau and Cantelon, 'Capitalism, Commercialism, and the Olympics', p.354.
38. V. Simpson and A. Jennings, *The Lords of the Rings: Power, Money and Drugs in the Modern Olympics* (London: Simon & Schuster, 1992).
39. Hill, *Olympic Politics*.
40. Ueberroth, *Made in America*.
41. Simpson and Jennings, *The Lords of the Rings*.
42. T. Alkemeyer and A. Richartz, 'The Olympic Games: From Ceremony to Show', *OLYMPIKA*, 2 (1993), p.85.
43. Simpson and Jennings, *The Lords of the Rings*.
44. Ueberroth, *Made in America*.
45. Olympic Marketing Matters, 'The finances of the IOC: Where the Money Goes', *The Olympic Marketing Newsletter*, 15 (June 1999), p.7.

46. D. Booth, 'Gifts or Corruption?: Ambiguities of Obligation in the Olympic Movement', *OLYMPIKA*, 8 (1999), pp.43–69; A. Burroughs, 'Winning the Bid', in R. Cashman and A. Hughes (eds), *Staging the Olympics. The Event and its Impact* (Sydney: University of New South Wales Press, 1999), pp.35–45; H. Lenskyj, *Inside the Olympic Industry: Power, Politics, and Activism* (Albany, NY: State University of New York Press, 2000).

47. M. Evans, 'Sponsors May Force Coles to Quit', *Sydney Morning Herald*, 23 March 1999; G. Kitney, 'Car Giant's Threat to Pull Out of Games', *Sydney Morning Herald*, 10 March 1999; G. Korporaal, 'Samaranch Assures Key Sponsors About Reforms', *Sydney Morning Herald*, 12 March 1999.

48. Olympic Marketing Matters, 'The Olympic Crisis in Perspective', *The Olympic Marketing Newsletter*, 15 (June 1999), pp.1–4.

49. Greenpeace, *Green Olympics, Dirty Sponsors:. How McDonald's and Coca-Cola's Global HFC Pollution is Undermining the World's First Green Games at the Sydney 2000 Olympics* (Sydney: Greenpeace, 2000), p.1.

50. E. Seiter, *Sold Separately. Parents and Children in Consumer Culture* (Brunswick, NJ: Rutgers University Press, 1995), p.3; A. Bryman, *Disney and His Worlds* (London: Routledge, 1995).

51. K. Hill, 'On Your Marks for Sydney Superstore Spending Spree', *Sydney Morning Herald*, 18 September 2000.

52. See Salt Lake City Olympic Games website, accessed 9 March 2001: http://www.saltlake 2002.com.

53. Simpson and Jennings, *The Lords of the Rings*.

54. Olympic Marketing Matters, 'Olympic Sponsors' Partnerships with Broadcasters', *The Olympic Marketing Newsletter*, 12 (January 1998), p.8.

55. D. Booth and C. Tatz, '"Swimming with the Big Boys"?: The Politics of Sydney's 2000 Olympic Bid', *Sporting Traditions*, 11, 1 (1994), pp.3–24.

56. Kidd, 'Taking the Rhetoric Seriously', p.82.

57. E. Shaker, 'Corporate Content: Inside and Outside the Classroom', *Education, Limited. CCPA Education Project*, 1, 2 (1998), p.2.

58. Shaker, 'Corporate Content', p.2.

59. K. Schimmel and T. Chandler, 'Olympism in the Classroom: Partnership Sponsored Educational Materials and the Shaping of the School Curriculum', in J. Tolleneer and R. Renson (eds), *Old Borders, New Borders, No Borders: Sport and Physical Education in a Period of Change* (Aachen: Meyer and Meyer, 2000), p.428.

60. S.R. Steinberg and J.L. Kinchloe, *Kinderculture: The Corporate Construction of Childhood* (Boulder, CO: Westview, 1997), p.13.

61. Steinberg and Kinchloe, *Kinderculture*, p.13.

62. P. Welch, 'Cute Little Creatures: Mascots Lend a Smile to the Games', *Olympic Review*, 250–1 (1988), p.437.

63. 'The Mascots of the Games of the XXVII Olympiad', *Olympic Review*, 16 (February/March 1997), p.8.

64. 'Olympic News Notes', *Journal of Olympic History*, 1 (1999), p.46.

65. Ibid.

66. D. Godwell, 'The Olympic Branding of Aborigines: The 2000 Olympic Games and Australia's Indigenous People', in K. Schaffer and S. Smith (eds), *The Olympic Games at the Millennium: Power, Politics, and the Games* (New Brunswick, NJ: Rutgers University Press, 2000), p.245.

67. Salt Lake City Games website.

68. V. Paraschak, 'Aboriginal Inclusiveness in Canadian Sporting Culture: An Image Without Substance?', in *Sport as Symbol, Symbols in Sport: Proceedings of the 3rd ISHPES Congress, Cape Town, South Africa* (1995), p.347.

69. G. Waitt, 'Playing Games with Sydney: Marketing Sydney for the 2000 Olympics', *Urban Studies*, 36, 7 (1999), pp.1055–77; Godwell, 'The Olympic Branding of Aborigines'; D. Whitson and D. Macintosh, 'The Global Circus: International Sport, Tourism, and the Marketing of Cities', *Journal of Sport and Social Issues*, 23 (1996), pp.287–95; H. Wilson, 'What is an Olympic City? Visions of Sydney 2000', *Media, Culture and Society*, 18 (1996), pp.603–18.

70. Wilson, 'What is an Olympic City?'.

71. Whitson and Macintosh, 'The Global Circus', p.279.

72. M. Beazley, P. Loftman and B. Nevin, 'Downtown Redevelopment and Community Resistance: An International Perspective', in N. Jewson and S. MacGregor (eds), *Transforming Cities: Contested Governance and New Spatial Divisions* (London: Routledge, 1998), pp.181–92.

73. C. Rutheiser, *Imagineering Atlanta: The Politics of Place in the City of Dreams* (London: Verso, 1996); Lenskyj, *Inside the Olympic Industry*.

PART IV:
TELEVISION AND THE
COMMERCIALISATION OF SPORT

10

Media Sport, Globalisation and the Challenges to Commercialisation: Sport Advertising and Cultural Resistance in Aotearoa/New Zealand

STEVEN J. JACKSON, ANDREW GRAINGER

and RICHARD BATTY

The global popularity of sport has made it a powerful vehicle in the expansion of transnational commercial interests. While debate continues as to whether particular sporting events are demanded or imposed upon the increasingly satellited television audience, the reality is that people are tuning in. The fact that audiences are watching (or even assumed to be watching) means that they can be demographically cross-sectioned, commodified and sold to eager advertising and marketing conglomerates. In simple terms, the Olympics, World Cup soccer, the Super Bowl, X-Games and a host of other increasingly global media sporting spectacles are created and produced in order to attract television audiences whose capacity to consume is sold to prospective promotional agents. However, we are increasingly aware that the logic of this seemingly straightforward system is much more complex and consequential. We cannot, and should not, ignore the deeper cultural values and ideologies that are reproduced through mediated sport, because they are integral to naturalising and reproducing dominant notions of competition, global capitalism, nationalism and the gender order. In short, we cannot underestimate the immense impact that global media sporting spectacles have in reproducing power relations that shape our various social identities. Moreover, it is important that we recognise that sporting spectacles, along with many other aspects of culture, have been transformed into commodities by transnational corporations (TNCs). Collectively, these TNCs are contributing to the advancement of post-industrial capitalism – a political, economic and cultural system that is fundamentally changing the nature of the nation state and the international flow of people, products and ideas. In short, it is a paradigmatic shift in the way that we live our lives.

In this chapter we examine the commercialisation of sport from a New Zealand perspective. New Zealand provides a useful site of analysis because as a small, relatively isolated British colony, its sport has, until very recently, been largely structured within the ideals of amateurism or at best semi-professionalism. In the first part of the chapter we focus on the changing nature and position of New Zealand's national game, rugby, as it confronts and at times embraces the new forces of commercialism. Furthermore, we examine the most recent changes to rugby as it locates itself within the global economy. Then, in the second part we examine how, in the face of powerful transnational corporate promotional culture, signs of local resistance are emerging. Specifically, we examine case studies of global sporting advertisements that have been banned or publicly challenged in a local context. To begin, and to put the issue in context, we provide a brief introduction to the nature of commercialised global sport.

Though some would argue that changes in the logic and organisation of commercialised sport during the nineteenth century were revolutionary, they were relatively incremental and comprehensible by today's standards. Change is occurring so quickly that those at the forefront of producing global sport, as well as those charged with critiquing and challenging its impact on contemporary social life, often have little time to reflect and consider its consequences. Nevertheless, there is no denying that sport, as an aspect of popular culture, has changed in the way it is produced, represented and consumed.

The globalisation of the sport-media complex has created enormous opportunities for transnational corporations and their associated marketing arms.[1] However, while both the base of potential consumers and means of distribution have certainly expanded, there are new challenges facing those involved in the world of international commercial sport. Notably, these challenges are of both a theoretical and applied, or industry-based, nature. For example, considerable debate has emanated from discussions about the impact of globalisation and the relationship between the global and the local.[2] Central to these debates is the seemingly limitless power of the media to provide access to global commodities, images and ideas and the potential effects these have on local culture. Global sport, including its televisual production and associated marketing, is one such commodity that has been the subject of increasing scholarly and industry attention.[3] While there are many facets to the global sport commodity, our focus is the role of advertising. Arguably, advertising is at the forefront of global capitalism and as such represents a key site for examining the power, politics and contradictions associated with globalisation. Consequently, we focus on the mechanisms and machinations of transnational sport advertising in order to gain a better understanding of the processes and challenges to the increasingly commercialised nature of global media sport.

The presence, indeed omnipresence, of advertising within the realm of sport is testimony to the strong links between commercialisation, the sport industry and the wider economy. One only needs to consider some of the following examples to see that the commodification and commercialisation of sport is a *sign of the times*:[4]

- The emergence of virtual advertising enables different, and even competing, global transnational corporations to share 'imaginary' marketing space during televised sports broadcasts.
- Every available space on an athlete's body and equipment is now for sale. From Tiger Woods's Nike 'swooshed' golf balls to the soles of a knocked-out boxer to the bras of female World Cup soccer players (Nike, USA), transnational corporations are constantly seeking to have their signs displayed within sporting contexts. The fact that there are people employed to measure each and every sponsor's sound bite and image is further testimony to the economy of sporting signs and spaces.
- In 1995 the IOC established the Olympic Television Archive Bureau (OTAB) a repository of over 20,000 hours of film and television footage of the modern Games. Astute sponsors, marketing firms and television production companies can now purchase images of the past so that they can be used in advertising and other commercial projects. In this way sporting images of the past become part of the promotional efforts of the present through the marketing of nostalgia.

Clearly, global sport companies are going to great lengths to brand their products and reach new markets. Yet, while current political and economic conditions have tipped the scales in their favour, transnational corporations and their associated advertising and marketing support systems are not without challenges. Thus, as previously noted, in the latter part of this chapter we examine particular examples of global-local disjunctures – that is, how global sport marketing campaigns are challenged and resisted on a local level. Next, we examine the way in which global commercial forces have shaped rugby in New Zealand.

The Commercial Transformation of New Zealand's National Game

Rugby has been synonymous with New Zealand for over a century. Indeed, it has been asserted that 'the New Zealand rugby nation predated, and in part facilitated, the emergence of the New Zealand nation itself'.[5] Imported and spread by British elites, the game quickly assumed a different identity in the new colony. Rather than a game for society's privileged, rugby's popular, if sometimes mythical, historical status in New Zealand has been attributed to its ability to bring together 'men' of all backgrounds, including Maori. Equally important to rugby's emerging centrality within New Zealand were significant overseas tours, in particular 1905 and 1924.[6] These sporting tours provided a major public stage through which the colony could demonstrate its physical superiority over the 'mother country', thereby helping to forge a sense of national identity. The success of further tours helped ensure that the game was entrenched as part of the social fabric for years to come.

However, in 1981 rugby's position within New Zealand faced its first big challenge. The 1981 Springbok tour divided the nation between those who loved the game and wanted to separate sport and politics and those who saw rugby's darker side. Among the protesters were citizens fighting against the apartheid policies of a racist South Africa along with groups like WAR (Women Against Rugby), who challenged the violent, sexist culture of the game and a patriarchal New Zealand society.

According to some sources, the 1981 Springbok tour decentred rugby and a period of rebuilding followed as the game's administrators attempted to win back the New Zealand public.[7] The popularity of the game was damaged even further, however, when the New Zealand Rugby Football Union (NZRFU) decided to send a team to South Africa in 1985. Ultimately, the tour was cancelled after a court injunction brought by two lawyers argued that the tour was not in the best interests of the game and therefore was in breach of the governing body's stated object of promoting, fostering and developing the game in New Zealand. However, an unsanctioned, rebel team (the 'Cavaliers') toured South Africa in 1986, causing considerable embarrassment for the NZRFU. Notably, several allegations were made that players were paid to go on the tour, thus revealing early signs of a creeping commercialism.

The national game and its administrators needed something to purge the memories of the South African controversies.[8] It came in the form of the inaugural Rugby World Cup hosted by New Zealand and Australia in 1987. Aside from all its other benefits, the tournament provided an opportunity to reinvent the national game. Backed by increasing global and local commercial interests, rugby administrators worked hard to win back the public. Judging by sponsorship interest, subsequent participation rates and television ratings it succeeded. The performance of the dominant All Black team that went on to win the tournament contributed significantly to restoring public pride in rugby.

However, the success of the 1987 Rugby World Cup in part contributed to the emergence of new challenges to the game. First, it helped increase the profile of rugby beyond the handful of traditional rugby-playing nations. The International Rugby Board (IRB) has continued to develop that profile through the World Cup and, more recently, the International Seven-a-side competition, to the point where they now boast a rugby presence (albeit limited) in over 100 countries. That international development, however, has had the effect of draining some talent from the more established powers of the game – New Zealand players and coaches have been lured to all parts of Europe, Asia and the Americas. A second impact of the 1987 and 1991 World Cup tournaments was to increase the profile of individual players, leading to the targeted recruitment of a handful of key stars by professional rugby league clubs. Between 1990 and 1995 several high-profile All Black players were enticed into 'defecting' to the rival sporting code.

By 1993 the NZRFU was acknowledging that while the status of rugby was improving there were a number of significant challenges they needed to address. A major change in direction was heralded with a steering committee being formed to conduct a strategic planning exercise coordinated by the Boston Consulting Group. The group described the forces for the restructuring of rugby as 'overwhelming'. While the report of the committee (*Taking Rugby into the 21st Century: Strategic Choices Facing the New Zealand Rugby Football Union*) did not specifically advocate a move towards professionalism (it would have been sacrilege to use the term professional in what had always prided itself on being an amateur sport), there were a number of indications in that direction: 'While rugby is still officially an amateur sport, it is important to ask whether this can be sustained'.[9] The steering committee compared rugby to sporting leagues and competitions in other parts of the world (Australia, Europe, North America), nearly all of which were professional. Players were referred to as 'employees' and the report raised concerns over issues of 'employee welfare'. The need to combat the 'open cheque books' of rugby league clubs was recognised as well as the NZRFU's ability to influence the IRB with respect to the financial compensation of players.

The language of commercialisation and commodification was evident throughout the steering committee's report. The All Blacks were referred to as a 'valuable asset' to be protected from 'over-exposure'. Initial signs of market segmentation were evident, with fans being divided into two different exploitable groups: 'dedicated supporters' and 'theatre-goers'. Draft systems were advocated so that players could be moved around to ensure the evenness of competition that the market demanded. The need to focus on the commercial aspects of the national sport – by increasing revenues, adapting the rules and scheduling of games to meet TV requirements and catering for sponsors' requests – was emphasised in the report's recommendations. Consequently, a streamlined 'professional' management organisation was advocated and the union set about restructuring in 1995, with the new system finally put into place early in 1996. However, despite the best-laid plans for a gradual transition to a professionalised, commercialised era of rugby, by the time the new structure was in place other problems had overtaken the NZRFU.

In the early 1990s key media interests were beginning to identify the value and unexploited potential of rugby as a global television commodity.

This prompted two rival groups to embark on what Fitzsimmons has described as the 'Rugby War'.[10] In the lead-up to the 1995 Rugby World Cup, the World Rugby Corporation (WRC) worked behind closed doors to secure media and player contracts and was well on its way to luring away a significant segment of the New Zealand, Australian and South African rugby union elite player base. This forced the hand of the NZRFU and the other rugby nations. Players were hurriedly signed up to contracts and the race was on to create the competitions necessary, and generate the funds required, to support the new professional game. Averting the biggest crisis of its century-old existence, the NZRFU, in conjunction with the ARFU and SARFU (Australian and South African Rugby Football Unions), signed a ten-year, NZ $800-million deal with Rupert Murdoch's News Corporation. For a number of reasons, the deal is considered to be a major turning point for the sport of rugby generally and New Zealand's national game in particular. First, the agreement forced the International Rugby Board (IRB) to end its antiquated charade of an amateur ethos (referred to even within the rugby administration as 'shamateurism'), and full professionalism was embraced. Second, the deal with Murdoch provided the financial stability to retain players along with the media technologies to take the game global. And, third, while the new contract provided opportunities, it was also a potential threat because New Zealand's national game was now inextricably linked to the global economy, making it directly susceptible to foreign influence and control. One of the first impacts felt was in relation to the ownership of, and access to, televised rugby.

At the time when the 1993 steering committee report was written, television rights and sponsorship already accounted for the majority of the NZRFU's revenue. While broadcasts of the national game remained on free-to-air TV for the first three years of the professional era, renegotiated TV rights deals saw the ownership of live broadcasting of most domestic, and all international, games signed over to subscription-TV network SKY in 1998. The disappearance of live coverage of the national game drew comment and criticism from the public and politicians. Calls were made for legislation that would protect live free-to-air rights in the same way that major national and international event rights are protected in Australia, the United States and Europe. To put the issue in context, it is important to understand that subscription to SKY-TV was not only limited by financial constraints; there were regions of the country where people could not get reception, effectively excluding them from watching live test matches. Ultimately, the debate subsided and no action was taken.

It should also be noted that the NZRFU had embraced sponsorship of the national team some time before rugby officially turned professional. The traditional silver fern emblem that had appeared on every All Black Jersey since 1887 was joined in 1992 by the 'Canterbury of New Zealand' logo and then later by the emblem of New Zealand's main export beer brand, Steinlager. The arrival of professionalism saw the union turn its attention to negotiating new sponsorship deals.

The most significant development in this regard occurred in 1998 as the NZRFU moved to change its principal corporate sponsor. Locally-based manufacturer Canterbury of New Zealand had, through its parent company, a history of involvement with the All Blacks stretching back over 75 years. When the contract to supply the clothing for New Zealand teams came up for renewal, Canterbury had the right to respond to any bid. With the movement of the major global footwear and apparel producers into rugby (Nike sponsors the English and South African teams, Reebok sponsors Wales) it seemed inevitable that the All Black contract would become hot property. Canterbury would not be able to compete against the likes of Nike, which was the clear front-runner boasting an insurmountable resource base. However, a last-minute bid by global sports company adidas was even too much for Nike to counter and the All Black sponsorship changed hands.

To a large extent, it was the link between rugby and national identity that attracted adidas to New Zealand Rugby. Adidas CEO Robert Louis-Dreyfus suggested that outside soccer-crazy Brazil, 'no other country links with sport as New Zealand does with Rugby and the All Blacks'.[11] That, along with the *image* of the All Blacks, led Adidas to enter into its biggest team contract, estimated at over NZ $100 million over the next five years. The agreement demonstrated the economic and cultural currency of gaining global exposure through the integrated media technologies of Rupert Murdoch. As a global sporting commodity (and the most powerful within world rugby), the New Zealand All Blacks became a very attractive 'brand'. Indeed, Saatchi and Saatchi head of television Howard Greive, who was responsible for the producing the new Adidas advertising campaign argued that 'the All Blacks can deliver something to their brand that no other team or individual can in sport'.[12]

From an outsider's perspective, adidas faced at least two major challenges. First, as a global company it needed to establish a local identity and find a way of linking their brand with the legendary All Blacks. Second, it needed to find an innovative way of introducing adidas. All Blacks to the world. Adidas carefully, but expediently, stamped its mark on the All Blacks. A multifaceted campaign was launched to coincide with the commencement of the sponsorship, including event promotions along with TV, radio and print advertisements. Adidas even contributed to the underwriting of a documentary about the All Blacks called *Haka*. The documentary, which featured footage of the first game of the new sponsorship, was sold to TV stations throughout the world. According to adidas Vice President Martin Brewer, the documentary focused on the history, passion and tradition of the All Blacks.[13] These initiatives aside, the most important release by adidas was the introduction of new product, including the new team strip.

On 1 July 1999 the new All Black jersey was released. Prior to the release Craig Lawson, adidas NZ Managing Director, indicated that the new jersey would be in keeping with the traditions of All Black Rugby: 'We respect the sanctity of the All Black Jersey ... we have been very respectful of the whole image of All Black rugby in everything we've done'.[14] The solid black jersey featured the characteristic Silver Fern (the symbol of New Zealand sports teams) on the left breast and the adidas logo on the right. The key point of difference from the previous All Black jersey was in the collar. Gone was the white collar characteristic of All Black jerseys over the past 75 years; instead it was replaced with a black Chinese-style collar, reminiscent of the jerseys worn by the 1905 originals. While the change was only minor, it was quickly seized upon by former players and sports journalists alike who noted the likeness to teams of old.[15] Adidas's worldwide Rugby Category Manager, Neil Nottingham, stressed that the company had 'done its research' before deciding to make the new jersey completely black. He too noted the jersey's resemblance to the 1905 model, saying the key was to retain the All Black heritage.[16]

Adidas executives were quick to point out that they had refrained from putting the trademark adidas three stripes on the new jersey. The New Zealand public were left in little doubt, however, as to the depth of the adidas association with New Zealand rugby. The sponsorship deal also involved the New Zealand 'A' side, the world-champion New Zealand women's team (the Black Ferns) as well as the New Zealand Maori, the Colts (New Zealand juniors), and New Zealand Schools sides. Some of these teams (most notably the New Zealand Maori) have a history and tradition almost as long as the All Blacks. However, adidas 'respect for tradition' obviously ends with the All Blacks, since the three stripes appear on all these teams' uniforms. New Zealand's five 'Super-12' sides that compete in a regional competition with South African and Australian teams were also part of the package. Furthermore, adidas also became the naming sponsor of the new 'adidas Rugby Academy' in Palmerston North. Adidas executives were very happy with the overall launch. CEO Robert Louis-Dreyfus indicated a desire to build gradually on the company's relationship with the All Blacks. He commented that adidas recognised the strength of the All Black image but were wary of 'diluting the All Blacks brand'. Consequently it intended to extend the merchandising of the team by expanding the range of All Black-related products 'little by little'.[17]

There were two key features or themes evident in adidas's emergence into New Zealand and its sponsorship of the All Blacks. First, there was the emphasis on 'Black' not only in terms of the team's jersey but also in terms of event promotions. The second key feature was the idea of tradition and history. Adidas used several different approaches, including a strategic use of nostalgia, in order to construct the image of a long-standing relationship between the brand and the All Blacks. Two new television commercials were launched both of which were tied into local test matches.

A song titled 'Bless 'em All', the 'Captains' commercial in which it served as the audio track and the new All Black jersey were all prominent features in the first game of the adidas era that took place on 10 July 1999 in Dunedin against South Africa. In the lead-up to the game, fans had been encouraged to observe a 'blackout' (another historical/wartime reference) by wearing black clothing, displaying black supporter cards and painting their faces. Lyric sheets featuring the adapted version of 'Bless 'em All' were distributed and local radio personalities led renditions of the song. A temporary big screen was installed at one end of the ground and the 'Captains' commercial was screened repeatedly before the game and during half-time.

After the teams ran out on to the field the All Blacks assembled to perform their traditional challenge to the opposition, the *Haka*. However, unlike typical performances of the *Haka*, this one was amplified and played through speakers to the stadium audience. In addition, the *Haka* that was performed was slightly different to the one that New Zealand rugby supporters had become accustomed to over recent years and to the one performed just a few weeks previously in a game against France. The New Zealand rugby public was quick to seize on the difference, but the speculation that it was related to the new sponsor contract was denied. Amid all the hype that surrounded the event, a game of rugby was played, the result being an All Black victory over South Africa by 28 to nil. The 20 adidas executives (including the CEO) who were present apparently left very satisfied.[18] The Dunedin test match played an important role in launching the adidas brand, but it was the ensuing release of two new advertisements that were central to their local and global strategy.

The first television advertisement, 'Captains', appeared following the release of the new All Black jersey. In keeping with the theme of history and tradition, the commercial was staged in an old locker room and featured six former All Black captains pulling on chronologically appropriate versions of the All Black jersey. As each of the captains (Charlie Saxton, Fred Allen, Sir Wilson Whineray, Sir Brian Lochore, Graham Mourie, Wayne Shelford, Sean Fitzpatrick and Taine Randell) pulled the jersey over their head they were 'reincarnated' as the next captain, concluding with 1999 captain Randell wearing the new adidas jersey. Adidas's global advertising manager, Linda Shatteman, said the Saatchi-produced commercial 'demonstrated that adidas respects and understands the traditions of All Black rugby'.[19]

In the months that followed, a second commercial was launched featuring the *Haka* and entitled 'Black'. The black-and-white advertisement uses interchanging images of Maori warriors, complete with *moko* (facial tattoo) and actual game footage of current All Black players doing the *Haka*. The images and soundtrack were very dramatic. According to Howard Greive, Saatchi's head of television, the concept was to 'create a sort of primal scary ad'.[20] In an interview with *AdMedia* magazine Greive further noted that:

> One of the key words that adidas were keen to go with was authenticity – so that's why we shot a game and that's why we shot the *Haka*. ... We knew that if we could just show people what it is actually like to be confronted by the *Haka* and to watch the All Blacks play their game – then you don't have to manufacture anything. All you have to do is show it.[21]

Presumably Greive fails to see the irony of his statements about authenticity. His team of cinematographers, including two specialists from the National Football League, went to enormous lengths in order to manufacture notions of tradition and authenticity in the adidas advertisement. The advertisement was released in both the local and overseas markets and gained enormous attention. In addition, corresponding poster and billboard campaigns were launched in conjunction with the television advertisement. One dramatic image revealed a huge black-and-white billboard in central London featuring various All Blacks doing the *Haka* with nine tribal warriors montaged into the background. Another billboard showed a huge *moko*-faced Maori warrior glaring angrily at all who gazed upon him with the adidas trifoil logo and the NZRFU trademark silver fern subtly located on the left and right hand sides of the image respectively. Unfortunately for both adidas and the All Blacks, France pulled off an incredible upset, ending the dream of a second Rugby World Cup for New Zealand. Subsequently the All Blacks underwent a process of rebuilding after losing the 2000 Bledisloe Cup and the Tri-Nations series. Still, the All Blacks are a commercial success with respect to drawing crowds and enticing people to purchase the adidas brand.

To this point we have discussed how New Zealand rugby was transformed from a largely amateur game to a highly commercialised global sporting commodity. While there were certainly some challenging moments en route to their current enviable position, there was little in the way of local resistance for new sponsor adidas. However, in July 2000, a year after their corporate debut, controversy arose that had the potential to trouble adidas for the foreseeable future. Specifically, we refer to two concerns raised by members of the Maori tribe Ngäti Toa. The first concern relates to a legal challenge regarding trademark and copyright authority over the use of the *Haka*. In effect, the Ngäti Toa tribe, whose ancestral chief, Te Rauparaha, is credited with inventing the version of the *Haka* transformed and used by the All Blacks, are seeking financial compensation (estimated at $NZ1.5 million) for its commercial use, particularly in adidas advertising.[22] The other concern is less financial and more a matter of cultural sensitivity. The use of the *moko* (facial tattoo) on the warriors in the advertisements is viewed as offensive to some Maori because it is not intended for commercial use; rather the *moko* symbolically displays aspects of the tribal heritage of the person wearing it.[23] Although these protests are coming from a relatively small number of people, their concerns are no less legitimate. What they demonstrate is that despite the economic power of adidas, a global company, there are examples of resistance to the commercialisation of sport on a local level.[24] Although some might interpret the Maori claim for financial compensation as just another form of commercialism, it could also be viewed as a strategy that recognises that while the forces of global capitalism might be too powerful to fight, Maori can strive to maintain some control over the representation of their culture. Moreover, they may also be able, through legal and other channels, to obtain some degree of remuneration that could, in turn, be used to protect, develop and advance other aspects of their culture. Because rugby is New Zealand's national game, it will likely remain a contested terrain of interests, including transnational corporations hoping to reach new markets and those wishing to challenge various forms of power relations that the game reproduces. The simultaneous commercial success of and Maori backlash against adidas highlight the complexity of the global/local nexus in New Zealand. Notably, while adidas is the most recent case, it is not the first example of local resistance to global sporting commodities in New Zealand.

Over the past seven years there have been a number of global sporting companies that have encountered opposition in New Zealand, not with respect to their 'products' per se, rather in relation to their advertising campaigns.[25] While we have already illustrated how adidas has encountered local resistance, in the next section we examine how other global sporting companies, including Nike and Reebok, have had to deal with having their advertisements banned from television. In part, these examples reveal the power, politics and contradictions that emerge when global commodities meet local culture. However, they also illustrate, albeit indirectly, how global, commercialised sport is being challenged and opposed.

Global Sport, Advertising and Local Resistance

Transnational corporations and their marketing consultants have become increasingly aware of the problems associated with trying to *fit* into local cultures. While it has become a popular notion, the 'think global, act local' philosophy oversimplifies the complexity of political systems, cultural values and market forces. The reality is that different cultural products mean different things to different people, in different places, at different times. Perhaps most significant is the fact that local cultural values play a key role in how global commodities are viewed and consumed. And while it is often difficult to articulate the precise nature and meaning of cultural values, the presence of particular institutions, governing bodies and laws provide insights into local concerns.

New Zealand, similar to most nations, has a set of regulatory bodies that are responsible for monitoring and censoring media content as a means of protecting the public and upholding particular standards of decency. One of the most contentious issues with respect to media content in New Zealand centres on debates about media violence. Indeed, New Zealand has quickly gained a reputation for upholding one of the, if not *the*, most conservative state broadcast policies with respect to the issue of media violence.[26] In part, this has been a response to deregulation and the increased importation of foreign, particularly American, television programmes, which are often heavily criticised for their perceived levels of violence. Notably, this philosophical and political stance has carried over into the realm of advertising and, more importantly, with respect to the current discussion, is impacting on transnational sporting interests. Next, we provide case studies of Nike and Reebok advertisements that were banned from New Zealand television screens due to excess violence. However, before doing so it is important that the reader have some basic understanding of how the key New Zealand advertising regulatory bodies operate, including the manner in which they handle public complaints.

In New Zealand, the Advertising Standards Authority operates as a self-regulating body consisting of media professionals with a diverse background. However, in addition to this body New Zealand has established two related agencies: the Television Commercials Approvals Bureau (TVCAB) and the Advertising Standards Complaints Board (ASCB). The TVCAB serves as a first-stage screening organisation. All television commercials to be aired on New Zealand television must gain the approval of the TVCAB. And while it operates as part censor, it also serves as an advocate for advertising firms. It does this by encouraging firms to submit scripts for their commercials in advance so that potential problems can be identified before money is spent on production. However, even advertisements that have been authorised for screening by the TVCAB are subject to public complaint once they are screened. It is at this stage that the ACSB becomes involved. This board reviews all cases of public complaint with respect to established codes of practice. Any member of the public has the right to file a complaint and, based on the case's merit, it may be heard by the full ASCB board. When a legitimate complaint is granted a hearing, the alleged infringing company is allowed to respond and defend its position. Next we present a specific example of a sport advertisement, titled 'Nike Coach', that received a public complaint and was subsequently banned.

Just Don't Do It: The Banning of a Nike Advertisement

In 1994 Nike released an advertisement for the Australian and New Zealand markets. The American-produced advertisement featured a rugby football coach in the process of 'psyching' up his team during a pre-game address. He stresses to his players that they must 'visualise your opponent as your worst enemy. The person you absolutely despise the most … the absolute most.' Occasionally cutting from the locker room, the coach's speech is interspersed with scenes of the players tackling the various people who supposedly represent their worst enemies. Among them are a traffic warden, an Australian talk-show host, former England cricketer Ian Botham and a New Zealand 'All Black' rugby player. The commercial ends with the players tackling a final 'enemy' — the coach himself. As the screen fades to black, and the Nike 'Just do it' slogan appears, we hear him, in strained tones, telling his players that 'You boys are quick learners'.

In order to be screened on New Zealand television, the commercial had initially been viewed and approved by the TVCAB. However, although it was cleared for screening, it later became the subject of a public complaint made to the ASCB. The complainants in this case maintained that not only did the commercial fail to convey the product being sold, but also suggested that it could possibly prompt violence, especially on the sports field. There appeared to be at least three strands to their argument. First, a possible violation of the specific advertising code that addresses the offensive representation of violence. Second, the advertisement is challenged because it does not explicitly feature the product for sale (a factor the ASCB later ruled as unnecessary under local regulations). And finally, they directly confront Nike by questioning the ambiguity of their 'Just do it' signature slogan.

In its defence Nike argued that the advertisement had received a positive response from both the public and from those directly involved in the game of rugby. More significantly, it also argued that it would not intentionally jeopardise its global profile by producing a violent commercial. As it maintained, '[Nike] have an international reputation to uphold and all advertising produced is carefully scrutinised. … In fact, we briefed the agency [Wieden and Kennedy] to pay great attention to eliminating any foul play or violence from the advertisement.'[27] However, while acknowledging that the advertisement was intended to be a 'spoof', the ASCB was firmly of the view that the representation of people being tackled, the majority of whom were not rugby players, was violent. It was of the opinion that the combination of inciting phrases, coupled with tackling, was offensive. Furthermore, it asserted that there was a general public concern with violence on and off the sports field and that this added to the inappropriateness of the commercial. Accordingly, the board ruled that the commercial breached codes for offensive advertising and it was subsequently withdrawn.

While the 'Coach' commercial represents only one of several locally banned sport-related advertisements, it is perhaps the most vivid example of just how strict New Zealand advertising regulations are with regard to the portrayal of violence. Certainly, it is evidence of wider efforts by New Zealand advertising censors to make it clear to advertisers that gratuitous violence of any form is unacceptable, regardless of the way it may be framed or presented. This notwithstanding, what may be more significant to note from this case is that, like several other Nike advertisements that have been the subject of complaint, the 'Coach' commercial faced no restrictions in other countries in which it screened, including Australia and the United States. Thus, even when occurring on a regional basis between nations with seemingly very similar cultures (such as New Zealand and Australia), global advertising and marketing campaigns are still subject to local interpretation, legislation and resistance.

New Zealand's resistance to 'globally' disseminated representations of violence in sports-shoe advertising could, therefore, in fact best be described as just one example of the way in which exposure to global commodities and images may stimulate attempts to rearticulate or define national cultural identity. At the same time these signs of resistance might also be interpreted as a form of resistance to commercialised, commodified sport. Such arguments seem particularly true in relation to what some view as 'American' influences on sport. The particular resistance to problems associated with America is illustrated in our second example, the banning of the Reebok Shawn Kemp 'Kamikaze' advertisement.

Resisting America: The Case of Reebok's Shawn Kemp 'Kamikaze' Advertisement

In 1995 Reebok submitted an advertisement to the TVCAB. In this case the commercial was rejected before it ever went on air; hence there was no official complaint laid, nor a need for an ASCB hearing. Nevertheless, the commercial gained considerable publicity, including a focused discussion on TV3's *Ralston*, a segment of the evening news that addresses topical and controversial issues.

In brief, the commercial features a one-on-one game of basketball between the NBA's Shawn Kemp (who, at the time, was playing for the Seattle Supersonics) and an animated, high-tech 'grim reaper' figure who challenges opponents by warning that 'only those with superhuman ability may enter my court'. Kemp takes up the challenge, stating 'I've got next', which results in the hooded skeleton-figure transforming into a warrior. A physical contest ensues and Kemp, with the aid of his Reebok 'Kamikaze' basketball shoes, drives hard to the basket emitting what has been described as a 'primal scream', causing the warrior to explode.

The TVCAB ruled that the ad contained excessive and gratuitous violence. While the official TVCAB transcript was not available for this case, the basis of the decision-making process can be surmised from various publicly recorded media reports and discussions on the subject. For example, in an official memorandum to Reebok (NZ) Ltd's advertising agency, MOJO, the TVCAB's executive director, Winston Richards, explained:

> Our view, consistent with our previous decisions and with relevant determinations of the Advertising Standards and Complaints Board, is that the level of aggression and violence are totally unacceptable in an advertisement for sports shoes. ... The basic concept of a shoe advertisement which turns basketball into a battle is likely to be unduly offensive to a significant section of the community ... and therefore amendments to this advertisement are unlikely to make it acceptable.[28]

According to Reebok's Marketing Manager, Jeremy O'Rourke, the ad simply combines two popular teenage activities – basketball and video games – and translates these through Shawn Kemp's 'kamikaze' style of play in order to reach their intended target market. This argument did not sway the TVCAB. For example, during his appearance on TV 3's *Ralston* Winston Richards countered Reebok's O'Rourke by noting that

> basketball is theoretically a non-contact sport. ... It doesn't really matter that the character is computer generated ... the key is the violence ... it does carry the standard techniques for enhancing violence in cinematic-type terms ... it has all the elements of enhanced violence through sound effects and the obscured activity where you're not quite sure what happens.[29]

According to Richards, the fact that the violence in the advertisement is part of a fantasy competition between a sporting hero and an animated video character is largely irrelevant. The banning of the commercial – or more accurately the refusal to approve it for airing – was clearly a shock to

Reebok. Reebok (NZ) Ltd general manager Ian Fulton said he was 'staggered'.[30] Reebok had invested a lot of time and energy in the 'kamikaze' campaign, and posters, based on the television commercial, were already in circulation in sports stores and on the streets. In Fulton's words, 'It is painful to see this work go to waste because of the television ban.'[31]

There are several interesting features surrounding this case. First, although the ad was prohibited from screening on New Zealand television, it was approved for showing in local movie theatres. As Reebok's Ian Fulton said at the time, 'It is already screening with success in New Zealand cinemas. In my view the Kamikaze commercial would be enjoying the same response if it was able to screen on television. It seems so contradictory to have differing standards for cinema and television.'[32] Indeed, there are separate regulations concerning the screening of advertisements on television and in movie cinemas.

A second noteworthy point is that although it is not stated in the official memorandum sent to Reebok, statements by the TVCAB's Executive Director, Winston Richards, in newspaper and television interviews allude to the 'American' source of the violence in advertising production. For example, he states: 'There seems to be a trend over the past couple of years, originating in America, to have increasingly violent and aggressive sport-shoe commercials and in our view they are inappropriate.'[33] Later, when challenged with the fact that the same advertisement was playing successfully in almost every other Reebok market, Richards replied: 'It is an American commercial that is certainly played in America and Australia. But we are more conservative when it comes to violence than America, and quite properly so in my view, and more conservative than Australia, and that is quite clearly spelled out in Complaints Board decisions.'[34] Richards not only targets America as the source of the violence within advertising; he clearly demarcates New Zealand as different from both the US and Australia with respect to local policy on the problem. Here Richards employs the term 'conservative' to connote a national censorship policy, though as we will demonstrate, this position is often hypocritical and inconsistent.

There are quite a few apparent contradictions in existing New Zealand media regulation policy. First, as previously mentioned, the Reebok advertisement prohibited from being screened on television was shown in New Zealand movie theatres, despite the fact the audiences may be very similar. Second, critics of media violence, both in New Zealand and overseas, often attack the aggressive representations in fictional portrayals of cartoons, movies and, and in this case, sport-related advertisements. Yet rarely do they criticise the real violence within sports such as rugby union and rugby league, where violence causes real injuries, pain and suffering. Third, there does appear to be some evidence to suggest that global, largely

American, mediated commodities are perceived and labelled as being more violent than similar domestic products. No doubt it is possible that New Zealand media commodities – films, sports, advertisements – are indeed less violent than those imported, and certainly one would expect this given the strict codes being enforced. However, this is clearly not always the case and there are several examples from locally produced movies (*Once Were Warriors* and its sequel *What Becomes of the Broken Hearted*; *Heavenly Creatures*), action adventure programmes (*Xena: Warrior Princess* and *Hercules* were produced in New Zealand), sport (rugby union and rugby league) and even advertisements.[35]

In combination, the aforementioned issues reveal concerns about the impact of global cultural commodities, including violent forms of entertainment, on local culture. To this extent the prohibition or banning of global sport advertisements serve as examples of what Appadurai refers to as global-local disjunctures.[36] Here, we use the term disjuncture to refer to sites of incongruency, conflict and resistance at the global/local nexus. At the same time the contradictions highlighted point to an ambiguous, sometimes biased but certainly questionable, set of social policies regarding the censorship of media violence. While it is difficult to make a direct connection between New Zealand's censorship of American-produced media violence and resistance to forces of commercialisation, we note that violence has become just another commodity that can be sold in various forms of entertainment, including sport. Moreover, it has become one of the new strategies being used by the advertising industry to sell commodities.[37]

Conclusion

New media technologies continue to redefine our conceptions and experiences of time and space. These technologies enable distant people, processes and products to have a more dramatic and immediate effect on our everyday lives than ever before. In the age of post-industrial capitalism this has contributed to a logic, and increasingly global practice, focused on the search for cheaper modes of production, efficiency and new markets. In turn, this has led to the commodification of culture and experience. As society becomes increasingly defined as consumers rather than citizens, transnational corporations and their attendant advertising and marketing support systems are developing new strategies with which to attract and persuade. The result is that advertisements are developed as a means of capturing our memories, dreams and even fears so that they can be re-sold through objects of consumption. However, as the sign wars intensify, there is increasing pressure for advertisers to find new themes that will attract and hold attention even if it means shocking or offending.[38] Consequently, society is now witnessing the appropriation and exploitation of almost every aspect of culture: violence, sex, drugs, disease, suicide and death are now all too common features in contemporary advertising. Yet, as we have illustrated, there are signs of resistance and, in the case of New Zealand, even the complaint of one individual can bring a multi-million dollar campaign to a halt. Notably, while New Zealand may be more sensitive to the issue of violence in the media, including advertisements, it is not alone. During the Sydney 2000 Olympics the NBC television network withdrew a Nike advertisement called 'Horror' because they were receiving so many complaints from the American public. Perhaps Nike intended the ad to create controversy, thereby luring a particular segment of the market. However, public reaction would suggest that a line had been crossed and, while the key issue seemed to be violence, it is impossible to separate out the fact that it was the use of violence in pursuit of commercialisation that was being challenged. Despite this example of resistance, sport will continue to be a key site through which transnational corporations expand their interests. Moreover, the advancement of new media technologies ensures that advertising will be at the forefront of their global marketing strategies. The image-based nature of contemporary social existence would suggest that these are the signs of our sporting times.

NOTES

1. D.L. Andrews, 'The (Trans)National Basketball Association: American Commodity-Sign Culture and Global-Local Conjuncturalism', in A. Cvetkovich and D. Kellner (eds), *Articulating the Global and the Local: Globalization and Cultural Studies* (Boulder, CO: Westview Press, 1997), pp.72–101.
2. See M. Albrow and E. King, *Globalization, Knowledge and Society* (London: Sage, 1990); L. Grossberg, 'Cultural Studies, Modern Logics, and Theories of Globalisation', in A. McRobbie (ed.), *Back to Reality? Social Experience and Cultural Studies* (Manchester: Manchester University Press, 1997); S. Hall, 'The Local and the Global: Globalization and Ethnicity', in A.D. King (ed.), *Culture, Globalization and the World-System* (London: Macmillan, 1991); R. Robertson, *Globalization: Social Theory and Global Culture* (New York: Sage, 1992).
3. P. Donnelly, 'The Local and the Global: Globalization in the Sociology of Sport', *Journal of Sport and Social Issues*, 23 (1996), pp.239–57. S. Jackson and D. Andrews, 'Between and Beyond the Global and the Local: American Popular Sporting Culture in New Zealand', *International Review for the Sociology of Sport*, 34, 1 (1999), pp.31–42; J. McKay, G. Lawrence, T. Miller and D. Rowe, 'Globalization and Australian Sport', *Sport Science Review*, 2 (1993), pp.10–28. J. Maguire, 'Globalization, Sport Development, and the Media/Sport Production Complex', *Sport Science Review*, 2 (1993), pp.29–47. J. Maguire, 'Sport, Identity Politics, and Globalization: Diminishing Contrasts and Increasing Varieties', *Sociology of Sport Journal*, 11 (1994), pp.398–427; D. Rowe, 'The Global Love-Match: Sport and Television', *Media, Culture & Society*, 18, 4 (1996), pp.565–82.
4. S. Jackson and D. Andrews (eds), *Sport, Culture and Advertising: Identities, Commodities and the Politics of Representation* (Westport, CT: Greenwood Press, 2003).
5. G. Fougere, 'Sport, Culture and Identity: The Case of Rugby Football', in D. Novitz and W. Wilmott (eds), *Culture and Identity in New Zealand* (Wellington: Government Print, 1989), p.113.
6. J. Phillips, *A Man's Country?* (Auckland: Penguin, 1987).
7. G. Fougere, 'Sport, Culture and Identity'; also S. Thompson, 'Challenging the Hegemony: New

Zealand Women's Opposition to Rugby and the Reproduction of a Capitalist Patriarchy', *International Review for the Sociology of Sport*, 23 (1988), pp.205–12.

8. J. Kirwan, *Kirwan: Running on Instinct* (Auckland: Moa Beckett Publishers, 1992).

9. *Taking Rugby into the 21st Century: Strategic Choices Facing the New Zealand Rugby Football Union* (Boston Consulting Group, 1993).

10. P. Fitzsimons, *The Rugby War* (Sydney: HarperSports, 1996).

11. R. Lilley, 'Adidas Thinks Big Over All Blacks', *National Business Review*, 16 July 1999, p.11.

12. 'Primal Team', *Admedia*, 14, 9 (October 1999), pp.22–3.

13. N. Wallace, 'All Blacks, Southern Fans and Venue Impress New Sponsors', *Otago Daily Times*, 12 July 1999, p.24.

14. D. Holden, New Strip "Black and Black"', *The Press*, 1 July 1999, p.29.

15. P. Gifford, 'New All Black Jersey Evokes Long and Feared Tradition', *Sunday Star Times*, 4 July 1999, p.B4; also K. Tutty, 'All Black Jersey Needs More Trials', *The Press*, 2 July 1999, p.22.

16. 'Black Collar "Return to Heritage": New Look Jersey Explained', *Otago Daily Times*, 12 July 1999, p.17.

17. Lilley, 'Adidas Thinks Big'.

18. Wallace, 'All Blacks, Southern Fans and Venue'.

19. 'Hymn Over Heresy', *The Independent*, 7 July 1999, p.24.

20. 'Primal Team', p.23

21. Ibid., p.22.

22. N. Reid, '$1.5m for Haka', *Sunday News*, 11 June 2000, p.1.

23. 'Who Owns the Haka', *Backchat*, programme 16, series 3 (Television One, 18 June 2000).

24. S. Jackson and B. Hoko, 'Sport, Tribes and Technology: The New Zealand All Blacks *Haka* and the Politics of Identity', *Journal of Sport and Social Issues* (2002).

25. A. Grainger and S. Jackson, 'Sports Marketing and the Challenges of Globalization: A Case Study of Cultural Resistance in New Zealand', *International Journal of Sports Marketing & Sponsorship*, 2, 2 (2000), pp.111–25; A. Grainger and S. Jackson, 'Resisting the Swoosh in the Land of the Long White Cloud', *Peace Review*, 11, 4 (1999), pp.511–16.

26. K. Weaver, 'The Television and Violence Debate in New Zealand: Some Problems of Context', *Continuum: The Australian Journal of Media and Culture*, 10, 1 (1996), pp.64–75.

27. New Zealand Advertising Standards Complaints Board, Complaint 94/152 (Nike 'Rugby Coach'), 18 July 1994, p.1.

28. 'Reebok Commercial Banned in New Zealand', Reebok Inc press release, 19 June 1995, p.1.

29. Ralston segment of TV3 News, 19 June 1995.

30. 'Reebok Commercial Banned', p.1.

31. Ibid., p.2.

32. Ibid., p.1.

33. 'Sport Shoe Advert Ban Stuns Reebok', *The Dominion*, 20 June 1995, p.7.

34. Ralston segment of TV3 News, 19 June 1995.

35. For example, in 1995 McDonald's released a commercial for its new MegaFeast burger featuring All Black rugby star Jonah Lomu. The commercial shows Lomu battling against animated buildings, eventually destroying them. In style and content this was very similar to the Reebok 'kamikaze' commercial, yet no controversy emerged.

36. A. Appadurai, 'Disjuncture and Difference in the Global Cultural Economy', *Theory, Culture & Society*, 7 (1990), pp.295–310.

37. S. Jackson, 'Sport, Violence and Advertising in the Global Economy', *Working Papers in Sport and Leisure Commerce*, 4 (University of Memphis, 1999), pp.1–20.

38. R. Goldman and S. Papson, *Sign Wars* (New York: Guildford, 1996).

11

Televised Sport in a Global Consumer Age

MICHAEL SILK

There is all around us today a kind of fantastic conspicuousness of consumption and abundance, constituted by the multiplication of objects, services and material goods, and this represents something of a fundamental mutation in the ecology of the human species. Strictly speaking, the humans of the age of affluence are surrounded not so much by other human beings, as they were in previous ages, but by *objects*. Their daily dealings are not now so much with their fellow men [*sic*], but rather – on a rising statistical curve – with the reception and manipulation of goods and messages.

Jean Baudrillard[1]

Consumption is a myth. That is to say, it is *a statement of contemporary society about itself*, the way our society speaks about itself. And, in a sense, the only objective reality of consumption is the *idea* of consumption; it is this reflexive, discursive configuration, endlessly repeated in everyday speech and intellectual discourse, which has acquired the force of *common sense*. Our society thinks itself and speaks itself as a consumer society. As much as it consumes anything, it consumes *itself* as consumer society, as *idea*. Advertising is the triumphal paean to that idea.

Jean Baudrillard[2]

As Baudrillard emphasises, we are surrounded by a 'fantastic' conspicuousness of consumption and abundance.[3] As a cultural product, mediated sport is in no way distinct or separate from the idea of a consumer society. Indeed, mediated sport forms have not only been wholly appropriated into the very order of corporate capitalism; they are in fact an important constituent, and constitutor, of the engines and processes of global corporate capitalism. Somewhat modifying Baudrillard then, mediated sport production, with its constituent parts – signs, goods, services, products, people and other paraphernalia – can be thought of as the very essence of, or the 'triumphal paean' to, the *idea* of a consumer society. That is, it is *common sense* to think about mediated sport today as being produced in accordance with the logics inherent in accumulating capital. As such, mediated sport, as a mythologised hypercommercialised product, is a reflexive and discursive configuration that speaks and thinks itself as a consumer society – it is a *statement of contemporary society about itself.* Rather than provide an apologetic account of the debasement of sport and the media into consumer culture, this chapter aims to address the relationships between hypercommercialised mediated sport forms and the cultural sphere. That is, the chapter aims to rethink the relationship between economies and cultures in addressing the transformations, or as Baudrillard puts it, the 'fundamental mutation in the ecology of the human species' that takes place in, and through, a global consumer age.

This may proffer a problem for many cultural thinkers and scholars, for this involves breaking with some of the cornerstones of modernity and recognising the importance of the relationships between *cultures* and *economies*. That is, understanding mediated sport within global consumer culture *is understanding* the substantial realignments in political, economic, cultural and symbolic life brought about in, and through, an intensified or accelerated phase of globalisation. Mediated sport is a rich arena for investigating these very processes, for there has been a proliferation of broadcast channels that are reaching an ever wider audience within an accelerated phase of globalisation, processes that have potential to disrupt, transform or fragment contemporary cultural identities.[4]

To achieve an understanding of the relationships between economies and culture requires a theoretical sophistication that, with a few notable exceptions, has not been formally embraced within the scholarly discussion of mediated sport. Such an approach to comprehending sport, media and consumer culture requires the building of bridges between cultural studies and critical political economy. This position may well bring criticism from scholars on both sides of the political economy and cultural studies 'divide'. However, like Grossberg, this chapter takes as its starting point that capitalism has always figured centrally in cultural studies work. The differences have actually been in the way certain political economists have practised political economy.[5] To comprehend the relationships between the media, sport, culture and commodification, an approach is required that can engage with the engines, processes and transformations in the late capitalist economy, marked by 'flexible' regimes of accumulation[6] and by transnational corporations replacing the nation state as arbitrators of production. To address the relationships between *cultures* and *economies*, the approach taken to address mediated sport must be contextual and historically grounded, deriving from particular social conjectures, *and* at the same time be able to respond to the shifts and tensions in late capitalism. This involves a cultural studies approach that is more of a 'sensibility'[7] rather than a definable and coherent practice. As such, this chapter stresses a strategic cultural studies sensibility, an approach or practice that aims to explain the transformations and processes of (late) capitalism in particular locations through the application of a loose set of transferable theoretical and interpretative tools. Specifically, this approach is used to address the relationships between (corporate transnational) capitalism, media sport and cultural transformations.

Without question the modern media play a pivotal role in the continual production and reproduction of identities, yet cultural studies has often seen itself rooted in, and to, particular national formations. The new global economy of culture, however, entails the de-territorialisation of culture and its subsequent re-territorialisation, with the latter seriously undermining any equation of culture with location or place.[8] If cultural studies fails to embrace the ways in which the economy is now being restructured on a global scale, it will remain locked within a Fordist paradigm and scholars investigating areas such as mediated sport will increasingly be unable to understand and respond to and the accompanying changes in the spheres of cultures and politics.[9] As Grossberg has argued, cultural studies must begin to question the terms it is locked into if it is to face one its most urgent challenges – namely the issue of globalisation.[10] Grossberg continues:

> As cultural studies responds to the new political terrain opened up by the contemporary globalisation of culture, and transforms itself accordingly, it will face a disruptive challenge. If cultural studies was founded in part as a response to the inadequacy of political economy theories of the relations between culture and economics, it has too often given up any attempt to take economic relations seriously. ... The globalisation of culture makes the cost of displacing the economic too high. Cultural studies has to return in some way to its original problematic – to rethink the relations between the economy and culture without automatically slotting the economic into the bottom line.[11]

To address mediated sport within a globally oriented consumer climate, this chapter sets out to rethink the relationships between mediated sport, economy and culture. Despite the complexities involved, the tensions, ambiguities and contradictions one is likely to encounter (and there are many within this chapter and within intellectual circles as a whole), comprehending mediated sport in the twenty-first century requires reformulating the theoretical distance between the economic and cultural spheres. Gruneau has pointed out that many of the more established pre- and post-war forms of cultural 'identity' (associated for example with class, gender, race, nation, sexual preference) have become destabilised and subjected to new forms of negotiation.[12] It is the contemporary industries of media and entertainment that have become increasingly significant sites for these negotiations. In this context, sport, particularly mediated sport, has become more important than ever as a site for dramatising diverse and often contradictory forms of social identification, not only with nations and cities, but also with race, class and a dizzying array of consumer goods and lifestyles.[13] To articulate the relationships between economies and cultures as constituted through, and by, mediated sport requires pointing to the changing relations of capital, the changing nature of consumption and the changing nature of the global relations of both political and economic power.[14] This involves addressing the ways in which mediated sport is embodied within intersecting market-, political- and consumer-oriented local/global initiatives and the relationships this has with the mobilisation and permeation of place-bound identities. To comprehend these relationships, the chapter explicates critical political economy and cultural studies approaches to analysis of media sport, transformations and negotiations within, and between, transnational corporations, media networks and sport and addresses the impact that a globally oriented hypercommercialised mediated sport can have upon cultural identities.

Levelling the Land: A 'Return to Something Nasty Down Below'

It was suggested in the introduction to this chapter that to comprehend the relationship between commodification and mediated sport it is important to address the central dynamics of global capitalist relations *with* the production of the sport media. This understanding can greatly enhance knowledge of the ideological and cultural meanings inherent in the media product. Understanding these relationships however requires returning to questions of economie*s and* cultures in a way that develops beyond a simplistic distinction between owners of the means of production and waged labour.[15] In their critique of cultural studies, Ferguson and Golding suggest that culture has entirely lost its moorings from the bedrock of history and that social science, political force and economic dynamics all appear to have been evaporated by the intense heat of textual 'interrogation'.[16] Those in cultural studies generally, and those that have addressed mediated sport, have tended to be locked in textual analysis, despite Johnson emphasising, in his seminal cultural studies position piece,[17] the import of production. Such an approach does not adequately account for how the cultural practices of media production take place under the conditions of global transnational corporate capitalism. To contextualise the debate between political economists and cultural studies scholars requires a return, as ever, to the landmark work of Raymond Williams.

Williams sought to engage an exploration of cultural power with political economy. He recognised that a critical political economy of communications was indispensable to his political project, but he never managed to integrate it fully into his theoretical schema.[18] In terms of mediated sport, drawing on Williams, comprehension is required of the active relationships that constitute the *practice* of production – the *conditions* of practice and the *components* of the product.[19] Despite Raymond Williams's legacy, most cultural studies work has focused on media artefacts, or the output of cultural practice, rather than its conduct.[20] With the exception of a few studies in televised sport,[21] media sport production has all but been banished from view, the rationale of cultural production itself and the place and thoughts of cultural producers neglected by the majority of analyses.[22] The 'evaporation' of the political economic sphere in analysis of mediated sport forms is at odds with the legacy of Raymond Williams. Williams argued that we have to break from the common procedure of isolating the object and then discovering the components.[23] To this end, cultural studies has spent surprisingly little time investigating how the cultural industries actually operate on a day-to-day basis. Indeed, Garnham argues that cultural studies' rejection of the manipulation model between producer and consumer has made it difficult to take the mediators seriously as a distinct social group with its own cultural norms, sets of practices and interests and embedded in a distinct labour process.[24] Thus, it has little to say about how the symbols that circulate in our culture are actually constructed or about the possible impact of the global restructuring of the field of cultural production.[25] Murdock contends that you do not have to subscribe to the more apocalyptic or fanciful visions of postmodern theory to accept that we are faced with substantial realignments and changes in economic, political and symbolic life, both within nation states and within the world system as a whole.[26]

Media economies in general, the political economy argument goes, are driven by a logic of capitalism and a pursuit of maximal profit, in which advertising plays a primary role.[27] The central ambition of political economy is to trace in detail how the central dynamics of capitalism, and the shifting balances between markets and public provision, shape the making and taking of meaning in everyday life at every level – across the multiple sites of production and consumption – and how they facilitate, compromise or block the building of a truly democratic common culture.[28] Political economy highlights the fact that capitalist societies are organised according to a dominant mode of production that structures institutions and practices according to the logic of commodification and capital accumulation so that cultural production is profit and market-oriented.[29] Kellner outlines how the forces of production (such as media technologies and creative practice) are deployed according to dominant relations of production in determining what sort of cultural artefacts are produced and how they are consumed.[30] As such, critical political economy is able to locate the boundaries of action within the economic structure of the industry.[31] Cultural studies, however, tends to point towards the logic of capital accumulation, but instead of focusing on the ownership, it looks at the programmes – the messages – that are produced.[32] Turner argued that the lines between the two approaches have become blurred and that there have always been moments of cooperation, even a merging of the two traditions.[33]

The conceptual 'blurring' of the political economy and cultural studies approaches to cultural production is able to address these realignments in economic, political and cultural life and provide more holistic ways of comprehending the link between economies *and* cultures. Further, McRobbie argues that to understand such processes, cultural studies must utilise the insights of political economy.[34] In so doing, she proposes that a more reliable set of cultural maps, graphs, ethnographies and facts and figures about media culture will be forwarded.[35] In analysing media sport this can aid in determining the *reasons behind* which meanings circulate and which do not, which stories are told and about what, which arguments are given prominence and what cultural resources are made available to whom. The analysis of these processes is vital to an understanding of the power relationships involved in culture and their relationships to wider structures of domination.[36]

Some, however, argue that cultural studies has struggled to come to terms with the conditions generated by globalisation and capitalist postmodernity. McRobbie concludes that there has been relatively little theoretical engagement with any of the emergent global and socio-political formations of the 1990s.[37] Given this, it is important to situate analysis of cultural texts within their system of production and distribution. According to Ferguson and Golding,[38] a 'multiperspectival'[39] approach is needed to energise research and theory in an era of new communications technologies and global/local information exchange. The approach conquers the far from satisfactory perpetuation of a false dichotomy between a cultural studies fixed on populism and difference and a monotheistic political economy fixed on class and economies.[40] It was along this line that Hall proposed it was time to 'return the project of cultural studies from the clean air of meaning and textuality and theory to the something nasty down below'.[41]

In mediated sport, this approach can highlight the dominant mode of production that structures media institutions and practices, and thus the cultural and ideological messages inherent within the product, according to the logic of commodification and capital accumulation so that cultural production is profit- and market-oriented.[42] This allows for a conceptual engagement between economies and the transformations in cultures. Specifically, the need for cultural studies to take the insights of critical political economy seriously is clearly signalled by the popularity of the notion of 'cultural industries'.[43] The goods these industries manufacture play a pivotal role in organising the images and discourses through which we make sense of the world. The hypercommerical, transnational televised sport product is no exception, organised and produced around the logic of capital accumulation. The cultural industries do not simply make commodities; through various media forms they make available the repertoire of meanings through which the social world, including the world of commodities, is understood and acted on.[44] Indeed, prompted by the opening of previously closed or protected consumer markets around the world, and vigorously promoted by ubiquitous advertising carried by various media forms, consumerism itself has emerged as one of the main contemporary cultural systems.[45] These processes not only have the potential to permeate and disrupt organically grounded identities but also can introduce new nomadic identities and ways of looking into countries whose recent cultural history has been dominated by nation-building.[46] It is the rationale behind cultural production, framed by technological and regulatory processes and capital flows, that has tended to be absent from analyses of the sport media. Comprehending the profit- and market-oriented conditions of sport production, however, can greatly enhance knowledge of the product created and thus the possible impact that these new discourses may have on cultural identities. Thus, within this chapter, mediated sport is seen as constitutive of, and constitutors of, the broader political, economic, cultural and symbolic transformations taking place within, and through, an accelerated phase of globalisation. Before addressing the dislocation and relocation of contemporary cultures, characterised by the relationships between the sport media and the increasing inter-nationalisation of the flow of capital and commodities, it is important to briefly contextualise these processes in the commodification of the sport media, the interrelated ownership of the sport media and the rights negotiations that take place between networks and sport organisations.

The Televised Sport Marketplace: Transnational Corporate Capitalism and Cultural Identities

Following Grossberg and his colleagues,[47] an adequate understanding of the relationship between sport and the media can only be grasped if we address how the media functions to produce particular kinds of products and how they are influenced by interactions with other situations. This involves looking at how the media, as economic organisations, both require and produce money and how this in turn influences the way they function and the kind of messages they produce. Indeed, Grossberg et al. question the extent to which the media can perform other functions – information and entertainment – adequately if their major role is to make money.[48] In media sport, such questions become important in deciphering the actual product created by television professionals. To what extent, for example, would a media network be subject to the corporate goals and interests of a parent company, advertiser or sponsor?[49]

Jhally has termed the interlocking of sports, media and commerce the 'audience commodity'.[50] The audience commodity describes the interplay between advertising revenues provided to the media as well as direct sponsorship of events, the purchase of broadcasting rights and the elusive and concentrated audience that sports programming is attempting to capture.[51] It has been argued that the media produce audiences that are sold to advertisers.[52] The advertiser becomes the customer and the audience is merely a product. J. Williams applied this perspective to televised sport, stating that this is especially true in televised sport in which the flow of sports coverage and its forms are increasingly dictated by the demands of advertisers.[53] It is proposed from this perspective that a (symbiotic) relationship between sport and television has developed which can be seen as a fusion between media, sport and advertising. This relationship can also be contradictory, because it is also a contractual relationship, in which conflicts of interest are endemic. The media appreciate the value of sport to sell advertising; just as the sports industry appreciates the free publicity derived from the coverage. The media, however, would like to buy the sport material for as little as possible, while the sports industry fights to retain a proprietary interest in what it produces for public consumption.[54] Televised sports audiences offer desirable demographics for advertisers. Furthermore, televised sport can be a live, unscripted, dramatic and colourful spectacle, all of which catch the audience's eye.[55] Televised sport is therefore a useful tool with which to attract advertising revenues. Wenner stated that if a broadcaster has done his [*sic*] job well – and invariably it is 'he' – the sports fan will be attentively viewing when a commercial message appears.[56] This contention can be extended if one considers that many such messages are contained within the broadcast itself, such as when a sponsor's name appears on a player's shirt or advertising board. With the fusion between sport and the commercial sector being so entrenched, the viewer would do well to distinguish the sport from the commercial message.

Televised sport has also heightened the visibility of star performers, which in turn has led to athletes endorsing commercial products and advertisers aligning themselves with popular sports.[57] Televised sport has become an alternative way of product promotion through, for example, signature sponsorship that consists of a company connecting itself to a programme.[58] The growth of televised sports sponsorship constitutes an economic force that has generated a 'cultural transformation'.[59] Specifically, while certain sports have changed, the economic impetus has also changed the way these sports are represented, as media networks attempt to produce 'glossy spectacles' that will attract the targeted viewer and thus please commercial backers. To satisfy the economic forces impinging on the production of mediated sport, and the increased competition from a proliferation of domestic and 'foreign' broadcast channels, producers feel a need to produce a show – an entertainment spectacle. To create this media event, televised sport producers employ the three interrelated production practices: visual, verbal and presentational.[60] These three interrelated production practices work together to augment the live event and create a show. As Maguire stated, 'The media/sport production complex enhances the excitement/spectacle value of the sport ... in the following ways: cutting and editing of the live match, use of camera positions, angle and focus, use of slow motion, use of graphics, music, interviews and "expert" analysis.'[61]

Perhaps the most influential player in the contemporary sport media is the Australian-born tycoon Rupert Murdoch. Through his News Corporation empire, Murdoch has controlling interests in television networks British Sky Broadcasting (BSkyB), Star TV (which covers Asia), the Fox family of networks that cover North America, Australia and Latin America, the British-based Foxtel, German-based Vox and the Australian-based Channel Seven. Through News Corporation, Murdoch's global reach is phenomenal: 'In the course of 24 hours, News Corporation reaches nearly half a billion people in more than 70 countries. Virtually every minute of the day, in every time zone on the planet, people are watching, reading and interacting with our products.'[62] Murdoch is not alone in reaching a global audience through mediated sport. The Disney Corporation's ESPN reaches 127 million people in 50 countries per broadcast day. Ted Turner rivals Murdoch as one of the most powerful media magnates in contemporary society. Turner founded the Goodwill Games and the Atlanta Thrashers professional ice hockey team and launched the first 24-hour television news station Cable News Network (CNN). His empire was acquired by entertainment giant Time Warner in a deal valued at US$7.6 billion., a deal which saw Turner become vice-chairman of Time Warner's board of directors.

A combination of political, economic, technological and legal change has fuelled the global market for (sports) programming. Further, as has been outlined above through Turner and Murdoch, this climate has made possible the cross-border ownership of television stations and the global dissemination of some television channels.[63] Indeed, the rivalry between an ever-expanding range of networks fighting for audience share, and thus the advertisers' dollar, has been an important factor in the escalating cost for the rights for sporting competitions. Table 11.1 outlines some of the recent sports rights negotiations between leagues and media networks. This economic climate has caused some networks to be excluded from screening

TABLE 11.1 RECENT TELEVISION SPORTS RIGHTS

Sporting competition	Time period	Monetary value	Major players
National Football League (NFL)	1998-2005	$17.6 billion (US)	Fox, CBS, ESPN, ABC
National Basketball Association (NBA)	1998-2002	$4 billion (US)	NBC, TNT, TBS
Major League Baseball (MLB)	1996-2001	$1.7 billion (US)	NBC, Fox, ESPN. Prime Liberty
Olympic Games	2003 (Summer), 2006 (Winter) and 2008 (Summer)	$2.3 billion (US)	NBC
English Premier League Soccer	2001-2003	£1.64 billion (GBP)	BSkyB, NTL, ITV

live sport altogether. In Britain, for example, the British Broadcasting Corporation (BBC) has not been able to compete with the capital offered by Murdoch's BSkyB for live sporting events. The BBC is a publicly-funded entity and thus cannot justify the increased expenditure of licence-payers' money on sporting rights. As a result, in the last few years the BBC has lost Ryder Cup golf, English Premier League soccer, English rugby union internationals and rugby league to BSkyB. Additionally, the BBC lost Grand Prix motor racing, the Football Association Challenge Cup and test match cricket to commercial stations within the British Isles. The BBC is able to continue showing some live sports as events such as the Oxford-Cambridge boat race and the Epsom Derby horse race have been listed as 'protected' events by the British government and will therefore continue to be on 'free-to-air' television. In addition to transforming the media landscape, the economic, political, technological and legal conditions that have allowed for increased competition, media deregulation and the global dissemination of television channels have resulted in alterations to the sporting landscape.

The most striking example of the transformation in sporting cultures was seen in the organisation of rugby. Specifically, the transition from amateurism to professionalism can be traced to the corporate forces that were attempting to restructure rugby league in Australia.[64] The changes centred on the emerging pay-television market in Australia, where two major consortiums, Optus Vision (owned by Kerry Packer) and Foxtel (owned by Rupert Murdoch) were preparing to go to air and were urgently looking for a 'product' that would attract subscribers. In early 1995, Packer held both free-to-air and pay television rights to broadcast the Australian Rugby League (ARL) until the year 2000. Murdoch's reaction was to create his own league that would rival the ARL – Super League – and create a product for his network. An unprecedented war followed Murdoch's announcement as players from both rugby league and rugby union were offered previously unseen amounts of money to sign with Super League. To maintain union players, the New Zealand Rugby Football Union (NZRFU) had to find someone to bankroll their plans to pay their players. The unions of the southern hemisphere turned to Murdoch and signed a deal guaranteeing them $500m in return for a decade's worth of television rights. In soccer, the corporate ownership of clubs in Europe is nothing new, with many major transnationals owning or holding sizeable stakes in many top clubs. For example, the Italian club Juventus are allied with car manufacturer Fiat, Dynamo Kiev with Microsoft, Marseille of France with Adidas, Ajax Amsterdam with sport management group IMG and the Spanish club Barcelona with the Sony Corporation. Media networks have also allied themselves with major European clubs. Real Madrid are part-owned by the Spanish telecommunications giant Telfonica, Paris St Germain with Canal Plus, Anderlecht of Belgium with Direct TV, and British clubs Arsenal, Liverpool, Rangers and Celtic with Carlton Media, Granada Television, Time Warner and the Mirror Group respectively. In the UK, various television networks purchase as much of a stake as is allowed by regulators to a media network (less than ten per cent) in as many clubs as is possible in the attempt to influence television rights negotiations. Cable channel NTL, for example, owns 9.9 per cent in English clubs Aston Villa, Newcastle United and Middlesbrough, while BSkyB owns 9.9 per cent in Leeds United, Sunderland, Manchester City, Chelsea and Manchester United. Further, BSkyB has also signed a deal with Manchester United's shirt sponsor, the mobile phone company Vodaphone, to offer Sky on-line news, entertainment and sports news content to Vodaphone's eight million British customers. Indeed, through News Corporation's Star TV network and utilising the popularity of Manchester United in Asia, Vodaphone see this sponsorship as an opportunity to penetrate the massive economies of scale to be derived from the mobile-phone market in Asia. As Peter Bamford, Chief Executive of Vodaphone UK Limited, explained, 'Manchester United is one of the best sporting brands in the world. … This sponsorship goes far beyond a pure shirt sponsorship and will bring a new range of mobile information services to a loyal massive supporter base.'[65]

Economies and Cultures: Cultural Identities and Hypercommodified Global Sport Media

It is not so much these remarkable figures, sporting transformations and negotiations that form the central concerns of this chapter. This context is crucial, for it reveals the scale and appropriation of mediated sport within the global capitalist order. However, the central thrust of this chapter is the rethinking of the relations between these economies *and* culture.[66] Various chapters within this volume have provided a far more comprehensive account of the hypercommercialising tendencies of sporting cultures and the appropriation of sport into the 'avaricious tentacles of corporate capitalism'[67] than is offered here. Rather, this chapter illustrates the ways in which the delivery of a hypercommodified sport, through consumer-oriented global mass media, can affect cultural identities. Barker coherently draws together the economic and cultural relationship in suggesting that

> [t]he case for exploring the economic and cultural significance of television is particularly acute at present because of changes in the patterns of global communications including a significant rise in transnational television. In turn, the globalisation of the institutions of television raises critical questions about culture and cultural identities. Thus, the globalisation of television has provided a proliferating resource for both the deconstruction and reconstruction of cultural identities. That is, television has become a leading resource for the construction of identity projects.[68]

Perhaps crucial in Barker's conceptualisation is his emphasis on the way in which television, perhaps the major disseminator of cultural meanings within contemporary society, can provide resources for both the deconstruction and reconstruction of cultural identities. It is precisely this duplicitous, or perhaps at times contradictory, tendency that the remainder of this chapter investigates within the realm of mediated sport. Specifically, the central argument is that the hypercommercialised media sport empire is not necessarily creating some type of homogenised sporting ultra-culture. Scholars have argued that new economic relations of production, distribution and consumption, and the recreation of new commodity markets have effectively dismantled or transcended existing geographical and cultural borders.[69] However, at the same time that nation states seem to be in decline,[70] paradoxically there seems to be a resurgence of 'nation'.[71] Sporting events, especially as represented on television and in other media forms, straddle this paradox for they serve as time-space compressed sites for the temporary mobilisation of nation states as they often pit one country against another.[72] Rowe and colleagues, for example, point to major sporting events, such as the Olympic, Pan-American, World Student, European and Commonwealth Games, the World Cups of soccer, rugby union, cricket and so on as the most concentrated and powerful intersections of media, nation and sport.[73] At the same time, though, such transnational meetings do have the potential to flatten out difference and encourage social disintegration in which forces of order and incorporation are always negotiated and contested by forces of fragmentation.[74] Thus, the relationships between sport, media and commerce are far more complex, as Barker so eloquently elucidated:

> the relationship between globalisation, television and cultural identity is a complex one in which a whole range of competing identities are in play from absolutist ethnic or religious identities to hybrid cross-cultural identities. ... In the context of globalisation, both the physical movement of peoples and the electronic distribution of 'culture' contribute to the development of just such hybrid identities.[75]

To begin to comprehend the production, distribution and consumption of contemporary identity politics in, and through, hypercommodified media, it makes sense to address the practices of those involved in the creation of such mediated sport products. Somewhat modifying the sentiments of Morley and Robins,[76] then, there is a need to evaluate the influence that emergent world markets and products – stimulated by expanding global image industries and supplied by increasingly sophisticated traditional delivery systems – have on the experience of everyday lives within particular cultural settings. It is the everyday lives and practices of those involved in the production of media sport that are of interest in this chapter. The ideological practices of individuals, key state officials and representatives of transnational corporations, organisations and capitalist classes in mobilising particular cultural, national, gendered racial identities and lifestyles centred more on consumer choices figure strongly in this. It is television, or perhaps more accurately, an increasingly commodified and consumer oriented televised sport, which is central to the temporary mobilisation of contemporary cultural identities or lifestyle preferences. The question, then, of the seemingly contradictory mobilisation and disappearance of the nation state, as Rowe et al. suggest, is not abstract.[77] Rather, it is a matter of the relative power of different groups, be they a nation's government, a sporting organisation or a transnational corporation, to define cultural identities or tastes, and their abilities to mobilise their definitions through their control of cultural institutions.

In response to an increased rivalry between cities, regions and nations, image and profile can be used to gain competitive advantage in the global economy. Through sporting events, cities and nations work hard to present themselves as preferential locations for industrial investment (particularly the new culture industries prefigured on information and images) and for other kinds of more flexible mobile ventures such as conferences, conventions and tourism. In attempting to regenerate cultures, attractions and spectacular structures, cities and localities mobilise every aesthetic power of illusion and image in an attempt to mask the intensifying class, racial and ethnic polarisations going on underneath.[78] That is, given the increased pressure on cities to adopt an entrepreneurial stance to attract mobile global capital, localities are actively involved in initiatives to refurbish and refine national and local identities.[79] In terms of national cultures, this has involved the reinvention of tradition and the reshaping and refurbishment of the ethnic core of the people.[80] In sporting terms, one has only to think of the presentation of the Aryan race through the 1936 Olympics, the exploitation or assimilation (and subsequent commodification and promotion) of 'first nations' and aboriginal cultures at the 1988 Calgary Winter Olympics and the Sydney 2000 Summer Olympics, the strategies of the Malaysian government to promote 'one nation' through the television coverage of the 1998 Commonwealth Games and, of course, the possibilities for the Chinese government in 2008 to promote a purified version of Chinese culture that masks various polarisations and human-rights violations. The strategies, then, of those with power/knowledge to recreate a place *and* a culture that is marketable in the 'network society' is bringing change to what Robins terms 'spaces of identity'.[81]

That sporting events have been used for such political and economic gain is without question. Indeed, television delivery has been at the forefront of initiatives and struggles to promote a particular way of life, a culture and so on. One has only to think back, for example, to Leni Riefenstahl's films of the 1936 Berlin Olympic Games, to the struggles various networks had inserting their own commentary over Russian pictures of the 1980 Moscow Olympics or to practically any opening ceremony of a major sporting event to create a picture of the intentional penetration of a particular way of life, no matter how received, to another part of the world. What, however, is new is the ways in which various organisations (governmental and corporate) are involved in the reinvention of place and cultural identity in response to conditions brought about by an accelerated phase of globalisation in an attempt to attract more mobile global capital and investment. For example, MacNeill's analysis of the 1988 Calgary Winter Olympics revealed that the cultural producers were involved in a remaking of Canadian culture and a reaffirming of nationhood through Olympic ice hockey.[82] MacNeill proposed that the broadcast crew worked hard to provide a particular interpretation of hockey along legitimised storylines that could be profitably *sold* to advertisers.[83] It is proposed then that new economic relations of distribution and consumption and the creation of new commodity markets influence cultural production within transnational corporate capitalism. That is, like other forms of cultural and material production, media sport is committed to maximising profit by developing systems of production and distribution that can respond quickly to the different demands of smaller groups and consumers. As a result, identities can become fractured, pluralised and hybridised, and populations that were silent and marginalised in the past have moved to the centre of the historical and cultural stage. Grossberg et al. propose that in such conditions, no human activity is free from capitalism, commodification and the profit motive, no space in people's everyday lives remains outside these economic processes.[84] Indeed, according to Jameson, this is most apparent in the case of culture and communication, which have become totally commercialised – the result being that no society has ever been saturated with signs and messages like this one.[85] It is thus commonsensical to apply this argument to the production of media sport products and address whether media networks are responding to what Harvey, Rail and Thibault term a 'global logic'.[86]

Harvey proposes that in the face of flux and the ephemerality of capital accumulation, it is hard for cultural producers to maintain place-bound identities.[87] Despite the resonance, fixity and re-imagining of the nation in the logics of transnational corporate capitalism, there are, at the same time, processes that make it more difficult for cultural producers to promote a form of national identity, no matter how superficial, depthless or inauthentic. An important facet of this relationship is between media networks, corporate sponsors and advertisers. The work of Appadurai,[88] Harvey[89] and Featherstone[90] has shown how, rather than an accidental or unintended emergence of signs in distinct localities, transnational corporations increasingly direct advertising and images towards various parts of the globe in an attempt to appeal to specific differentiated audiences and market. These conditions have the potential to alter the production practices of those involved in recreating televised sport for various markets. In a previous study for example, I outlined how, under the logics of transnational corporate capitalism, the Canadian Sports Network (TSN) attempted to derive massive economies of scale from the creation of a bland 'global' product that negated reference to the Canadian nation state.[91] Further, the organisation of media sport production around the logics of market forces and profit accumulation makes available a gamut of meanings through which we can comprehend the world. As was previously outlined, consumerism itself has emerged as a contemporary cultural system, a system that introduces new nomadic identities and ways of seeing. Clearly globalisation has increased the range of sources and resources for identity construction, which allows for the production of hybrid identities in post-traditional global societies where bounded cultures and places, although very much still with us, are cut across by the circulation of other global cultural discourses.[92] Drawing on Maffesoli,[93] Featherstone proposes that the production of identities involves a more complex range of unities and blends in which some of the old communalities may wither away or, at the least, find themselves juxtaposed alongside other (recreated) traditions and value complexes.[94] Perhaps most importantly, it is global television that offers a wealth of subject positions and symbolic resources for identity formation.[95] As an exemplar of a 'global logic' and the fracturing of identities through a hypercommercialised televised sport product, it is relevant to present a brief example of the ways in which one broadcaster produced a major sporting event.

Spectacles of Accumulation and Legitimation: Competing Discourses at Kuala Lumpur 98

This example, focusing on the practices of Television New Zealand (TVNZ) at the 1998 Kuala Lumpur Commonwealth Games, is offered in an effort to provide some empirical weight to the debates in this chapter.[96] However, it is acknowledged that the example focuses on one small broadcaster producing a product for a particular locality. Thus, specific economic, political and cultural conditions that will not be the same for other broadcasters frame the ways in which TVNZ operated. However, it is possible to draw out from the example key insights that point to the production of sport and the production of more complex, hybrid identities and lifestyles within a hypercommodified televised sport product produced for a geographically bounded consumer. Of course, this points to the need for more empirical studies that critically investigate the production of sport for various (inter)national marketplaces. As might be expected, the TVNZ crew was involved in an exercise to legitimise the broadcasts of the games for domestic consumption. This strategy of localisation was deeply bound with the institutionalised values and practices that the crew members brought with them to Kuala Lumpur. That is, among the crew was a logic, or institutional wisdom, that framed their production of the event for a New Zealand audience. These practices took place in relation to an industry-wide belief system about producing televised sport in a commercial, competitive environment. The meanings embodied within these practices were taken for granted by all: to highlight the New Zealand performances at the games, especially the successful ones. Bound with the localisation of the games, the crew worked hard to integrate advertisers and sponsors within the programming; indeed it was accepted as an important and necessary part of the representation of Kuala Lumpur '98 Like MacNeill's analysis of the 1988 Winter Olympics,[97] the spectacle of legitimation, recreating the broadcasts for domestic consumption, was deeply bound with the spectacle of accumulation, the logic inherent in the accumulation of capital.[98] That is, the crew reconstructed a set of meanings that were dedicated to inculcating and exemplifying values of national historical unity that stressed continuity despite profound social change.[99] Specifically, TVNZ commodified tradition and marketed it as pastiche or as simulacrum, appropriating past images in an attempt to accumulate capital and solidify its place in the competitive media marketplace. Through the commercial production process, TVNZ attempted to reconstruct a particular version of the past and reproduced a 'preferred' sense of national identity based on an historically rooted sense of place.[100] This stressed historical unity despite profound change and reproduced a preferred sense of New Zealand and of TV One (TVNZ's flagship channel) as the home of the nation's sporting success and excellence.

However, the main broadcast sponsor associated with brand TV One is Air New Zealand, whose brief was to sell the Asian market to the New Zealand consumer. Air New Zealand desired to be associated with positive images of Malaysia, and Asia as a whole, in an attempt to sell the destination to the New Zealand consumer. As such, the TVNZ broadcasts were a series of productions that emphasised a brand name, Air New Zealand, with a preferred representation of Malaysian identities and cultural symbols as a 'spectacle for the global tourist'.[101] As a result, the marketing of Asia by Air New Zealand for the domestic consumer framed the narrative constructions and resultant meanings of the games. As such, in a global consumer culture, it was common sense to the broadcaster to reproduce or recreate Asia for the local consumer through a televised sport broadcast. In this case, then, the spectacle of legitimation, the practice of legitimising the broadcast for domestic consumption, operated through the spectacle of accumulation. To maintain a *consistent* and *coherent* narrative and to conform to Air New Zealand's initiatives, TVNZ worked hard to ensure its narratives 'flowed' and made 'editorial sense'. Further, the broadcasts made economic sense, for they served to *position* the viewer towards consuming a particular set of meanings about Malaysia, a set of meanings bound with the initiatives of Air New Zealand.[102] TVNZ's broadcasts clearly attempted to conjure up images of the New Zealand nation state, and temporarily mobilise the collective memory. Yet, at the same time, the broadcasts operated to bypass the New Zealand nation state altogether and focus on the mobilisation and recreation of Malaysia state in favour of the accumulation of capital. The meanings embodied within these practices were significantly influenced, resulting in the TVNZ product containing 'preferred' interpretations of Malaysia over 'local' New Zealand performances.

Concluding Comments: Cultural Production in
Global Consumer Culture

This chapter set out to rethink the relationships between economies and cultures. Specifically, through discussion of hypercommodified mediated sport forms, the intention has been to problematise the influence that cultural production within global consumer culture has upon cultural identities. It is argued that substantial realignments within the global economy have increased the possibilities for certain cultural and national identities to be exploited, masked or marginalised. Following Kevin Robins it can be proposed that a 'global-local nexus'[103] has emerged in which the local becomes a fluid and relational space. As such, local cultural identities have increasingly become constituted through their relationship to global political, economic, cultural and symbolic forces. The example of the TVNZ production of the 1998 Commonwealth Games provides tentative empirical interpretation of the conditions that transnational corporate forces created for the production practices of a broadcaster at a major sporting event centred on 'nations', observations that raise important questions for the construction of hybrid identities (including discourses of consumerism) and the dissolution of organically ground identities. Under the logics of transnational capitalism, then, the manner in which discourses of belonging are represented has become exteriorised through, and internalised within, the promotional strategies of transnational corporations. In the case highlighted in this chapter, this involved a televised sport event being represented under the rubrics of a broadcast sponsor, a logic that challenged discourses of locality and provided greater possibilities for belonging.

It has been the aim of this chapter to link these wider corporate, economic and political spheres with the production of sport for a media audience. While not making any claims about how any particular audience might contend or reject such images and discourses, the intent has been to address the impact these conditions have on media sport production. Specifically, it was important to evaluate the influence that emergent world markets and products – stimulated by expanding global image industries, and supplied by increasingly sophisticated traditional delivery systems – have had on the everyday lives, experiences and practices of those involved in the production of media sport. While it has been possible to point to the ways in which cultural producers' practices are structured by the institutions and circuits of commodified cultural production, distribution and consumption, these conditions are far from adequately understood in the production of sport for television. Rather, too much emphasis has been placed upon the text in analysis of the sport media, with little concern for the conditions that have made possible any particular broadcast. Following Raymond Williams,[104] then, what are required are empirically oriented studies that link the rationale behind cultural production, framed as it is by technological, regulatory and capital flows and processes, with the actual components of the product. Comprehending these profit- and market-oriented conditions of sport production will greatly enhance knowledge of the product created and thus the possible impact that these new discourses may have upon cultural identities. In this sense, it might be possible to open up our comprehension of televised sport within global consumer culture and begin to address some of the contradictions apparent in the continual production and reproduction of identities within globalisation processes. At least, scholarly analysis of the sport media must take cultural producers seriously as a distinct social group with their own cultural norms, sets of practices and interests that are embedded in a distinct labour process. Specifically, this requires analysis of the production of hypercommodified media sport forms by a new class of cultural producer – a cultural group for whom consumer culture has acquired *common sense*, a group whose objective reality is the *idea* of consumption, a reality that is endlessly repeated in everyday speech and discourse.

NOTES

1. J. Baudrillard, *The Consumer Society* (London, Sage, 1998), p.25 (emphasis in original).
2. Ibid., p.193 (emphasis in original).
3. Ibid.
4. C. Barker, *Global Television: An Introduction* (Oxford: Blackwell, 1997).
5. L. Grossberg, 'Cultural Studies Versus Political Economy: Is Anyone Else Bored with this Debate?', *Critical Studies in Mass Communication*, 12 (1995), pp.72–81.
6. D. Harvey, *The Condition of Postmodernity* (Oxford: Blackwell, 1989).
7. J. Howell, D. Andrews and S. Jackson, 'Cultural and Sports Studies: An Interventionist Perspective', in J. Maguire and K. Young (eds), *Perspectives on the Sociology of Sport* (Greenwich, CT: JAI Press, forthcoming).
8. L. Grossberg, 'Cultural Studies, Modern Logics and Theories of Globalisation', in A. McRobbie (ed.), *Back to Reality: Social Experience and Cultural Studies* (Manchester: Manchester University Press, 1997).
9. N. Garnham, 'Political Economy and the Practice of Cultural Studies', in M. Ferguson and P. Golding (eds), *Cultural Studies in Question* (London: Sage, 1997).
10. Grossberg, 'Cultural Studies, Modern Logics'.
11. Ibid., p.9.
12. R. Gruneau, *Class, Sports, and Social Development*, 2nd edn (Champaign, IL: Human Kinetics, 1999).
13. Ibid.
14. Grossberg, 'Cultural Studies, Modern Logics'.
15. Ibid.
16. M. Ferguson and P. Golding. 'Cultural Studies and Changing Times', in Ferguson and Golding, *Cultural Studies in Question*.
17. R. Johnson, 'What is Cultural Studies Anyway?', *Social Text*, 16 (1986), pp.38–80.
18. R. Williams, *Problems in Materialism and Culture: Selected Essays* (London: Verso, 1980).
19. Ibid.
20. Ibid.
21. R. Gruneau. 'Making Spectacle: A Case Study in Televised Sport Production', in L. Wenner (ed.), *Media, Sports, and Society*, pp.134–54 (Newbury Park, CA: Sage, 1989); M. MacNeill, 'Networks: Producing Olympic Ice Hockey for a National Television Audience', *Sociology of Sport Journal*, 13 (1996), pp.103–24; B. Stoddart, 'Sport, Television, Interpretation and Practice Reconsidered: Televised Sport and Analytical Orthodoxies', *Journal of Sport and Social Issues*, 18 (1994), pp.76–88.
22. Ferguson and Golding, 'Cultural Studies and Changing Times'; S. Frith, 'The Cultural Study of Popular Music', in L. Grossberg, C. Nelson and P. Treichler (eds), *Cultural Studies* (London: Routledge, 1992); see also J. Carey, 'Reflections on the Project of (American) Cultural Studies', in Ferguson and Golding, *Cultural Studies in Question*.
23. Williams, *Problems in Materialism and Culture*.
24. Garnham, 'Political Economy'.
25. Ibid.
26. G. Murdock, 'Cultural Studies at the Crossroads', in McRobbie, *Back to Reality*.
27. G. Murdock and P. Golding, 'Culture, Communication and Political Economy', in J. Curran and

M. Gurevitch (eds), *Mass Media and Society* (London: Edward Arnold, 1991), pp.15–32.
28. G. Murdock, 'Base Notes: The Conditions of Cultural Practice', in Ferguson and Golding, *Cultural Studies in Question*.
29. D. Kellner, 'Overcoming the Divide: Cultural Studies and Political Economy', in Ferguson and Golding, *Cultural Studies in Question*.
30. Ibid.
31. Garnham, 'Political Economy'.
32. L. Grossberg, E. Wartella and D. Whitney, *Media Making: Mass Media in a Popular Culture* (Thousand Oaks, CA: Sage, 1998).
33. G. Turner, *British Cultural Studies: An Introduction*, 2nd edn (Boston, MA: Unwin Hyman, 1996).
34. A. McRobbie, 'All the World's a Stage, Screen, or Magazine: When Culture is the Logic of Late Capitalism', *Media, Culture, and Society*, 18 (1996), pp.335–42.
35. Ibid.
36. Garnham, 'Political Economy'.
37. McRobbie, 'All the World's a Stage'.
38. Ferguson and Golding, 'Cultural Studies and Changing Times'.
39. D. Kellner, *Media Culture: Cultural Studies, Identity and Politics Between the Modern and the Postmodern* (London: Routledge, 1995); Kellner, 'Overcoming the Divide'.
40. Ferguson and Golding, 'Cultural Studies and Changing Times'.
41. S. Hall, 'Cultural Studies and its Theoretical Legacies', in Grossberg, Nelson and Treichler, *Cultural Studies*, pp.277–294.
42. Kellner, 'Overcoming the Divide'.
43. Murdock, 'Cultural Studies at the Crossroads'.
44. Ibid.
45. Ibid.
46. Ibid.
47. Grossberg, Wartella and Whitney, *Media Making*.
48. Ibid.
49. Ibid.
50. S. Jhally, 'The Spectacle of Communication: Material and Cultural Factors in the Evolution of the Sports/Media Complex', *Insurgent Sociologist*, 3 (1984), pp.41–57; S. Jhally, 'Cultural Studies and the Sport/Media Complex', in Wenner, *Media, Sports, Society*, pp.70–93.
51. Jhally, 'Cultural Studies and the Sport/Media Complex'.
52. Jhally, 'The Spectacle of Communication'; L. Wenner, 'The Audience Experience with Sports on Television', in Wenner, *Media, Sports, and Society*, pp.13–48.
53. J. Williams, 'The Local and the Global in English Soccer and the Rise of Satellite Television', *Sociology of Sport Journal*, 11 (1994), pp.376–97.
54. J. Wilson, *Playing by the Rules: Sport, Society, and the State* (Detroit, MI: Wayne State University Press, 1994).
55. Wenner, 'The Audience Experience'.
56. Ibid.
57. G. Whannel, 'The Unholy Alliance: Notes on Television and the Remaking of British Sport, 1965–1985', *Leisure Studies*, 5 (1986), pp.129–45; G. Whannel, *Fields in Vision: TV Sport and Cultural Transformation* (London: Routledge, 1992).
58. J. Hargreaves, *Sport, Power and Culture* (Oxford: Polity Press, 1986).
59. Whannel, *Fields in Vision*.
60. Ibid.
61. J. Maguire, 'Globalisation, Sport Development and the Media/sport Production Complex', *Sport Science Review*, 2 (1993), p.39.
62. News Corporation website, online at http://www.newscorp.com (accessed June 2000).
63. D. Held, A. McGrew, D. Goldblatt and J. Perraton, *Global Transformations: Politics, Economics and Culture* (Oxford: Polity Press, 1999).
64. See P. Fitzsimmons, *The Rugby War* (Sydney: HarperCollins, 1996) for a detailed explication of these processes.
65. Vodaphone, 'Vodaphone and BSkyB to Pursue New Relationship', online at http://www.vodaphone.net (accessed June 2000).
66. Grossberg, 'Cultural Studies, Modern Logics'.
67. See Andrews, Chapter 1 in this volume.

68. C. Barker, *Television, Globalization and Cultural Studies* (Buckingham: Open University Press, 1999), p.3.
69. Harvey, *The Condition of Postmodernity*; D. Morley and K. Robins, *Spaces of Identity: Global Media, Electronic Landscapes and Cultural Boundaries* (London, Routledge, 1995).
70. Held et al., *Global Transformations*.
71. D. Rowe, J. Mckay and T. Miller, 'Come Together: Sport, Nationalism and Media Image', in L. Wenner (ed.), *MediaSport* (London and New York: Routledge, 1998).
72. Ibid.
73. Ibid.
74. I. Ang, 'Global Media/Local Meaning', *Media Information Australia*, 62 (1991), pp.4–8; Rowe et al., 'Come Together'.
75. Barker, *Global Television: An Introduction*, p.170.
76. Morley and Robins, *Spaces of Identity*.
77. Rowe et al., 'Come Together'.
78. F. Bianchini and H. Scwengel, 'Re-imaging the City', in J. Corner and S. Harvey (eds), *Enterprise and Heritage: Crosscurrents of National Culture* (London: Routledge, 1992), pp.212–34; Harvey, *The Condition of Postmodernity*; Whitson and Macintosh, 'The Global Circus: International Sport Tourism and the Marketing of Cities', *Journal of Sport and Social Issues*, 20 (1996), pp.239–57.
79. K. Robins, 'Tradition and Translation: National Culture in its Global Context', in Corner and Harvey, *Enterprise and Heritage*.
80. M. Featherstone, *Undoing Culture: Globalisation, Postmodernism, and Identity* (London: Sage, 1995).
81. Robins, 'Tradition and Translation'.
82. M. MacNeill, 'Networks: Producing Olympic Ice Hockey for a National Television Audience', *Sociology of Sport Journal*, 13 (1996), pp.103–24.
83. Ibid.
84. Grossberg, Wartella and Whitney, *Media Making*.
85. F. Jameson, *Postmodernism, or the Cultural Logic of Late Capitalism* (London: Verso, 1991).
86. J. Harvey, G. Rail and L. Thibault, 'Globalization and Sport: Sketching a Theoretical Model for Empirical Analyses', *Journal of Sport and Social Issues*, 20 (1996), pp.239–57.
87. Harvey, *The Condition of Postmodernity*.
88. A. Appadurai, 'Disjuncture and Difference in the Global Economy', *Theory, Culture & Society*, 7 (1990), pp.295–310; A. Appadurai, *Modernity at Large: Cultural Dimensions of Globalisation* (Minneapolis, MN: University of Minnesota Press, 1996).,
89. Harvey, *The Condition of Postmodernity*.
90. Featherstone, *Undoing Culture*.
91. M. Silk, 'Local/Global Flows and Altered Production Practices: Narrative Constructions at the 1995 Canada Cup of Soccer', *International Review for the Sociology of Sport*, 34 (1999), pp.113–24.
92. C. Barker, *Global Television: An Introduction*.
93. M. Maffesoli, 'The Ethics of Aesthetics', *Theory, Culture & Society*, 8 (1991), pp.7–20; M. Maffesoli, *The Time of the Tribes* (London: Sage, 1995).
94. Featherstone, *Undoing Culture*.
95. Barker, *Global Television: An Introducton*; Kellner, *Media Culture*.
96. See M. Silk, 'Together We're One: The Place of the Nation in Media Representation of Kuala Lumpur 98', *Sociology of Sport Journal*, 18 (2001), pp.277–302..
97. MacNeill, 'Networks: Producing Olympic Ice Hockey'.
98. Jhally, 'Cultural Studies and the Sport/Media Complex'.
99. Rowe et al., 'Come Together'.
100. S. Hall, 'Cultural Studies: Two Paradigms in Cultural Studies', in T. Bennett (ed.), *Culture, Ideology, and Social Processes* (London: Batsford, 1989), pp.19–39.
101. A. Firat, 'Consumer Culture or Culture Consumed', in J. Costa and G. Bamossy (eds), *Marketing in a Multicultural World* (London and Thousand Oaks, CA: Sage, 1995).
102. Silk, 'Together We're One'.
103. Robins, 'Tradition and Translation'; K. Robins, 'What in the World is Going On?' in P. Du Gay (ed.), *Production of Culture/Cultures of Production* (London: Sage, 1997).
104. Williams, *Problems in Materialism and Culture*.

12

Media Ownership of Teams:
The Latest Stage in the Commercialisation
of Team Sports

BILL GERRARD

Professional team sports have become a set of commodities to be bought and sold in the marketplace.[1] The professional team sports industry is a complex micro-economy consisting of a set of interdependent markets. Teams buy the services of players and coaches. Fans buy game tickets, subscriptions to TV sports channels and team merchandising. TV companies buy sports broadcasting rights to deliver games to the stay-at-home fans. Big business buys executive suites, corporate hospitality and sponsorship opportunities. At the top end of the team sports hierarchy, it is a seller's market. There is a limited supply of star players and top coaches. And there are relatively few big teams with large fan bases and valuable broadcasting and sponsorship rights. The star players, top coaches and big teams have considerable market power, and are able to extract high economic rents.

The teams themselves have become commodities to be bought and sold, with big teams commanding high acquisition values. For example, the annual Forbes report in June 2000 on the value of Major League Baseball (MLB) teams ranks the New York Yankees as the most valuable team with an estimated current value of $548 million.[2] The average value of a MLB team is $233 million, implying that the total current value of MLB teams is $7 billion. The largest soccer team in the world, Manchester United in England, has a record market capitalisation on the London Stock Exchange of £1.02 billion ($1.5 billion).

One of the most significant aspects in the recent development of the professional team sports industry has been the acquisition of teams by media groups.[3] This has been an international development in several sports but has been most prevalent in the North American major leagues and European soccer. The ownership of teams by media groups could potentially have a very profound impact on the future direction of professional team sports, particularly on the sporting and financial viability of leagues. To the extent that media groups are attracted to owning and controlling the image rights of the biggest teams and are prepared to invest heavily in pursuit of sporting success, this could undermine the competitive balance of leagues as the smaller teams become reduced to perennial doormats. In addition, the media-owned teams may spark another acceleration in the wage-price spiral in professional team sports, undermining the financial viability of all professional sport teams.

This chapter examines some of the economic implications of the ownership of teams by media groups in the context of the developing commercialisation of team sports. It traces the development of team sports as a commodity from their initial professionalisation of team sports through to the current era of commercialisation of team sports. It is argued that media ownership of teams is best understood as a response to the extreme uncertainty in the professional team sports industry arising from both the internal dynamic of the industry and the external environmental turbulence primarily caused by technological change.

To this end the next section outlines a framework for understanding the development of team sports as a commodity. Three stages are identified: regulated professionalism; deregulated professionalism; and commercialism. The following section focuses on the media ownership of teams as the latest emerging trend in the commercialisation of sport. The acquisition of pro sports teams by media groups represents an example of upstream (or backward) vertical integration. The economic theory of vertical integration is discussed and applied to the media ownership of teams. In particular, attention is given to why the professional team sports industry appears to be bucking the trend in other industries, where many firms are undertaking vertical de-integration. The next section provides a case study of vertical integration in English professional soccer with an emphasis on the acquisition of ownership stakes in teams by media groups as a tactic in the competition for broadcasting rights. The paper concludes with a discussion of what the future may hold for professional team sports and its fans as the media ownership and control of teams extends.

The Commercialisation of Team Sports

The development of team sports as a commodity can be useful analysed in terms of three stages. The first stage, regulated professionalism, for most major sports covers the period from the mid-nineteenth century, when professional team sports first developed, through to the 1950s and the emergence of television as a mass medium. The second stage of deregulated professionalism covers the period from the 1950s through to the 1980s as televised sport grew rapidly and the internal regulatory mechanisms within many sports became progressively less restrictive, particularly with the achievement of free agency by players. The third and current stage of the development of team sports is that of commercialism from the late 1970s onwards in most major sports. The chronology is indicative, a representative summary of developments across the leading team sports in North America, Europe and other leading industrialised nations reflecting broadly similar patterns of external environmental change in socio-economic conditions and technological progress especially in the media and telecommunications. For any individual team sport in any specific country, the transition from one stage to another is dependent on the timing of key structural changes such as the relaxation of restrictions on player bargaining rights, league re-organisation and major broadcasting and sponsorship deals.

Stage One: Regulated Professionalism

The professionalisation of team sports began in the mid-nineteenth century largely as a result of the socio-economic developments consequent on the Industrial Revolution. Industrialisation created an urbanised working class. As wages increased and working hours were reduced through statutory controls and other changes in working practices, workers gradually had more time and money to spend on leisure. Consequently there was a rapid growth in the demand for spectator sports involving highly skilled athletes. But the demand to watch top-quality sport with top players changed the entry requirements for participants. Regular participation in public sporting events was no longer limited to a rich elite who could afford to indulge in sport. Sporting participation became a meritocracy with entry based on skill. The mass demand for spectator sports created the opportunity for skilled players to earn their living from sport able to devote themselves on a full time basis to training and playing. Thus was born the professional skilled athlete.

But the payment of players had a profound impact on the nature of sport. Sport became a commodity to be sold to spectators to generate the revenues to cover player costs. This led to the first 'enclosure' movement in sport. Professional sport could not be played on the village green open and freely available to all spectators. Professional sport by its very nature must be exclusive, available only to those spectators prepared to pay for the right to watch the contests. Hence the professionalisation of sport saw the relocation of the principal sporting venue away from the open village green to the closed urban sports stadium with pay-to-view turnstiles. Gate revenues became the major source of team income to cover the cost of player wages.

Teams became financial organisations with income and expenditures, assets and liabilities. The financialisation of teams has several long-term implications. The initial formation of teams required a significant financial investment, particularly for those teams that acquired land and built their own stadium. The need to raise finance meant that teams had to form themselves into business companies, with initial investors taking equity stakes in teams. Originally teams were formed as mutual associations of amateur players who wished to play competitively against other teams. Professionalisation transformed teams into business companies with owners, creating a separation between team participation and team control. Players are paid employees producing the sporting performance, but the owners have the ultimate financial control of the team. Inevitably this creates potential conflicts, not only between players and owners but also between owners and fans.

Unlike amateur teams, professional teams have several groups of stakeholders with different and often conflicting objectives. Fans typically are concerned only with sporting performance, but the owners of professional teams have both sporting and financial objectives. These two objectives are often mutually consistent, but periodically team owners and their senior management may face difficult choices between on-the-field sporting performance and off-the-field financial performance. Teams can attempt to improve sporting performance by spending more on playing talent, but eventually there comes a point where additional expenditure on playing talent, even if it achieves greater sporting success, cannot generate sufficient additional revenues to cover the increased player costs. This is the fundamental performance trade-off in professional team sports. The extent to which teams are prepared to sacrifice financial performance in pursuit of better sporting performance depends on the preferences of the owners. Vrooman has described a preference for improved sporting performance over maximising financial performance as the sportsman-owner effect.[4] In general, until relatively recently, the professionalisation of sport has been associated by the predominance of the sportsman-owner effect with team owners setting only the minimal financial targets of breaking even and long-run survival.

As well as creating the team-management problem of resolving the potential conflicts between different stakeholders, the professionalisation of team sports also created a league-management problem, the resolution of potential conflicts between the private interests of individual teams and their collective interests as a league of teams. Professional team sports have a peculiar economics.[5] Sporting contests are jointly produced by independent competitors. It takes two teams to produce an individual game and several teams to produce league and knock-out tournaments. Successful leagues must strive to maintain a reasonable degree of competitive balance between teams to ensure that game and league outcomes remain uncertain. Without uncertainty of outcome, individual games and tournaments overall become highly predictable, losing an essential element of their appeal to fans. Winning is important to teams and their fans but the emotional and financial value of winning is often crucially dependent on the closeness of the competition. Fans of winning teams may become bored if winning becomes almost guaranteed because of the lack of effective competition from other teams. This phenomenon is often referred to as the New York Yankees paradox in recognition of the general perception that attendances at Yankees games began to decline during their period of post-war domination, only for this trend to be reversed as the Yankees' sporting performance declined.

Competitive balance in a sports league is a collective good. It is not the natural outcome of teams pursuing their own private interests. Teams differ in their capacity to generate revenue. The economics of individual teams is largely a matter of history and geography. Teams based in large metropolitan areas with a history of past achievement tend to have the largest fan bases and are able to generate large revenues. In the pursuit of sporting success, the big-revenue teams will naturally tend to use their financial power to attract the star players. But the concentration of the star players in a few big-revenue teams can undermine the competitive balance of leagues, with a potential loss of revenues for all teams if fans begin to lose interest. In addition, excessive competition between the big-revenue teams for star players will bid up player wages, thereby further undermining the financial viability of leagues.

Leagues have recognised from their very inception that there is an imperative to avoid excessive economic competition between their member teams in order to protect the collective interest in maintaining the sporting and financial viability of leagues. Leagues developed a set of internal regulatory mechanisms to maintain competitive balance and prevent financial failure. Broadly speaking, two types of regulatory mechanisms have been developed by leagues: revenue-sharing and player labour-market restrictions, including player reservation systems and wage controls. The principal form of revenue-sharing in professional team sports has been shared gate receipts, the principal source of team revenue. Shared gate receipts represent a form of cross-subsidisation of small-revenue teams by the big-revenue teams. Effective cross-subsidisation reduces the financial disparity between teams, thereby allowing smaller teams to be more competitive in the market for playing talent and more able to recruit and retain star players.

Player labour-market restrictions involve more direct controls on the recruitment, retention and remuneration of players. Most sports leagues introduced player labour-market restrictions at the time of their formation or very soon afterwards to maintain competitive balance by restricting the concentration of star players at the big-revenue teams, as well as to control the growth of player costs to ensure the financial viability of the leagues. Player labour-market restrictions are of two general types: player reservation systems and wage controls. Player reservation systems involve the administrative allocation of players between teams. Teams are given exclusive rights to recruit and/or retain their allocated players. In contrast, free agency involves the market allocation of players between teams, with players able to negotiate with any team at the end of their current contract. Under player reservation systems, a player can only move to a new team if his existing team is prepared to release him and this may require payment of a 'transfer fee' or some form of barter arrangement such as player or draft-pick swaps. Examples of player reservation systems include the reserve rule in major-league baseball, the drafting system for new players entering the major leagues, and the retain-and-transfer system in European soccer.[6] All of these systems were originally designed to ensure that all teams had equal access to the pool of available playing talent irrespective of financial size. But these player reservation systems, by severely limiting the bargaining power of players (effectively a player has only a single buyer for his playing services), also helped control the growth of player wages. In addition, leagues also introduced direct controls on wages including maximum wage levels for individual players and salary caps for total team expenditure on players. Again these direct wage controls sought to maintain competitive balance and financial viability.

The success of player reservation systems in maintaining competitive balance remains a matter of controversy. Rottenberg proposed what is now referred to in the sports economics literature as Rottenberg's invariance proposition.[7] He argues that the equilibrium distribution of playing talent across teams in a league is invariant to whether the league operates under a player reservation system or free agency. Rottenberg's theoretical model of a sports league assumes that both teams and players are wealth maximisers. Under wealth maximisation, players will move to the teams where their marginal revenue product (MRP) is highest. The equilibrium distribution of playing talent occurs when the MRP of playing talent is equalised across teams. The equilibrium distribution is unaffected by the structural regime in the market for playing talent. The star players will move to the big-revenue teams to maximise their MRPs irrespective of whether teams or players control the movement of players between teams. A wealth-maximising small-revenue team will trade its star player to a big-revenue team if the return from trading the player exceeds that from retaining the player. The structural regime affects only the income distribution between teams and players, not the distribution of playing talent between teams. In effect, the structural regime allocates the ownership of the property rights over a player's playing services and, hence, determines who earns the economic rents from these playing services. Under a player reservation system, teams earn the economic rent through their monopsonistic market power. Under free agency, star players earn the economic rents as monopolistic suppliers of highly skilled playing services. The empirical evidence on the effects of free agency on the distribution of playing talent is inconclusive.[8]

Stage Two: Deregulated Professionalism

The transition of professional team sports from a highly regulated commodity to a free-market commodity began in the post-war era. Partly the transition was a consequence of external environmental change, particularly the growth of television as a mass medium. Television brought new opportunities to professional team sports through the opportunity to bring live games and edited highlights into the home. No longer was the opportunity to watch sport to be restricted to those prepared to travel to the stadium. The armchair fan was born. The emergence of new market opportunities for professional team sports gave new momentum to the internal dynamic created by the ongoing conflict between teams and players over income distribution. Throughout the 1960s and 1970s, player associations in leading team sports throughout the world demanded the removal of the restrictions on their bargaining rights and the introduction of free agency. Free agency and arbitration was introduced in major-league baseball in 1976. Full free agency was achieved in the NBA (basketball) in 1983. In English professional soccer, the maximum wage was abolished in 1961 and the retain-and-transfer system was reformed following a High Court ruling in 1963 that it represented a restraint of trade. Soccer players got 'freedom of contract' in England in 1977, but this was a very diluted form of free agency that still required transfer fees to be paid for out-of-contract players moving to another team. Free agency has only been achieved in European soccer following the Bosman ruling by the European Court of Justice in 1995.

The gradual removal of player labour-market restrictions has had the expected effect on player wages.[9] As the bargaining power of players has increased, so inevitably has the rate of growth of player wages. Zimbalist, for example, estimates that free agents in major-league baseball now receive wages in excess of their MRP, compared to earlier estimates by Scully and other studies that suggested the top baseball players only received around 15 to 20 per cent of their MRPs under the reserve rule in the 1960s and 1970s.[10] This represents an annual average growth rate of around ten per cent in player wages over and above the underlying revenue growth in major-league baseball since the introduction of free agency. A similar trend has emerged in European soccer. In England, the wages of professional soccer players grew at an annual average rate of less than three per cent from 1900 through to the abolition of the maximum wage in 1961. Since 1961, the annual average rate of player wage growth for the top players has been around 15 per cent. And since the introduction of Bosman free agency in 1995, player wage growth in the English Premiership has averaged around 35 per cent annually, which, just as in major-league baseball, exceeds revenue growth by around ten per cent annually.

The acceleration of player wage growth has had repercussions throughout the professional team sports industry. Teams have come under increased pressure to generate and retain more revenues. This has inevitably resulted in higher gate prices. In addition the big-revenue teams have sought to reduce the extent of any revenue-sharing arrangements in their leagues in order to retain a greater proportion of their revenues. But the lessening of the degree of cross-subsidisation between teams has tended to reduce the degree of competitive balance in leagues. Overall, the era of deregulated professionalism saw the emergence of a wage-price spiral in professional team sports with teams locked into a vicious circle of higher wage growth, forcing them to charge higher prices for gate admissions and their image rights. In turn players use their increased bargaining power to push for ever higher wages. Inevitably, deregulated professionalism undermined the sporting and financial viability of leagues as the regulatory mechanisms for protecting the collective interests of teams were gradually dismantled.

Stage Three: Commercialism

The commercialisation of team sports from the late 1970s onwards is the inevitable outcome of the interplay between the industry's internal dynamic and external environmental change. The growth in the demand for televised sport has been phenomenal. Coupled with this growth in demand, there has been huge technological change in the telecommunications and media industry. New delivery platforms have emerged with the development of cable and satellite broadcasting. Digital TV signals are replacing analogue signals. This technological change has produced the second 'enclosure' movement in professional team sports. Sport has entered the era of the electronic turnstile, with subscription and pay-per-view TV. Sport is crucial to the success of new delivery platforms and digital TV. Sport is the single biggest driver globally in the take-up of subscriptions to satellite, cable and digital TV. Rupert Murdoch of News Corporation put it very succinctly when he said that sport is the 'battering ram'. As a consequence the value of sport broadcasting rights has grown exponentially. For example, in 1960 the broadcasting rights for American football in the NFL and AFL combined were valued at $4.7 million. By 1975 the total value of the broadcasting rights had grown to $58.2 million. Fifteen years later, the rights were worth $948 million. Currently the NFL's broadcasting rights gross more than $2 billion annually. The broadcasting rights for other major-league sports and European soccer have followed similar trends. The huge increase in the market for televised sport has had a knock-on effect on the value of other image rights, particularly sport sponsorship, now estimated to worth in excess of $20 billion worldwide.

In contrast to professionalisation, the defining characteristic of the commercialisation of team sports has been the change in the corporate objectives of teams, away from maximising sporting performance subject to a break-even or minimum-loss financial constraint. Commercial sports teams are profit-led businesses seeking to increase shareholder value. Commercialism signifies the decline of the sportsman-owner effect, with the ownership of teams dominated more by investment funds and corporate ownership than private individuals. In some cases, particularly professional soccer in England, the change in ownership has involved stock-market flotation of the team as a public company on the stock market. Under more commercially orientated ownership and management regimes, team investment in playing squads is subject to similar financial appraisal processes as other capital projects. Commercial sports teams attempt to invest in playing talent only up to that point at which shareholder value is maximised.

The maximisation of revenue opportunities by teams has led to further deregulation in sports leagues as the big-revenue teams strive for greater control of their image rights and revenue streams. One consequence in many domestic leagues throughout the world has been the creation of breakaway 'super' or 'premier' leagues controlled by the top teams. This has inevitably created conflict with the governing authorities. In European soccer, this has gone one stage further, with active discussion by the biggest clubs across Europe about the creation of a transnational European Super League outside the established governing structure. The conflict between teams and governing authorities has also focused on the control of image rights with the big teams seeking greater control of their own image rights, especially broadcasting rights. To the extent that the big teams gain more control over their own image rights, this further reduces the degree of cross-subsidisation in leagues, exacerbating the problem of maintaining competitive balance.

But the greater commercial orientation of teams has not necessarily ensured greater financial stability. The star players have also become profit-led businesses employing an array of legal and financial advisers to maximise their earnings streams. Free agency allows the star players maximum scope to exploit their bargaining power to maintain and increase their share of teams' revenue streams. The wage-price spiral in the professional team sports industry has further accelerated. Alan Sugar, a former chairman of the English soccer club Tottenham Hotspur, has famously described this as the 'prune-juice' effect. The revenues that flow into teams very quickly flow out again in player salaries. Thus commercialism has in many cases tended to further undermine the sporting and financial viability of leagues by exacerbating the disparity between teams and heightening the conflict between players and teams.

The Media Ownership of Professional Sports Teams

An emerging trend in the commercialisation of team sports has been the acquisition of team ownership stakes (either partial or total) by media groups. It is a trend that is common to both the North American major leagues and British and European soccer. A survey in February 2000 of the North American major leagues found that 29 major-league teams are owned wholly or partially by media groups.[11] These ownership stakes are held by 19 different media groups, with nine media groups having stakes in two or more teams from different major leagues. Time Warner currently has stakes in three teams: the Atlanta Braves (MLB), the Atlanta Hawks (NBA) and the Atlanta Thrashers (NHL). In British soccer, media groups have stakes in ten English Premiership teams and one Scottish Premiership team. Media groups also own stakes in soccer teams in France, Italy, Greece and Switzerland. So why should media groups wish to own stakes in professional sports teams?

Media ownership of teams is an example of vertical integration in which firms operating at one stage of the value chain move into another stage either through acquisition or by setting up a new operating unit. Teams produce the content that media groups distribute. Hence media ownership of teams represents backward (or upstream) vertical integration as media groups move into a prior stage of the value chain. By contrast, sports teams that set up their own TV channels are undertaking forward (or downstream) vertical integration.

Economic theory suggests three broad reasons for vertical integration: organisational efficiency, technical efficiency and market power.[12] Firms may vertically integrate if it is more cost-effective to coordinate sequential stages of the value chain internally rather than relying on external market coordination. This is the main thrust of the market-failure/transaction-costs theory of vertical integration developed by Williamson and derived from Coase.[13] Coase argued that there are two alternative methods of coordinating economic activities – internally within firms using administrative procedures or externally through the market using the price mechanism. Firms represent the internal administrative coordination of economic activities. Firms exist because the transaction costs of coordinating economic activities through the market exceed internal administrative costs. Market coordination requires the identification of suitable trading partners and the negotiation of mutually acceptable contracts. These transaction costs may be relatively high, particularly if there is high market uncertainty and/or contracts are difficult to specify and costly to renegotiate. From this perspective, firms prefer to coordinate sequential stages of the value chain through ownership rather than the market whenever vertical integration yields higher expected returns due to lower internal administrative costs and/or lower uncertainty.

Vertical integration may also be motivated by gains in technical efficiency if different stages of the production process are merged as, for example, in the case of iron and steel production. However there is no necessity a priori that firms should integrate vertically in order to achieve potential technical efficiency gains. These gains could be secured using other forms of vertical coordination such as joint ventures between independent firms. The use of ownership to coordinate, rather than more arm's-length contractual relationships, needs to be explained, again suggesting the possible importance of market transaction costs.

Increased market power provides another possible explanation of vertical integration, although again these arguments require to be supplemented by a transaction-cost explanation of ownership as the preferred mode of coordination. Vertical integration can significantly increase the market power of firms by foreclosure of rivals' markets and increased barriers to entry for new competitors. Firms who own a key supplier or distributor may deny access to their competitors or only allow access on disadvantageous terms. In addition, if vertical integration offers substantial production and/or overhead cost reductions, this may act as a deterrent to new entry by firms outside the industry that may require substantial higher capital investment in order to compete with the vertically-integrated incumbent.

The possible gains from vertical integration were one of the factors behind the merger boom in the 1970s and 1980s. However, many mergers failed to achieve the expected increased returns. As a consequence, the last decade has seen a reversal of the trend with many firms downsizing, concentrating on their core businesses and divesting more peripheral activities. This has included vertical de-integration and a return to outsourcing from independent suppliers. In part vertical de-integration has been motivated by recognition that internal administrative costs are not necessarily lower than market transaction costs. Internalising economic activities in a large administrative body creates a multitude of principal-agent problems and a potential significant loss of organisational efficiency and a consequent rise in production and administrative costs. In such cases organising economic activities externally through the market coordination of independently owned business units might be more cost-effective.

So why is the professional team sports industry bucking the trend and becoming more vertically integrated just as other industries are moving in the opposite direction? There appear to be two key drivers of vertical integration in the professional team sports industry: the strategic importance of securing access to sports broadcasting rights coupled with extreme uncertainty. Sports broadcasting rights are absolutely vital to the commercial development of new media distribution networks. Without access to live coverage of major sports events, new media distribution networks face an uphill struggle to attract viewers and advertisers. Ownership of teams can provide security of access to sports broadcasting rights to the extent that teams possess significant control of their own rights. Ownership of teams also provides a hedge against future uncertainty in the professional sports industry. The industry faces not only uncertainty from the internal dynamic generated by the conflict over income shares between teams, players and governing authorities but also the environmental uncertainty created by the rapid rate of technological change, particularly the convergence of television and the Internet. Teams, ultimately, are the fundamental long-term assets in the professional team sports industry. Ownership of teams puts media groups in a key position to influence future changes in the industry.

The impact of media ownership of teams depends primarily on the influence exerted on the corporate objectives of teams. Media groups may have two alternative possible influences on team objectives. One possibility is that media groups could adopt a 'loss-leader' strategy to their teams, putting the priority on sporting performance. Alternatively media groups could adopt a 'profit-maximisation' strategy with the priority on financial performance. A loss-leader strategy would represent a return of the sportsman-owner effect with over-investment in playing talent. In contrast a profit-maximisation strategy would involve greater emphasis on the control of player costs. The presence of several loss-leader teams may undermine the sporting and financial viability of a league. Loss-leader teams are likely to dominate the market for star players. The resulting concentration of star players in a few leading teams will significantly reduce the degree of competitive balance in the league. The intense bidding for star players will also create further player cost inflation throughout the league, accelerating even more the wage-price spiral with potentially serious implications for the financial survival of the smaller teams that are not being bankrolled by large media groups.

Media ownership of teams may alienate the fans. Although the fans of loss-leader teams may enjoy greater glamour and success, the fans of smaller teams are likely to be alienated by their 'doormat' status. Fans of the league as a whole may become alienated by the loss of competitive balance. The fans of the media-owned teams may become alienated by the loss of their teams' independence and identity. Teams often have very strong historical links with their local community. Teams can be an important part of social identification, creating a strong sense of tribalism in the fan base. Corporate control of teams by media groups can be viewed by fans as a very serious threat to their very sense of being, provoking strong, even militant, reactions. Witness, for example, the extent of fan opposition to BSkyB's attempted takeover of Manchester United discussed below.

A crucial factor affecting the impact of media ownership of teams is whether the broadcasting rights are owned individually by teams or collectively by the league. League ownership of broadcasting rights is generally more beneficial to fans as a whole for two reasons. First, teams are first and foremost monopoly suppliers to their own team fans. Fan loyalty to their own teams gives considerable market power to teams, especially to those teams with large fan bases. In contrast, leagues have less monopoly power since they supply to a wider cross-section of team fans and game fans (i.e. fans with an allegiance to the sport not a specific team). Leagues, therefore, are likely to face a more elastic demand as well as competition from other leagues and sports. Hence a league-ownership regime is likely to lead to lower prices than a team-ownership regime. Second, league ownership of broadcasting rights provides a mechanism through the distribution of TV revenues to facilitate cross-subsidisation of smaller teams to maintain and enhance competitive balance. A team-ownership regime is likely to significantly increase the financial disparity between teams and, consequently, cause a loss of competitive balance. The TV rights ownership regime is a key determinant of both the motivation for, and financial value of, media ownership of teams. If teams individually control their own broadcasting rights, then ownership of teams gives ownership of broadcasting rights. If leagues own the broadcasting rights, ownership of teams will give media groups only some degree of influence over the league's decision on the sale of its broadcasting rights. Hence the motivation for media ownership of the biggest teams will be strongest in those leagues in which teams retain significant control of their own broadcasting rights. Furthermore, the financial value of a team to a media owner also depends crucial on the TV rights regime. The financial value of a professional sport team equals the present value of the team's future net income stream. That net income stream will be significantly higher if teams own their own broadcasting rights and are able to earn monopolistic profits from supplying games to their own team-fans.

Case Study: Media Ownership of English Premiership Soccer Teams

Unlike the major leagues in North America, English professional soccer is organised as a merit hierarchy with promotion and relegation between and within leagues at the end of each playing season based on league performance. Until 1992, the Football League represented the top of the merit hierarchy. The Football League is the oldest professional soccer league in the world, having been formed originally in 1888. Until 1992 the Football League comprised 92 teams organised into four divisions with promotion and relegation between these divisions. In 1992 the 22 teams in the top division broke away from the Football League to set up the FA Premier League (FAPL) under the auspices of the Football Association, the overall governing body for soccer in England. The FAPL maintained the merit hierarchy by retaining a system of promotion and relegation with Division One of the Football League. The principal motivation for the creation of the FAPL was the desire of the top clubs to gain greater control over the revenues generated by the sale of TV and sponsorship rights.

Prior to the formation of the FAPL, the Football League had negotiated a four-year contract with ITV in 1988 to show 18 live games per season. This contract was worth £44 million ($66 million). The FAPL negotiated its own TV deal in 1992 and eventually agreed a five-year deal with the satellite broadcaster BSkyB for 60 live games per season to be shown on subscription TV. The contract was worth £191.5 million ($287 million). In addition the sale to the BBC of the rights to show edited highlights as well as a separate deal for international rights raised total TV revenues to around £300 million ($450 million) to be shared between the 22 Premiership teams. The BSkyB deal was a landmark deal for both soccer and BSkyB. Before it acquired the exclusive rights to live Premiership soccer, BSkyB was in severe financial trouble. Premiership soccer rights transformed BSkyB into the largest and most successful provider of subscription and pay-per-view TV in the UK. Premiership soccer is the most important driver of TV subscriptions in the UK. Without Premiership soccer, it is unlikely that any new delivery platform can succeed. Hence the intensity of the auction for its rights.

Any collective arrangement for selling broadcasting rights necessarily requires a distribution mechanism to allocate the TV revenues between teams. The FAPL has developed a distribution mechanism that attempts to balance the conflicting objectives of equality and reward. Equality helps facilitate competitive balance by allocating TV revenues equally across teams irrespective of size and league performance, thereby cross-subsidising the smaller teams. However, the danger of equal shares irrespective of league performance is the loss of incentives for teams to maximise their sporting performance. Performance-related distribution of TV revenues is required to maintain the competitive integrity of leagues. The FAPL resolved the tension between equality and reward by allocating 50 per cent of the TV revenues equally between teams, 25 per cent on the basis of final league position (i.e. performance-related) and 25 per cent as facility fees based on the number of TV appearances of teams. The facility fees are largely size- and performance-related, since the bigger and more successful teams tend to be shown more often.

BSkyB successfully bid to retain the contract for exclusive rights to live Premiership soccer in 1997, agreeing a four-year deal for 60 live games per season worth £670 million ($1 billion). BSkyB's retention of the Premiership soccer contract in 1997 was almost a foregone conclusion given its dominant position in UK sports broadcasting. However, despite the lack of effective competition, the 1997 TV deal represented more than a fourfold increase in the value of the Premiership rights since 1992. Partly this was a reflection of the success of the Premiership and BSkyB over the previous five years. But it was also in part a recognition by BSkyB of the increased likelihood of more effective competitive challenges in the near future to its dominant position in the UK sports broadcasting rights market.

Since 1997 there has been a period of great environmental turbulence in the UK sports broadcasting market, which has created extreme uncertainty for BSkyB and the FAPL. Partly this uncertainty has been due to technological and commercial developments in the media industry, but also importantly it has been caused by a legal challenge to the collective sale of sports broadcasting rights. The Office of Fair Trading (OFT) referred the 1997 deal between the FAPL and BSkyB to the Restrictive Practices Court (RPC) as a collusive agreement against the public interest. The OFT argued that the collective sale of sports broadcasting rights combined with exclusivity is anti-competitive. The OFT sought an RPC ruling against league-ownership regimes and acceptance of a presumption in favour of teams selling their broadcasting rights individually. The RPC eventually ruled in the summer of 1999 against the OFT, finding that in the case of English Premiership soccer the collective sale of TV rights is in the public interest. In part, the RPC ruling recognises the inherent collective nature of broadcasting rights in professional team sports. Part of the significance and value of any individual game lies in its context as a league game, implying that all teams in the league contribute to the value of all individual games not just the two teams competing in any specific match. Hence all teams can legitimately claim to be joint producers of any league game with a share of the property rights. The RPC ruling also recognises the importance of collective arrangements for maintaining and enhancing competitive balance in leagues. Finally the RPC accepted that the increased TV revenues achieved by the FAPL had been used to improve Premiership soccer to the benefit of fans by providing the financial resources to attract top international players from foreign leagues and to fund stadium construction and improvement.

Although BSkyB successfully defended its exclusive Premiership contract in the courts, it continues to face other technological and commercial challenges. BSkyB's dominant position in subscription and pay-per-view TV in the UK is being gradually eroded by the growth of cable TV, particularly the emergence of the US media group NTL as a significant competitor in the UK market. Another potential long-term source of competition is provided by the development of digital terrestrial television, although the initial entrant in the UK market, On Digital (later rebranded as ITV Digital), was a commercial failure. In the longer run, the convergence of television and Internet technologies creates the possibility of yet another potentially significant delivery channel for live sports events.

BSkyB's response to the emergence of serious competitive threats was to launch a bid for Manchester United plc, the largest soccer team in the world and the dominant team in the FAPL. BSkyB's bid in September 1998 valued Manchester United at £623.5 million ($1.03 billion) and was accepted by the directors of Manchester United plc but such was the scale of public concern that the government referred the bid to the Monopoly and Mergers Commission (MMC) for investigation.[14] The MMC ruled against the proposed merger in March 1999 and its findings were endorsed by the Secretary of State for Trade and Industry. Thus BSkyB's bid was effectively blocked. The immediate consequence was the withdrawal of a pending bid by NTL to acquire a controlling stake in another Premiership team. Newcastle United.

The MMC ruled against the proposed merger between BSkyB and Manchester United on a variety of grounds.[15] The MMC concluded that BSkyB's ownership of Manchester United would reduce the competition for Premiership soccer broadcasting rights irrespective of whether or not these rights continued to be sold collectively. The MMC also concluded that the proposed merger would have two adverse effects on soccer. First, it would reinforce the trend towards greater financial inequality between teams, weakening the smaller teams and reducing competitive balance. Second, it would give BSkyB direct influence on decisions affecting the organisation of soccer and this influence might not always be exercised to the long-term benefit of soccer.

The MMC cited the possibility of a 'toehold effect' as one of the ways in which the vertical integration of BSkyB and Manchester United could adversely affect competition between broadcasters for Premiership TV rights. A toehold effect exists when a bidder in an auction has an ownership stake in the property being sold and that stake, even if relatively small, increases the likelihood of that bidder winning the auction.[16] Bidders with a toehold ownership stake have an incentive to bid above the property value since part of the bid price would be automatically reimbursed to the bidder through its ownership stake. Thus a toehold stake would allow the bidder to bid more aggressively, necessitating other bidders without a toehold stake to bid above the property value in order to win the auction. Thus competitors are more likely to be deterred from entering the auction. And, even if they do enter the auction, there is a higher probability of the 'winner's curse' occurring, with the winning bid being in excess of the 'true' property value.

Following the rejection of the proposed merger, BSkyB has embarked on an alternative strategy of acquiring minority stakes in several Premiership teams. League rules permit ownership stakes in more than one team provided that no single stake exceeds ten per cent of the team's equity. BSkyB currently have ownership stakes in five soccer teams: Manchester United, Leeds United, Manchester City, Sunderland and Chelsea. Other media groups are adopting a similar strategy. NTL have ownership stakes in four soccer teams – Newcastle United, Middlesbrough, Aston Villa and Leicester City – while Granada, one of the leading ITV companies, has an ownership stake in Liverpool. The 'follow-the-leader' strategy by NTL is clearly aimed at preventing BSkyB from exerting 'insider' influence on future decisions regarding soccer broadcasting rights. The strategy had an immediate success. The 2001–2004 contracts for Premiership broadcasting rights were awarded in the summer of 2000 with BSkyB retaining the exclusive first-choice rights to show 66 live games per season on subscription TV. However, the Premiership also awarded NTL second-choice rights to show 40 live games per season on a pay-per-view basis (although NTL subsequently withdrew its bid). Including the edited highlights rights acquired by ITV, the total value of the three-year deal was in excess of £1.6 billion ($2.4 billion), excluding international rights.

Both BSkyB and NTL have also taken steps to create a strategic advantage in the long term as regards the technological convergence of television and the Internet. Increasingly it is becoming likely that, in the future, sports TV broadcasting will be replaced by narrowcasting through the Internet. The latest Premiership broadcasting deal specifically excludes Internet rights. Teams now have the rights to show delayed transmission of their games on their websites. To the extent that the Internet eventually becomes the dominant delivery platform for live sports coverage, then control of team websites will become crucial. BSkyB acquired Sports Internet, the UK-based company that manages many of the leading sports websites including those of several Premiership teams. Sports Internet also owns Opta, the leading supplier of soccer statistics, as well as interests in online betting. NTL are following a different strategy. It agreed to wholly fund a joint venture to develop their Internet opportunities for the Football League. NTL also agreed a similar deal with Glasgow Rangers, one of the leading Scottish soccer teams. Further strategic alliances between existing teams, media groups and Internet companies are highly likely.

What Next for Professional Team Sports?

Looking in the crystal ball, it seems clear that environmental change and the internal dynamic of the industry will continue to undermine the sporting and financial viability of existing leagues. The accelerating wage-price spiral shows no signs of slowing. Star players will continue to exploit their bargaining power under free agency to maximise their earnings. Teams will continue to respond by hiking up the prices charged for their commercial properties – gate tickets, executive suites and corporate hospitality, merchandising and broadcasting and other image rights. Collective arrangements and revenue-sharing agreements will come under ever increasing pressure from the big-revenue teams. In particular, team ownership of Internet rights may become the major driver towards greater financial inequality between teams and the consequent loss of competitive balance. This may given even further momentum towards the creation of breakaway transnational 'super leagues' consisting of the biggest teams regionally or internationally. The creation of a European super league in soccer remains a distinct possibility.

The importance of securing access to sports broadcasting rights is unlikely to be diminished. Thus the trend towards increased media ownership of teams is unlikely to be reversed, especially if teams gain greater control individually of their broadcasting rights. Media ownership may re-introduce the sportsman-owner effect in the biggest teams, but this may serve to further undermine competitive balance and financial viability. It may also alienate the fans – not only the fans of the smaller 'doormat' teams but also the fans of the media-owned teams resentful of the corporate control of their local teams.

The future prospects for leading team sports are not, therefore, necessarily unproblematic despite the continued growth in revenues. However, despite the alienation of some fans, particularly the traditional lower-income fans who have been marginalised economically by higher gate prices and TV subscription fees, fans ultimately have the potential to control the future of professional team sports through the exercise of consumer sovereignty. Team allegiance is a 'free good' in the sense that a fan can claim allegiance to a team without ever directly contributing financially to that team. Fans are not necessarily financial supporters of a team. Teams face an ongoing imperative to transform fans' allegiance into active support and revenue streams. Ultimately teams must provide what the fans are prepared to pay to watch in a stadium or at home on TV. If teams and their media owners lose touch with what their fans want, they will lose financially. If fans want the traditions of their teams and sports to be maintained, then they need only to refuse to buy tickets or subscriptions for anything different. The economic power of fans is the ultimate protective mechanism for sports. Accordingly in response to any suggestion that media ownership of teams could transform the major leagues into sporting theatricals resembling the WWF, ultimately all that can be said is that it will not happen if the fans do not want it to. Media ownership of teams does pose severe threats to the sporting and financial viability of leagues, but media groups have a real incentive to defend the integrity of leagues in order to maintain the supply of top-quality, competitive team sports to the fans. After all, when all is said and done, without the fans there would be no professional team sports industry and no profits. Media owners of teams forget this basic fact of sporting life at their financial peril.

NOTES

1. B. Gerrard, 'Team Sports as a Free-Market Commodity' *New Political Economy*, 4 (1999), pp.273–8.
2. M.K. Ozanian, 'Too Much to Lose', *Forbes*, 165, 14 (2000), pp.94–100.
3. D.K. Stotlar, 'Vertical Integration in Sport', *Journal of Sport Management*, 14 (2000), pp.1–7.
4. J. Vrooman, 'A Unified Theory of Capital and Labour Markets in Major League Baseball', *Southern Economic Journal*, 63 (1997), pp.594–619.
5. W.C. Neale, 'The Peculiar Economics of Professional Sports', *Quarterly Journal of Economics*, 78 (1964), pp. 1–14.
6. P.D. Staudohar, *Playing for Dollars: Labour Relations and the Sports Business* (Ithaca, NY: Cornell University Press, 1996); P.J. Sloane, 'The Labour Market in Professional Football', *British Journal of Industrial Relations*, 7 (1969), pp.181–99.
7. S. Rottenberg, 'The Baseball Player's Labour Market', *Journal of Political Economy*, 64 (1956), pp.242–58.
8. R. Fort and J. Quirk, 'Cross-Subsidisation, Incentives, and Outcomes in Professional Team Sports', *Journal of Economic Literature*, 33 (1995), pp.1265–99; T. Hylan, M. Lage and M. Treglia, 'The Coase Theorem, Free Agency, and Major League Baseball: A Panel Study of Pitcher Mobility from 1961 to 1992', *Southern Economic Journal*, 62 (1996), pp.1029–42; A. Krautmann and M. Oppenheimer, 'Free Agency and the Allocation of Labour in Major League Baseball', *Managerial and Decision Economics*, 15 (1994), pp.459–69. J. Vrooman, 'A General Theory of Professional Sports Leagues', *Southern Economic Journal*, 61 (1995), pp.971–90.
9. R. Anderson and J.J. Siegfried, 'The Implications of Athlete Freedom to Contract: Lessons from North America', *Economic Affairs*, 17 (1997), pp.7–12; R. Simmons, 'Implications of the Bosman Ruling for Football Transfer Markets', *Economic Affairs*, 17 (1997), pp.13–18.
10. A. Zimbalist, 'Salaries and Performance: Beyond the Scully Model', in P.M. Sommers (ed.), *Diamonds Are Forever: The Business of Baseball* (Washington, DC: The Brookings Institution, 1992); G.W. Scully, 'Pay and Performance in Major League Baseball', *American Economic Review*, 64 (1974), pp.915–30.
11. K. Kilbride, 'Comparing Media Ownership of Football Clubs in England and Europe', *Euro Football Finance 2000 Conference Documentation* (London: SMi, 2000).

12. R. Clarke, *Industrial Economics* (Oxford: Basil Blackwell, 1985).
13. O.E. Williamson, 'The Vertical Integration of Production: Market Failure Considerations', *American Economic Review Papers and Proceedings*, 61 (1971), pp.112–23; R. Coase, 'The Nature of the Firm', *Economica*, 4 (1937), pp.386–405.
14. A. Brown and A. Walsh, *Not For Sale: Manchester United, Murdoch and the Defeat of BSkyB* (Edinburgh: Mainstream, 1999).
15. Monopolies and Mergers Commission, *British Sky Broadcasting Group plc and Manchester United plc: A Report on the Proposed Merger* (London: The Stationery Office, 1999).
16. P. Klemperer, 'Auctions with Almost Common Values: The "Wallet Game" and Its Applications', *European Economic Review*, 42 (1998), pp.757–69.

PART V:
SPORT SPONSORSHIP

13

'Money for Nothing and Your Cheques for Free?'[1] A Critical Perspective on Sport Sponsorship

TREVOR SLACK and JOHN AMIS

Since the 1984 Olympic Games the concept of marketing has become of central importance in the world of sport. The contemporary discourse that is promoted by politicians, the media, sport managers and indeed many athletes is no longer just about winning medals or producing best performances. It is about such issues as the size of television contracts, the licensing and merchandising of official products and the marketing of ancillary goods and services (concessions, parking and corporate hospitality). One particularly significant component of the sport marketing mix is the sponsorship of individual athletes, teams, events and organisations. While exact figures on the size of the sponsorship market are difficult, if not impossible, to ascertain, estimates suggest that as sport has become increasingly commercialised the amount of spending on sponsorship worldwide has risen from $5.6 billion in 1984 to approximately $25 billion in 2000.[2] Parallel to the increased amount of spending on sponsorship has been a significant growth in academic interest in the phenomenon. Studies have focused on a range of topics, with the most frequent areas of enquiry being: defining and characterising sponsorship, corporate motivations and objectives of sponsorship, measuring the effectiveness of sponsorship, strategic aspects of sponsorship and legal and ethical considerations of sponsorship.[3]

In some ways the increased amount of academic interest in sponsorship is a positive development for sport. However, in other ways the type of research being conducted is a significant cause for concern. Research into sport sponsorship is best described in the same way as some of the more critical management scholars have described research in mainstream marketing – devoid of any social and historical context, staunchly positivistic, exhibiting a low level of theory development and lacking in self-reflectivity.[4] For most researchers sport sponsorship is seen as a neutral harmless task in which sponsors provide money to sport and in turn get to link their product to an athlete, team or event. Sport is seen to benefit because it receives a needed infusion of money. Commercial sponsors benefit because of their association with the popularity of sport, the visibility of the event or the high profile nature of the athlete(s) involved. All of these are factors that it is believed will ultimately help sell more product. As Milne and McDonald explain, 'Sponsorship has been defined as a business relationship between a provider of funds, resources, or services and a sport event or organization that offers the sponsor some rights and an association that may be used for commercial advantage.'[5]

The conceptual underpinning of such an understanding of the process of sport sponsorship is based in the notion that these types of transactions (and other marketing practices) involve an exchange relationship. McCarville and Copeland for example suggest that 'sponsorship involves an exchange of resources with an independent partner in hopes of gaining a corresponding return for the sponsor'.[6] Lee, Sandler and Shani define sponsorship as involving 'the provision of resources (e.g. money, people, equipment) by an organisation directly to an event, cause or activity in exchange for a direct association (link) to the event cause or activity. The providing organisation can then engage in sponsorship-linked marketing to achieve either their corporate, marketing or media objectives.'[7] Howard and Crompton in their book *Financing Sport* entitle their chapter on sponsorship 'Nature of the Sponsorship Exchange'.[8] By basing ideas about sponsorship on the concept of exchange, scholars who have studied this practice have provided an image of neutrality and of choices that are limited only by the skill of the people involved in the sponsorship transactions. Such a view ignores the underlying inequalities of power that are part of the sponsorship process, presents an overly simplistic account of the complexities of such interactions and neglects to address how structures of domination and exploitation shape and mediate these relationships.[9]

Consequently, the purpose of this chapter is to begin to address some of these issues by presenting a more critical analysis of sport sponsorship than that which currently exists in the literature. To this end we focus first on the way in which sponsorship is underpinned by the creation of false needs; we then look at how sponsorship is linked to capital accumulation; this is followed by an examination of how sponsorship can change the way some sports are experienced and practised. Next, we look at how the ability of some organisations and individuals to enact sponsorship agreements is limited; this is followed by discussion of how sponsorship may impact on fans. We finish with a brief commentary about how sponsorship activities are sometimes inconsistent with a company's products and practices and then offer some concluding remarks.

How Sponsorship is Underpinned by the Creation of False Needs

One of the conditions of modern economies is that their markets are essentially saturated. Most of us have access to as many brands of hamburgers, chocolate bars and soft drinks as we need, a wide range of choice in beers, variety in the type of cars we can buy, a wide selection of athletic footwear and clothing designed for every possible sport and ability level, and shampoos and deodorants made from almost every possible ingredient. When our need for these types of products is satisfied, the companies that produce them have to create new artificial needs. These needs are induced by others whose job it is to suggest to us that our social status, our individuality and our self-identity will be incomplete unless we fulfil these needs. It is here that marketing techniques such as sponsorship become important. Creating new needs is very much about building associations and the use of symbols and imagery. As Hansen points out,

> Once real needs have been satisfied and products perfected to the point that significant improvements are no longer possible, competition takes place on the level of symbols and images. A product's design and the aesthetic symbols which constitute its image can however, only be successful if they are accepted by the majority of the proposed target group.[10]

It is these types of condition that make sport sponsorship such an appealing vehicle for marketing products. The emotion and excitement that exemplify the imagery of sport, the gold medals, victory podiums, 'swooshes' and Olympic rings that provide desirable and easily recognisable symbols – all can be directed to targeted audiences.[11]

The contradiction here is that in presenting these symbols and images to targeted groups, sponsors aim to appeal to our need for individuality. The advertising that accompanies sponsorship invites consumers into 'fantasies of individualism, although the promise of individualism is likely premised on conformity of consumption preferences'.[12] It is, as Savan suggests, an invitation to 'join us and become unique'.[13] The consumption of sport products that is promoted through sponsorship is constructed then not only to satisfy a perceived material need but to do so in a way that can serve to enhance individual identity. Messages from leading brands 'promise individuality, personal growth or a set of ideas to live by'.[14] Nike sponsorships for example emphasise self-empowerment and achievement through the associated use of its slogans such as 'Just do it', 'There is no finish line' and 'You don't win silver – you lose gold'. Reebok's less successful 'U B U' campaign and Converse's 'It's what's inside that counts' were based on a similar premise. As Miller et al. note, this individualism rests on the 'conformity of consumption preferences' that in turn are based on the creation of false needs.[15]

Sponsorship is used to construct how, as consumers, we perceive our needs. These needs are socially constructed by marketers rather than objectively given, as such sponsorship involves the constitution of artificial needs rather than just a process of responding to given needs. It then uses associations with the symbolism and imagery of sport to suggest that the sponsor's product can satisfy these needs that have been created. This symbolism and imagery creates myths which encourage consumers to believe that their personal identities are associated with and dependent on the ownership and consumption of the sponsor's product.[16]

Sponsorship and Capital Accumulation

In their book *Monopoly Capitalism*[17] Baran and Sweezy argue that western economies have entered into a period of over-production. Consequently, as noted above, false needs have to be created among people so that they buy commodities that they do not really need in order that capitalism can survive. Marketing techniques such as sponsorship are functionally necessary to the continuation of advanced capitalist economies because they provide the means by which individuals are persuaded to purchase goods. The creation of false needs ensures that goods continue to be sold in saturated markets, but corporations in advanced capitalist societies also turn to new markets in order to ensure a continued process of capital accumulation. Sport sponsorship is used in both these processes. Lawrence and Rowe suggest that within advanced capitalist societies sport has distinct qualities that help facilitate the process of capital accumulation.[18] These include the commodification of athletes to be bought and sold according to their ability to generate profit for clubs and corporations, and the utilisation of sport by the mass media to attract audiences for the purpose of exposing them to consumer goods (either through sponsorship or advertising) which are often quite unrelated to the sport itself.

As an example of this, Andrews points out that in the early 1990s the American market for professional basketball had been saturated. Jackson and Andrews cite Don Sperling, director of NBA Entertainment, as saying: 'Domestically we're tapped. … Ratings have peaked. Attendance has peaked. The market here has peaked.'[19] As a result, the NBA and its associated sponsors turned to the global economy in order to maintain their profit levels.[20] An overseas division, 'NBA International', was formed, deals to broadcast games were signed with national networks in individual countries, and regional deals were struck with satellite and cable broadcasters such as Star Sports, ESPN International, and SkySports. 'By the start of the 1994–5 season the NBA was being broadcast in either one-hour, two-hour or live game packages in 141 countries to an estimated audience of over 5550 million households.'[21] In 2001 the NBA had expanded to 206 countries across 128 networks and 42 languages.[22] To enhance capital accumulation in its sponsoring companies, the NBA has ensured that when its games are broadcast in national or regional markets these companies are offered commercial slots in the broadcast. As Andrews points out, this practice allows both partners (the NBA and its sponsor) to benefit. This he suggests is particularly the case in situations where a corporate sponsor such as McDonald's or Coca-Cola develops promotions which directly engage with the NBA as both partners benefit from the 'intertextual association derived from the proximity of two All-American commodity-signs'.[23]

In part to legitimise its growing global presence and to help create foreign interest in its sponsors' products, the NBA has increased the number of foreign players on its team's rosters from three in the 1993–4 season to 52 players from 31 countries and territories in the 2000–1 season. The impact that these players are having on the promotion of the NBA in their home countries cannot be underestimated. Pau Gasol, for example, a Spaniard playing for the Memphis Grizzlies, is, according to local journalist Antoni Daimiel, 'headline news ... a part of the mainstream five or six times a day'. Interest in Gasol and his counterparts has resulted in Spanish television showing five NBA games a week, up from the solitary weekly game shown back in 1986.[24] Similar worldwide interest has led to the NBA directly employing more than 200 foreign employees operating from offices in Taiwan, Singapore, Barcelona, Hong Kong, Tokyo, Melbourne, Paris, London, Toronto, and Mexico City.[25] Its revenue from its 150 global licensing partners and 15–20 sponsors was over $3 billion in 1997 – ten times the $300 million generated a decade earlier. One of the key factors that contributed to the ability of the NBA and its key sponsors to maintain the level of capital growth in these new markets was the entry of the so called 'Dream Team' in the 1992 Olympic Games. The involvement of players such as Michael Jordan, Charles Barkley and Scottie Pippen ensured global exposure for the team and continued profits for the athlete's sponsor Nike and the other corporations who endorsed the NBA and/or individual players. The success of this concept was emphasised by the way in which subsequent 'Dream Teams' were put together for the 1996 and 2000 Olympics despite mounting criticism that assembling such a dominant group of multi-millionaire athletes was diametrically opposed to the ideals of Olympic competition.[26] The National Hockey League has employed a similar strategy in promoting the 'Dream Team' concept, using high-profile athletes to promote the league on a global Olympic stage and thus raising the profile of itself and its corporate sponsors.

In addition to the NBA, Coca-Cola also provides an example of the way in which corporations use sport sponsorship to ensure continued capital accumulation. Like other companies, Coke is constantly looking for ways to secure its hold on existing markets and penetrate new markets. Its major thrust in sport sponsorship has its roots in 1974, the year Brazilian industrialist João Havelange was elected president of the International Federation of Football Associations (FIFA). In his campaign for president, Havelange had promised African and Asian nations that more of them would be included in the World Cup; he also promised the creation of a World Youth Championship and a number of development programmes. To fulfil his promises Havelange needed money. He turned to a man who had become his friend, adidas boss Horst Dassler, and Dassler's business partner Patrick Nally. Nally was eventually able to sign an agreement with Coca-Cola for a worldwide sponsorship programme. The deal gave Havelange the money he needed to keep his promises to the African and Asian nations through hosting tournaments and running local development programmes. These regions, while peripheral to football's main Western European theatre, were central to Coca-Cola's global marketing strategy and specifically its penetration of new markets.[27] The timing of this initiative was particularly important for Coca-Cola as in 1977 a *Business Week* article 'had warned of "The Graying of the Soft Drink Industry" [and] demographers had forecast a gloomy future'.[28] Coke had also suffered setbacks as a result of political problems in Iran, Nicaragua and Guatemala and criticisms of its labour policies.[29] The new football sponsorship provided the company with a means of penetrating new markets and thus ensuring continued capital accumulation.

Perhaps the best example of the way in which sponsorship has been used to enhance capital accumulation comes from the actions of adidas and its former CEO the late Horst Dassler, the man his business partner Patrick Nally called 'the puppet master of the sporting world'.[30] Early on, in the 1950s and 1960s, Dassler realised that the best way to promote his athletic footwear was to get top athletes to wear it. He retained a group of representatives,[31] many of them highly placed within the sporting world, to influence national federation officials to let adidas sponsor their national teams. Dassler gained in two ways from the associations he set up. First in the more lucrative markets Dassler was able to sell his product. However, in the less affluent markets, such as Africa and Asia, Dassler was able to generate a different type of capital – political capital. Through his sponsorship of national teams Dassler was able to wield considerable influence over key members of national federations and a number of IOC members. As a result, when the IOC met in 1985 to decide the marketing rights for the 1988 Olympic Games, it was the adidas controlled ISL Marketing that was awarded the contract despite the fact that it had only been in existence for two years.[32] ISL subsequently went on to acquire the marketing rights to the World Athletics Championships and the Soccer World Cup.[33]

Marketing practices such as sponsorship, as has been shown, can play a central role in stimulating and legitimising the consumption of goods and as such contributing to the process of capital accumulation within the sponsoring companies. In many ways this is not surprising, as contributing to 'the bottom line' is one of the main aims of sponsorship. However, in societies where mass consumption dominates, it has been argued that there is often a growing indifference to more basic needs. For example, when companies sponsor celebrity athletes to endorse their products, they are essentially suggesting that the purchase of this product will increase the consumer's chance of being like the star athlete. The need for the product becomes associated with success in the sport and values such as proper training, discipline and teamwork may be marginalised.

Consumption of sponsored goods can also be presented as a panacea for many of life's ills, in that the consumption of such goods is seen as offering the potential for personal freedom. In this regard Bauman has suggested that choice, and especially consumer choice, exemplifies a new view of freedom in contemporary social life and that the freedom attributed to an individual is constituted by his/her ability to be a consumer.[34] However, such choice also acts as a form of repression for individuals who do not have the resources to become involved in these choices. In addition, as Keat notes, the idea of consumer sovereignty can act as a guise for other 'more pressing projects such as the restoration of the fortunes of capital accumulation'.[35]

Changing the Way Sport is Experienced and Practised

There is much in the sport sponsorship literature to suggest that sport benefits considerably from the commercial support it receives. At one level it is hard to disagree with this argument. Enhanced levels of commercial sponsorship have led to increased media exposure for sport; spectators in many parts of the world get to watch athletes they would not normally see if it were not for corporate dollars; and some athletes themselves have benefited in that they are now no longer state-supported amateurs but are able to receive some level of financial compensation for their efforts. However, the few academics that have been critical of sponsorship have suggested that it has changed the experience of sport and the way in which some sports are played.

For example, as commercial forces have become more prevalent, sponsors are asking athletes to compete more frequently. If top athletes do not perform, television companies are not interested in covering the event; if television companies do not cover the event, sponsors fail to receive the exposure they seek, and hence sponsors pressure athletes to compete. Sack and Staurowsky show how in the United States college athletes are required to compete in extensive collegiate sport schedules, which limit their educational experiences, because of the money that their teams can gain through commercial sponsorship.[36] Predictably, such pressures become more intense in professional sport. In early 1999, for example, Chelsea's French defender Frank Leboeuf complained that he had already played so many matches that season his body had packed up. In May 1999, Yegveny Kafelnikov, at that time the number one tennis player in the world, was fined for not trying at the Czech Open. Just before this, at an irrelevant tournament in Monte Carlo, Kafelnikov had competed against a French teenager and won only three games, admitting that the only thing that mattered to him was the French Open.[37]

There have also been suggestions that some athletes have 'played hurt' in order to appease sponsors who expect them to compete in certain events. The most recent and celebrated case involved the Brazilian football star Ronaldo who played in his country's loss to France in the 1998 World Cup Final. Aldo Rebelo, a Brazilian Congressman and head of an inquiry into football in the country, believed that Nike exerted undue influence over the Brazilian team. It was suggested that the psychological pressures of the Nike contract contributed to the convulsions (some believe an epileptic fit) that star player Ronaldo is alleged to have suffered on the day of the final – a game in which he played but one in which he failed to exhibit his normal high standard of performance.[38] Ronaldo (who also had a personal sponsorship deal with Nike) denied that he was placed under any pressure[39] and Nike came out of the enquiry relatively unscathed. The enquiry did, however, reveal that national coach Mario Zagallo had an individual contract with Nike for a year up to the World Cup finals. His role in the selection of Ronaldo was subject to debate and the fact that he was on Nike's payroll could only add weight to accusations that the sportswear company may have had some input into team selection in France.

A slightly different twist on the way in which the financial pressures produced by sponsorship money affect athletes involved Kenyan steeplechaser Bernard Barmasai. In 1999, Barmasai competed in the IAAF Golden League series. The series of seven matches had a prize of $1 million for anyone who won all seven races. Barmasai had won the first five races and was competing in the sixth in Zurich. In the final stages of the race Barmasai was challenged by teammate Christopher Koskei. Barmasai, who stated that 'I knew he [Koskei] was good in the final 100 metres' is alleged to have told Koskei 'leave it to me'. 'That is why he slowed down. It is good for me if I win and it is good for my friend' Barmasai is reported as saying.[40] Opponents of the Golden League series have suggested that with large sums of sponsorship money available and athletes from different countries sharing the same agent, such deals are not uncommon. The 100 metre runner Ato Bolden dismissed the league as too crowded and benefiting only a small group of individuals while the rest receive nothing.[41]

In addition to changing the experience of sport for some athletes, sponsorship has also changed the way some sports are played. Sponsors who are involved in televised events often dictate when and where games are staged. Nike by virtue of its £104-million sponsorship of Brazilian football can dictate where, when and against whom the national team will play twice per year until 2006 (this was originally to be five times).[42] Crucially, Nike has also been able to insist on appearance by some of the team's top players.[43] When the United States was awarded the Soccer World Cup finals there were fears that in order to make the game more appealing to sponsors the goal would be widened and matches would be played in four quarters. None of these changes came about, but FIFA did enact stricter interpretations of foul and violent play in order to limit the more physically intimidating aspect of the game. The world governing body also made some subtle changes to the offside rule favouring attacking play; adopted a strict line on how to deal with injured players; and awarded three points to teams for first-round wins. As Sugden and Tomlinson note, 'these innovations matched the image of soccer in the USA which sponsors were keen to promote – a free flowing, creative game with few of the trappings of overt aggression and violence characteristic of other top-level professional team sports'.[44]

Football is not the only sport that has been subject to changes: golf, cricket, athletics, rugby union, rugby league, volleyball, and rowing are among the sports that have seen multiple changes in attempts to increase their attractiveness to television audiences and sponsors. Golf provides perhaps the most obvious example with 'head to head' duels between Tiger Woods and other leading players, sometimes under floodlights; 'skins' games featuring four leading players competing for money on each hole; and a proliferation of team events all designed to widen golf's already massive television appeal. Cricket has seen a greater emphasis on one-day matches, particularly on the Indian subcontinent, one of the largest markets for televised cricket in the world. Rowing has adopted the Super Sprints, which have modified the traditional 2000-metre format to one that is akin to a relay race in order to make the sport more appealing to spectators and to television and sponsors. Tennis has seen its scoring system changed, with tie-breaks introduced to shorten matches and make them more interesting. Rugby league switched from winter to summer and rugby union embraced professionalism. All are factors that, Polley suggests, are the result of a 'desire to increase the various sports' attractiveness to paying spectators, television audiences, and ultimately sponsors'.[45]

Limited Ability to Enact Sponsorship Agreements

While some sports, sporting organisations, teams and athletes have undoubtedly benefited from sponsorship moneys, the notion of sponsorship is, as noted earlier, rooted in the idea of an exchange. To most observers this involves an equal exchange of goods and services. However, the power of some athletes and organisations to transact an exchange is limited. As Alvesson and Willmott, writing about marketing in general, explain, the idea that marketing transactions such as sponsorship are based on exchange 'obscures, or at least fails to address, the social relations of inequality that privilege or exclude participation in *marketized* transactions' (emphasis in original).[46] Clearly some sporting organisations and athletes are more able to engage in these transactions than others. Not surprisingly, the organisations that have been most successful in securing corporate sponsorship have been those that are concerned with the more high-profile sports. In a study of Canadian corporations, Copeland et al. found that nearly 70 per cent of their respondents were sponsoring elite-level 'amateur' or professional sport.[47] Berrett and Slack found that the national-level sporting organisations that were most likely to receive sport sponsorship were those that had a large amount of television coverage and/or had a large participant base.[48] Smaller sports organisations and those that have a lower public profile are usually unable to attract high levels of support from corporate bodies. Hargreaves has even suggested that in the larger and higher-profile organisations that are able to gain sponsorship, this can lead to uneven development, because there is no guarantee that the moneys obtained will filter down to the lower levels of the sport.[49] Polley makes a similar point when he suggests that major sponsorships tend to be concentrated at the elite level and as such do not benefit the grass roots, where they are most needed.[50] Professional football in England provides a good example of this. While the top Premiership clubs seem awash with money and are able to pay their top players well over one million pounds a year, a number of Nationwide League clubs have recently been up for sale, and several have been in administration.[51]

So while a few popular sports do well from corporate support, the vast majority of sporting organisations struggle to gain any type of help. For example, in 1998 US speed-skating coach Gerard Kemkers bemoaned the fact that although long-track speed skating had generated more US Winter Olympic medals than any other sport, the team had no corporate sponsors. US skaters were having to fit low-paying jobs into 30-hour training weeks, and many were said to have bills of between $2,500 and $5,000 as a result of the need to purchase new hinged-blade 'clap skates'. 'We would be happy with $100,000' – a figure that pales in comparison to the funds received by sports such as skiing, ice hockey and figure skating – Kemkers was quoted as saying.[52] In a similar vein, following a 25 per cent reduction of state funding to sport by the Canadian government in the mid 1990s, sporting organisations were expected to turn to the corporate sector for support. While some sports like soccer (a high-participation sport in Canada) were able to secure corporate help, many were unable to attract such support and athletes were faced with paying their own way. Ann Peel, head of the Canadian Athletes Association, was quoted as saying: 'Athletes are being told there are tough choices. ... If you want this training camp you pay for it ... if you need new equipment tough luck.'[53]

In the same way that the financial differences between the few sporting organisations that are able to secure significant corporate sponsorship deals and the vast majority who cannot is large, so too is the differential between the funding of individual athletes. Top athletes in high-profile sports can earn millions of dollars, but the difference between the top athletes and those just below them is large. In 1999, Paul Lawrie, the winner of the British Open Golf Championship, received £350,000; the last player in the tournament got £700. In the same year, the men's winner at Wimbledon received £455,000; players who were knocked out in the first round received £6,830. The amount of sponsorship money that would be available to these athletes as a result of their successes, or lack thereof, would be equally very different. While images of Tiger Woods's multi-million dollar sponsorship deals paint a rosy picture, the reality is that comparatively few athletes make large sums of money through sponsorship. Often particularly hard hit are female athletes. A 1999 study funded by Sport England and carried out by the Sports Sponsorship Advisory Service, showed that 82 per cent of 200 British blue-chip companies were not actively interested in sponsoring women's sport.[54] While athletes like Martina Hingis, Venus Williams and Anna Kournikova have made considerable sums out of sponsors; Williams having signed a $40 million deal with Reebok and Kournikova allegedly earning over £7 million in 2000, it is often sexuality rather than athleticism that sponsors are buying. Kournikova, generally considered the highest earner in terms of sponsorship money, has yet to win a Grand Slam singles title.[55] Even Williams, by anybody's standards a superb athlete, re-imaged herself after the Reebok deal. Appearing at the Australian Open shortly after signing the contract with Reebok Williams wore 'a black bra top highlighting her cleavage, with the company logo at nipple height'.[56] Other less 'attractive' female athletes are unable to come close to these types of sponsorship deals. As Coakley notes, 'the endorsement record of Martina Navratilova shows also that being a lesbian dramatically decreases one's advertising value'.[57]

The selling of sexuality is not a new phenomenon in marketing. Bourdieu's notion of physical capital is useful in helping understand why 'sexual attractiveness' is valued over athleticism in sponsoring women's sport.[58] For Bourdieu the body represents a form of physical capital. The physical capital obtained through participation in activities such as sport can be converted into social, cultural or economic capital.[59] Shilling suggests that the conversion of physical capital into other forms of capital is influenced by gender.[60] It is harder for women than men to convert the physical capital that they obtain through sporting prowess into economic capital. While athletic ability is valued, it is not as valued as the combination of athletic ability and 'sexual attractiveness' which is more easily converted into economic capital. As Hargreaves notes, 'whereas for men athletic ability is the main determinant of earning ability, for most female performers the additional dimension of sexual attractiveness is what secures sponsorship and media coverage'.[61] Indeed the Sports Sponsorship Advisory Service report mentioned above suggested that women athletes 'play the sex appeal card to attract more media coverage and therefore more sponsorship'.[62]

Disadvantaging the Fan

While sponsorship has undoubtedly brought a number of benefits to sports fans, it has also served to create some situations in which fans are disadvantaged. At a very basic level, it is possible to argue that the sponsorship money that top athletes and teams receive is indirectly paid for by the fans. Although it varies by country, many company expenses such as sponsorship can be accounted for in such a way that they become tax-deductible. As a result, sponsorship outlays can be used to offset profits in other areas, thus decreasing a company's tax bill. The consumer has no choice, even if he or she is a not a fan of the team, event or athlete being endorsed: it is they who ultimately pay the sponsorship bill. As Schlossberg points out in writing about the professional sports stadiums and arenas for which sponsors have purchased the naming rights, sponsors pay 'for the privilege of putting their names on them, while fans are paying more and more for the privilege of being exposed to these marketing communications messages. Yes, people pay for the privilege of being advertised to.'[63]

Many commentators have argued that the introduction of commercial practices such as sponsorship into sport, particularly professional team sports, means that for the fan some of the essence of sport is lost. As Davies poignantly argues about football:

> [It] is not about profit and loss. It is about glory and excitement, about loyalty and legends, about local identity and family history, about skills and talents, none of which can be computed on balance sheets. Football doesn't have a product. Every year [Manchester] United fans

have their ashes scattered on the turf at Old Trafford. How often do you see that happening at Tesco's?[64]

In Marxist terms, practices such as sponsorship are said to have an alienating effect on fans. As a result of sponsorship and the attendant increased television exposure, spectators become physically passive, watching sport on their television from home but rarely participating. The consumption of sport then becomes an experience that takes place in the consumers' heads rather than on the terraces and in the stands.[65] Carn et al., writing about football, argue that the drive for profit that underpins the embrace of sponsorship encourages 'the club to erode the emotional bond between club and the traditional supporter'.[66] This 'fan equity' is the traditional economic basis of the club because the passion shown by the spectators at the ground is what produces the spectacle that makes football a televisual product. However, fans lured by the televised product, which sponsorship demands, see the game as entertainment not as an emotional attachment. The net effect of sponsor-driven televised sport may then 'be to destroy "fan equity" by driving them from the grounds to which they may never subsequently return'.[67] It also has had the effect of marginalising traditional working-class fans and attracting more middle-class supporters who are willing to pay the massively increased ticket prices and quietly watch games in all-seater stadia. More tickets are purchased by corporations anxious to entertain clients, creating a less passionate fan base famously derided by Manchester United captain Roy Keane as prawn-sandwich eaters who would be unable to spell football, let alone understand it.[68] As such the emotion that produces the spectacle, so dear to sponsors, may ultimately disappear and this will not only harm the sponsor but the financial basis of the club.

Fans may also suffer as a result of the contractual agreements that are struck between sponsors and organising committees such as those of the Olympic Games, the World Cup or other major sporting festivals. Often these contracts require that in return for their financial contribution sponsors get access to prime seating at the events. Preuss notes that apart from the tickets supplied to them, sponsors are often able to purchase additional tickets. In Calgary in 1988, approximately ten per cent of all tickets went to sponsors; in Barcelona the figure was around 12.6 per cent; in Atlanta it was ten per cent. Coca-Cola received 80,000 tickets (which would be for prime seats at the premier events). This, as Preuss notes, was more than the number (45,000) provided for the whole of Germany.[69] Such allocating of prime seats means that, as was the case in Atlanta and Sydney, fans had to enrol in a lottery and pay for their tickets whereas 'the captains of international business whose hundreds of millions of dollars in sponsorship [had] bought the games, lock, stock and logo' were allocated free seats for prime events, such as the opening and closing ceremonies.[70]

A slightly different scenario is playing out in many US university sports programmes and professional sport franchises. Here, as part of sponsorship deals, companies often have access to luxury boxes to watch the game. The allocation of these seats to sponsors hurts fans in a number of ways. First, while the fan pays for his or her ticket from discretionary income, sponsors are able to claim such expenditure as a business-entertainment deduction on the principle that it is a way of securing clients.[71] Second, fans are hurt because in many stadiums the revenue from luxury boxes goes directly to the team, not to the public authority, which often paid for the stadium and to which fans pay taxes.[72] Third, fans may suffer because the space which is required for luxury boxes is now no longer available for regular, lower-priced seats, thus reducing the available opportunities for seating.

Sponsorship Inconsistencies with Sponsors' Products and Practices

As McDaniel, Mason and Kinney outline elsewhere in this collection, there has been a long association between sport sponsorship and tobacco, alcohol and gambling. In large part, the involvement of these industries in sponsoring sport has been in an attempt to legitimise their products and obscure the negative association between such products and public health.[73] While there has been considerable debate in both the academic literature and the popular press about the relative pros and cons of such sponsorship, there has been little consideration, in the academic literature, of the contradictions that arise from other product sponsors being involved in sports and sporting events. Here we focus briefly on two of the biggest sponsors of sport: McDonald's and Coca-Cola. We focus on the way in which their involvement in the sponsorship of sport and sports events can be viewed as inconsistent with aspects of their product and/or mode of operation.

Coca-Cola is the longest-running sponsor of the Olympic Games. The most recent Games in Sydney, of which Coca-Cola was a major sponsor, was the first to be billed as the 'Green Games'. The official guidelines called for the Olympic site to be free of global-warming hydrofluoro-carbons (HFCs). Yet early in 2000, Greenpeace revealed that two of the major Olympic sponsors, Coca-Cola and McDonald's, were undermining the environmental guidelines for the world's first Green Games by using HFCs in their refrigeration systems at the Olympic site. Campaigners around the world joined the Greenpeace website campaign to prevent Coca-Cola from using dangerous HFC gases. Protests were held, letters and emails written, and in late June 2000 Coca-Cola announced that it was adopting a new refrigeration policy. The company would phase out all potent greenhouse-gas HFCs by the Athens 2004 Olympics. Rupert Posner, Greenpeace's Olympics campaigner, suggested 'if Coca-Cola can make this change, so too can other Olympic sponsors such as McDonald's'.[74]

Like Coca-Cola, McDonald's has also had an extensive involvement with the Olympic Games and like Coca-Cola it was extensively involved in the 'Green Games'. It has also been heavily criticised for its environmental practices. Accusations have been made that it destroys rainforests to make way for cattle ranching, that the production and disposal of the packaging it uses have detrimental environmental effects, and that it is cruel to animals.[75] Such actions would sit in direct contradiction to the tenets of the 'Green Games'. There have also been criticisms that McDonald's exploits children with its advertising and that its central product, the hamburger, contributes to a number of health problems.[76] Likewise Coca-Cola has been criticised for the excessive promotion of its product in schools and the possible health consequences of its product.[77] While sponsorship of the sports events, teams, organisations and individuals that these companies engage in may not be a direct reaction to the criticisms that are levelled at their operations and their products, the contradictions inherent in such actions reduce the integrity of the sponsorship. Such sponsorships may also subtly help gloss over the type of broader social issues that are linked to these companies and their products.

Conclusion

Our purpose in this chapter is not to suggest that sponsorship does not contribute to the development of sport. Statements to this effect would be foolish and detrimental to the efforts of many socially responsible companies that have engaged in helping to promote and develop sport. However, what we do argue is that those who uncritically accept the logic of sponsorship and fail to take account of the way in which corporate money changes the experience of sport and the way sport is played are engaging with an overly simplistic and naïve view of this relationship.

Researchers who have tried to understand the impact of sponsorship have done so using the positivistic approach that characterises much of the study of marketing. Seeing the world as an objective reality, they have conducted questionnaire research to verify that sponsorship works because spectators are able to recall the names and symbols of the corporations funding the athlete, team event or organisation. Their work has in a Kuhnian sense been based on 'normal science'. A more penetrating critique, which takes into account the subjective experience of both players and spectators, is needed. It is also necessary to look critically at the motives of sponsors.

Sponsorship is different from philanthropy: it is a strategic action from which the sponsor expects commercial benefits to accrue. Looking critically at this process will, we believe, show that the cheques are not free but can come at a cost to the sport and often involve broader social costs. A critique of the type we are proposing will need to move away from the bland surveys that characterise much of what passes for sponsorship research, to engage with more interpretative approaches. Such approaches will have to question the ontological and epistemological assumptions that have been explicit in sponsorship research as practised to date.

To this end, in a slight modification of what Firat, Dholakia and Bagozzi had to say about marketing in general, we conclude with the following thought:

> Today sponsorship needs a thorough deconstruction. ... For a healthy process of criticism and deconstruction, we must not be afraid to pose as questions what we have assumed were answers, and we must not pull back from being radical in every sense. We must go to the practice we call sponsorship and question its very roots, asking questions that will enable a thorough and robust understanding of those roots. We must be radical in seeking novel and revolutionary alternatives to our set ideas.[78]

NOTES

1. This slight play on one of the lines from the Dire Straits song 'Money for Nothing', on the *Brothers in Arms* album, was suggested by our colleague Dr Tim Berrett.
2. W. Fenton, 'In a Downturn or Just Pausing for Breath?: An Objective Look at the State of the Sports Marketing Industry', *International Journal of Sport Marketing & Sponsorship*, 3 (2001), p.345.
3. T.B. Cornwell and I. Maignan, 'An International Review of Sponsorship Research', *Journal of Advertising*, 27 (1998), pp.1–21.
4. See M. Alvesson and H. Willmott, *Making Sense of Management* (London: Sage, 1996). J. Arndt, 'On Making Marketing Science More Scientific: The Role of Observations, Paradigms, Metaphors, and Puzzle Solving', *Journal of Marketing*, 49 (1985), pp.11–23. G. Morgan, 'Marketing Discourse and Practice: Towards a Critical Analysis', in M. Alvesson and H. Willmott (eds), *Critical Management Studies* (London: Sage, 1992), pp.136–58.
5. G.R. Milne and M.A. McDonald, *Sport Marketing: Managing the Exchange Process* (Sudbury, MA: Jones and Bartlett, 1999), p.122.
6. R.E. McCarville and R.P. Copeland, 'Understanding Sport Sponsorship Through Exchange Theory', *Journal of Sport Management*, 8 (1994), pp.102–14.
7. M. Lee, D. Sandler and D. Shani, 'Attitudinal Constructs Towards Sponsorship: Scale Development Using Three Sporting Events', *International Marketing Review,* 14 (1997), pp.124–33.
8. D.R. Howard and John L. Crompton, *Financing Sport* (Morgantown, WV: Fitness Information Technologies, 1995). pp.223–264.
9. Alvesson and Willmott, *Making Sense of Management*.
10. K.P. Hansen 'The Mentality of Management: Self-Images of American Top Executives', in S.R. Clegg and G. Palmer (eds), *The Politics of Management Knowledge* (London: Sage, 1996), p.43.
11. See D. Shilbury, S. Quick and H. Westerbeek, *Strategic Sport Marketing* (St Leonards, NSW:

Allen & Unwin, 1998), p.175–82 for a brief explanation of targeting audiences in relation to television sponsorship.
12. R. Goldman and S. Papson, *Nike Culture* (London: Sage, 1998), p.2.
13. L. Savan, *The Sponsored Life* (Philadelphia, PA: Temple University Press, 1994), p.9.
14. P. Doyle, 'Building Value-Based Branding Strategies', *Journal of Strategic Marketing*, 9 (2001), pp.255–68.
15. T. Miller, G. Lawrence, J. McKay and D. Rowe, *Globalization and Sport* (London: Sage, 2001), p.57.
16. Alvesson and Willmott, *Making Sense of Management*.
17. P. Baran and P. Sweezy, *Monopoly Capitalism* (Harmondsworth: Penguin, 1966).
18. G. Lawrence and D. Rowe 'The Corporate Pitch: Televised Cricket Under Capitalism', in G. Lawrence and D. Rowe (eds), *PowerPlay: The Commercialisation of Australian Sport* (Sydney: Hale & Iremonger, 1986), pp.166–7.
19. A Voisin, 'NBA Takes Active Role in Dealing with AIDS Issue', *Atlanta Journal and Constitution*, 3 December 1991, p.F-1, cited by S. Jackson and D. Andrews, 'Between and Beyond the Global and the Local', *International Review for the Sociology of Sport*, 34 (1999), pp.31–42.
20. D. Andrews, 'The [Trans]national Basketball Association: American Commodity-Sign Culture and Global-Local Conjuncturalism', in A Cvetovich and D. Kellner (eds), *Articulating the Global and the Local: Globalization and Cultural Studies* (Boulder, CO: Westview Press, 1997), pp.72–101 See also Miller et al., *Globalization and Sport*, 38
21. M. Hiestand, 'NFL Clears Way for In-Stadium Highlights Shows', *USA Today*, 13 December 1994, p.3C, cited by Andrews, 'The [Trans]national Basketball Association'.
22. Miller et al., *Globalization and Sport*.
23. Andrews, 'The [Trans]national Basketball Association'.
24. K. Haack 'From Martin to Memphis, Gasol continues trend', online at www.nba.com/news. gasol_feature_011112.html, accessed 30 January 2002.
25. S. Hill and G. Rifkin, *Radical Marketing* (New York: HarperPerennial, 1999), p.124.
26. 'Dream Team Doomed?' Associated Press, 26 October 2000, online at www.abcnews.go.com/sections/sports/DailyNews/dreamteam001026.html, accessed 30 January 2002.
27. J. Sugden and A. Tomlinson, *Great Balls of Fire: How Big Money is Hijacking World Football* (Edinburgh: Mainstream Publishing, 1999), p.60.
28. M. Pendergrast, *For God, Country and Coca-Cola* (London: Weidenfield, 1993).
29. Ibid.
30. V. Simpson and A. Jennings, *The Lords of the Rings* (Toronto: Simon & Schuster, 1992), p.23.
31. Included in this group were IOC members Dick Pound and Professor Anwar Chowdhry, the latter also President of the International Amateur Boxing Association.
32. T. Slack, *Understanding Sport Organizations* (Champaign, IL: Human Kinetics, 1996).
33. ISL subsequently went bankrupt in early 2001.
34. Z. Bauman *Freedom* (Milton Keynes: Open University Press, 1988).
35. R. Keat, 'Scepticism, Authority, and the Market' in R. Keat, N. Whiteley and N. Abercrombie (eds), *The Authority of the Consumer* (London: Routledge, 1994), pp.23–42, cited by S. Miles, *Consumerism – as a Way of Life* (London: Sage, 1998), p.155
36. A. Sack and E. Staurowsky, *College Athletes for Hire* (Westport, CT: Praeger, 1998).
37. E. Bell and D. Campbell, 'For the Love of Money', *The Observer*, 23 May 1999, p.22.
38. A. Bellos, 'What Happened to the Beautiful Game? *The Guardian*, 14 January 2001, p.16.
39. B. McKenna, 'Ronaldo Denies World Cup Sponsor Pressure', *The Independent*, 11 January 2001, p.26.
40. 'Kenyan Athlete to Pay Dearly for Race Fixing', online at www.nationaudio.com/News/EastAfrican/300899/Sports/Sports5, accessed 21 January 2001.
41. Ibid.
42. Bell and Campbell, 'For the Love of Money'.
43. A. Bellos, 'How Nike Bought Brazil', *Guardian*, 9 July 2001; online at www.guardian.co.uk/Archive, accessed 30 January 2002.
44. J. Sugden and A. Tomlinson, *FIFA and the Contest for World Football* (Cambridge: Polity Press, 1998), p.213.
45. M. Polley, *Moving the Goalposts* (London: Routledge, 1998), p.83.
46. Alvesson and Willmott, *Making Sense of Management*, p.121.
47. R. Copeland, W. Frisby and R. McCarville, 'Understanding the Sport Sponsorship Process from

a Corporate Perspective', *Journal of Sport Management*, 10 (1996), pp.32–48.
48. T. Berrett and T. Slack, 'A Framework for the Analysis of Strategic Approaches Employed by Non-profit Sport Organisations in Seeking Corporate Sponsorship', *Sport Management Review*, 4 (2001), pp.21–45.
49. J. Hargreaves, *Sport, Power and Culture* (Oxford: Polity Press, 1986).
50. Polley, *Moving the Goalposts*, p.64.
51. D. Fifield, 'York Fight for Survival Typifies Financial Crisis', *Guardian*, 10 January 2002, p.30.
52. T. Weir, 'US Coach Says Sponsorship Would Do a World of Good', *USA Today*, 2 January 1998, p.2C.
53. B. Cheadle, 'Athletes Asked to Share Burden', *Edmonton Journal*, 23 December 1995, p.D2.
54. A Gillan, '"Sex appeal" Pays in Sport', *The Guardian*, 26 August 1999, p.4.
55. Kournikova did win the 1999 and 2002 Australian Open doubles title with Martina Hingis.
56. S. Barwick, 'Venus Keeps Sponsors Out in Front', *Daily Telegraph*, 17 January 2001, p.9.
57. J. Coakley, *Sport in Society*, 6th edn (Boston, MA: McGraw-Hill, 1998), p.359.
58. While gender is contained in Bourdieu's analysis, his work has not focused specifically on issues of patriarchal domination. Rather women are analysed as members of a social class, which is defined in contrast to membership in other class categories. Regardless, several writers on women's involvement in sport (see J. Hargreaves, *Heroines of Sport* [London: Routledge, 2000] and S. Gilroy, 'Working on the Body: Links Between Physical Activity and Social Power', in G. Clarke and B. Humberstone [eds], *Researching Women and Sport* [Basingstoke: Macmillan, 1997] pp.96–112]) have made use of Bourdieu's work.
59. P. Bourdieu, *Distinction* (London: Routledge & Kegan Paul, 1984).
60. C. Shilling, *The Body and Social Theory* (London: Sage, 1993).
61. J. Hargreaves, *Sporting Females* (London: Routledge, 1994), p.206.
62. Gillan, '"Sex appeal" Pays in Sport'.
63. H. Schlossberg, *Sports Marketing* (Oxford: Blackwell, 1996), p.176.
64. H. Davies, 'Merchandise United', *The Guardian*, 4 April 1995, pp.1–3, cited by Miles, *Consumerism – as a Way of Life*, p.129.
65. Miles, *Consumerism – as a Way of Life*.
66. P. Carr, J. Findlay, S. Hamil, J. Hill and S. Morrow, 'The Celtic Trust', in S. Hamil, J. Michie, C. Oughton and S. Warby (eds), *The Changing Face of the Football Business* (London: Frank Cass, 2001), p.75.
67. Ibid., p.76
68. 'Angry Keane Slates Man Utd Fans', 9 November 2000, online at www.news.bbc.co.uk/sport/hi/English/football/champions_league/rewind_1014000, accessed 30 January 2002.
69. H. Preuss, *The Economics of the Olympic Games* (Sydney: Walla Walla Press, 2000), p.153.
70. A. Jennings, *The New Lords of the Rings* (London: Pocket Books, 1996), p.4.
71. J. Cagan and N deMause, *Field of Schemes* (Monroe, ME: Common Courage Books, 1998), p.50.
72. M. Rosentraub, *Major League Lo$ers* (New York, NY: Basic Books, 1997), p.96.
73. D.R. Howard and J.L. Crompton, *Financing Sport*, (Morgantown, WV: Fitness Information Technology, 1995). See Chapter 10.
74. 'Coca-Cola Cleans Up – Thank You', online at www.cokespotlight.org/html/news/uppdates, accessed 15 November 2001.
75. See, online, www.mcspotlight.org/issues/environment/ and www.mcspotlight.org/case/
76. E. Schlosser, *Fast Food Nation* (London: Allen Lane, 2001).
77. M. Kaufman, 'Fighting the Cola Wars in Schools', *Washington Post*, 23 March 1999, p.Z12.
78. A.F. Firat, N. Dholakia, R.P. Bagozzi (eds), *Philosophical and Radical Thought in Marketing* (Lexington, MA: D.C. Heath, 1987), pp.xvii–xviii.

14

Spectator Sport's Strange Bedfellows: The Commercial Sponsorship of Sporting Events to Promote Tobacco, Alcohol and Lotteries

STEPHEN R. McDANIEL, DANIEL S. MASON
and LANCE KINNEY

As other contributors to this book have noted, sport has increasingly become bound up in the global process of commercialisation. One increasingly prominent component of commercialised modern sport[1] lies in the realm of sports marketing. The intrusion of event signage, athlete endorsements, product placements, 'official' sponsor designations, personal seat licences, buying/selling media rights and other aspects of this new business have changed the ways in which we see and understand sport. Indeed, organised sport is now a vehicle to promote other, broader business interests. This commercial encroachment has not been without criticism or commentary, particularly where the business interests are concerned with products or services that arguably contradict the very values that sport is alleged to represent.

This chapter critically examines the complex and often puzzling nature of the commercial relationships that have developed over the years, between sport organisations and the marketers of so-called 'sin products' (i.e. tobacco, alcohol and gambling). It discusses the associated policy concerns, controversies and arguable hypocrisy inherent in these relationships. In doing so, it raises questions as to whether or not certain areas of the sports industry are compromising virtue for revenue by helping companies market products that are potentially harmful to public health, or if such practices are antithetical to other core values of the sport organisations involved in such sponsorship practices. Moreover, it examines whether commercial practices like sponsorships have changed the institution of sport or if it is society that has changed as a result of an increased focus on health and social issues and related expectations concerning business practices and public policy.

We begin with an overview of the concept of sports marketing and sponsorship strategy. We focus specifically on the ways in which this practice has provided new revenue streams for sports teams and leagues. The long-standing relationship between sport and certain 'socially stigmatised product categories' is then discussed. Our emphasis is on how these associations have remained despite the apparent contradictions between healthy physical activity and possible health/social concerns over the products involved in event sponsorships. We conclude by offering some data on contemporary views about this issue and a discussion of the efficacy of regulation and regulatory practices.

Sport, Marketing and Event Sponsorship

Although corporations have used sport as a vehicle to help promote their brands since the mid-nineteenth century, the practice has become more commonplace in recent years. As audiences of print and broadcast media have fragmented (or demassified) with the growing number of media options available to them and traditional advertising media have become increasingly cluttered, marketers have turned to what has been termed 'lifestyle marketing'. Lifestyle marketing targets consumers based upon their lifestyles and interests, whether it be the corporate sponsorship of the fine arts, popular music or sporting events. Given the centrality these activities have in consumers' lives, sponsors are able to cut through the 'noise' of traditional advertising and reach people on a deeper and more emotional level by connecting their brand(s) to event properties.

Event sponsorship, or event marketing, has been defined as 'a cash and/or in-kind fee paid to a property in return for access to the exploitable commercial potential associated with that property'.[2] A variety of consumer-oriented objectives are often associated with such sponsorships, including increasing consumers' awareness of a sponsor's brand and improving its image, as well as the ability to use promotional tie-ins and sampling at events.[3]

Sponsorship strategies are also noted for an ability to associate sponsors with particular usage situations and an ability to cut through the clutter associated with other marketing communication techniques.[4] By carefully selecting events, marketers can gain exposure to difficult-to-reach target markets and demonstrate a commitment to supporting the target's lifestyle and interests.[5] In addition to consumer-oriented objectives, Sandler and Shani note that other objectives can be served, including corporate image building or media exposure.[6] Sponsorship is noted to operate differently from conventional advertising in that event-title sponsorship, such as the Nokia Sugar Bowl, and/or arena signage viewed at the event or via television broadcasts offer little opportunity to relay a selling message.[7]

Recent spending estimates illustrate the phenomenal growth of sponsorship as a marketing tactic; expenditures across all types of events were estimated at $6.8 billion for 1998, of which 67 per cent involved sport.[8] This staggering figure illustrates why sponsorship is one of the fastest-growing areas of marketing communication. In addition, it shows that sponsorship sales provides a lucrative revenue stream for sport organisations. While this form of commercialisation has become more ubiquitous it does not mean it has necessarily been embraced by all.

As Davidson notes, even when marketing practices are geared towards socially acceptable products, such business practices are often subject to criticism.[9] For example, some see marketing as a waste of resources, others are wary of the 'powerful' effects of advertising and there are those who see it as promoting questionable values related to consumption and materialism. Moreover, others have argued that sponsorship of amateur sporting events, such as college sports or the Olympics, have made them overly commercial.[10] Consequently, it is not surprising that when conventional marketing practices, like sport sponsorship, are used to promote potentially problematic product categories, such as tobacco, alcohol or gambling, such activities are viewed with even greater disdain.

Historical Ties between Sport, Tobacco, Alcohol and Gambling

While these three product categories have had a long-standing relationship with sport, the ways in which each has enjoyed social acceptability has certainly changed over time. As the subject of this chapter is the issue of using sport to promote tobacco, alcohol and lotteries, it is important to examine how long these industries have been associated with sporting activities. In addition, one would surmise from some of the topics addressed in this book that sport has been changed by the encroaching commercial element in sport. However, as this section will show, there have been long-standing commercial relationships between sport and tobacco, alcohol, and gambling. In fact, evidence suggests that these relationships extend back for centuries. For example, entrepreneurs have tried to further their own business interests using sport at least since the emergence of modern team games during the mid-nineteenth century.

Today, few question the social and physical benefits of sport and exercise, yet at one time sport and leisure practices such as drinking and gambling were all condemned as wasteful, if not blasphemous behaviours. Early critics suggested that when one or more of these activities occurred, violence and other acts of social unrest often ensued.[11] As a result, statutes of early English medieval kings often contained church bans on games and tournaments.[12] Carter, in a study of coroners' records from thirteenth-century

England, found frequent examples where alcohol consumption by participants and spectators led to violent behaviour.[13] Until the nineteenth century, organisers of sport were forced to address unruly crowds who were seen as a danger in the facilities constructed specifically for sport. As Vamplew explains, 'No doubt gambling losses and alcohol had contributed to many a crowd fracas at pre-enclosed [non-gated horse] race meetings'.[14] Some early sports, particularly fighting and blood sports, were considered to be organised primarily for the purpose of gambling.[15] As a result, reformers sought to control unwanted behaviour in society, including alcohol consumption, violence, gambling and some sporting forms.

In early colonial times in what would become the United States, the landed gentry would engage in gambling activities, including cards, dice and horse racing, during their leisure time – legal gambling was limited to men of property.[16] Similarly, drinking and gambling were an integral part of the working class, who were able to circumvent anti-gambling laws by frequenting coffee-houses, saloons and billiard halls. Perhaps the earliest 'sponsors' of sporting events – those who used sport in order to further their other business interests – were tavern and alehouse owners who knew that organising games would attract spectators and participants, many of whom would imbibe the other products available at the tavern. These patrons would also frequently gamble; by wagering on events, the intensity of the sporting experience was increased.[17] In England, gambling had long been an integral (if undesirable) part of the day-to-day lives of many. State-run lotteries had even been created, although this practice was banned during the 1820s.[18]

By the onset of the twentieth century, reformers also began to see the merits that sport and physical activity held for a society that was re-establishing itself in urban areas. As such, sport and its associated health benefits began to be seen as a means of self-improvement. This new outlook was in contrast to Puritanical views of 'amusements' being counterproductive to society. To promote this new ideology, reformers and other leaders began to provide parks, playgrounds and other urban facilities for public usage.[19] In this manner, sport emerged as an important part of a healthy lifestyle, and was viewed less as a threat to society. In fact, sport was thought to be so beneficial that the playground movement and public school systems were training-grounds for teaching individuals leadership, teamwork and other desirable qualities, while assimilating immigrants in countries such as the US.[20]

However, gambling and consumption were still considered societal problems, and as modern team sports emerged, it was not long before questions arose as to the legitimacy of game outcomes due to the influence of gambling interests. In other words, although organisers of sport recognised that gambling was a part of the leisure experience and generated further interest in sporting events, some distance between theses practices needed to be made in order to maintain some semblance of integrity related to game outcomes. While this would be easy to do for sports such as football or baseball, other sports were much more directly dependent upon gambling interests. Recognising this situation, gambling's association with certain sports such as horse racing enjoyed a growing acceptance by the US press through the mid-1860s.[21] Thus, gambling was viewed as a 'necessary evil' that would ensure the survival of the sport.[22] By some estimates, total betting on races in the US reached $200 million by the 1890s.[23] Although gambling was not universally endorsed by the press, an increase in gambling on sporting events was seen more as 'a reflection of the American proclivity to speculate on almost everything'.[24] However, by the early twentieth century, reformers led by New York Governor Hughes attempted to eliminate public gambling.[25]

During the very same period, entrepreneurs also began viewing sport as a means of generating revenues. Open play areas began to be enclosed as organisers of athletic contests began charging spectators to attend various matches to finance increasing facility costs and, in some sports, demands by players for remuneration. Thus, promoters were put in a delicate situation; in many cases they relied on gambling interests to keep interest in games and attendance high, yet they needed to dissociate the events from the gambling element to maintain the integrity of the contests.

In some instances, the influence of gambling interests went beyond that of recognising the need for gambling to increase interest in matches. Even sports such as baseball, which did not seem to have the same natural ties to gambling as horse racing, were not immune to controversy. According to Riess, at the onset of the twentieth century 'baseball was an important nexus between urban machine politics and organised crime, albeit a lesser one than prize fighting or horse racing'.[26] There were also accusations of game fixing by players throughout the first two decades of the twentieth century.[27] One of the most notorious examples from the US remains the 'Black Sox' scandal of 1919, where eight members of the Chicago White Sox allegedly agreed to fix the World Series for $100,000. Although all eight members were later acquitted, incoming baseball commissioner Kenesaw Landis banned all of them from baseball, including all-time great 'Shoeless' Joe Jackson.[28] The most recent highly-publicised scandal in baseball remains the banishment of Pete Rose, the sport's all-time leader in hits, due to his gambling on baseball and other sporting events. For this and other controversies, Ostertag argues that baseball has been perhaps the most vocal opponent of state-sanctioned sports gambling.[29]

Baseball has not been the only sport unable to avoid gambling scandals. For example, each of the other major North American professional sports leagues (basketball, football and ice hockey) has, over the years, had to address gambling scandals. Perhaps the most significant contribution to this problem was the advent of the point spread, invented by bookies during the 1940s to minimise losses and to encourage more betting on collegiate basketball games.[30] The point spread also allowed players to manipulate a game's final score without changing the outcome. As a result, several prominent scandals have occurred in collegiate basketball, including one in 1951 involving New York college teams.[31]

In the meantime, alcohol and tobacco companies had been quick to recognise that the consumers of their own products were often those who chose to attend and participate in sporting contests. It thus followed that sport could be a convenient tool to promote such products. In fact, the sports trading card industry has its roots in cigarette packaging, where cards were inserted into packages to encourage collecting and to protect the cigarettes from being crushed when shipped. As the first decades of the twentieth century progressed, technological advancements in production and communication facilitated the increasing popularity of some sports and the emergence of these activities as integral components of popular culture. In doing so, the potential of association with sports such as baseball became increasingly lucrative for sponsorship interests. For this reason, many outstanding baseball players, including Nap Lajoie, Lou Gehrig and Babe Ruth supplemented their earnings through endorsing tobacco products.

However, fearing that players' direct association with these products might undermine the integrity of the sports themselves, professional sports leagues began forbidding players from such endorsements. This was perhaps in response to increasing awareness of the harmful effects of tobacco usage and alcohol abuse. Thus in recent decades in North America, collective bargaining agreements between leagues and their respective players' associations contain specific 'morality' clauses that ensure that players will not associate with gambling, tobacco or alcohol companies. However, this has not stopped former athletes such as Willie Mays, Bill Russell or John Elway from endorsing breweries at the conclusion of their playing careers. Willie Mays, who recently endorsed Coors beer, was banned from baseball by then-commissioner Bowie Kuhn shortly after being inducted into the Baseball Hall of Fame for acting as a goodwill ambassador for an Atlantic City casino. However, he was reinstated by the incoming commissioner Peter Ueberroth a few years later. Interestingly, these additional restraints on players have occurred as state lotteries have become more widespread; obviously, leagues have acted to continue to dissociate themselves from gambling scandals and other activities that might undermine the uncertainty of game outcomes.

As has been briefly shown in this section, sport has had a long-standing association with tobacco, alcohol and gambling; over time, each has been viewed with varying degrees of scrutiny and disdain. In many cases, the frequency and visibility of these associations have been determined simply by the degree to which public opinion and state intervention have attempted to control and/or limit such ties. It is important to make the distinction that sport, despite initially being considered uneconomic and wasteful, began to be seen as an important contributor to developing character and healthy lifestyles. This view of physical activity emerged during the mid- to late nineteenth century and continues today. However, another underlying theme throughout the centuries has been that sport's organisers have seen tobacco, alcohol and gambling interests as a 'necessary evil'. In other words, while there certainly has to be some dissociation from these products, the importance of and reliance upon them have never been denied. In cases where incidents related to abuse of these products have occurred, leagues and organisers have been forced to address a subject that is known to maintain an interest and demand for the very contests whose integrity is in question.

Current Issues and Trends in the Use of Sport Sponsorship to Promote 'Sin Products'

Tobacco Sponsorship

Despite the historical ties with sport, manufacturers of tobacco products have seen their ability to market their products increasingly controlled by public policy. Tobacco manufacturers in the US (and other countries) have been restricted from purchasing advertising on radio and television since the early 1970s and they have turned to outdoor and print advertising, as well as promotions, such as event sponsorships, to gain exposure for their brands. According to recent sponsorship industry reports, tobacco companies account for around four per cent of all sponsorships.[32] Of the three product categories examined in this chapter, tobacco has received the most negative attention as of late, because of its well-documented health implications. Opponents of tobacco promotion argue that event marketing targets (or at the very least, reaches) children and potentially obfuscates health concerns by associating smoking with sport, while mentions of sponsor brand names and mediated arena signage subvert cigarette advertising bans in the electronic media.[33] For example, using a content analysis of a televised auto race, Blum found that a cigarette sponsor's brand name was visible (or mentioned) over 5,933 times during the course of one telecast. In this case, the sponsor was able to draw attention to its product even though its ability to advertise on television is prohibited.

The tobacco industry maintains that its sponsorships are using conventional marketing communications to promote a legal product, while sponsoring events (e.g. auto racing) with audience demographics that are over 90 per cent adult.[34] In addition, they contend that the purpose of this strategy is to influence brand switching and not to induce children to begin smoking.[35] Although a good deal of research has examined the effects of traditional advertising as it pertains to promoting tobacco products, only a few studies have been conducted on tobacco sponsorship effects.[36] This work suggests that such promotions may influence children's awareness of tobacco brands and sponsorship activities. However, the degree to which such sports-oriented promotions might obscure the potential health concerns related to this product is unclear.[37]

Some of the above arguments have resulted in the initiation of sweeping regulations on tobacco advertising and sponsorship worldwide. Several countries, including Australia, Canada, France, Iceland, New Zealand, Norway, Sweden and the US, already have bans or restrictions on tobacco companies' use of sport sponsorship.[38] The European Union recently voted to ban all tobacco sponsorships and advertising, effective October 2001.[39] Likewise, a recent legal settlement in the US restricts tobacco companies from sponsoring team and youth sports as well as selling sports-related apparel. In addition to government bans, many amateur and professional sporting organisations have opted for self-regulation in terms of tobacco sponsorship.[41] In fact, tobacco is the most commonly restricted product category in event marketing, with an estimated 30 per cent of event properties refusing to accept sponsorships from such companies.[42]

Beer and Alcohol Sponsorships

As previously noted, marketers of alcoholic beverages have long been associated with sport. However, the amount of money directed towards sports marketing (i.e. advertising and sponsorships) has increased along with the public's interest in sports. The relevance of this marketing tactic to the brewing industry is evidenced by Miller Beer's commissioning a major study of US sports fans in the early 1980s.[43] Moreover, companies like Anheuser-Busch and Coors own sports franchises and stadiums. In terms of sponsorship activity, the alcoholic beverage category is currently responsible for almost twice as much spending as tobacco products (i.e. seven per cent of all sponsorship spending), and this category also outspends marketers of non-alcoholic beverages (who account for six per cent).[44] When these sponsorship expenditures are combined with the amounts devoted to alcohol advertising in electronic and print media, it is evident that spectator sports are far more dependent on money from beer/alcohol companies than they are from tobacco interests. Of course, there are different concerns associated with the use of alcohol versus the use of tobacco; nevertheless, product consumption by minors is problematic with either category.

Within the sponsorship policy debate, there seems to be an implicit notion that certain products are more problematic than others (e.g. hard liquor as opposed to beer). For instance, the International Olympic Committee (IOC) refuses to accept sponsorships from tobacco and spirit companies because they are not considered congruent with Olympic ideals. Yet the IOC allows a brewing company, Anheuser-Busch, to associate its products with the games. Likewise, over half of the colleges and universities in the US have contracts with beer companies.[45] However, according to statistics from the US Department of Health and Human Services, alcohol (of all types) is the number-one drug problem in the US, responsible for over 105,000 deaths[46] and $166.5 billion in economic costs annually.[47]

As with the promotion of tobacco products, marketing alcoholic beverages is controversial because of the implications for youngsters. For example, it is estimated that junior and senior high-school students in the US consume 35 per cent of all wine coolers and 1.1 billion cans of beer each year,[48] despite laws which require a person to be 21 in order to purchase and consume alcohol legally. For the above reasons, it could be argued that sponsorships associating alcohol with sport have as far-reaching health implications as those involving tobacco.

Research involving fifth- and sixth-grade students in the US suggests that television sports viewing may indirectly increase youngsters' intentions to consume alcohol via embedded advertising that increases their brand awareness for beer.[49] Another study found white male adolescents reported a consistent preference for beer ads with sports content.[50] According to other research, based on a review of some 443 hours of televised sports, there were more commercials for alcoholic beverages than for any other beverage category, with mediated arena signage for alcohol sponsors appearing at a rate of 3.3 times an hour.[51]

Although sport seems to offer an ideal vehicle to promote products and attract new consumers, the influence of event sponsorship on the trial and adoption of products, like alcohol, is not well substantiated.[52] Moreover, brewers argue that they are marketing a legal product to adults that, when used responsibly, does not present a problem. They also point to their funding of public-service messages emphasising the importance of responsible drinking and the legal drinking age. However, given some of the concerns noted above about using sport to help promote alcoholic beverages, there are still groups that feel such sponsorships are not appropriate.

The US National Council on Alcoholism and Drug Abuse issued a formal protest against Anheuser-Busch's sponsorship of the 1996

Olympic Games in Atlanta.[53] Similarly, the National Coalition of
Hispanic Health and Human Services Organisations voiced concerns
over A-B's involvement with World Cup soccer.[54] The company also
sought an exemption to France's rules prohibiting alcohol advertising
and billboards, in order to have stadium signage when that country
hosted the 1998 World Cup soccer tournament. This was also opposed by
substance-abuse groups in that country.[55] In 1998, US Secretary of Health
and Human Services Donna Shalala urged members of the National
Collegiate Athletic Association (NCAA) not to accept alcohol
sponsorships.[56] More recently, several groups in Utah expressed their
concern over the brewer's association with the Winter Olympics, held in
Salt Lake City in 2002.[57]

Lotteries and Sport Sponsorship

Lotteries returned to the US in the early 1960s and about a decade later in
Canada. At the time of this writing there are 38 lotteries in the US sponsored
by state governments and the District of Columbia, who use part of the
revenue for funding education and sports facilities. Unlike tobacco and
alcohol, state lotteries are currently not subject to the same types of
advertising restrictions and 30 of them sponsor sports. In Canada, lotteries
are run in each province, and some of the profits go to help both their
amateur and professional sport organisations.

   Just as the juxtaposition of tobacco or beer with sports might seem odd
in some respects, business relationships involving sports and gambling
activities, like state-sponsored lotteries, are peculiar as well. As Frey
(1992) notes, most sporting organisations try to distance themselves from
other forms of gambling for fear of tainting the integrity of their product
(which is dependent on the uncertainty of outcomes)[58]. Sports betting in the
United States is only legal in Nevada and there is currently a movement
afoot in the US to ban sports wagering altogether. However, it would
appear that many sport organisations in North America hold the same
benign view of lotteries, compared to sports wagering, as they hold
towards beer (versus spirits), because none of the leagues and governing
bodies prohibit their members from accepting sponsorships from state or
provincial lotteries.

   While lotteries are different from sports betting in terms of their
potential directly to damage sports, the two are both forms of gambling and
research suggests that they can be addictive and have potentially harmful
health and social consequences – similar to alcohol or tobacco. For
example, a University of Chicago study found a statistically significant
relationship between the availability of state lotteries and the prevalence of
at-risk gambling.[59] Likewise, a 1990 study by the Maryland Task Force on

Gambling Addiction found that 22 per cent of callers to a compulsive gambling hotline were lottery addicts.[60] Another study funded by the British Columbia Lottery Corporation in 1994 suggested that gambling at an early age and continuous forms of gambling (e.g. instant lottery games and video lottery) were risk factors for problem gambling.[61]

Current estimates hold that around five million US adults are pathological gamblers with another 15 million at risk of joining them.[62] It is estimated that the annual cost of problem and pathological gamblers is US$5 billion, in addition to US$40 billion estimated in lost productivity, social services and bad debt over their lifetime.[63] These figures do not include the negative emotional and psychological impact on the families of problem gamblers, which is difficult to quantify. And just as under-age smoking and drinking is a concern in the US and abroad, it appears that adolescents are having problems with gambling as well. For example, Ladouceur, Dube and Bujold found that over 60 per cent of 1,300 primary-school students surveyed in Quebec reported playing the lottery, with 40 per cent reporting gambling once a week or more.[64] Similar studies in the US have found that between 27 per cent and 35 per cent of 15- to 18-year-olds had purchased lottery tickets for themselves in Minnesota, Louisiana, Texas and Connecticut.[65] Meanwhile, a recent Canadian study found that gambling-related problems are four times more prevalent among those between the ages of 12 and 19 than people 18 to 74.[66]

In addition to the concerns regarding lotteries and under-age consumers, there are also those who argue that state-sponsored lotteries function as a regressive tax on the poor, as they cannot afford to spend their money on such activities.[67] For example, one study found that the higher the income of gamblers, the more likely they were to report gambling for entertainment, while lower-income respondents were more likely to see gambling as an investment.[68] It has also been noted that state lotteries have cannibalised charitable gambling, such as church bingo.[69] Moreover, promises concerning the use of lottery earnings to fund public concerns like education are not always fulfilled either, as a study by *Money* magazine found that states without lotteries devote a larger part of their budget to education than states with lotteries.[70]

Proponents of lotteries argue that many of the above claims are false or greatly exaggerated.[71] Moreover, they contend that most people enjoy the lottery responsibly and that pre-existing pathologies are responsible for people abusing lotteries. They also point to the important streams of revenue that this form of gaming provides for state and provincial governments, which subsequently benefits their residents. In addition, many states set aside money from their earnings to help deal with research and treatment of problem gamblers.[72]

There are currently no available data on the level of sports sponsorship spending by government-sponsored lotteries in the US and Canada. However, based on information from the promotions departments of state and provincial lotteries in both countries, they currently have sponsorship agreements with sports teams and arenas in the Canadian Football League (two teams), Major League Baseball (11 teams), the National Basketball Association (11 teams), the National Football League (11 teams), the National Hockey League (ten teams) and the NCAA (nine teams), as well as various minor-league sports organisations and auto racing.[73] In fact, none of the major sports leagues in North America prohibit their members from helping to promote this type of gambling activity, including the governing body of intercollegiate athletics in the US. This is particularly interesting since NCAA president Cedric Dempsey has noted that the widespread acceptance of gambling has made it difficult to create a ban on sports wagering and has acknowledged the potential health problems associated with gambling behaviour.[74] Dempsey's stance and the NCAA's push for prohibiting sports gambling therefore both seem at odds with allowing member organisations, such as the US Air Force Academy, Florida State University, Marshall University, New Mexico State University, Penn State University, the University of Louisville, the University of New Mexico, the University of Virginia and West Virginia University, to have sponsorship agreements with state lotteries at the time of writing.[75]

The NCAA's (and various professional sports leagues') implicit views on the differences between lotteries and sports betting are similar in many ways to the IOC's current stance that beer sponsors are somehow more consistent with Olympic ideals than tobacco or spirit companies. This stance may be due in part to the fact that it has only been in recent years (1994) that gambling addiction has been recognised as a psychiatric disorder by mental-health professionals, similar to alcohol or drug addiction. In fact, what is considered by some to be a landmark policy study on gambling behaviour in the US was only recently published, in 1999[76]. Comparatively, the US Surgeon General's report on the relationship of smoking and cancer was issued in 1964 (at a time when just over 50 per cent of the adult male population smoked).[77]

Public Opinion on Sponsorships and Their Regulation

As shown above, data suggest that the use and/or abuse of tobacco, alcohol and lotteries products can produce a number of negative social and economic effects on society, although industry and public health officials disagree as to the role marketing plays in this. It is also important therefore to understand and consider how the public views such products and their associations with sport. This will also serve to help place in context recent public policy regarding sponsorship.

In terms of public opinion on the product categories themselves, a recent Gallup poll found that, when Americans were asked which creates the most problems for society, 77 per cent reported alcohol and 12 per cent reported tobacco (while nine per cent reported both and two per cent had no opinion).[78] A similar poll found that 55 per cent of US respondents agreed that legalised gambling was creating a compulsive gambling problem nationally; yet over 70 per cent reported that it was not immoral, or harmful in moderation, with a little over half agreeing that it provided money for social programmes.[79] Interestingly enough, only 26 per cent of those respondents reported supporting the outlawing of sports betting in the US. Conversely, a 1995 poll of residents in Alberta, Canada, found that 68 per cent felt that increased access to gambling would create more problems than it was worth,[80] and 48 per cent of them viewed gambling as an 'evil influence'.[81]

In terms of general public opinion on sponsorship, a 1993 Roper Poll revealed that 76 per cent of US respondents felt that sponsorship was a fair price to pay to keep ticket prices down.[82] The majority of them (68 per cent) were not concerned about the kinds of companies that sponsor sports events, with only 14 per cent disapproving of alcohol and tobacco sponsorships.[83] In fact, 73 per cent were opposed to government efforts to ban certain companies from sponsoring sports.[84] Subsequently, 78 per cent of respondents reported that owners and operators of sporting facilities should have the final say on what type of company sponsors an event.[85] A 1995 Associated Press poll of 1,007 American adults found 73 per cent of respondents supporting the proposition that the tobacco industry should pay for campaigns to discourage teenage smoking. However, only 42 per cent supported banning the tobacco industry's use of sport sponsorship to promote their products.[86] Similarly, a 1996 study in Canada found that the majority of Canadians felt that legal business enterprises should be allowed to sponsor events and wanted the government to cut spending on events, including sports.[87] The above survey results suggest that while many are opposed to the promotion of tobacco products, the majority of people are reluctant to allow the government to restrict commercial speech in this context and/or place a greater financial burden on the public in the process. As suggested by the above data, an intriguing factor affecting views on restricting tobacco and alcohol sponsorship of sport is the notion of self-interest. In a review of studies on self-interest and public policy, Green and Gerken found that self-interest did not have a significant influence upon most political and social attitudes.[88] In contrast, based on two surveys of California residents (conducted in 1984 and 1987), they found significant differences between smokers and non-smokers on opinions towards policy issues related to smoking (e.g. restricting smoking in public places and tax increases on cigarettes). McDaniel and Mason applied the above notion to public opinion on sport sponsorships, finding that the more alcohol and tobacco use added to respondents' enjoyment of sport spectating, the more likely they were to favour sponsorships promoting those product categories.[89]

A more recent public opinion survey (1999) suggests that US consumers hold differing opinions about the importance of context on sponsorship practices, in terms of intercollegiate athletics versus professional sports organisations.[90] On the general notion of corporate sponsorship, American consumers are more supportive of business involvement with professional sports, as 66 per cent of respondents holding an opinion indicated that they agree that it is appropriate for corporations to sponsor professional sports events, while 13 per cent disagreed with this practice. Support for sponsorship of college athletics is somewhat lower, with 54 per cent feeling that corporate involvement is acceptable. The majority of respondents (64 per cent) did not feel that sponsorships lower sports event ticket prices.

As with the general notion of sports sponsorship, the US public appears more accepting of alcohol's association with professional sports. When asked specifically about alcohol's involvement with professional sports, 46 per cent reported supporting this tactic with 38 per cent opposing it. Conversely, when alcohol sponsorships of collegiate sports were considered, 37 per cent of the sample supported such promotions, as compared to 49 per cent who opposed the practice. However, self-interest did appear to play some role in alcohol sports sponsorship attitudes. When self-identified alcohol beverage drinkers considered alcohol and college sports sponsorship, 45 per cent supported involvement while 45 per cent were opposed. Support increased for alcohol and professional sports event associations, with 57 per cent of the drinkers judging these sponsorships as acceptable.

The same pattern is observed for tobacco brands at the professional level (current NCAA regulations prevent member schools from accepting tobacco brand sponsorships.) When the full sample is considered, 40 per cent of respondents welcomed tobacco's involvement at the professional level, with 49 per cent opposing tobacco. However, if the respondent indicated he/she smoked, support was likely to be stronger, as 55 per cent of respondents who smoked supported tobacco sponsorship of professional sporting events. Fully 78 per cent of the sample was opposed to government oversight of all sponsorship activities.

It appears that both US and Canadian respondents are concerned over health and social issues related to the marketing of so-called 'sin products'. However, it is interesting to note that US respondents report alcohol as being a more pressing social concern than tobacco and respondents in both countries do not seem to favour government intervention. It is unclear whether this is due to financial self-interest (i.e. reducing ticket prices or the public burden of supporting sport) or the concern to preserve free commercial speech – or some combination of the two. At any rate, it appears that public opinion data do not convincingly support either side of the argument in this sponsorship debate.

Discussion and Conclusions

This chapter has sought to bring to light several of the issues and controversies related to the sponsorship of sport by the marketers of tobacco, alcohol and lotteries. While we noted that the institution of sport has had long-standing relationships with all of these product categories, the rather cyclical nature of public perceptions, proliferation and subsequent regulation regarding the above stigmatised industries were also illustrated. This review also suggests that there are a number of considerations and questions raised by examining the seemingly incompatible associations between sport and arguably unhealthy product categories. And as with many public-policy issues, there is a relativity to what might be considered 'right' or 'wrong' in this instance, depending on one's perspective. The rights and needs of all major stakeholders therefore need to be considered.

It appears that current concerns regarding sponsorships involving tobacco, alcohol and lotteries often vary based on perceptions of health risks associated with the different product categories. As previously noted, while it is generally accepted that the mere use of tobacco poses health problems, it is the abuse of products such as beer/alcohol or lotteries which creates concerns. Consequently, tobacco is the most regulated product category when it comes to such promotions, although it remains to be seen whether or not the rather fine-grained distinctions that many sports organisations make in accepting sponsorships from beer companies (but not spirits) or state lotteries (but not casinos) are tenable.

One central question that arises when considering sponsorships involving socially stigmatised products such as those reviewed here is the appropriateness of government regulation. There is a growing body of research on the implications of product usage for tobacco, alcohol and gambling. Moreover, there is also a growing body of research on the effects of advertising for such products, where messages contain selling propositions and other imagery. However, it is much more difficult to isolate the effects of more subtle forms of promotion, such as event sponsorship, from the effects of other marketing strategies and social influences (such as family and peers).[91] Consequently, the notion of government regulation of sponsorship activities, without strong empirical support, seems problematic in most democratic societies.[92] In addition, the public opinion data presented herein suggest that such actions are not necessarily condoned by the public.[93] Moreover, some scholars question the efficacy of such health policy strategies altogether, as it is argued that they create a false sense of security by dealing with a complex issue in too simplistic a manner.[94] It would seem, then, that other solutions should be considered first.

The tobacco, alcohol, and gambling industries are operating in an increasingly restrictive regulatory environment worldwide. Continued research on the effects of such products and subsequent concern for social health issues, as evidenced by public interest groups such as www.thetruth.com and the recent scrutiny of tobacco marketing issues (including sport-related sponsorship) in the US, could also portend a re-examination of alcohol and gambling issues worldwide. In addition, new practices such as online gambling bring new global policy concerns. Even in the absence of policy decisions, league and/or event organisers may also take it upon themselves to address sponsorship issues and self-regulate in order to maintain a new level of corporate citizenry, especially given that a large part of their audience is made up of under-age consumers. Consequently, the sport business context may be an important issue to consider, in terms of the organisation, its culture and its mission (e.g. differences between professional sports versus amateur or intercollegiate athletics).

Although it is easy to argue that most modern sports are commercial to varying degrees, it is clear that sporting organisations paint different pictures of themselves, and public opinion data suggest that the North American public differentiates between professional sports and intercollegiate athletics in terms of supporting commercial associations with makers of certain products. For example, data from recent polls suggest that more respondents felt sponsorships are more appropriate for professional teams than college teams, with the same being true for sponsorships involving beer.[95] Moreover, it would seem that professional sports organisations have a different mission from intercollegiate athletics, and that the former might be more focused on the bottom line than the latter. In fact, some schools have started turning down sponsorships from beer companies.[96] In the near future, all sports organisations may want to consider doing the same with lottery sponsorships, as the ubiquity of all forms of gambling may make it increasingly difficult for them in their quest to eliminate sports wagering (given the public opinion data on the latter form of gambling). The crux of the matter seems to be short-term financial gain versus the long-term outlook concerning the integrity of contests as well as the image of sports organisations.

Finally, in addition to the role of government and the accountability of sports organisations, what role does the sports consumer play in this equation? Data suggest that public opinion is concerned to varying degrees about the health and social ramifications of tobacco, alcohol, and gambling but does not favour government regulation of sponsorship; likewise, it appears that people appreciate the financial benefits of sponsorship revenues. However, it remains to be seen whether the general public will want to help absorb the economic consequences of social problems created by people who use/abuse the products promoted through sport just so these sponsorship revenues (and/or lottery sales) can subsidise sports organisations and their facilities.

This discussion brings us full circle to the intent of this book – an examination of the commercialisation of sport. Indeed the times are changing, but in the case of tobacco, alcohol, and gambling interests, each has had an enduring presence with consumers and organised, modern sport. However, as outcries over overcommercialisation and health concerns related to these products continue to grow, the manner in which these relationships persist will certainly change. Many of the alleged problems associated with these products and their relationship to sport have in fact been concerns voiced over the past 150 years; it is only with new information related to the health and social costs of these products that policy has restricted the ability of marketers to promote them. In addition, it could also be argued that a new era of corporate governance that has a stakeholder rather than shareholder focus has meant that sporting organisations may increasingly restrict partnerships with these products in order to project themselves as good corporate citizens.

Perhaps the most interesting issue that emerges from this discussion is the place that sport holds in society. Without a doubt, modern organised sport has been about more than fair play, health/fitness and the other alleged qualities associated with sport that have been espoused since the late nineteenth century. In the twentieth century the sports that were tied to corporate sponsors have been more about commercial interests and flaunting the merits of political systems than they were about sportsmanship and play for its own sake. Yet despite the now-public airing of the IOC's dirty laundry, we still cling to the Olympics as something more than commercial spectacle. As we have shown in this chapter, commercial modern sport has developed alongside many other questionable interests, which have included tobacco, alcohol, and gambling. Thus the problems associated with their interrelationships are not necessarily new; they are more pronounced within a context of public concern, increasing regulation, and a desire to continue incorrectly to consider commercial spectator sport as something purer and above other forms of mass entertainment. It is this distinction that reaffirms the importance of sport to people worldwide.

NOTES

1. Modern sport is characterised by standardised rules, faciltities and equipment; formal organisation; media coverage; record keeping; and the presence of spectators.
2. L. Ukman, *The IEG's Complete Guide to Sponsorship: Everything You Need to Know About Sports, Arts, Event, Entertainment and Cause Marketing* (Chicago, IL: IEG, Inc., 1995), p.1.
3. See M.H. Cunningham and S.F. Taylor, 'Event Marketing: State of the Industry and Research Agenda', *Festival Management and Event Tourism*, 2 (1995), pp.123–37; G. Levin, 'Sponsors Put Pressure on for Accountability', *Advertising Age*, 21 June 1993; A.A. Schreiber, *Lifestyle and Event Marketing: Building the New Customer Relationship* (New York: McGraw-Hill, 1994); W.L. Shanklin and J.R. Kuzma, 'Buying that Sporting Image', *Marketing Management*, Spring 1992, pp.59–67.
4. D.M. Sandler and D. Shani, 'Sponsorship and the Olympic Games: The Consumer Perspective', *Sport Marketing Quarterly*, 2 (1993), p.38.
5. T. Meenaghan, 'The Role of Sponsorship in the Marketing Communications Mix', *International Journal of Advertising*, 10 (1991), p.43; D.W. Marshall and G. Cook, 'The Corporate (Sports) Sponsor', *International Journal of Advertising*, 11 (1993), p.319. See also J. Jensen, 'Sports Marketing Links Need Nurturing', *Advertising Age*, 65, 13 (1994); Schreiber, *Lifestyle and Event Marketing*.
6. See D.M. Sandler and D. Shani, 'Sponsorship and the Olympic Games: The Consumer Perspective', *Sport Marketing Quarterly*, 2 (1993), pp.38–43.
7. See G.B. Hastings, 'Sponsorship Works Differently from Advertising', *International Journal of Advertising*, 3 (1984), pp.171–6; Ukman, *The IEG's Complete Guide to Sponsorship*.
8. International Events Group (IEG) Sponsorship Report (1998), online at www.sponsorship.com.
9. D.K. Davidson, *Selling Sin: The Marketing of Socially Unacceptable Products* (Westport, CT: Quorum Books, 1996).
10. See M. McAllister, 'College Bowl Sponsorship and the Increased Commercialization of Amateur Sports', *Critical Studies in Mass Communication*, 15 (1998), pp.357–81; M.R. Real, 'Is Television Corrupting the Olympics?' *Television Quarterly*, 28 (1996), pp.2–12.
11. For a discussion of Puritan influences on sporting practices in America, see A. Guttmann, *A Whole New Ballgame: An Interpretation of American Sports* (Chapel Hill, NC: University of North Carolina Press, 1988).
12. J.M. Carter, 'Sports and Recreations in Thirteenth-Century England: The Evidence of the Eyre and Coroners' Rolls – A Research Note', *Journal of Sport History*, 15 (1988), p.167.
13. See Carter, 'Sports and Recreations in Thirteenth-Century England'.
14. W. Vamplew, 'Sports Crowd Disorder in Britain, 1870–1914: Causes and Controls', *Journal of Sport History*, 7 (1980), p.13.
15. R. Munting, 'Social Opposition to Gambling in Britain: An Historical Overview', *International Journal of the History of Sport*, 10 (1993), p.295.
16. B.G. Rader, *American Sports: From the Age of Folk Games to the Age of Televised Sports* (Upper Saddle River, NJ: Prentice-Hall, 1999), p.10.
17. Ibid., p.28.
18. M. Clapson, *A Bit of a Flutter: Popular Gambling and English Society, c.1823–1961* (Manchester: Manchester University Press, 1992), p.187.
19. See Rader, *American Sports*, pp.98–115.
20. Ibid.
21. M.A. Adelman, *A Sporting Time: New York City and the Rise of Modern Athletics, 1820–70* (Urbana, IL: University of Illinois Press, 1986), p.88.
22. Ibid.
23. J.R. Betts, *America's Sporting Heritage: 1850–1950* (Reading, MA: Addison-Wesley Publishing, 1974), p.222.
24. Adelman, *A Sporting Time*, p.162.
25. In Canada, gaming was prohibited under the Criminal Code passed in 1892, which contained specific provisions pertaining to gambling: M.Y. Seelig and J.H. Seelig, '"Place Your Bets!" On Gambling, Government and Society', *Canadian Public Policy – Analyse de Politiques*, 24 (1998), p.92. A similar prohibition was later passed in the US: *National Gambling Impact Study Commission Report: Lotteries*, online at www.ngisc.gov/research/lotteries.html.
26. S.A. Riess, *Touching Base: Professional Baseball and American Culture in the Progressive Era* (Urbana, IL: University of Illinois Press, 1999), p.87.

27. Ibid., pp.87–96.
28. Ibid., pp.92–6.
29. T.J. Ostertag, 'From Shoeless Joe to Charlie Hustle: Major League Baseball's Continuing Crusade Against Sports Gambling, *Seton Hall Journal of Sport Law*, 2 (1992), p.33.
30. A.J. Figone, 'Gambling and College Basketball: The Scandal of 1951', *Journal of Sport History*, 16 (1989), p.45.
31. See Figone, 'Gambling and College Basketball'.
32. IEG Selling More Sponsorship Seminar, 1998.
33. See A.B. Blum, 'Marlboro Grand Prix: Circumvention of the Television Ban on Tobacco Advertising', *The New England Journal of Medicine*, 324 (1991), pp.913–16; J. Hoek, P. Gendall and M. Stockdale, 'Some Effects of Tobacco Sponsorship Advertisements on Young Males', *International Journal of Advertising*, 12 (1993), pp.25–35; D.R. Howard and J.L. Crompton, *Financing Sport (*Morgantown, WV: Fitness Information Technology, 1995); F. Ledwith, 'Does Tobacco Sports Sponsorship of Television act as Advertising for Children?' *Health Education Journal*, 43 (1984), pp.85–8; K.S. Meier, 'Tobacco Truths: The Impact of Role Models on Children's Attitudes Toward Smoking', *Health Education Quarterly*, 18, 2 (1991), pp.173–82.
34. T.W. Robertson, 'Should Tobacco Companies Market Through Sports', *Team Marketing Report*, June 1996, p.8.
35. See Howard and Crompton, *Financing Sport.*
36. Hoek, Gendall and Stockdale, 'Some Effects of Tobacco Sponsorship', pp.25–35; Ledwith, 'Tobacco Sports Sponsorship of Television', pp.85–8.
37. S.R McDaniel and G. Heald, 'Young Consumers' Responses to Event Sponsorship Advertisements of Unhealthy Products – Implications of Schema-Triggered Affect Theory', *Sport Management Review*, 3 (2000), 163-84.
38. Hoek, Gendall and Stockdale, 'Some Effects of Tobacco Sponsorship', pp.25–35; Howard and Crompton, *Financing Sport.*
39. 'The European Union Bans Tobacco Sponsorships', *Sports Business Update*, 203 (8 December 1997).
40. *Sports Industry News*, 17 May 1996, p.193.
41. Howard and Crompton, *Financing Sport.*
42. Ibid., p.282.
43. *Miller Lite Report on American Attitudes Toward Sports* (1983)
44. IEG Selling More Sponsorship Seminar.
45. Dave Curtin, 'Beer-money Brouhaha Brewing at Area Schools', *Denver Post*, 3 October 2000, online at www.denverpost.com/news/news1003b.htm
46. Center for Science in the Public Interest, 'Alcohol Advertising Facts' (n.p., May 1986).
47. National Institute on Alcohol Abuse and Alcoholism, 'Updated Estimates for 1995', *The Economic Costs of Alcohol and Drug Abuse in the United States – Executive Summary* (1998).
48. Center for Science in the Public Interest, 'Youth Drinking and Attitudes' (October 1994).
49. J.W. Grube and L. Wallack, 'Television Beer Advertising and Drinking Knowledge, Beliefs, and Intentions Among Schoolchildren', *American Journal of Public Health*, 84, 2 (1994), pp.254–9.
50. M.D. Slater, D. Rouner, K. Murphy, F. Beauvais, J. Van Leuven and M. Domenech Rodriguez, 'Male Adolescents' Reactions to TV Beer Advertisements: The Effects of Sports Content and Programming Context', *Journal of Studies on Alcohol*, July 1996, pp.425–33.
51. P.A. Madden and J.W. Grube, 'The Frequency and Nature of Alcohol and Tobacco Advertising in Televised Sports, 1990 through 1992', *American Journal of Public Health*, 84 (1994), pp 297–9.
52. See D.W. Stewart and R. Rice, 'Nontraditional Media and Promotions in the Marketing of Alcoholic Beverages', in E.E. Martin and P. Mail (eds), *Effects of the Mass Media on the Use and Abuse of Alcohol: NIAAA Research Monograph No. 28* (Bethesda, MD: National Insititute on Alcohol Abuse and Alcoholism, 1995), pp.209–38.
53. D.M. Carter, *Keeping Score: An Inside Look at Sports Marketing* (Grants Pass, OR: The Oasis Press, 1996).
54. Ibid.
55. *Sports Industry News*, 18 April 1997, p.142.
56. 'Frederick Sees Mixed Message in Alcohol Sponsorship', *Kansas City Star*, 11 September 1999.
57. 'California Group Joins Olympic Beer Fight', *Salt Lake City Tribune*, 27 June 1998.
58. See G.J. Smith and D.S. Mason, 'Double Bind: The Kinky Relationship Between Gambling and Big-Time Sports', paper presented at the 10th International Conference on Gambling and Risk Taking, Montréal, Québec, 31 May–4 June 1997.

59. National Opinion Research Center, *Report on Gambling's Community Impact* (Chicago, IL: University of Chicago, 1998), online at ww.norc.uchicago.edu/new/gambling.htm
60. V.C. Lorenz, 'State Lotteries and Compulsive Gambling', *Journal of Gambling Studies*, 6 (1990), pp.383–96.
61. See Seelig and Seelig, '"Place Your Bets!"', p.96.
62. National Coalition Against Legalized Gambling, *Facts About Gambling*, online at www.ncalg.org/pages/fact_about_gambling.htm
63. National Opinion Research Center, *Report on Gambling's Community Impact.*
64. R. Ladouceur, D. Dube and A. Bujold, 'Gambling Among Primary School Students', *Journal of Gambling Studies*, 10 (1994), pp.363–70.
65. *National Gambling Impact Study Commission Report: Lotteries.*
66. See Seelig and Seelig, '"Place Your Bets!"', pp.91–106.
67. C.T. Clotfelter and P.J. Cook, *Selling Hope: State Lotteries in America* (Cambridge, MA: Harvard University Press, 1989), p.159.
68. See Seelig and Seelig, '"Place Your Bets!"'.
69. *National Gambling Impact Study Commission Report: Lotteries.*
70. Ibid.
71. Duane V. Burke, 'Top Ten Myths About Lottery (and Why They Are Not True)', (1999), online at www.naspl.org/burke899.html
72. NASPL, *Problem Gambling Services*, online at www.naspl.org/contribs.html
73. Personal communications, March–June 2000.
74. Online at http://sportsillustrated.cnn.com/football/college/news/1998/08/05/ncaa_gambling/
75. Personal communications, March–June 2000.
76. *National Gambling Impact Study Commission Report.*
77. 1st Surgeon General's Report, online at www.tobacco.org/History/1964-01-11_1st_SGR.htm
78. Frank Newport, 'More Than a Third of Americans Report Drinking Has Caused Family Problems' (3 November 1999), online at www.gallup.com/poll/release/pr991103.asp
79. Public Agenda Online: 'Gambling', online at www.publicagenda.org/issues/frontdoor.cfm?issue_type=gambling
80. See Seelig and Seelig, '"Place Your Bets!"'
81. J. Woodward, 'Know When to Fold 'Em: Alberta Opinion Polls Show Growing Belief that Gambling is Bad Bet', *Alberta Report*, 22, 49 (November 1995), p.32.
82. Carter, *Keeping Score*, p.143.
83. Ibid., p.144.
84. Ibid., p.145.
85. Ibid.
86. *Marketing News*, 25 September 1995, p.5.
87. J. Barker, 'New Research Focuses on Tobacco Sponsorship', *Canadian FundRaiser*, 13 November 1996.
88. D.P. Green and A.E. Gerken, 'Self-Interest and Public Opinion Toward Smoking Restrictions and Cigarette Taxes', *Public Opinion Quarterly*, 53 (1989), pp.1–16.
89. S.R. McDaniel and D.S. Mason, 'An Exploratory Study of Influences on Public Opinion Towards Alcohol and Tobacco Sponsorship of Sporting Events', *Journal of Services Marketing*, 13 (1999), pp.481–99.
90. L. Kinney and S.R. McDaniel, 'American Consumer Attitudes toward Corporate Sponsorship of Sporting Events', in L. Kahle and C. Riley (eds), *Sport Marketing and the Psychology of Marketing Communication* (Mahwah, NJ: Lawrence Erlbaum, 2004) pp.211–22.
91. Stewart and Rice, 'Nontraditional Media and Promotions'.
92. J.C. Luik, 'Tobacco Advertising Bans and the Dark Face of Government Paternalism', *International Journal of Advertising*, 12 (1993), pp.303–24.
93. Kinney and McDaniel, 'Consumer Attitudes'.
94. Luik, 'Tobacco Advertising Bans'.
95. Kinney and McDaniel, 'Consumer Attitudes'.
96. Curtin, 'Beer-money Brouhaha Brewing'.

15

Let the Market Decide: Sport Sponsorship and its Implications for Moral Autonomy

MICHAEL K. MAUWS

Towards the end of June 2000, a 24-year-old golfer by the name of Tiger Woods became the focus of countless newspaper, magazine and web articles. Woods had just won the prestigious US Open by a record-setting 15 strokes and, in doing so, had firmly established himself among the finest golfers ever to play the game. Not surprisingly, much of the commentary revolved around Woods's amazing performance on the links of Pebble Beach. Sportswriters were scrambling for their thesauruses as they searched for new superlatives to use in place of the worn and hackneyed phrases used to describe the more mundane events of the sporting world. On this occasion, there was little doubt that something historic had transpired and every journalist was anxious to define the terms with which this event would be remembered.

But at that moment, virtually all agreed that it would be years before Woods's golf game reached its peak. And for this reason, his future performances were all but guaranteed to overshadow his performance at the 100th US Open. As a result, the real story that day was not that which appeared in the sports pages, it was that which appeared in the business pages. It was said that Woods was destined to become the sports world's first billionaire. As long ago as 1996, Nike's chairman Phil Knight had predicted that Woods *could* become golf's first billionaire. At the time, it seemed somewhat far-fetched, even if Michael Jordan *was* earning over $70 million in salary and sponsorships that year. But after Woods's performance at the US Open, what had previously been seen as merely possible was now being seen as inevitable. Considering his youth; considering the increasing prize money now available; most importantly, considering the ever-increasing sums being paid to sponsor him, it was now hard to deny that Woods was destined to become a billionaire in the not-too-distant future with the vast majority of this wealth coming from his sponsorship income.

So what are we to make of this observation? Should it concern us? For example, should we care when a single individual is paid in excess of $20 million just to have a car manufacturer's name printed on his golf bag? Should we be upset if this same person receives approximately $100 million just to sport a stylised check mark on his hat and shirt? Were it just this one individual, perhaps we could see this as an aberration and choose to ignore it. However, the fact is that this is anything but an aberration. The sums being spent on sport sponsorship continue to rise. More and more professional athletes are on the receiving end of increasingly lucrative endorsement contracts. And this does not apply just to professional sports. While the sums involved are often smaller, an increasing number of 'amateur' athletes are being funded by or at least rewarded with sponsorship income. Thus, as the co-dependency of athletes and corporations continues to evolve, it may be worth reflecting upon the nature of this relationship and its implications, particularly with respect to the athletes involved.

In this chapter I do just that. More specifically, what I examine are the ethical implications that arise from athletes' access to, and in many cases dependence upon, sponsorship revenues. The perspective from which I do so is that which has come to be known as 'post-structuralism'.[1] I will say more about this perspective in the section that follows but, for now, it is important to note that ethics, from a post-structuralist perspective, has little to do with a code of conduct applicable to all. For post-structuralists, the study of ethics still entails an exploration of how one ought to live one's life;[2] however, post-structuralists tend to diverge from other theorists in their steadfast refusal to universalise any one answer to this question. Thus, my aim here is not to examine the implications of sponsorship with respect to any universal code of athletic conduct but, rather, to examine them in relation to how the individuals we know as high-performance athletes[3] make decisions about how they are to live their lives.

Towards this end, in the first section of this chapter I provide a brief introduction to the post-structuralist perspective for the benefit of those to whom it may be unfamiliar. I conclude this section with a brief review of Shogan's[4] post-structuralist rendering of the making of high-performance athletes, and those already familiar with post-structuralism may want to proceed immediately to this point. In the second section, I present sponsorship as a disciplinary practice, by which I simply mean to say that it serves to influence or discipline individuals' behaviour. In the third section I address the loss of moral autonomy alluded to in the title of this chapter. I touch briefly upon both the liberal and communitarian traditions, but the bulk of my comments reflect the post-structuralist tradition, particularly as instantiated in the work of Bauman.[5] I conclude the chapter with some questions that might be asked by those who are, like myself, concerned with the increasing interconnectedness that is developing between sport and commercial activity.

Post-structuralism: A Primer

The term 'post-structuralism' is among those whose exact meaning is the source of some controversy. Unfortunately, a full review of the post-structuralist perspective is clearly beyond the scope of this chapter. Those who are interested in learning more may want to consult the wide variety of books now available on postmodernism, many of which address the latter's similarities and differences with post-structuralism.[6] In addition, many recent books on research methodologies in the social sciences devote a few pages, if not an entire chapter, to discussing post-structuralist perspectives.[7] A widely cited, if somewhat dense, explication of the French post-structuralism that informs this chapter can be found in Dews.[8] Finally, some may find it useful to consult Sturrock's discussion of structuralism[9] to more fully appreciate what it is that makes the perspective adopted here *post* structuralism.

A cursory understanding of structuralism's central tenet is very much a necessity in order to comprehend the post-structuralist perspective. Structuralism originated in the discipline of linguistics and is often associated with the work of Saussure.[10] In very crude terms, what differentiates the structuralist position is its suggestion that the connection between symbols and their referents is arbitrary. Therefore, the meanings associated with symbols do not derive from the nature of their referents, but from somewhere else. For structuralists, this 'somewhere else' is the entire system of signs of which these symbols are a part. In other words, the meaning of a symbol is determined by its relations with all the other symbols of which the sign system is comprised.

Post-structuralism, in all its variations, has discarded much of what structuralism has to offer.[11] However, this notion that it is relationships rather than referents that define the meanings of terms is central to all versions of post-structuralism. Thus, for many post-structuralists, the aim is to do away with *things* so as to focus on what really matters, i.e. what we *say* about things.[12] We may see and touch the things themselves, but the world we *know* is not that of physical projects but, rather, the objects constructed in discourse. Thus, for post-structuralists, it is our ways of speaking, and the practices through which these ways of speaking are translated into actions, that are central in understanding the workings of the social world. It is the objects of discourse that really matter as opposed to the physical objects around which that discourse appears to revolve.

Central in the literature of post-structuralism are the writings of Michel Foucault.[13] As with post-structuralism more generally, a full review of Foucault's oeuvre is beyond the scope of this chapter.[14] All that needs to be noted here is the core focus of Foucault's work which, according to him, is the relationship between the subject and power.[15] In speaking of the 'subject', what Foucault has in mind is, loosely speaking, our understandings of ourselves. He occasionally speaks of sites of subjectivity and, by this, he means the positions we occupy when we think, speak and act. It is in relation to these positions that we come to know ourselves and through them that our sense of self emerges. As Weedon describes it, '[a]s we acquire language, we learn to give voice – meaning – to our experience and to understand it according to particular ways of thinking [and] particular discourses. ... These ways of thinking constitute our consciousness, and the positions with which we identify structure our sense of ourselves.'[16] These positions, however, are not natural entities preceding our entry into the world; instead, they are the product of discursive struggles and are continually being contested and reformulated by the accumulated and accumulating utterances of a wide assortment of social actors. Building on the core tenet of structuralism described above, the meaning of these positions – which is to say, their 'nature' – is defined in relation to the growing body of texts related to them; more specifically, the positions themselves emerge at the juncture of these texts and have no reality apart from them.[17] Thus, who we are is not determined by our birth but, rather, by the knowledge that emerges out of these discursive struggles. This knowledge shapes future discussions and, in doing so, plays an important role in the constitution of social positions and the subjectivities of the individuals who occupy them.

What the foregoing implies is that, if power is the capacity to influence outcomes, then knowledge is a pervasive and important form of power. In fact, so close is the relationship between these terms that Foucault occasionally combines them in the single term power/knowledge.[18] This is very different from the expression 'knowledge is power' which suggests that power derives from differential access to knowledge. Power/knowledge is about the *sharing* of knowledge and how, through its being shared, knowledge becomes constitutive.

Partially as a result of this focus on knowledge, many associate Foucault's writings, particularly his early writings,[19] with the history of ideas. However, in the light of the foregoing, it is also possible to see how his early work contributes towards a better understanding of the subject of social action. In fact, his focus on the subject and power is closely aligned with the work of so-called discursive psychologists whose interest is in understanding the phenomena that arise when different sociocultural discourses are integrated within an identifiable human individual situated in relation to those discourses.[20] The latter are interested in the person that emerges at the conjuncture of these discourses; they are interested in the forms of self-understanding that arise given the discursive resources available to human individuals. They may not speak of power and domination but, nevertheless, it is not difficult to see that discursive psychologists are, like Foucault, exploring the relationship between the subject and power.

To the degree that he is interested in unmasking the structures of domination (in the form of discursive formations) that shape individuals' understandings of the world, Foucault's project has much in common with the work of the Frankfurt School.[21] However, unlike the critical theorists associated with the latter, Foucault holds out no promise of us ever stepping outside these structures and knowing our 'true' nature – what the critical theorists refer to as 'emancipation'. To know, for Foucault, is always to know in relation to a particular subject position and the discourses out of which it has been constituted. And for this reason, it is not the task of the social scientist to clear away these discourses but, rather, to simply to lay bare the workings of these discourses and the practices that support them.

The Production of High-Performance Athletes

In her recent book, Shogan provides a preliminary sketch of the discourses and practices that constitute the subject position she calls 'the high-performance athlete'.[22] As she herself admits, her analysis is heavily influenced by Foucault's writings. Thus, her first few chapters provide us with a rough outline of how Foucault's insights might be usefully employed to illuminate the production of the sites of subjectivity occupied by the people we know as high-performance athletes.

Following the lead of Foucault, a central focus of Shogan's analysis is the 'disciplinary practices' by which 'docile bodies' are produced. In this regard, it is interesting to note that nearly two thousand years ago, Epictetus had the following to say about the path to Olympic victory:

> You will have to put yourself under *discipline*: to eat by rule, to avoid cakes and sweetmeats; to take exercise at the appointed hour whether you like it or not, in cold and heat; to abstain from cold drinks and from wine at your will; in a word, *to give yourself over to the trainer as to a physician*.[emphases added]

Little has changed in the intervening period. For as Shogan points out, 'A disciplined athlete is able to perform prescribed skills with minimum error and maximum intensity in dynamic, often stressful circumstances. In order for discipline to create skilled performers, individuals must be subjected to detailed control of time, space and modality of movement.'[23]

In speaking of 'discipline' here, a double entendre is intended as there is both the disciplinary knowledge of high performance sport and the physical discipline associated with athletic training in play. Ultimately, they are two sides of the same coin, as the latter almost always have their origins in the former. In any case, Shogan's concern is with the effects that result from the *subjects* of athletics being *subjected* to these practices:

> While disciplines produce performers who are superbly skilled, both the mechanical training to achieve skills and the automatic way in which skills are performed supports a concern that, while athletes are active with respect to movement, they are often passive in making decisions about the acquisition of movement skills and in reflecting on their continued involvement with technologies that produce these skills. Disciplines may be productive of bodies that can perform amazing skills but, during the acquisition and performance of skills, *athletes seem to have little or no agency*.[24]

Some might argue that this is simply the price athletes pay in order to be among the world's best. As Shogan herself admits, all of us, including academicians, are subjected to disciplinary practices as we try to excel in our respective endeavours. Thus, we need to keep in mind that it is not disciplinary practices per se that require scrutiny but, rather, the specific effects of particular configurations of practices.

In the case of high-performance sport, the fact that we subject individuals to these practices, and the fact that we continue to fund research related to achieving better and better performances, indicates that physical performances are highly valued in our society. Thus, the purpose of Shogan's analysis is to make us aware of the costs of those performances. Ultimately, what she is interested in is 'how an array of ethical issues also emerges when demands to improve performance envelop athletes, coaches, administrators, and scientists in decisions about how far to push the limits of performance'.[25] The ethical issues she has in mind arise when individuals fail to conform to the definition of 'high-performance athlete' being prescribed. And as she notes, '[f]ail they must because, despite the potentially homogenizing effect of technologies of high-performance sport, athletes come to sport as hybrids, reflecting diversity both within and among themselves. *No athlete is only an athlete*.'[26]

It is this final remark – that 'no athlete is only an athlete' – that is perhaps most relevant to the discussion at hand. For as we shall see, one of the effects of the rise of sport sponsorship is that, increasingly, athletes are being asked to be athletes *at all times*. Or to put this more bluntly, they are being asked to be *nothing more* than athletes. It is not enough that a large portion of their lives is regimented in the interests of achieving peak physical performances; now, if lucrative sponsorship contracts are to be secured, the rest of athletes' lives must be regimented in the interests of achieving corporate objectives. The question, thus, is whether this is too much to ask of athletes.

Sponsorship as a Disciplinary Practice

The capacity of money to affect athletes' behaviour has long been recognised in the world of sports. For example, as recently as 1962 English cricket maintained a sharp distinction between 'gentlemen' (those who played for the love of the game) and 'players' (those who played for money), going so far as to provide separate dressing rooms despite the fact that all played for the same team. Another example is the case of Jim Thorpe, an American athlete who was stripped of his Olympic gold medals for the decathlon and track-and-field pentathlon in 1912 because he had once been reimbursed for playing baseball. Other illustrations abound, but all serve to make the point that, until quite recently, money was widely understood to compromise the 'purity' of sports.

Needless to say, things have changed considerably in the sporting world. No longer will one find separate locker rooms for players and gentlemen. More to the point, we now have multi-million dollar NBA players winning Olympic gold medals, thereby signalling that the amateur ethos in sport is quickly waning, if not already dead. As for how this came about, virtually any explanation must acknowledge the influence of Mark McCormack and his privately held company, IMG. This company represents many of the finest athletes in the world. Starting with Arnold Palmer in the 1960s, IMG has become a multi-million dollar company by signing up athletes and convincing corporations that tying their promotional efforts to sports stars is good business. As *The Economist* summed it up, '[w]hen it comes to turning the sporting efforts into rivers of cash, no one does it better than IMG'.[27] There are other influences to be considered here as well, such as the proliferation of mass media outlets and the resulting competition for content, but all that really needs to be noted is that the sporting world is now awash with money and a significant portion of it is finding its way into the bank accounts of athletes. To get some idea of just how much money, consider that, by 1997, more than $1 billion dollars per year was being spent on endorsement contracts, with Nike alone spending close to $100 million.[28]

History aside, the issue is simply, how is this wealth affecting the athletes on whom it is being spent? Has it changed the nature of the game for them and, even more importantly, has it changed the way they choose to live their lives? If the headlines in *Forbes* magazine are any indication, it is difficult to imagine that the behaviour of players, and their attitude towards their sport, could somehow remain unaffected by the money involved. According to a 1996 article, 'Despite what Dennis Rodman, Charles Barkley, Deion Sanders and a rogues' gallery of other thuggish professional athletes might have you believe, the nice guys are finishing first where it counts: the product endorsement deals that determine whether an athlete is merely well paid or gets very rich.'[29] If this is true, then it is likely that elite athletes are at least thinking twice before engaging in any reprehensible behaviours. Even if so-called nice guys do not actually finish first, the fact is that their agents and managers, not to mention the media, are telling them this is the case. Thus, athletes are at least being made aware that anything bordering on unsportsmanlike behaviour can cost them dearly when it comes to endorsement contracts.

No doubt some would argue that sponsorship has been a positive influence on sport if it can be shown to be contributing to sportsmanlike behaviour. However, what needs to be noted is that, six years before its 'nice guys finish first' story, the headline on the cover of *Forbes* read 'Sports Today: Throw a Tantrum, Make a Buck'. Thus, it is not enough to question whether the incentive of endorsement contracts is bringing about desired behaviours since, at some point, those very same contracts will be used to promote the opposite behaviours. So what we must question instead is the bigger issue related to the role of economic incentives in sport more generally.

If it were simply about players' performance on the court, field or pitch, sponsorship income could be dismissed as simply another component of players' remuneration packages. However, what makes this component different is that, increasingly, endorsement contracts are encroaching upon a larger and larger portion of players' lives. Perhaps there was a time when star athletes were simply role models within their respective sports. It seems unlikely but, in any case, in today's context, athletes are being expected to model how one should live one's life *in its entirety*. What makes this situation particularly problematic is that it is no longer the lives of the athletes that are being presented to the public. Instead of being role models, in a somewhat bizarre reversal, the situation is now closer to being one in which athletes are trying to emulate the lives their sponsors' customers want to see modelled. This is, of course, an overstatement. Nevertheless, to some degree, athletes' behaviour is being affected by their sponsors' demands and, more specifically, by the threat of contracts being terminated should sponsors conclude that the athletes' images are no longer a reflection of desired corporate images.

In this regard, one does not have to look very far to find examples of athletes paying the price for failing to live their lives in the ways corporations deem acceptable. In some cases, it is hard not to see this as justice being meted out. When Aston Villa striker Stan Collymore publicly attacks his girlfriend, it seems entirely appropriate for Diadora to reconsider its sponsorship arrangements with him; when it is discovered that Middlesbrough's Paul Gascoigne has been beating his wife, to have his contract with adidas cancelled hardly seems sufficient punishment. The same thing might be said of the racist remarks of baseball player John

Rocker, and many other players who have engaged in similarly reprehensible behaviour. In cases such as these, we have little difficulty accepting the financial penalties players are made to pay in the form of sponsorship revenues foregone. The corporations, in this case, are simply doing what any decent person would do in similar circumstances: like the rest of us, they are making it clear that this sort of behaviour is unacceptable.

But where do we draw the line? And what if we are unable to agree where that line should be drawn? While virtually all can agree that physical assault and hate crimes are not to be tolerated, the verdict is less clear with respect to many of the other actions for which athletes are being punished. For example, Brett Favre, while quarterback for the Green Bay Packers, admitted that he had become addicted to painkillers. Given the physically punishing nature of Favre's sport, it would be easy to see an addiction such as this as an occupational hazard. Sponsors, however, saw it differently: Favre estimates the admission cost him $2 million, a figure others suggest is conservative.[30] Some might argue that this is an appropriate penalty for allowing oneself to become addicted to drugs of any sort, even if the addiction does originate with the demands of sport. However, many others would take the opposite position: addictions such as this are a part of sport that needs to be brought into public view and, therefore, athletes such as Favre should not be penalised for facilitating this.

The case of NBA star rebounder Dennis Rodman provides an even better illustration of sponsorship's potentially harmful effects on athletes' behaviour. Even those unfamiliar with Rodman's athletic prowess are likely to recognise him by his constantly changing hair colour and his numerous piercings and tattoos. They are also likely to know that Rodman is known as a regular cross-dresser, having frequently been photographed in women's clothing. These behaviours, as odd as some might find them, serve an incredibly important role within the world of sport. For more than any other individual, Rodman has problematised virtually every known stereotype of what athletes look like and how they live their lives. More importantly, he has made it clear that athletes are *more than just athletes*; i.e. 'athlete' is only one of these individuals' identities. Rodman makes it clear that athletes are not uniform bodies needing to be moulded by the normalising practices of coaches and trainers;[31] they are, in Shogan's terms, *hybrids* whose differences provoke resistance. Thus, for the sake of other athletes, and particularly the young athletes who are more likely to be searching for role models, athletes such as Rodman make the incredibly important statement that one is, first and foremost, an individual: 'athlete' is simply one of the identities through which one's individuality is defined.

Unfortunately, Rodman and those like him have been forced to pay a high price for their contributions towards a more tolerant society. Were

Rodman not so notoriously difficult to get along with – which in itself may be a further indication of intolerance within the world of sport – his 'penalty' alone would be in the millions of dollars. Regardless of the amount, what is clear is that Rodman's sponsorship revenues are not in line with his athletic abilities and, in part, this can be attributed to what others see as being unconventional behaviour. Rodman, at least, is willing to pay this price. But how many others are curbing their behaviour because they find this price too steep? And more importantly, how many young people are hesitating to express themselves because they can find so few role models willing to do the same? Answering these questions is very much an empirical problem but, if we did the research, what we would be likely to find is that, both directly and indirectly, both explicitly and implicitly, both on the court and off, athletes' behaviour is being affected by the increasing amounts being spent on sponsorship. And while it is not possible to say unequivocally that the effects are good or bad, what we can say with some certainty is that it is the potential for material gain that is behind the effects. So in the end, the question that arises is simply this: what are the chances for moral behaviour when it is economic gain as opposed to doing the 'right' thing that guides athletes' decisions?

The point of the foregoing is simply that sponsorship's presence is affecting athletes' behaviours. In both subtle and explicit ways, it is helping to produce sites of subjectivity such that athletes' moral autonomy is being compromised. The contracts athletes are being asked to sign extend the boundaries of the court, rink or field well beyond the portion of the day spent training and playing; these contracts make 'athlete' a 24/7 occupation. As both role models and citizens, athletes are losing control of their lives. In the current context, homogeneity and conformity are the ideals to be pursued; diversity and hybridity are, at best, secondary concerns. But even if we could agree as a society that these are values worth rewarding, as we shall see, there is a danger in having athletes exhibit these values only because it pays to do so.

The Loss of Moral Autonomy

What we are to make of sponsorship's effects on athletes' behaviour depends upon the ethical perspective we adopt. In recent years the anchor points of ethical debate have been the liberal and communitarian traditions.[32] There are of course variations within each tradition but, in general, the divide between those who give primacy to the individual – the liberals – and those who give primacy to the collective – the communitarians – has been seen as the most important. (It needs to be noted that this is a *very* crude account of the differences between these two positions; nonetheless, it suffices for the purposes at hand.) However, in the 1990s, Bauman began to carve out a third perspective, inspired in part by his insightful and disturbing account of the Holocaust.[33] Although he does not specifically align himself with post-structuralist perspectives, the latter fit well with his position on moral responsibility. Thus, it is Bauman's perspective that is most relevant to this discussion. Nevertheless, before we explore it, it is worth reviewing briefly what the liberal and communitarian perspectives imply with respect to the sponsorship issue described herein.

In somewhat crude terms, the goal of the liberal position is to place as few constraints as possible on the behaviour of individuals, while recognising that the freedom of some will be contingent upon curbing the freedom of others. In some cases, individuals may voluntarily choose to forego some of their freedom, usually in exchange for a benefit of some kind, but this is not a major concern for liberals. What is a concern is when individuals' freedom is compromised without their consent; in this case, one is faced with a decision between limiting the freedom of those who act and limiting the freedom of those who are adversely affected.

In the case of sport sponsorship, I suspect that most liberals would have little difficulty with athletes receiving enormous sums of money in exchange for their endorsing products and companies, nor would they have any difficulty with athletes receiving less money should their behaviour be deemed less than exemplary. From the liberal perspective, making less money is simply a consequence of a voluntarily chosen course of action; if athletes want to maximise their earnings, they should choose their actions accordingly.

However, the situation may be slightly more complex than this. After all, a convincing argument in favour of the liberal position is its potential benefits for society. As John Stuart Mill eloquently noted more than a century ago, 'There are but few persons, in comparison with the whole of mankind, whose experiments, if adopted by others, would be likely to be any improvement on established practice. But these few are the salt of the earth; without them, human life would become a stagnant pool.'[34] So even though liberals might condone the increasing co-dependency of sponsors and athletes on the grounds that this relationship is entered into voluntarily, its capacity to dampen individuals' enthusiasm for experiments in living might prove to be cause for concern.

For their part, what communitarians are likely to object to here is simply the potential for the lure of lucre to override considerations of community norms. In very simple terms, the emphasis within the communitarian tradition is on framing one's behaviour in terms of its implications for the community's well being. Individual autonomy is encouraged in this tradition, but only within the bounds of what is considered to be in the community's best interests. Thus, sponsorship income poses no threat provided it is being used to encourage behaviours deemed acceptable to the community (e.g. 'Nice guys finish first'), but becomes a problem when it brings about less desirable behaviour (e.g. 'Throw a tantrum, make a buck'). In other words, sponsorship itself is of little concern from a communitarian perspective; what really matters from this perspective is simply whether behaviour is or is not at odds with what the community has deemed to be its best interests.

Postmodern Ethics

Space does not permit a review of the respective limitations of the liberal and communitarian traditions. However, from a post-structuralist perspective, the difficulty with both is that, ultimately, their objective is a code of conduct to which all can adhere. Regardless of whether this amounts to a list of dos or don'ts, and regardless of how limited or extensive this list might be, it still amounts to a set of absolutes to which all are expected to adhere. This would not be a problem were it not for the fact that it is not clear from where the authority for such a list might derive. If nothing else, post-structuralist critiques have severely problematised the sort of grand narratives exemplified by universal codes of conduct.[35] If these codes of conduct could be seen as 'arbitrary' arrangements favouring particular outcomes and interests, there might not be a problem here; however, if not initially, then in the end, they are often seen as unassailable truths whose original inspiration has long since been forgotten. The search for a universal code of conduct can, among other places, be traced to Mount Sinai and the two tablets delivered up by Moses. In many regards, the commandments inscribed upon those tablets have been the model for hundreds of years of theorising on ethics and moral responsibility. The essence of this model is compliance or adherence: so long as one has adhered to the commandments (or rules and so on), one can be said to have behaved ethically.

But if our model of moral inquiry is to come from the Bible, we have, according to Bauman, chosen the wrong story as our inspiration. Instead of Mount Sinai, it is to the Garden of Eden that we should have looked for our model of ethical behaviour.[36] As will be recalled, while in the garden, Adam and Eve had no reason to contemplate the ethical content of their actions; it was only after being cast out that they were forced, for the first time, to contemplate 'good' and 'evil', 'right' and 'wrong'. Whereas everything was unequivocally good within the garden, things were ambiguous and ambivalent outside of it. And for Bauman, it is this equivocality that is at the heart of moral deliberation, meaning that the recognition of such is the precursor of morally responsible behaviour.

Bauman's self-proclaimed 'postmodern' ethics has many affinities with writers such as Buber and Logstrup. However, it is primarily from the work of Levinas that he is drawing.[37] Regardless, what interests Bauman is the notion of a moral impulse or moral imperative that is *prior to* any knowledge we might have of who we or others are, or of what it might be appropriate for us to do. The moral impulse, as he describes it, is an unlimited and unconditional responsibility for the Other. In contrast with liberal traditions, it is not predicated upon any sense of reciprocity; and in contrast with communitarian traditions, it transcends community or tribal distinctions. It is an impulse we experience when confronted with an Other's face; it is the impulse to do everything we possibly can to help the Other. And it is this impulse, in Bauman's account, that is at the heart of human sociality. The difficulty with this impulse is that it potentially leaves us with the perpetual feeling that we have not done enough, that we could always do more. So in this regard, ethical inquiry is really about deciding how much is enough; in brief, we want to be able to sleep at night knowing we have done our part.

What Bauman is suggesting is that human beings are, existentially, moral beings. This does not mean that we are fated to do the 'right' thing, whatever that might be. However, it does mean that we are inherently moral in the sense that we must at least decide whether or not to do what is right. Given that our moral impulse carries with it an unlimited responsibility for each Other we come into contact with, it is clear that in practice there must be limits to what we do for the Other. So it is here, according to Bauman, that ethical deliberation enters the picture, whether that be in the liberal or communitarian tradition. It is here, for example, that our definitions of 'us' and 'them' come into play as we try to limit those in relation to whom we must act on our moral responsibility. Liberal and communitarian discourses, discourses of nationalism, race, gender and religion, whether intentional or not, all serve the purpose of bringing into being sites of subjectivity that make us deaf to the ethical 'demands' of particular groups of Others and allow us to focus instead on the groups of Others of which we are or want to be a part.

And what of those groups for whom we are willing to recognise our moral responsibility? As alluded to above, it is not clear how much we should be doing for them, nor is it clear *what* we should be doing for them. Codes of ethics, while useful as rules of thumb, are still just that – rules of thumb. In Bauman's postmodern perspective, there are no absolutes; there are no behaviours whose moral repercussions are unequivocal. Thus, for the individual who wishes to act on his or her moral impulse, the world is the same as it was for Adam and Eve after being cast out: it is a world in which each of us must decide for ourselves the appropriate course of action.

From a post-structuralist perspective, the challenge that sponsorship poses is that it contributes towards the emergence of sites of subjectivity in which actions are chosen, whether consciously or not, on the basis of their economic content rather than their moral content. Although some might argue that, in the end, what really matters is putting an end to domestic violence and racial hatred, Bauman would argue – and clearly I agree with him – that developing individuals' sense of moral responsibility must be the long-term goal. Society changes far too quickly for us to ever be able to put in place rules to eliminate all undesirable behaviours; even if this were not the case, both agreeing on what is desirable, and trying to remember all the rules this entails, pose equally insurmountable challenges. Thus, ethical 'failures' are bound to result when we pursue this strategy. Ethical 'failures' are still bound to result when we seek to develop individuals' sense of moral responsibility but, in this case, they will at least be the product of human limitations rather than ignorance.

What we need to keep in mind is that the moral impulse is a very quiet voice within us and, as such, one that is easily drowned out by the cacophony of voices suggesting other courses of action. So even though economic incentives, such as sponsorships, may be used to promote desirable behaviours, the problem is that, over time, we forget why it is that those behaviours were desirable in the first place. In the end, we are left doing those things for the simple reason that it is economically beneficial to do so. And once this point is reached, it is easy to see how undesirable behaviours could be similarly promoted through the use of the very same incentives (e.g. Throw a tantrum, make a buck). Thus, to the degree that sponsorship supplants moral responsibility as the basis for choosing between alternative courses of action – *even if it leads to the same course of action* – it is undesirable in that the possibility of ethical 'failure' increases and the development of moral responsibility decreases.

I recognise that many have equated the rise of postmodernism with the death of ethics. And if ethics is equated with a universal code of conduct to which one can blindly adhere, then Bauman is among those sounding the death knell. However, what Bauman is also doing is suggesting that it is only when we give up on the idea of others providing us with a code of conduct that we can finally begin to address our moral responsibility in all its specificity. Thus, as he notes, although this may be the twilight of ethics, it may also be the dawn of morality.

Conclusion

The argument I have sought to make here is, in the end, quite a simple one: money changes everything. Money changes why we play sports; it changes why we value sportsmanlike conduct; and, increasingly, it changes why athletes live their life apart from sports as they do. For those who claim to know what the right thing is to do in these contexts, perhaps this is not a bad thing. However, on a personal note, I have enough difficulty figuring out what I should do, let alone what others should be doing. In light of this observation, I am extremely suspicious when someone else claims to know what I should be doing, or what others should be doing. And when they need to offer major incentives to have others do what they claim is right, I become that much more suspicious. In any case, the fact is that fewer and fewer seem to be playing sports for the sheer joy of the game. Even at the level of the schoolyard, it seems the promise of endorsement contracts many years down the road is present in competitive sports. And when this happens, the potential of sports to facilitate our development as human beings and citizens is greatly diminished. Playing sports might still be fun at this point, but it becomes recreation and nothing more.

There are other issues that arise out of this discussion that space does not permit me to discuss. There is one, however, that I would like to at least draw attention since it might not be as obvious as some of the others. In brief, what is the effect of trying to artificially fabricate perfect role models in the form of sports stars? Through endorsement contracts and 'break' clauses, this is effectively what sponsors are trying to do: they are trying to get athletes to mimic what 'society' thinks is the perfect human being. This may serve the purpose of providing role models but, at the same time, we need to keep in mind that it also promotes the sort of hagiography that leads the youth to blindly mimic whatever it is that their heroes choose to do. It also blinds us to the more harmful effects of competitive sport, such as the acceptance of physical violence. So from this perspective, there is much to be said about celebrating the imperfections of athletes and trying to learn from them. Encouraging youth to evaluate elite athletes rather than blindly mimicking them will go a long way towards developing their moral capacities.

As for Tiger Woods, all I can say is that I hope he is still able to find some enjoyment in the game that seems destined to make him a billionaire. It seems odd to be feeling pity for someone making that much money but, admittedly, that is what I feel when I watch Mr Woods play golf. It may take me two strokes to do what he can do with one, but I'd like to think that the fact that I am playing for the sheer joy of the game somehow makes me a better golfer than Tiger Woods.

NOTES

1. See P. Dews, *Logics of Disintegration: Post-Structuralist Thought and the Claims of Critical Theory* (London: Verso, 1987) and also J. Sturrock, *Structuralism* (London: Paladin, 1986).
2. For example, M. Foucault, *The History of Sexuality: The Use of Pleasure*, trans. R. Hurley, Vol. 2 (New York: Vintage, 1985).
3. D. Shogan, *The Making of High-Performance Athletes: Discipline, Diversity, and Ethics* (Toronto: University of Toronto Press, 1999).

4. Ibid.
5. Z. Bauman, _Postmodern Ethics_ (Oxford: Blackwell, 1993); Z. Bauman, _Life in Fragments: Essays in Postmodern Morality_ (Oxford: Blackwell, 1995); Z. Bauman, 'On Communitarians and Human Freedom. Or, How to Square the Circle', _Theory, Culture & Society_, 13, 2 (1996); Z. Bauman, 'What Prospects of Morality in Times of Uncertainty?', _Theory, Culture & Society_, 15, 1 (1998).
6. For example, P.M. Rosenau, _Post-Modernism and the Social Sciences: Insights, Inroads, and Intrusions_ (Princeton, NJ: Princeton University Press, 1992).
7. For example, M. Crotty, _The Foundations of Social Research: Meaning and Perspective in the Research Process_ (London: Sage, 1998).
8. Dews, _Logics of Disintegration_.
9. Sturrock, _Structuralism_.
10. F. de Saussure, _Course in General Linguistics_ (Lasalle, IL: Open Court, 1983).
11. R. Hodge and G. Kress, _Social Semiotics_ (Ithaca, NY: Cornell University Press, 1988).
12. M. Foucault, _The Archaeology of Knowledge_, trans. A. Sheridan (London: Routledge, 1972).
13. For example, M. Foucault, _The Order of Things: An Archaeology of the Human Sciences_, trans. A. Sheridan (New York: Vintage, 1970); M. Foucault, _Discipline & Punish: The Birth of the Prison_, trans. A. Sheridan (New York: Random House, 1979).
14. See H.L. Dreyfus and P. Rabinow, _Michel Foucault: Beyond Structuralism and Hermeneutics_, 2nd edn (Chicago, IL: University of Chicago Press, 1982) for an overview of Foucault's work. Some may find the intellectual portrait to be found in J. Miller, _The Passion of Michel Foucault_ (New York: Doubleday, 1993) a better starting point for understanding Foucault's perspective(s).
15. M. Foucault, 'The Subject and Power', in Dreyfus and Rabinow (eds), _Michel Foucault_.
16. C. Weedon, _Feminist Theory and Poststructuralist Practice_ (Oxford: Basil Blackwell, 1987), p.33.
17. See P. Bourdieu, 'Some Properties of Fields', in P. Bourdieu (ed.), _Sociology in Question_ (London: Sage, 1993).
18. For example, M. Foucault, _Power/Knowledge: Selected Interviews and Other Writings, 1972–1977_ (New York: Pantheon Books, 1980).
19. For example, M. Foucault, _Madness and Civilization: A History of Insanity in the Age of Reason_, trans. R. Howard (New York: Vintage, 1965); Foucault, _The Order of Things_; Foucault, _The Archaeology of Knowledge_; M. Foucault, _The Birth of the Clinic_, trans. A. Sheridan (New York: Vintage, 1973).
20. R. Harré, 'Discursive Psychology', in J.A. Smith, R. Harré and L. Van Langenhove (eds), _Rethinking Psychology_ (London: Sage, 1995), p.22; see also K.R. McGannon and M.K. Mauws, 'Discursive Psychology: An Alternative Approach for Studying Adherence to Exercise and Physical Activity', _Quest_, 52, 2 (2000).
21. For an introduction to the Frankfurt School, see D. Held, _Introduction to Critical Theory: Horkheimer to Habermas_ (Berkeley, CA: University of California Pres, 1980).
22. Shogan, _The Making of High-Performance Athletes_.
23. Ibid., p.13.
24. Ibid., pp.13–14.
25. Ibid., p.ix.
26. Ibid., p.ix, emphasis added.
27. 'The Paymasters', _The Economist_, 6 June 1998.
28. R. Lane, 'Nice Guys Finish First', _Forbes_, 16 December 1996.
29. Ibid., p.236.
30. Ibid.
31. Cf. P.A. Adler and P. Adler, 'Intense Loyalty in Organizations: A Case Study of College Athletics', _Administrative Science Quarterly_, 33 (1988).
32. A 'postmodern' rendering of the liberal position can be found in R. Rorty, _Contingency, Irony, and Solidarity_ (Cambridge, MA: Cambridge University Press, 1989); A. MacIntyre, _After Virtue: A Study in Moral Theory_ (Notre Dame, IN: University of Notre Dame Press, 1981) is a notable proponent of the communitarian position.
33. Z. Bauman, _Modernity and the Holocaust_ (Cambridge: Polity, 1989); see also Bauman, _Postmodern Ethics_; Bauman, _Life in Fragments_; Bauman, 'On Communitarians and Human Freedom'.
34. J.S. Mill, _On Liberty_ [1859] (Arlington Heights, IL: Crofts Classics, 1947), p.64.
35. For example, Foucault, _The Order of Things_; J.-F. Lyotard, _The Postmodern Condition: A Report_

of Knowledge (Minneapolis, MN: University of Minnesota, 1984); Rorty, *Contingency, Irony, and Solidarity*.

36. Bauman, 'What Prospects of Morality?'
37. M. Buber, *The Writings of Martin Buber* (New York: Meridian, 1956); M. Buber, *I and Thou* (New York: Charles Scribner's Sons, 1958); K.E. Logstrup, *The Ethical Demand* (Philadelphia, PA: Fortress, 1971); E. Levinas, *Totality and Infinity: An Essay on Exteriority* (London: Kluwer, 1969).

Index